Applied Computational Intelligence and Soft Computing in Engineering

Saifullah Khalid
CCSI Airport, India

A volume in the Advances in Systems Analysis,
Software Engineering, and High Performance
Computing (ASASEHPC) Book Series

Published in the United States of America by
    IGI Global
    Engineering Science Reference (an imprint of IGI Global)
    701 E. Chocolate Avenue
    Hershey PA, USA 17033
    Tel: 717-533-8845
    Fax: 717-533-8661
    E-mail: cust@igi-global.com
    Web site: http://www.igi-global.com

Library of Congress Cataloging-in-Publication Data

Names: Khalid, Saifullah, 1981- author.
Title: Applied computational intelligence and soft computing in engineering /
  Saifullah Khalid, editor.
Description: Hershey, PA : Engineering Science Reference, [2018] | Includes
  bibliographical references.
Identifiers: LCCN 2017014626| ISBN 9781522531296 (hardcover) | ISBN
  9781522531302 (ebook)
Subjects: LCSH: Engineering--Data processing. | Soft computing. |
  Computational intelligence.
Classification: LCC TA345 .A675 2018 | DDC 620.00285/63--dc23 LC record available at https://lccn.loc.gov/2017014626

This book is published in the IGI Global book series Advances in Systems Analysis, Software Engineering, and High Performance Computing (ASASEHPC) (ISSN: 2327-3453; eISSN: 2327-3461)

Advances in Systems Analysis, Software Engineering, and High Performance Computing (ASASEHPC) Book Series

Vijayan Sugumaran
Oakland University, USA

ISSN:2327-3453
EISSN:2327-3461

MISSION

The theory and practice of computing applications and distributed systems has emerged as one of the key areas of research driving innovations in business, engineering, and science. The fields of software engineering, systems analysis, and high performance computing offer a wide range of applications and solutions in solving computational problems for any modern organization.

The **Advances in Systems Analysis, Software Engineering, and High Performance Computing (ASASEHPC) Book Series** brings together research in the areas of distributed computing, systems and software engineering, high performance computing, and service science. This collection of publications is useful for academics, researchers, and practitioners seeking the latest practices and knowledge in this field.

COVERAGE

- Software engineering
- Computer Networking
- Enterprise information systems
- Virtual Data Systems
- Parallel Architectures
- Distributed Cloud Computing
- Computer System Analysis
- Human-computer interaction
- Computer graphics
- Performance Modelling

IGI Global is currently accepting manuscripts for publication within this series. To submit a proposal for a volume in this series, please contact our Acquisition Editors at Acquisitions@igi-global.com or visit: http://www.igi-global.com/publish/.

Titles in this Series

For a list of additional titles in this series, please visit: www.igi-global.com/book-series

Large-Scale Fuzzy Interconnected Control Systems Design and Analysis
Zhixiong Zhong (Xiamen University of Technology, China) and Chih-Min Lin (Yuan Ze University, Taiwan)
Information Science Reference • copyright 2017 • 223pp • H/C (ISBN: 9781522523857) • US $175.00 (our price)

Microcontroller System Design Using PIC18F Processors
Nicolas K. Haddad (University of Balamand, Lebanon)
Information Science Reference • copyright 2017 • 215pp • H/C (ISBN: 9781683180005) • US $195.00 (our price)

Probabilistic Nodes Combination (PNC) for Object Modeling and Contour Reconstruction
Dariusz Jacek Jakóbczak (Technical University of Koszalin, Poland)
Information Science Reference • copyright 2017 • 312pp • H/C (ISBN: 9781522525318) • US $175.00 (our price)

Model-Based Design for Effective Control System Development
Wei Wu (Independent Researcher, USA)
Information Science Reference • copyright 2017 • 299pp • H/C (ISBN: 9781522523031) • US $185.00 (our price)

Comparative Approaches to Using R and Python for Statistical Data Analysis
Rui Sarmento (University of Porto, Portugal) and Vera Costa (University of Porto, Portugal)
Information Science Reference • copyright 2017 • 197pp • H/C (ISBN: 9781683180166) • US $180.00 (our price)

Developing Service-Oriented Applications Using the Windows Communication Foundation (WCF) Framework
Chirag Patel (Charotar University of Science and Technology, India)
Information Science Reference • copyright 2017 • 487pp • H/C (ISBN: 9781522519973) • US $200.00 (our price)

Resource Management and Efficiency in Cloud Computing Environments
Ashok Kumar Turuk (National Institute of Technology Rourkela, India) Bibhudatta Sahoo (National Institute of Technology Rourkela, India) and Sourav Kanti Addya (National Institute of Technology Rourkela, India)
Information Science Reference • copyright 2017 • 352pp • H/C (ISBN: 9781522517214) • US $205.00 (our price)

Handbook of Research on End-to-End Cloud Computing Architecture Design
Jianwen "Wendy" Chen (IBM, Australia) Yan Zhang (Western Sydney University, Australia) and Ron Gottschalk (IBM, Australia)
Information Science Reference • copyright 2017 • 507pp • H/C (ISBN: 9781522507598) • US $325.00 (our price)

701 East Chocolate Avenue, Hershey, PA 17033, USA
Tel: 717-533-8845 x100 • Fax: 717-533-8661
E-Mail: cust@igi-global.com • www.igi-global.com

Table of Contents

Detailed Table of Contents

Chapter 1

THD and Compensation Time Analysis of Three-Phase Shunt Active Power Filter Using
Adaptive Blanket Body Cover Algorithm 1

    S. Khalid, CCSI Airport, India

A novel Adaptive Blanket Body Cover Algorithm (ABBC) has been presented, which has been used for the optimization of conventional control scheme used in shunt active power filter. The effectiveness of the proposed algorithm has been proved by applying this in balanced, unbalanced and distorted supply conditions. The superiority of this algorithm over existing Genetic Algorithm results has been presented by analyzing the Total Harmonic Distortion and compensation time of both the algorithms. The simulation results using MATLAB model ratify that algorithm has optimized the control technique, which unmistakably prove the usefulness of the proposed algorithm in balanced, unbalanced and distorted supply system.

Chapter 2

Swarm-Intelligence-Based Optimal Placement and Sizing of Distributed Generation in
Distribution Network: Swarm-Intelligence-Based Distributed Generation 29

    Mahesh Kumar, Universiti Teknologi Petronas, Malaysia & Mehran University of
        Engineering and Technology, Pakistan
    Perumal Nallagownden, Universiti Teknologi Petronas, Malaysia
    Irraivan Elamvazuthi, Universiti Teknologi Petronas, Malaysia
    Pandian Vasant, Universiti Teknologi Petronas, Malaysia
    Luqman Hakim Rahman, Universiti Teknologi Petronas, Malaysia

In the distribution system, distributed generation (DG) are getting more important because of the electricity demands, fossil fuel depletion and environment concerns. The placement and sizing of DGs have greatly impact on the voltage stability and losses in the distribution network. In this chapter, a particle swarm optimization (PSO) algorithm has been proposed for optimal placement and sizing of DG to improve voltage stability index in the radial distribution system. The two i.e. active power and combination of active and reactive power types of DGs are proposed to realize the effect of DG integration. A specific analysis has been applied on IEEE 33 bus system radial distribution networks using MATLAB 2015a software.

Environmental regulations demand efficient and eco-friendly ways of power generation. Coal continues to play a vital role in power generation because of its availability in abundance. Power generation using coal leads to local pollution problems. Hence this conflicting situation demands a new technology - Integrated Gasification Combined Cycle (IGCC). Gasifier is one of the subsystems in IGCC. It is a multivariable system with four inputs and four outputs with higher degree of cross coupling between the input and output variables. ALSTOM – a multinational and Original Equipment Manufacturer (OEM) - developed a detailed nonlinear mathematical model, validated made this model available to the academic community and demanded different control strategies which will satisfy certain stringent performance criteria during specified disturbances. These demands of ALSTOM are well known as "ALSTOM Benchmark Challenges". The chapter is addressed to solve Alstom Benchmark Challenges using Proportional-Integral-Derivative-Filter (PIDF) controllers optimised by Genetic Algorithm.

Modern engineering often uses computer simulations as a partial substitute to real-world experiments. As such simulations are often computationally intensive, metamodels, which are numerical approximations of the simulation, are often used. Optimization frameworks which use metamodels require an initial sample of points to initiate the main optimization process. Two main approaches for generating the initial sample are the 'design of experiments' method which is statistically based, and the more recent metaheuristic-based sampling which uses a metaheuristic or a computational intelligence algorithm. Since the initial sample can have a strong impact on the overall optimization search and since the two sampling approaches operate based only widely different mechanisms this study analyzes the impact of these two approaches on the overall search effectiveness in an extensive set of numerical experiments which covers a wide variety of scenarios. A detailed analysis is then presented which highlights which method was the most beneficial to the search depending on the problem settings.

The idea of this chapter is the use of Gaussian type-1 fuzzy membership functions based approach for automatic hand gesture recognition. The process has been carried out in five stages starting with the use of skin color segmentation for the isolation of the hand from the background. Then Sobel edge detection technique is employed to extract the contour of the hand. The next stage comprises of the calculation of eight spatial distances by locating the center point of the boundary and all distances are normalized with respect to the maximum distance value. Finally, matching based on Gaussian fuzzy membership function is used for the recognition of unknown hand gestures. This simple and effective procedure produces highest accuracy of 91.23% for Gaussian membership function and a time complexity of 2.01s using Matlab R2011b run on an Intel Pentium Dual Core Processor.

Ginalber Serra, Federal Institute of Education, Science, and Technology, Brazil
Edson B. M. Costa, IFMA, Brazil

A self-tuning fuzzy control methodology via particle swarm optimization based on robust stability criterion, is proposed. The plant to be controlled is modeled considering a Takagi-Sugeno (TS) fuzzy structure from input-output experimental data, by using the fuzzy C-Means clustering algorithm (antecedent parameters estimation) and weighted recursive least squares (WRLS) algorithm (consequent parameters estimation), respectively. An adaptation mechanism based on particle swarm optimization is used to tune recursively the parameters of a fuzzy PID controller, from the gain and phase margins specifications. Computational results for adaptive fuzzy control of a thermal plant with time varying delay is presented to illustrate the efficiency and applicability of the proposed methodology.

Reshma Kar, Jadavpur University, India
Amit Konar, Jadavpur University, India
Aruna Chakraborty, St. Thomas' College of Engineering and Technology, India

This chapter discusses emotions induced by music and attempts to detect emotional states based on regional interactions within the brain. The brain network theory largely attributes statistical measures of interdependence as indicators of brain region interactions/connectivity. In this paper, the authors studied two bivariate models of brain connectivity and employed thresholding based on relative values among electrode pairs, in order to give a multivariate flavor to these models. The experimental results suggest that thresholding the brain connectivity measures based on their relative strength increase classification accuracy by approximately 10% and 8% in time domain and frequency domain respectively. The results are based on emotion recognition accuracy obtained by decision tree based linear support vector machines, considering the thresholded connectivity measures as features. The emotions were categorized as fear, happiness, sadness, and relaxation.

Anuradha Saha, Jadavpur University, India
Amit Konar, Jadavpur University, India

This chapter introduces a novel approach to examine the scope of tactile sensory perception as a possible modality of treatment of patients suffering from certain mental disorder using a Support Vector Machines with kernelized neural network. Experiments are designed to understand the perceptual difference of schizophrenic patients from normal and healthy subjects with respect to three different touch classes, including soft touch, rubbing, massaging and embracing and their three typical subjective responses. Experiments undertaken indicate that for normal subjects and schizophrenic patients, the average percentage accuracy in classification of all the three classes: pleasant/acceptable/unpleasant is comparable with their respective oral responses. In addition, for schizophrenic patients, the percentage accuracy for acceptable class is very poor of the order of below 12%, which for normal subjects is quite high (42%). Performance analysis reveals that the proposed classifier outperforms its competitors with respect to classification accuracy in all the above three classes.

    Santanu Dam, Future Institute of Engineering and Management, India
    Gopa Mandal, Kalyani Government Engineering College, India
    Kousik Dasgupta, Kalyani Government Engineering College, India
    Parmartha Dutta, Visva-Bharati University, India

This book chapter proposes use of Ant Colony Optimization (ACO), a novel computational intelligence technique for balancing loads of virtual machine in cloud computing. Computational intelligence(CI), includes study of designing bio-inspired artificial agents for finding out probable optimal solution. So the central goal of CI can be said as, basic understanding of the principal, which helps to mimic intelligent behavior from the nature for artifact systems. Basic strands of ACO is to design an intelligent multi-agent systems imputed by the collective behavior of ants. From the perspective of operation research, it's a meta-heuristic. Cloud computing is a one of the emerging technology. It's enables applications to run on virtualized resources over the distributed environment. Despite these still some problems need to be take care, which includes load balancing. The proposed algorithm tries to balance loads and optimize the response time by distributing dynamic workload in to the entire system evenly.

    Shailendra Singh, National Institute of Technical Teachers Training and Research Institute,
      India
    Sunita Gond, Barkatullah University, India

As this is the age of technology and every day we are receiving the news about growing popularity of internet and its applications. Cloud computing is an emerging paradigm of today that is rapidly accepted by the industry/organizations/educational institutions etc. for various applications and purpose. As computing is related to distributed and parallel computing which are from a very long time in the market, but today is the world of cloud computing that reduces the cost of computing by focusing on personal computing to data center computing. Cloud computing architecture and standard provide a unique way for delivering computation services to cloud users. It is having a simple API (Application Platform Interface) to users for accessing storage, platform and hardware by paying-as-per-use basis. Services provided by cloud computing is as same as other utility oriented services like electricity bill, water, telephone etc. over shared network. There are many cloud services providers in the market for providing services like Google, Microsoft, Manjrasoft Aneka, etc.

    Murugan Sethuraman Sethuraman, Wolkite University, Ethiopia

Intrusion detection system(IDS) has played a vital role as a device to guard our networks from unknown malware attacks. However, since it still suffers from detecting an unknown attack, i.e., 0-day attack, the ultimate challenge in intrusion detection field is how we can precisely identify such an attack. This chapter will analyze the various unknown malware activities while networking, internet or remote connection. For identifying known malware various tools are available but that does not detect Unknown malware exactly. It will vary according to connectivity and using tools and finding strategies what they used. Anyhow like known Malware few of unknown malware listed according to their abnormal activities and changes in the system. In this chapter, we will see the various Unknown methods and avoiding preventions as birds eye view manner.

Chapter 12

The increase of e-Learning resources such as interactive learning environments, learning management systems or intelligent tutoring systems has created huge repositories of educational data that can be explored. This increase generated the need of integrating machine learning methodologies into the currently existing e-Learning environments. The integration of such procedures focuses on working with a wide range of data analysis algorithms and their various implementations in form of tools or technologies. This paper aims to present a self-contained roadmap for practitioners who want to have basic knowledge about a core set of algorithms and who want to apply them on educational data. The background of this research domain is represented by state-of-the-art data analysis algorithms found in the areas of Machine Learning, Information Retrieval or Data Mining that are adapted to work on educational data. The main goal of the research efforts in the domain of Intelligent Data Analysis on Educational Data is to provide tools that enhance the quality of the on-line educational systems.

Foreword

Computational Intelligence (CI) is one among the foremost important powerful tools for research within the diverse fields of engineering sciences starting from traditional fields of civil, mechanical engineering to vast sections of electrical, electronics and computer engineering and above all the biological and pharmaceutical sciences. The existing field has its origin in the functioning of the human brain in processing information, recognizing the pattern, learning from observations and experiments, storing and retrieving information from memory, etc. In particular, the power industry being on the verge of epoch changing due to deregulation, the power engineers require Computational intelligence tools for proper planning, operation and control of the power system. Most of the CI tools are suitably formulated as some sort of optimization or decision making problems. These CI techniques provide the power utilities with innovative solutions for efficient analysis, optimal operation and control and intelligent decision making.

During the last decades, the application of artificial intelligence techniques and methods has proved to be beneficial for the expansion of our knowledge on the design process and the achievement of better products and artifacts. The combination of these fields leads to more complex architectures able to address multiple – and more complex – design issues such as representation, solution search, learning, etc.

This book has been authored with the intention of focusing on the latest advances and to highlight the opportunities provided by the implementation of soft computing techniques in engineering such as Adaptive Blanket Body Cover Algorithm (ABBC), particle swarm optimization (PSO) algorithm, Genetic Algorithm, metaheuristic and Statistical based Sampling in Optimization, fuzzy logic control, Detection of Music Induced Emotion Changes by Functional Brain Networks, EEG-Analysis using neural network and many more techniques.

I wish to express deep gratitude to all authors who were taking part in the preparation of the manuscript of the book for their efforts, for their job, and generosity with which the impart experience and knowledge with readers.

The special gratitude is deserved publishing house of IGI Global, in particular, the editor Dr Saifullah Khalid and the editorial advisory board, for providing the opportunity for authors to publish their newest results.

Keshav Sharma
Civil Aviation Training College, India

Foreword

Keshav Sharma *is working as a Principal at Civil aviation training college, Allahabad, India. He holds degrees of Masters of Science (Electronics) from Rajasthan University, M.Phil (Solid State Electronics) from University of Delhi, and Masters in Management from Indian Institute of Technology (IIT), Bombay. He switched over to Airports Authority of India on its formation in the nineties and served in various capacities at middle and senior management level in the areas of Air Traffic Control, ATC Automation, Air Safety and Airport Management for almost 25 years as Air Traffic Controller (Aerodrome, Terminal and En-Route RADARs) and as Airport Director of some of major Airports. Further, He is now pursuing Doctor of Philosophy (PhD) from the department of Aerospace Engg. IIT Bombay and has published papers in international conferences/ journals on the subject of ATCO's cognitive workload assessment. Mr. Sharma is a life member of Institution of Electronics and Telecommunication Engineers (IETE), India and Aeronautical Society of India (ASI) and has served as a member of various executive committees in these professional organizations for various programs.*

Foreword

Computational Intelligence (CI) focuses on the theory, design, application, and development of biologically and linguistically motivated computational paradigms combining elements of learning, adaptation, evolution and fuzzy logic. Computational intelligence is the foundation of artificial intelligence that has expanded to an extent to be recognized as a separate domain of research. In general, the typical artificial intelligence techniques follow top-to-bottom approach wherein the structure of models, solutions, etc. are worked from top. Computational intelligence, however, are generally bottom-up techniques where order and structure emerge from an unstructured beginning. The term *computational intelligence* encompasses terms such as neural networks, connectionist systems, genetic algorithms, evolutionary programming, fuzzy systems, swarm intelligence, artificial immune systems and hybrid intelligent systems, etc.

Soft Computing has emerged as a vital approach towards achieving intelligent paradigm of processing, especially where the key part is learning from expertise in the presence of uncertainties, fuzzy belief functions, and evolution of the computing ways for training the training agent itself. Fuzzy, neural and evolutionary computing are the three major streams of soft computing.

Computational intelligence is the fabric of soft computing conjointly used with real world applications called hard computing. Soft computing, as such, does not put conditions on the matter, however, conjointly provides guarantee for rectification of a deficiency, if there is any, and that gets compensated by its strength of the strategies.

This valuable compendium addresses the following research topics and techniques, and much more, in relation with "Applied Computational Intelligence and Soft Computing in Engineering".

- Adaptive Blanket Body Cover Algorithm
- Swarm Intelligence Based Distributed Generation
- Genetic Algorithm based performance optimization
- Sampling in Optimization
- Static Hand Gesture Recognition
- Fuzzy Controller
- Functional Brain Networks
- EEG-Analysis Using Neural Techniques
- Ant Colony Based Approach
- Cloud Computing
- Unknown Malware Attack Finding
- Machine Learning Data Analysis

A huge variety and diversified application areas indeed are unfolded in the twelve chapters.

Sincere appreciation and gratitude are extended to each of the authors for contributing valuable chapters. Sharing with academic fraternity their deep insight and expertise in advance technology will surely go a long way for betterment of mankind. It will also pave way for furtherance of research in this field.

I congratulate the Publishing house IGI Global, the Editor, Dr. Saifullah Khalid, and all the Editorial Advisory Board Members for creating this platform to the experts to publish their contributions and suggestions in emerging areas of applied computational techniques.

I am sure that the readers would be greatly benefitted through this book personally, professionally as well as socially.

Bharti Dwivedi
Institute of Engineering and Technology Lucknow, India

Bharti Dwivedi *received the B.E. and M.Tech degrees in electrical engineering from GEC (now NIT), Raipur, India and IIT, Kanpur, India in 1979 and 1985, respectively. She received the PhD degree in electrical engineering from GEC (now NIT), Raipur, India in 2001. She is Professor and Head of Department at Department of Electrical Engineering, Institute of Engineering & Technology, India. She is also the advisor of several students of Master/PhD Program in Electrical Engineering at the Institute of Engineering & Technology, Lucknow, India. Prof Dwivedi has been in the field of teaching and research for more than 35 years. She has more than 50 research papers and articles in national journals, international journals, conference proceedings, conference paper presentation, conference abstracts. She has also written few books in the field of electrical engineering. Prof Dwivedi is a reviewer for many prestigious international journals and conferences. Her research interest includes topics on, Neural Networks, Fuzzy Inference Systems, and application of power electronics in power system.*

Preface

Artificial Intelligence and Computational Intelligence seek a related long term objective: attain general intelligence, which is the intelligence of a machine that could perform any logical task, that an individual can; There's an obvious dissimilarity between them. There are two types of machine intelligence: the artificial one based on hard computing techniques and the computational one based on soft computing techniques, which facilitate adaptation to many circumstances.

Computational Intelligence is a set of biological and linguistic computational tools and methodologies to address complex and challenging real world problems to which traditional approaches may not be very effective. Therefore, they are regarded as promising techniques for solving complex problems. Computational Intelligence describes a large, diverse, and evolving field of theories and techniques, all inspired in one way or the other by nature. Computational intelligence is a methodology involving computing that provides a system with an ability to learn and/or to deal with new situations, such that the system is perceived to possess one or more attributes of reason, such as generalization, discovery, association, and abstraction.

When the terms "intelligence" or "intelligent" are utilized by scientists, they're touching on an outsized assortment of human psychological feature behaviors—people thinking (Edward, 2003). Once life scientists speak of the intelligence of animals, they're asking us to decision to mind a group of human behaviors that they're declarative the animals capable of. Once computer scientists speak of computing, machine intelligence, intelligent agents, or (as I selected to try and do within the title of this essay) machine intelligence, we tend to also are touching on that set of human behaviors.

Though intelligence suggests that folks thinking, we'd be able to replicate an equivalent set of behaviors using computation. Indeed, one branch of contemporary psychological science is predicated on the model that the human mind and brain are complicated computational "engines," that is, we tend to ourselves are samples of machine intelligence. The idea, of course, is not new. It absolutely was mentioned by Turing within the Forties. Within the play concerning Turing's life, Breaking the Code (Whitemore, 1987), Turing is shown visiting his previous descriptive linguistics faculty and delivering an interview to the boys, during which he offers a vision of the thinking computer. The reminiscences of these of Turing's colleagues of the Forties who are still alive make sure that he spoke usually of this vision. In 1950, he wrote of it, in an exceedingly famed article (Turing, 1950), during which he projected a check (now known as the Turing test (TT)) for computational intelligence.

Within the check, a personality's judgment should be created regarding whether or not a group of determined behaviors is sufficiently almost like human behaviors that an equivalent word—intelligent—can with reason be used. The judgment is concerning behavior not mechanism. Computers aren't like human brains, however, if they perform equivalent acts and one performing artist (the human) is labelled intelligent, then the opposite should be tagged intelligent additionally.

I even have invariably likeable the Turing test as a result of it gave a transparent and tangible vision, was moderately objective, and created concrete the tie to human behavior by using the unarticulated criteria of a personality's decide. Turing Award winner Jim grey, who works in fields of engineering apart from AI, seems to agree. His list of challenges for the long run includes: "The Turing test: Win the imitation game half-hour of the time." considerably, he adds: "Read and perceive furthermore as a personality. Assume and write furthermore as a person's," (Gray, 1950). I'll have a lot of to mention concerning necessary conditions for these human activities later. However, there are issues with the Turing test (TT). Human intelligence is extremely multidimensional. However, the decide should fuse all of those dimensions into one judgment concerning the "humanness" of the behavior. The computer scientists who add the areas known as, or allied to, computing typically should study these dimensions one by one. Successes on anyone of the scale will solely be thought-about "partially intelligent" by Turing's criterion. Imagine doing a TT of procedure intelligence that was nearly as good as associate Einstein (who, after all, was Time magazine's "Man of the Century") in causation and making physical theories, however, was severely lacking in its ability to handle standard language. Still, associate applicable strategy for a scientific field to conduct its inquiry is divide-and-conquer—studies the dimensions of intelligence a lot of or less one by one. We tend to should be glad for a protracted time to return with "partial intelligence" in our artifacts as a natural consequence of this inevitable strategy. In dividing-and-conquering, these are some samples of the various human behaviors that we tend to either have divided out for study or have to be compelled to (Gentiner, 2003):

- The ability to draw abstractions from particulars.
- The ability to take care of hierarchies of abstraction.
- The ability to concatenate assertions and attain a replacement conclusion.
- The ability to reason outside this context.
- The ability to check and distinction 2 representations for consistency/ inconsistency.
- The ability to reason analogically.
- The ability to find out and use external symbols to represent numerical, spatial, or abstract data.
- The ability to find out and use symbols whose meanings are outlined in terms of different learned symbols.
- The ability to create and learn terms for abstractions furthermore as for concrete entities.
- The ability to invent and learn terms for relations as well as things.

Initially, it was believed that the machine learning processes would learn symbolic concepts built up out of symbolic entities, and relations. For example, in the late 1960s, I collaborated on the Meta-DENDRAL machine learning project, the result of which was a publication in the mainline literature of chemistry of a hitherto undiscovered symbolic model of the mass-spectral fragmentation of an interesting family of organic molecules (Buchanan, 1998). It was published because it was a contribution to mass-spectral fragmentation theory. In the years following, the machine learning field moved away from symbolic concepts toward the border of statistics, where the entities and relations were statistical in nature. This work had a large impact and helped to fuel the new field of data mining, but it had essentially no impact on the construction of the large knowledge bases at the core of CI. A team like Lenat's

CYC team continued to encode symbolic concepts manually, one by one. So the "missing science" is still mostly missing.

Design has been a human activity for thousands of years. In both its creative and routine forms, the scientific community has extensively studied design during the last decades for the establishment of general purpose and domain-independent scientific rules and methodologies. Demand for lightweight, efficient, and low cost structures seems mandatory because of growing realization of the rarity of raw materials and rapid depletion of convention energy sources. This requires engineers to be aware of optimization techniques. Designing, analyzing, and solving civil engineering problems can be very large scale and can be highly nonlinear, and to search out solutions to those problems is commonly terribly difficult. Within the past 20 years, soft computing ways have become a crucial category of economical tools for developing intelligent systems and providing solutions to difficult engineering issues. Intelligence built in computer programs covers Evolutionary computing, Fuzzy computing, Neuro-computing, which is also known as soft computing.

This book will provide an overview and original analysis of new developments and advances in several areas of computational intelligence. In addition to its detailed accounts of the most recent research, this book will provide useful applications and information on the benefits of applying computation intelligence techniques to engineering and technology.

The concepts, paradigms, and algorithms of computational intelligence and its constituent methodologies such as evolutionary computation, neural networks, and fuzzy logic, etc., are the focus of this book. In addition, this book emphasizes practical applications throughout, that is, how to apply the Computational Intelligence to practical problems in engineering and technology. There is a need to expose academician and researchers to CI and their multidisciplinary applications for better utilization of these techniques and their future development. This book not only deals with an introduction to the CI techniques along with their several applications but also tries to cover several novel applications of combining CI techniques and utilizing the hybrid forms in different practical areas like engineering systems used in military and civilian applications, manufacturing, biomedical and health care systems as well as engineering education.

This book seeks to provide a discussion forum for adopting the state of the art Computational Intelligence techniques in engineering and technology, developing the cutting edge techniques by using Computational Intelligence approaches, as well as exchanging of related ideas and discussing the future directions.

Although computational intelligence and soft computing are well-known fields, the novel applications of using computational intelligence and soft computing can be observed as an emerging field, which is the focus of this book.

The following research topics are well covered in this book:

- Adaptive Blanket Body Cover Algorithm
- Swarm Intelligence Based Distributed Generation
- Genetic Algorithm based performance optimization
- Sampling in Optimization
- Static Hand Gesture Recognition
- Fuzzy Controller
- Functional Brain Networks

- EEG-Analysis Using Neural Techniques
- Ant Colony Based Approach
- Cloud Computing
- Unknown Malware Attack Finding
- Machine Learning Data Analysis

The book is organized into 12 chapters. A brief description of each of the chapters is as follows:

Chapter 1: The chapter presents a novel Adaptive Blanket Body Cover Algorithm (ABBC), which has been used for the optimization of conventional control scheme used in shunt active power filter. The effectiveness of the proposed algorithm has been proved by applying this in balanced, unbalanced and distorted supply conditions. The superiority of this algorithm over existing Genetic Algorithm results has been presented by analyzing the Total Harmonic Distortion and compensation time of both the algorithms.

Chapter 2: The chapter addresses the issues of distributed generation (DG), which are getting more important because of the electricity demands, fossil fuel depletion and environment concerns. The placement and sizing of DGs have greatly impact on the voltage stability and losses in the distribution network. In this chapter, a particle swarm optimization (PSO) algorithm has been proposed for optimal placement and sizing of DG to improve voltage stability index in the radial distribution system. The two i.e. active power and combination of active and reactive power types of DGs are proposed to realize the effect of DG integration. A specific analysis has been applied on IEEE 33 bus system radial distribution networks using MATLAB.

Chapter 3: In this chapter performance optimization for non linear MIMO system has been discussed. Environmental regulations demand efficient and eco-friendly ways of power generation. Coal continues to play a vital role in power generation because of its availability in abundance. Power generation using coal leads to local pollution problems. Hence this conflicting situation demands a new technology - Integrated Gasification Combined Cycle (IGCC). The gasifier is one of the subsystems in IGCC. It is a multivariable system with four inputs and four outputs with a higher degree of cross coupling between the input and output variables. ALSTOM – a multinational and Original Equipment Manufacturer (OEM) - developed a detailed nonlinear mathematical model, validated made this model available to the academic community and demanded different control strategies which will satisfy certain stringent performance criteria during specified disturbances. These demands of ALSTOM are well known as "ALSTOM Benchmark Challenges". The chapter is addressed to solve Alstom Benchmark Challenges using Proportional-Integral-Derivative-Filter (PIDF) controllers optimized by Genetic Algorithm.

Chapter 4: This chapter presents metaheuristic and Statistical based Sampling in Optimization in the present scenario, modern engineering often uses computer simulations as a partial substitute to real-world experiments. As such simulations are often computationally intensive, metamodels, which are numerical approximations of the simulation, are often used. Optimization frameworks which use metamodels require an initial sample of points to initiate the main optimization process. Two main approaches for generating the initial sample are the `design of experiments' method which is statistically based, and the more recent metaheuristic-based sampling which uses a metaheuristic or a computational intelligence algorithm. Since the initial sample can have a strong impact on the overall optimization search and since the two sampling approaches operate based only widely different mechanisms this study analyzes the impact of these two approaches on the overall search effectiveness in an extensive set of numerical experiments which covers a wide variety of scenarios.

Chapter 5: This chapter shows the application of Gaussian type-1 fuzzy membership functions based approach for automatic hand gesture recognition. The process has been carried out in five stages starting with the use of skin color segmentation for the isolation of the hand from the background. Then Sobel edge detection technique is employed to extract the contour of the hand. The next stage comprises of the calculation of eight spatial distances by locating the center point of the boundary and all distances are normalized with respect to the maximum distance value. Finally, matching based on Gaussian fuzzy membership function is used for the recognition of unknown hand gestures. This simple and effective procedure produces the highest accuracy of 91.23% for Gaussian membership function and a time complexity of 2.01s using MATLAB.

Chapter 6: This chapter deals with a self-tuning fuzzy control methodology via particle swarm optimization based on robust stability criterion. The plant to be controlled is modeled considering a Takagi-Sugeno (TS) fuzzy structure from input-output experimental data, by using the fuzzy C-Means clustering algorithm (antecedent parameters estimation) and weighted recursive least squares (WRLS) algorithm (consequent parameters estimation), respectively. An adaptation mechanism based on particle swarm optimization is used to tune recursively the parameters of a fuzzy PID controller, from the gain and phase margins specifications.

Chapter 7: The emotions induced by music and an attempt to detect emotional states based on regional interactions within the brain have been discussed in this chapter. The brain network theory largely attributes statistical measures of interdependence as indicators of brain region interactions/connectivity. Two bivariate models of brain connectivity and employed thresholding based on relative values among electrode pairs, in order to give a multivariate flavor to these models, have been developed. The experimental results suggest that thresholding the brain connectivity measures based on their relative strength increase classification accuracy by approximately 10% and 8% in the time domain and frequency domain respectively. The results are based on emotion recognition accuracy obtained by decision tree based linear support vector machines, considering the thresholded connectivity measures as features. The emotions were categorized as fear, happiness, sadness, and relaxation.

Chapter 8: This chapter introduces a novel approach to examine the scope of tactile sensory perception as a possible modality of treatment of patients suffering from certain mental disorder using a Support Vector Machines with the kernelized neural network. Experiments are designed to understand the perceptual difference of schizophrenic patients from normal and healthy subjects with respect to three different touch classes, including soft touch, rubbing, massaging and embracing and their three typical subjective responses. Experiments undertaken indicate that for normal subjects and schizophrenic patients, the average percentage accuracy in classification of all the three classes: pleasant/acceptable/unpleasant is comparable with their respective oral responses. In addition, for schizophrenic patients, the percentage accuracy for the acceptable class is very poor of the order of below 10%, which for normal subjects is quite high (46%). Performance analysis reveals that the proposed classifier outperforms its competitors with respect to classification accuracy in all the above three classes.

Chapter 9: This book chapter proposes the use of Ant Colony Optimization (ACO), a novel computational intelligence technique for balancing loads of virtual machine in cloud computing. Computational intelligence (CI) includes the study of designing bio-inspired artificial agents for finding out a probable optimal solution. So the central goal of CI can be said as, a basic understanding of the principle, which helps to mimic intelligent behavior from nature for artifact systems. Basic strands of ACO is to design intelligent multi-agent systems imputed by the collective behavior of ants. From the perspective of operation research, it's a meta-heuristic. Cloud computing is a one of the emerging technology. It enables applications to run on virtualized resources over the distributed environment. Despite these still, some problems need to take care, which includes load balancing. The proposed algorithm tries to balance loads and optimize the response time by distributing dynamic workload in to the entire system evenly.

Chapter 10: This chapter discusses cloud computing, which is an emerging paradigm of today that is rapidly accepted by the industry/organizations/educational institutions etc. for various applications and purpose. As computing is related to distributed and parallel computing which is from a very long time in the market, but today is the world of cloud computing that reduces the cost of computing by focusing on personal computing to data center computing. Cloud computing architecture and standard provide a unique way for delivering computation services to cloud users. It is having a simple API (Application Platform Interface) to users for accessing storage, platform and hardware by paying-as-per-use basis. Services provided by cloud computing is as same as other utility oriented services like electricity bill, water, telephone etc. over a shared network.

Chapter 11: Intrusion detection system (IDS) has played a vital role as a device to guard our networks from unknown malware attacks. However, since it still suffers from detecting an unknown attack, i.e., 0-day attack, the ultimate challenge in intrusion detection field is how we can precisely identify such an attack. This chapter will analyze the various unknown malware activities while networking, the internet or remote connection. For identifying known malware various tools are available but that does not detect Unknown malware exactly. It will vary according to connectivity and use tools and find strategies what they used. Anyhow like known Malware few of unknown malware listed according to their abnormal activities and changes in the system.

Chapter 12: The increase of e-Learning resources such as interactive learning environments, learning management systems or intelligent tutoring systems has created huge repositories of educational data that can be explored. This increase generated the need for integrating machine learning methodologies into the currently existing e-Learning environments. The integration of such procedures focuses on working with a wide range of data analysis algorithms and their various implementations in form of tools or technologies. This chapter aims to present a self-contained roadmap for practitioners who want to have basic knowledge about a core set of algorithms and who want to apply them to educational data. The background of this research domain is represented by state-of-the-art data analysis algorithms found in the areas of Machine Learning, Information Retrieval or Data Mining that are adapted to work on educational data. The main goal of the research efforts in the domain of Intelligent Data Analysis on Educational Data is to provide tools that enhance the quality of the on-line educational systems.

Since Computational Intelligence in Engineering is a truly interdisciplinary field, scientists, engineers, academicians, technology developers, researchers, students, and government officials will find this text useful in handling their complicated real world issues by using Computational Intelligence methodologies and assisting in furthering their own research efforts in this field. Moreover, by bringing together representatives of academia and industry, this book is also a means for identifying new research problems and disseminating results of the research and practice.

The book editor is very grateful to the entire staff of IGI Global, for their confidence, interest, continuous guidance and support at all levels of preparation of this book's preparation. I wish all the readers a pleasant and enjoyable insightful and inspiring lecture of the contribution of this IGI Global book.

Saifullah Khalid
CCSI Airport, India

REFERENCES

Buchanan, B. G. (1998). Applications of artificial intelligence for chemical inference. XXII. Automatic rule formation in mass spectrometry by means of the meta-DENDRAL program. *J. ACS*, 61-68.

Edward, A. (2003). Some Challenges and Grand Challenges for Computational Intelligence. *Journal of the ACM, 50*(1), 32–40. doi:10.1145/602382.602400

Gentiner, D. (2003). Why we're so smart. In *Language in Mind: Advances in the Study of Language and Thought*. Cambridge, MA: MIT Press.

Gray, J. (1950). What Next? A Dozen Information-Technology Research Goals. *Journal of the ACM*, 41–57.

Turing, A. M. (1950). Computing machinery and intelligence. *Mind*, 59.

Whitemore, H. (1987). *Breaking the Code*. Amber Lane Press.

Chapter 1
THD and Compensation Time Analysis of Three-Phase Shunt Active Power Filter Using Adaptive Blanket Body Cover Algorithm

S. Khalid
CCSI Airport, India

ABSTRACT

A novel Adaptive Blanket Body Cover Algorithm (ABBC) has been presented, which has been used for the optimization of conventional control scheme used in shunt active power filter. The effectiveness of the proposed algorithm has been proved by applying this in balanced, unbalanced and distorted supply conditions. The superiority of this algorithm over existing Genetic Algorithm results has been presented by analyzing the Total Harmonic Distortion and compensation time of both the algorithms. The simulation results using MATLAB model ratify that algorithm has optimized the control technique, which unmistakably prove the usefulness of the proposed algorithm in balanced, unbalanced and distorted supply system.

INTRODUCTION

Non-linear loads cause the harmonics into the facility arrangement and these harmonics produce copiously of issues within the system. Once application of unbalanced and nonlinear loads will increase, supply gets distorted and unbalanced. These currents foul the provision point of the utility. Therefore, it is important to compensate unbalance, a harmonic and reactive component of the load currents. Whereas once supply is unbalanced and distorted, these problems worsen the system (Chen Donghua, 2005) (Saifullah & Bharti, 2014) (Saifullah Khalid, Application of AI techniques in implementing Shunt APF in Aircraft Supply System, 2013). By the appliance of shunt active power filter within the system can eliminate harmonic, reactive and unbalanced current still as improve the ability provide performance

DOI: 10.4018/978-1-5225-3129-6.ch001

and so the steadiness of system. Today, the soft computing techniques are used wide for optimization of the system applied or in control system; algorithms (Guillermin, 1996) (Abdul Hasib, Hew Wooi, A, & F., 2002) (Jain, Agrawal, & Gupta, 2002) (Norman, Samsul, Mohd, Jasronita, & B., 2004) used for locating the optimized values of the controllers variables, optimization of active power filter using GA (Chiewchitboon, Tipsuwanpom, Soonthomphisaj, & Piyarat, 2003) (Kumar & Mahajan, 2009) (Ismail, Abdeldjebar, Abdelkrim, Mazari, & Rahli, 2008) (Wang, Zhang, XinheXu, & Jiang, 2006), power loss diminution using particle swarm optimization (Thangaraj, Thanga, Pant, Ajit, & Grosan, 2010), neural network ANN Control (P, K, & Eduardo, 2001) (Rajasekaran, 2005) (Rojas, 1996) (Zerikat & Chekroun, 2008) (Seong-Hwan, Tae-Sik, YooJi-Yoon, & Gwi-Tae, 2001) applied in each machinery and filter devices.

In this chapter, 2 totally different soft computing techniques i.e. adaptive Blanket Body cover algorithm and Genetic algorithm are applied for reduction of harmonics and others downside generated into the balanced, unbalanced and distorted system attributable to the nonlinear loads (Chen Donghua, 2005). The results obtained with each the algorithms are far better than those of typical strategies. ABBC algorithm has given the better results as compare to GA and traditional scheme. The effectiveness of the planned scheme has been evidenced by the simulation results mentioned. The result justified their effectiveness.

In this chapter, ABBC algorithm has been wont to search the optimum value of PI controller parameters. For the case of GA, the optimum value of filter inductor has been calculated. The controlling theme has been modeled on the idea of Constant instantaneous Power control Strategy.

BACKGROUND

When one of the inital models based on instantaneous reactive power theory was reported, active filters had been advanced, The application of this technique allowts compensating independently the average or oscillating portions of the active (real) and reactive (imaginary) powers. One of the complications of the controllers based on the well-known PQ Theory is the practice of low-pass filters to distinct the average and oscillating portions of powers.

Literature Survey

The key papers that play a major role for the implementing Aircraft Power filters are listed below:

- **E.J. Woods, 1990:** Computer simulation results for a single channel of an aircraft electrical system with rectified power loads has been shown in this chapter. The computer model comprised of a generator, ac load with resistance and inductance, and a resistive dc load. The results are there in the form of computer generated plots which show system reaction (E.J.Woods, 1990).
- **Donghua Chen, Tao Guo, Shaojun Xie, Bo Zhou, 2005:** This chapter presents an aircraft shunt active filter, which provides a suitable answer for the neutral current in the three-phase system and the appropriate current controller. The preset frequency current controller implementing 3DSVM strategy is applied to balance the asymmetrical current. The simulation results induce that the discussed active filter can compensate the harmonics, reactive and unbalanced currents entirely (Chen Donghua, 2005).

- **Elisabetta Lavopa, Pericle Zanchetta, Mark Sumner, and Francesco Cupertino, 2009:** In this chapter, a new algorithm for fundamental frequency and harmonic components detection is discussed. The technique is based on a real-time accomplishment of discrete Fourier transform, and it permits fast and accurate evaluation of fundamental frequency and harmonics of a distorted signal with variable fundamental frequency. The proposed algorithm has been employed in MATLAB/Simulink for computer simulation (Lavopa & P., 2009).

- **Ahmad Eid, Hassan El-Kishky, Mazen Abdel-Salam, and Mohamed T. El-Mohandes, 2010:** This chapter presents a complete representation of the variable speed constant-frequency aircraft electric power system, which is developed to learn the performance characteristics of the system. The power quality characteristics of the studied aircraft electric power system with the proposed active filter are shown to be in fulfillment of the most recent military aircraft electrical standards MIL-STD-704F as well as with the IEEE Std. 519 (Ahmed & E. Z Nahla., 2009).

- **Eid, H. El-Kishky, M. Abdel-Salam, T. El-Mohandes, 2010:** This chapter presents a three-phase three-wire shunt active filter, which adjusts the load terminal voltage, eliminate harmonics, correct supply power-factor and balance the nonlinear unbalanced loads. The power quality of the studied aircraft electric system is shown to obey with IEEE-std 519 (Eid, El-Kishky, Abdel-Salam, & El-Mohandes, 2010).

- **Yingpeng Luo, Zhong Chen, Miao Chen, Jianxia Li, 2011:** This chapter has discussed control strategy of the cascaded inverter topology based aeronautical active power filter (AAPF). Furthermore, global framework and control performance of the proposed AAPF are given in detail (Yingpeng Luo, 2011).

- **Zhong Chen, Yingpeng Luo, Miao Chen, 2012:** This chapter is based on the analysis and modeling of the shunt APF with close-loop control and a feed forward compensation path of the load current is proposed to get better the dynamic performance of the APF. Experimental results have verified the feasibility of the proposed AAPF and the high presentation of the control strategy during steady-state and dynamic operations (Zhong Chen, 2012).

Issues, Controversies, Problems

Regrettably, power electronic loads have a fundamentally nonlinear nature, and they, therefore, draw a distorted current from the mains supply. Specifically, they draw non-sinusoidal current, which is not in proportion to the sinusoidal voltage. Consequently, the utility supplying these loads has to offer large reactive volt-amperes. Also, the harmonics produced by the load pollutes it. As nonlinear loads, these solid-state converters draw harmonic and reactive power part of the current from AC mains. The problem, which has been seen while using non-linear loads, is injected harmonics, reactive power burden, unbalance and excessive neutral current. Due to them, also to poor power factor, system's efficiency has also been reduced drastically. They also cause disturbance to other consumers and interference in nearby communication networks, excessive heating in transmission and distribution equipment, errors in metering and malfunctioning of utility relays. The inflict able tariffs levied by utilities against excessive VARs, and the threat of stricter harmonics standards have led to extensive surveys to quantify the problems associated with electric power networks having nonlinear loads. i.e. the load compensation techniques for power quality improvement.

KEY TERM (KT)

Following are the key terms, which will help the readers for understanding this chapter and related issues.

Power Quality

The term power quality is rather a general concept. Broadly, it may be defined as the provision of voltages and System design so that the user of electric power can utilized electric energy from the distribution system successfully, without interference on interruption. Power quality is defined in the IEEE 100 Authoritative Dictionary of IEEE Standard Terms as the concept of powering and grounding electronic equipment in a manner that is suitable to the operation of that equipment and compatible with the premise wiring system and other connected equipment Utilities may want to define power quality as reliability.

- **Power Quality Problems:** A recent survey of Power Quality experts has shown the concern that 50% of all Power Quality problems are related to grounding, ground current, ground bonds, ground loops, and neutral to ground voltages, or other ground associated issues.The following indications are pointers of Power Quality Problems:

    ○ A piece of equipment misoperates at the same time of day.
    ○ A circuit breakers trip deprived of being overloaded.
    ○ Equipment fails in a thunderstorm.
    ○ Automated systems halt for no apparent reason.
    ○ Electronic systems fail or fail to operate on a common basis.
    ○ Electronic systems work in one location but not in another location.

    The commonly used terms those describe the parameters of electrical power that describe or measure power quality are Voltage sags, Voltage variations, Interruptions Swells, Brownouts, Blackouts, Voltage imbalance, Distortion, Harmonics, Harmonic resonance, Inter-harmonics, Noise, Notching, Spikes (Voltage), Impulse, Ground noise, Common mode noise, Crest factor, Critical load, Dropout, Electromagnetic compatibility, Fault, Flicker, Ground, Raw power, Ground loops, Clean ground, Transient, Voltage fluctuations, Dirty power, Under voltage, Momentary interruption, Over voltage, THD, Nonlinear load, Triplens, Voltage regulation, Voltage dip, Blink, Oscillatory Transient etc.

- **Power Quality Standard:** Power quality is a worldwide issue, and keeping related standards current is a never-ending task. It typically takes years to push changes through the process. Most of the ongoing work by the IEEE in harmonic standards development has shifted to modifying Standard 519-1992.

    ○ **IEEE 519:** IEEE 519-1992, Recommended Practices and Requirements for Harmonic Control in Electric Power Systems, established limits on harmonic currents and voltages at the point of common coupling (PCC), or point of metering. The limits of IEEE 519 are intended to:

- Assure that the electric utility can deliver relatively clean power to all of its customers;
- Assure that the electric utility can protect its electrical equipment from overheating, loss of life from excessive harmonic currents, and excessive voltage stress due to excessive harmonic voltage. Each point from IEEE 519 lists the limits for harmonic distortion at the point of common coupling (PCC) or metering point with the utility. The voltage distortion limits are 3% for individual harmonics and 5% THD.

SYSTEM DESCRIPTION

The supply system (Balanced/Unbalanced/Distorted) may be a three-phase system with a supply frequency of 50 Hertz. Figure one shows the APF applied for improvement of the power quality beneath all supply conditions. Shunt APF compensates the harmonic currents within the system [22] (Khalid & Dwivedi, Power quality improvement of constant frequency aircraft electric power system using Fuzzy Logic, Genetic Algorithm and Neural network control based control scheme, 2013), (R. C. Dugan, 1996) (Saifullah Khalid, Power Quality: An Important Aspect, 2010), (Ghosh & Ledwich, 2002) and therefore improves the power quality. The shunt APF is completed by using one voltage supply inverters (VSIs) connected at point of common coupling (PCC) with a common DC link voltage (Mauricio Aredes, 1997) (Saifullah Khalid, Power Quality Issues, Problems, Standards & their Effects in Industry with Corrective Means, 2011) (Khalid & Dwivedi, A Review of State of Art Techniques in Active Power Filters and Reactive Power Compensation, 2007). The load into consideration may be a 3 sort of non-linear loads. 1st load used 6-pulse current source converter Bridge. Second is that the 3 phase diode bridge rectifier with the inductance of 300mH and third one is 3 phase diode bridge rectifier with the capacitance of 1000uF (Load 3). The values of the circuit parameters and load into account are given in Appendix.

CONTROL THEORY

The projected control of APF depends on Constant instantaneous Power control Strategy optimized with soft computing techniques like adaptive Blanket Body cover algorithm/ Genetic algorithm. Overall control theme using constant instantaneous power control strategy with the application of adaptive Blanket Body cover algorithm/Genetic algorithm has been dealt in following sections (Ghosh & Ledwich, 2002) (S.Khalid, 2009) (Saifullah khalid, 2013).

Design Using Novel Adaptive Blanket Body Cover Algorithm (ABBC) (Proposed)

Adaptive Blanket Body cover algorithm (ABBC) is proposed by the author for combinatorial optimization issues. Non-linear continuous optimization issues need a robust search methodology to resolve them and this new adaptive Blanket Body blanket algorithm (ABBC) has been developed for them.

In the ABBC algorithm, an eternal search space has been discretized and back-tracking and adaptive radius features are utilized to lift the performance of the search method.

In this Chapter, the proposed ABBC algorithm searches the optimum value of the proportional integral controller parameters i.e. Kp and Ki and therefore the objective function (OB) is determined such as to give their optimum value with the conditions of % overshoot, rise time and settling time. Objective function has an equation that has 3 variables i.e. % overshoot, rise time and settling time. Initially, the Boundary of Kp and Ki, their higher limits and lower limits, then radius value, conditions for ABBC back tracking, objective function and stop criteria has been outlined.

The shape of the blanket is supposed to be rectangular. We have assumed that the size of the blanket is such that it can be folded maximum twenty times solely. We have outlined some random values of Kp & Ki, which will be within the range of predefined initial values. As shown in Figure 1, the folds are named as X1, X2,.............X20. Each fold has different values of Kp & Ki.

This comparison direction has been inspired from the human nature of using the blanket to cover the body during chilled winter. The blanket has been initially folded to cover upper body. When the body senses the cold in the lower portion, the upper fold will be opened. Thereafter, the lower portion of the blanket will be folded to cover the body. When the full body senses the cold, only lower or upper portion fold alone cannot cover the whole body. So, the full blanket will be folded such that the layer of the blanket will be doubled.

The comparison will move downward direction up to the tenth fold, thereafter it will start from the twentieth fold in the upward direction up to eleventh fold. In the last step, the blanket will be folded half for a complete check of optimum values. Best value of each blanket fold will be compared with the initial value of next blanket fold. Then the best outcome will be saved and will be compared to next one. This process will repeat itself and will stop when stopping criteria fulfill.

We have observed that comparison of each blanket fold values goes through forty times as shown in Figure 1 and that is that the reason for selecting maximum searching iteration (40 iterations) for ABBC

Figure 1. Shunt active power filter used with Load 1, 2 and 3 under balanced/unbalanced/distorted supply

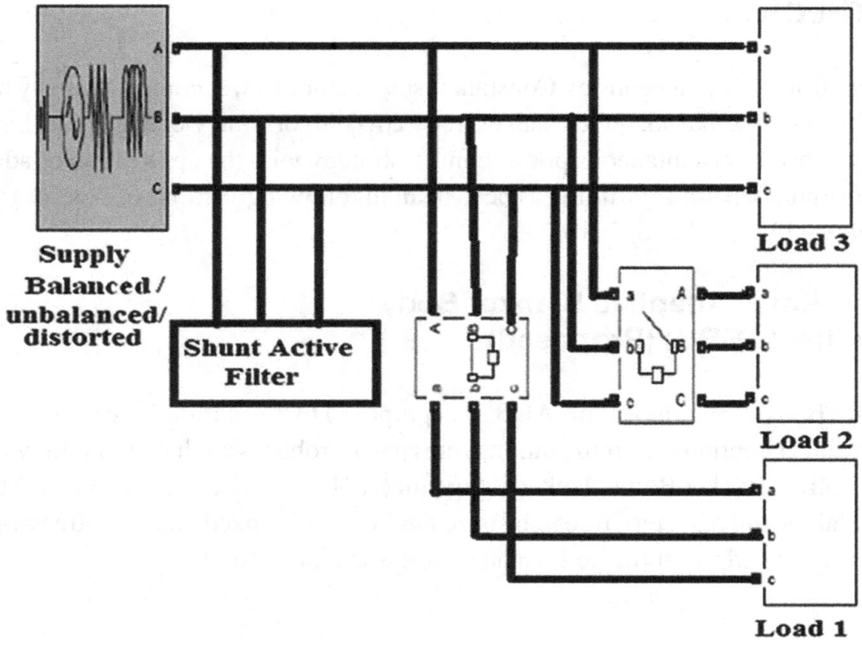

as the stop criterion. There's a predefined list named as Blanket fold list, which contains the values which are distributed over the folds of the blanket.

Figure 2 shows the flow chart for the search of parameters using adaptive body blanket cover (ABBC) algorithm. The values initially used for Kp and Ki were 0.1 and 45 respectively. After the calculation, ABBC algorithm gives the value 0.184 and 14.32. it's been ascertained that whereas using these ABBC calculated values of Kp and Ki, the THD of supply current and voltage are reduced staggeringly that proves that the values are optimum.

Function evaluations: since this chapter relies on the critical analysis supported THD of the supply it's been seen that the objective function taken has shown its effectiveness, which may be seen from the reduction of THD.

Computational time has conjointly been seen terribly less i.e. within seconds, all iterations are over and optimum values of Kp and Ki are often seen on MATLAB/Simulink complier. We will see that this method is extremely stable since it's been calculated offline and so are often used to replace the present values. Robustness of this algorithm is often understood by the great results and less computational time. Convergence analysis has been done offline. The range of iterations with variation in Kp and Ki values has been taken to prove the pliability of the algorithm. This algorithm is extremely convenient to use because of the programming and fewer computational time. The feasibleness and good thing about the algorithm are proved by the simulation results. It's in no time. The parameters i.e. Kp and Ki has been set at random at first and so it has been tuned by using this algorithm offline. Standard equations of Kp and Ki using settling time ($T_{Settling}$), rise time (T_{Rise}) and percent overshoot (P.O.) are used for locating the objective function within the program.

Figure 2. Blanket folds used for optimization

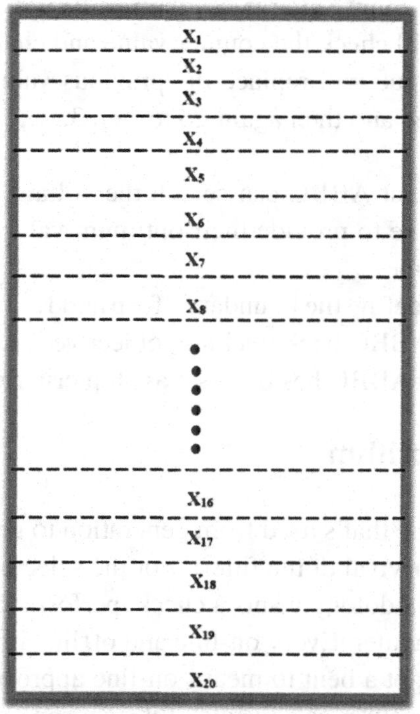

There has been a counter used, which will count the number of iterations and therefore the program will stop automatically once count is up to forty i.e. stopping criteria is forty iterations. Objective function (OB) is defined by

$$OB \text{ (settling time, rise time and percent overshoot)} = E + G + O \tag{1}$$

$$E + G + O = 1 \tag{2}$$

E, G and O are the priority coefficients of settling time, rise time and percent overshoot respectively.

In this chapter, the values of (E, G, and O are set to 0.33, 0.33, and 0.34, respectively. The ABBC search will try to find the best controller parameters to achieve the minimum OB value.

Step 1: Blanket fold list having values of K_p and K_i have been loaded and the counter has been made zero, which will check the number of iteration.

Step 2: the value of the objective function has been calculated for initial values of K_p and K_i.

Step 3: Resultant of step 2 has been compared with the calculated value of an objective function of Blanket fold list i.e. the first comparison from upward to downward, then downward to upward, thereafter half fold of the blanket, and comparison from upward to the downward direction.

Step 4: If the results are not better, it will be saved in blanket fold list and then counter will automatically increase and there will be a change in K_p and K_i values from the blanket fold list. These values will replace the previous values. The objective function for these values will be calculated and then again go to step 3.

Step 5: If the results are better than blanket fold list solutions, it will be saved as the best solution.

Step 6: If number of iteration i.e. count value is 40, the results with the optimum value of K_p and K_i will be shown otherwise it will check the counter value and change the K_p and K_i values from the blanket fold list and these value will replace the previous value and then objective function for these values will be calculated and then again go to step 3.

It will be seen in Figure four that ABBC can search the voltage controller parameters Kp and KI and the objective function is set like to provide their optimum value with the conditions of minimum overshoot, rise time and settling time.

Initially, we have a tendency to define the boundary of Kp and Ki, their higher limits and lower limits, then radius value, conditions for ABBC back tracking, objective function and stop criteria. Maximum searching iteration (40 rounds) for ABBC has been set as stop criterion.

Design Using Genetic Algorithm

GA could also be a search technique that's used from generation to generation for optimizing performs. In fact, GA works on the rule of survival of the fittest. For the selecting the parameters used in the controller using GA, the analysis methodology wants a check, performed on-line on the particular plant or off-line with simulations on a computer. Every on-line and offline methodology are having advantages and disadvantages each. If we've got a bent to means on-line approach, the foremost advantage is that the consistency of the final word answer, as a results of it's chosen on the idea of its real performances, whereas if we have a tendency to predict concerning its disadvantage, it always involve thousands of tests to attain an even result i.e. this optimization methodology will take long run for experiments to run on the real system. Simply just in case of the off-line approach, GA improvement relies on a so much plenty of precise model of the system in conjunction with all elements, all non-linearties, and limits of the controllers. It has to be compelled to, however, be well-known that a negotiation must be met in terms of simulation accuracy and optimization time. Offline, computer simulation using MATLAB Simulink has been applied to hunt out the optimum value.

Figure 3. Flow chart for finding the parameters using ABBC

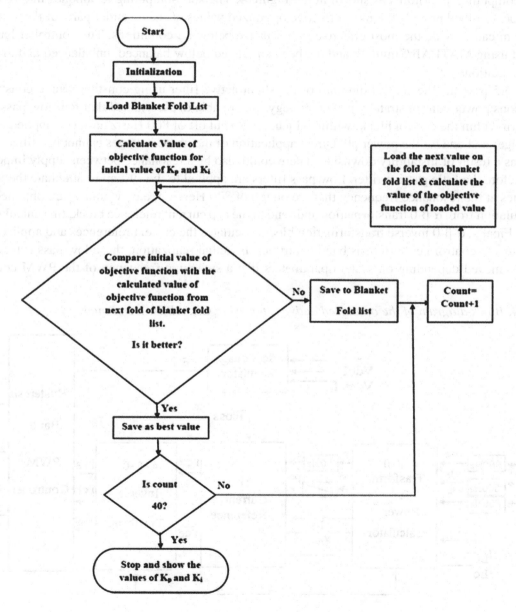

In this chapter, the GA is applied to figure out the appropriate APF parameters i.e. device filter (Lf). The boundary and limits of parameters inside the filter have been outlined and a program using genetic algorithm has been written to return up with the foremost effective value of the filter device.

Control Scheme

In this chapter, Constant instantaneous Power control Strategy (Saifullah Khalid, Comparison of Control Strategies for Shunt Active Power Filter under balanced, unbalanced and distorted supply conditions, 2013) (Mauricio Aredes, 1997) (Saifullah Khalid, Power Quality Issues, Problems, Standards & their Effects in Industry with Corrective Means, 2011) has been used for active power filer with the appliance of soft computing algorithms as shown in the Figure 4. The soft computing techniques like ABBC & GA are accustomed provide the most effective optimized values of the essential parts of the system so the system can provide the most effective performance below all conditions. The controller has been modeled using MATLAB/Simulink and it's been simulated below balanced, unbalanced and distorted supply conditions.

Figure 5 presents the control diagram of the shunt active filter using constant source constant instantaneous power control strategy power strategy. we are able to ascertained that four low pass filters are shown within the control block; within which, 3 with cut off of 800 Hertz has been applied to filter the voltages and one for the power p0. Direct application of the phase voltages cannot be utilized in the control as a result of instability downside. There could also be a resonance between supply impedance and therefore the little passive filter. Low pass filters are applied to the system to attenuate the voltage harmonics at the resonance frequency that are on top of 800 Hertz. p, q,p_0, v_α and v_β are obtained once the calculation from α-β-0 transformation and send to the α-β current reference block, that calculates $i'_{c\alpha}$ and $i'_{c\beta}$. Finally, α-β-0 inverse transformation block calculates the current references and applied to the PWM current control i.e. hysteresis band controller. In actual realization, these low-pass filters could also be removed depending on system parameters like a switching frequency of the PWM converter

Figure 4. Block diagram of the optimized active filter using GA, ABBC techniques

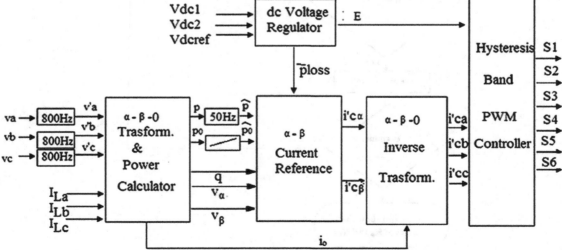

Figure 5. Control block diagram of the shunt active filter using Constant Instantaneous Power Control Strategy

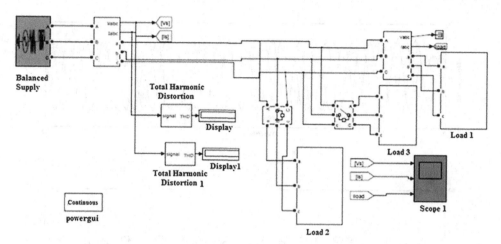

and a frequency response of the electronic circuit for voltage measurement. Later on, the APF has been optimized using soft computing technique i.e. ABBC & GA; that compensate the harmonics and unbalances and build the system among limits of IEEE 519-1992 standard.

SIMULATION RESULTS AND DISCUSSIONS

In this section, 3 sorts of supply system i.e. balanced, unbalanced supply and distorted supply (Mauricio Aredes, 1997) has been simulated in MATLAB/Simulink and their results are mentioned. 3 sort of loads has been used, One 6-pulse current source converter bridge (Load 1), One 3 phase diode bridge rectifier with the inductance of 300mH (Load 2) and one 3 phase diode bridge rectifier with the capacitance of 1000uF (Load 3). To check the dynamic ability of the novel Shunt Active Power filter, simulation of the balanced, unbalanced and distorted supply system has been done once all loads are connected with the system at the completely different time. In this chapter, Load one is often connected, Load 2 is at first connected and is disconnected when each 2.5 cycles and load three is connected and disconnected once each half cycle.

Simulation Results and Discussion of Three Phase Balanced Supply System

In this section, power supply system of 110V with source frequency 50 Hertz has been simulated.

Simulation Results and Discussion of Uncompensated System in Balanced Supply System

Modeling and simulation for an uncompensated system with balanced supply condition for 50 Hz supply for all three loads connected together at different time interval have been done. All the simulations have been done for 15 cycles.

Figure 6. MATLAB/SIMULINK model for all three loads connected together at different intervals for balanced supply condition

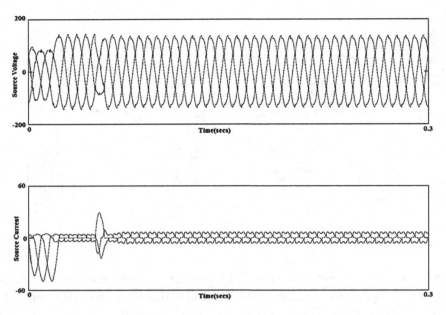

Figure 6 shows the Simulink Model of the uncompensated system with balanced supply condition. Whereas, Figure 7 presents the waveforms of source current and source voltage.

After doing simulation in MATLAB/Simulink, it's been discovered that THD of supply current is 25.63% and THD of supply Voltage were 4.1%. By perceptive this knowledge, we are able to simply perceive that they're out of the limit of IEEE 519-1992 limit. We've got seen that supply has been impure once totally different nonlinear loads are connected.

Simulation Results and Discussion of Shunt APF Using ABBC Algorithm in Balanced Supply System

From the simulation results shown in figure eight, it's been ascertained that the THD of supply current & supply voltage was 1.05% and 3.13% severally. The compensation time was 0.052 sec. At t=0.052 sec, we are able to see that the waveforms for supply voltage and supply current became sinusoidal.

From Figure 8, we will see the waveforms of compensation current, dc capacitor voltage and load current. The variation in dc voltage is clearly seen within the waveforms. As per demand for increasing the compensation current for fulfilling the load current demand, it releases the energy and thenceforth it charges and tries to regain its set value. If we tend to closely observe, we will conclude that the compensation current is really fulfilling the demand of load current and when the active filtering the supply current and voltage is forced to be sinusoidal.

Figure 7. Waveforms of source voltage and source current of all loads connected together at different time interval for balanced supply condition

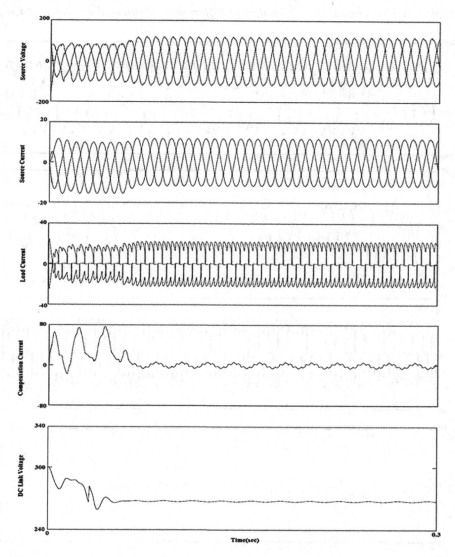

Simulation Results and Discussion of Shunt APF Using GA in Balanced Supply System

From the simulation results shown in figure nine, it's been ascertained that the THD of supply current & supply voltage was 1.46% and 3.25% severally. The compensation time was 0.055 sec. At t=0.055 sec, we are able to see that the waveforms for supply voltage and supply current became sinusoidal.

From Figure 9, we will see the waveforms of compensation current, dc capacitor voltage and load current. The variation in dc voltage is clearly seen within the waveforms. As per demand for increasing

Figure 8. Source voltage, source current, compensation current (phase b), DC link voltage and load current waveforms of active power filter using Constant Instantaneous Power Control Strategy using ABBC Algorithm with all three loads connected together at different time interval for balanced supply system

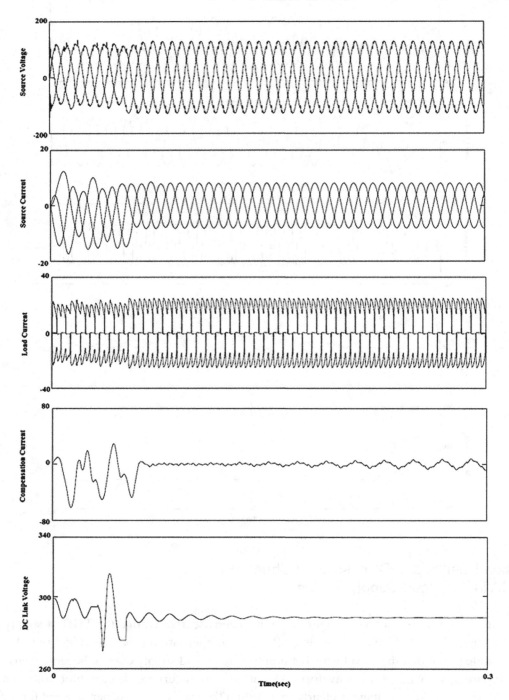

Figure 9. Source voltage, source current, compensation current (phase b), DC link voltage and load current waveforms of active power filter using Constant Instantaneous Power Control Strategy using Genetic Algorithm with all three loads connected together at different time interval for balanced supply system

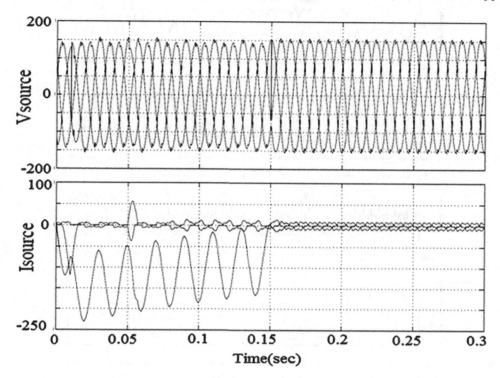

the compensation current for fulfilling the load current demand, it releases the energy and thenceforth it charges and tries to regain its set value. If we tend to closely observe, we will conclude that the compensation current is really fulfilling the demand of load current and when the active filtering the supply current and voltage is forced to be sinusoidal.

Simulation Results and Discussion of Three Phase Unbalanced Supply System

In this section, supply system of 110V, 50 Hertz with a step phase variation of 120^0 with begin and finish time of 0.01 to 0.15 sec severally i.e.an unbalanced supply system has been simulated.

Simulation Results and Discussion of Uncompensated System in Unbalanced Supply System

After doing simulation in MATLAB/Simulink while not connecting any filter (Figure 10) i.e. for uncompensated System, it's been ascertained that the THD of supply current found whereas using all 3 loads at the same time connected with the system at completely different time is 26% and THD of supply Voltage were 3.46%. By observant this information, we will simply perceive that they're out of the limit of IEEE 519-1992 limit. We've seen that supply has been impure once loads have been connected.

Figure 10. Source voltage and source current waveforms of uncompensated system for unbalanced supply

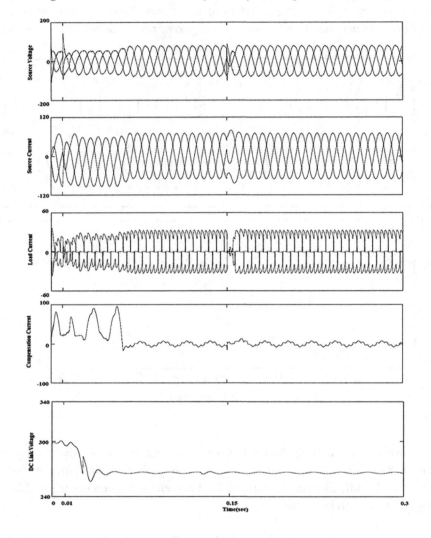

Simulation Results and Discussion About the Shunt APF Using ABBC Algorithm in Unbalanced Supply System

From the simulation results shown in Figure 11, it's been ascertained that the THD of supply current & supply voltage was 1.02% and 3.13% severally. The compensation time was 0.003 sec. At t=0.006 sec, we are able to see that the waveforms for supply voltage and supply current became sinusoidal.

From Figure 11, we will see the waveforms of compensation current, dc capacitor voltage and load current. The variation in dc voltage is clearly seen within the waveforms. As per demand for increasing the compensation current for fulfilling the load current demand, it releases the energy and thenceforth it charges and tries to regain its set value. If we tend to closely observe, we will conclude that the compensation current is really fulfilling the demand of load current and when the active filtering the supply current and voltage is forced to be sinusoidal.

Figure 11. Source voltage, source current, compensation current (phase b), DC link voltage and load current waveforms of active power filter using Constant Instantaneous Power Control Strategy using ABBC Algorithm with all three loads connected together at different time interval for unbalanced supply system

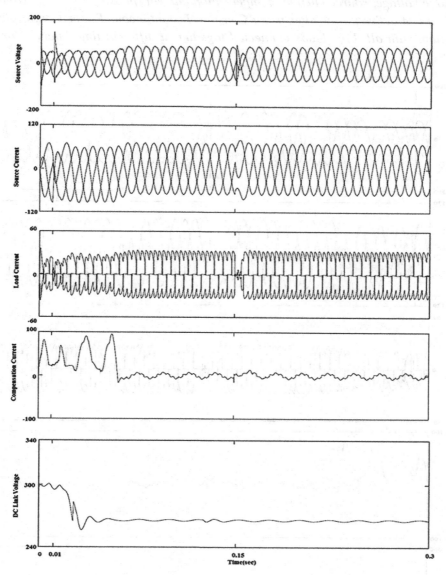

Simulation Results and Discussion about the Shunt APF Using GA in Unbalanced Supply System

From the simulation results shown in Figure 12, it's been ascertained that the THD of supply current & supply voltage was 1.46% and 3.31% severally. The compensation time was 0.007 sec. At t=0.007 sec, we are able to see that the waveforms for supply voltage and supply current became sinusoidal.

Figure 12. Source voltage, source current, compensation current (phase b), DC link voltage and load current waveforms of active power filter using Constant Instantaneous Power Control Strategy using Genetic Algorithm with all three loads connected together at different time interval for unbalanced supply system

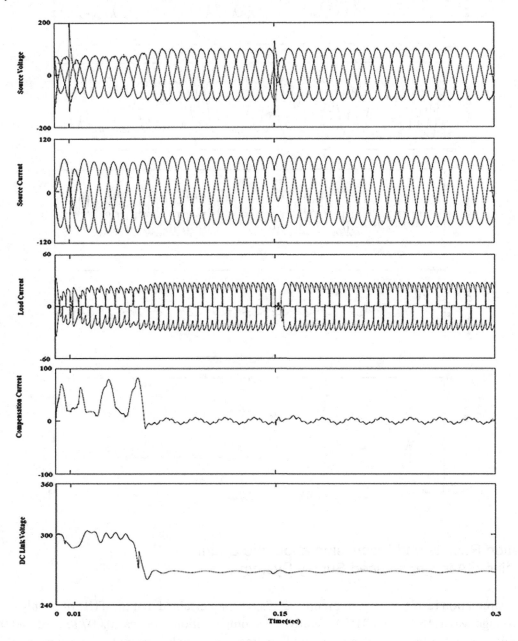

Simulation Results and Discussion of Three Phase Distorted Supply System

In this section, source system of 110V, 50 Hertz with phase A having an injection of third order harmonics and phase B having an injection of second order harmonics of amplitude 0.2 p.u. at begin time of 0.05 sec and finish time is 0.2 sec has been used.

Simulation Results and Discussion of Uncompensated System in Distorted Supply System

After doing simulation in MATLAB/Simulink while not using any filter (Figure 13) i.e. for uncompensated System, it's been ascertained that the THD of supply current found whereas using all 3 loads at the same time connected with the system at totally different time is 26% and THD of supply Voltage were 3.46%. By perceptive this knowledge, we are able to simply perceive that they're out of the limit of IEEE 519-1992 limit. We've seen that supply has been impure once loads have been connected.

Simulation Results and Discussion About the Shunt APF Using ABBC Algorithm in Distorted Supply System

From the simulation results shown in Figure 14, it's been ascertained that the THD of supply current & supply voltage was 1.05% and 3.13% severally. The compensation time was 0.004 sec. At t=0.0204 sec, we are able to see that the waveforms for supply voltage and supply current became sinusoidal.

Figure 13. Source voltage and source current waveforms of uncompensated system for distorted supply

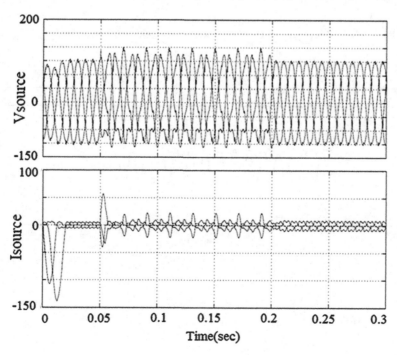

Figure 14. Source voltage, source current, compensation current (phase b), DC link voltage and load current waveforms of active power filter using Constant Instantaneous Power Control Strategy using ABBC Algorithm with all three loads connected together at different time interval for distorted supply system

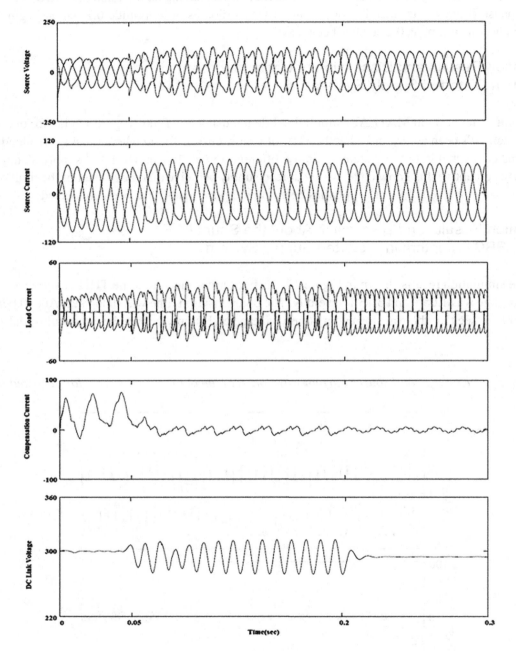

Simulation Results and Discussion About the Shunt APF Using GA in Distorted Supply System

From the simulation results shown in Figure 15, it's been ascertained that the THD of supply current & supply voltage was 1.43% and 3.25% severally. The compensation time was 0.005 sec. At t=0.205 sec, we are able to see that the waveforms for supply voltage and supply current became sinusoidal.

Figure 15. Source voltage, source current, compensation current (phase b), DC link voltage and load current waveforms of active power filter using Constant Instantaneous Power Control Strategy using Genetic Algorithm with all three loads connected together at different time interval for distorted supply system

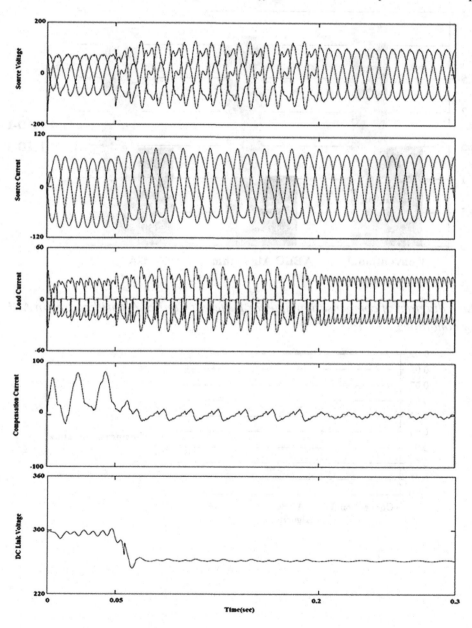

The simulation waveforms are shown above and also the result tabulated in table one and Table 2 confirms that the novel ABBC algorithm primarily based Shunt APF can perform well in balanced, unbalanced and distorted supply system and it dynamic ability and superiority over typical constant instantaneous power control current management technique and its optimized version using GA technique by perceptive its least THD and less compensation time.

Figure 16. Bar diagram of THD-I and THD-V for Different Control Algorithm used in APF under balanced supply conditions

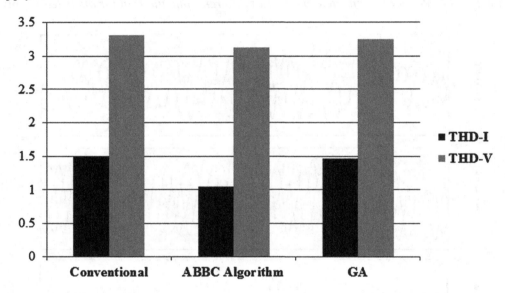

Figure 17. Line diagram of compensation time for Different Control Algorithm used in APF under balanced supply conditions

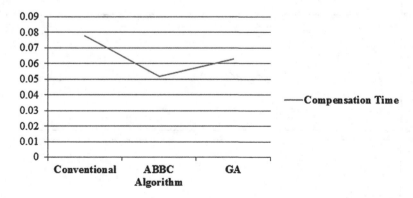

Figure 18. Bar diagram of THD-I and THD-V for Different Control Algorithm used in APF under unbalanced supply conditions

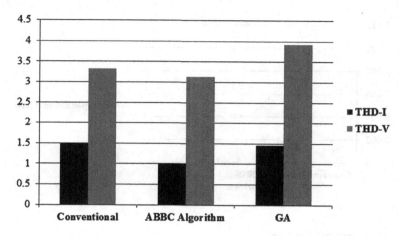

Figure 19. Line diagram of compensation time for Different Control Algorithm used in APF under unbalanced supply conditions

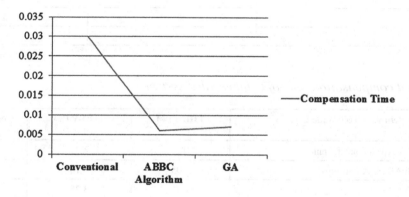

Figure 20. Bar diagram of THD-I and THD-V for Different Control Algorithm used in APF under distorted supply conditions

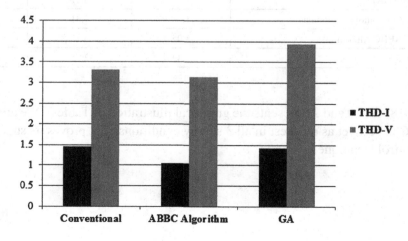

Figure 21. Line diagram of compensation time for Different Control Algorithm used in APF under distorted supply conditions

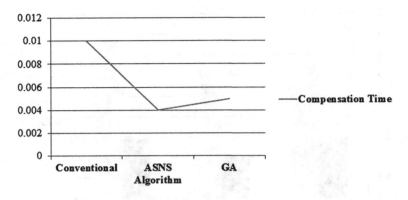

Table 1. THDs of uncompensated system

System Details	THD-I (%)	THD-V (%)
Balanced Supply	25.63	4.1
Unbalanced Supply	26.22	3.46
Distorted Supply	26	3.46

Table 2. THDs and compensation time of compensated system

Supply System with Technique Used	THD-I (%)	THD-V (%)	Compensation Time (sec)
Balanced Supply (with Conventional Technique)	1.5	3.31	0.078
Balanced Supply (with ABBC Algorithm)	1.05	3.13	0.052
Balanced Supply (with GA)	1.46	3.25	0.063
Unbalanced Supply (with Conventional Technique)	1.5	3.33	0.030
Unbalanced Supply (with ABBC Algorithm)	1.02	3.13	0.006
Unbalanced Supply (with GA)	1.46	3.31	0.007
Distorted Supply (with Conventional Technique)	1.46	3.31	0.010
Distorted Supply (with ABBC Algorithm)	1.05	3.13	0.004
Distorted Supply (with GA)	1.43	3.25	0.005

Figure 16, 17, 18, 19, 20 and 21 presents the graphical illustration of Table 2. We are able to observe clearly that ABBC is best yet as quickest in all 3 supply conditions, that proves its superiority over GA and traditional control technique.

CONCLUSION

A novel improved algorithm i.e. adaptive Blanket Body cover (ABBC) algorithm applied in shunt active power filter has been conferred, that works effectively under the balanced, unbalanced & distorted supply conditions. System optimization by using adaptive Blanket Body cover algorithm has well worked for the model using conventional constant instantaneous power control Technique. ABBC has effectively compensated the system. THD for source current and source voltage has been reduced significantly over a very little time of few seconds. While comparing with the conventional as well as advanced GA technique, it can be clearly said that ABBC is better as well as faster than both techniques. The simulation results clearly prove ABBC superiority over GA and conventional control technique.

REFERENCES

Abdul Hasib, A., & Hew Wooi, P. (2002). Fuzzy Logic Control of a three phasInduction Motor using Field Oriented Control Method. *Society of Instrument and Control Engineers, SICE Annual Conference*, 264-267.

Afonso, J. L., F. J. (1998). Genetic Algorithm Techniques Applied to the Control of a Three-Phase Induction Motor. *UK Mechatronics Forum International Conference*, 142-146.

Ahmed, A. H., & Nahla, E. Z. G. Y. (2009). Fuzzy Logic Controlled Shunt Active Power Filter for Three-phase Four-wire Systems with Balanced and Unbalanced Loads. World Academy of Science, Engineering, and Technology, 58, 621-626.

Chen Donghua, T. G. (2005). Shunt Active Power Filters Applied in the Aircraft Power Utility. *36th Power Electronics Specialists Conference*, 59-63.

Chiewchitboon, T., Soonthomphisaj, & Piyarat. (2003). Speed Control of Three-phase Induction Motor Online Tuning by Genetic Algorithm. *Fifth International Conference on Power Electronics and Drive Systems, PEDS 2003*, 184-188. doi:10.1109/PEDS.2003.1282751

Dugan, R. C. M. F. (1996). Electrical Power Systems Quality. New York: McGraw-Hill.

Eid, A., El-Kishky, H., Abdel-Salam, M., & El-Mohandes, T. (2010). VSCF Aircraft Electric Power System Performance with Active Power Filters. *42nd South Eastern Symposium on the System Theory*, 182-187. doi:10.1109/SSST.2010.5442838

Ghosh, A., & Ledwich, G. (2002). *Power Quality Enhancement Using Custom Power Devices*. Boston, MA: Kluwer. doi:10.1007/978-1-4615-1153-3

Guillermin, P. (1996). Fuzzy logic Applied to Motor Control. *IEEE Transactions on Industrial Application*, *32*(1), 51–56. doi:10.1109/28.485812

IEEE Standard 519-19921992*IEEE Recommended Practices and Requirements for Harmonic Control in Electrical Power Systems*. IEEE.

Ismail, B., Abdeldjebar, H., Abdelkrim, B., Mazari, B., & Rahli, M. (2008). Optimal Fuzzy Self-Tuning of PI Controller Using Genetic Algorithm for Induction Motor Speed Control. *International Journal of Automotive Technology*, *2*(2), 85–95. doi:10.20965/ijat.2008.p0085

Jain, S., Agrawal, P., & Gupta, H. (2002). Fuzzy logic controlled shunt active power filter for power quality improvement. *IEE Proceedings. Electric Power Applications*, *149*(5), 317–328. doi:10.1049/ip-epa:20020511

Khalid, S. N. (2009). Application of Power Electronics to Power System. New Delhi: University Science Press.

Khalid, S., & Dwivedi, B. (2007). A Review of State of Art Techniques in Active Power Filters and Reactive Power Compensation. *National Journal of Technology*, *3*(1), 10–18.

Khalid, S., & Dwivedi, B. (2013). Power quality improvement of constant frequency aircraft electric power system using Fuzzy Logic, Genetic Algorithm and Neural network control based control scheme. *International Electrical Engineering Journal*, *4*(3), 1098–1104.

Kumar, P., & Mahajan, A. (2009). Soft Computing Techniques for the Control of an Active Power Filter. *IEEE Transactions on Power Delivery*, *24*(1), 452–461. doi:10.1109/TPWRD.2008.2005881

Lavopa, E., Zanchetta, P., Sumner, M., & Cupertino, F. (2009). Real-time estimation of Fundamental Frequency and harmonics for active shunt power filters in aircraft Electrical Systems. *IEEE Transactions on Industrial Electronics*, *56*(8), 412–416. doi:10.1109/TIE.2009.2015292

Mauricio Aredes, J. H. (1997, March). Three-Phase Four-Wire Shunt Active Filter Control Strategies. *IEEE Transactions on Power Electronics*, *12*(2), 311–318. doi:10.1109/63.558748

Norman, M., Samsul, B., Mohd, N., & Jasronita, J., & B., O. S. (2004). A Fuzzy logic Controller for an Indirect vector Controlled Three Phase Induction. *Proceedings of Analog And Digital Techniques In Electrical Engineering*, 1–4.

P, P. J., K, B. B., & Eduardo, B. d. (2001). A Stator-Flux-Oriented Vector-Controlled Induction Motor Drive with Space-Vector PWM and Flux-Vector Synthesis by Neural Networks. *IEEE Transaction on Industry Applications*, *37*(5), 1308-1318.

Rajasekaran, S. P. (2005). *Neural Networks, Fuzzy Logic, and Genetic Algorithm: Synthesis and Applications*. New Delhi: Prentice Hall of India.

Rojas, R. (1996). *Neural Network- A Systematic Introduction*. Berlin: Spriger-Verlag.

Saifullah, K., & Bharti, D. (2014). Comparative Evaluation of Various Control Strategies for Shunt Active Power Filters in Aircraft Power Utility of 400 Hz. *Majlesi Journal of Mechatronic Systems*, *3*(2), 1–5.

Saifullah Khalid, B. D. (2010). Power Quality: An Important Aspect. *International Journal of Engineering Science and Technology*, *2*(11), 6485–6490.

Saifullah Khalid, B. D. (2011). Power Quality Issues, Problems, Standards & their Effects in Industry with Corrective Means. *International Journal of Advances in Engineering & Technology*, *1*(2), 1–11.

Saifullah Khalid, B. D. (2013). Application of AI techniques in implementing Shunt APF in Aircraft Supply System. *SOCROPROS Conference on Dec 26-28* (pp. 333-341). Roorkee: Springer Lecture Notes.

Saifullah Khalid, B. D. (2013). Comparison of Control Strategies for Shunt Active Power Filter under balanced, unbalanced and distorted supply conditions. *IEEE Sponsored National Conference on Advances in Electrical Power and Energy Systems (AEPES-2013)*, 37-41.

Saifullah Khalid, B. D. (2013). Comparative critical analysis of SAF using soft computing and conventional control techniques for high frequency (400 Hz) aircraft system. *IEEE 1st International Conference on Condition Assessment Techniques in Electrical Systems (CATCON)* (pp. 100-110). Kolkata: IEEE.

Seong-Hwan, K., & Tae-Sik, P. (2001). Speed-Sensorless Vector Control of an Induction Motor Using Neural Network Speed Estimation. *IEEE Transactions on Industrial Electronics, 48*(3), 609–614. doi:10.1109/41.925588

Thangaraj, R., Thanga, R. C., Pant, M., Ajit, A., & Grosan, C. (2010). Optimal gain tuning of PI speed controller in induction motor drives using particle swarm optimization. *Logic Journal of IGPL Advance Access*, 1-4.

Wang, G., Zhang, M., Xu, X., & Jiang, C. (2006). Optimization of Controller Parameters based on the Improved Genetic Algorithms. *IEEE Proceedings of the 6th World Congress on Intelligent Control and Automation*, 3695-3698.

Woods, E. J. (1990). Aircraft Electrical System computer Simulation. *Proceedings of the 25th Intersociety Energy Conversion Engineering Conference, IECEC-90*, 84-89. doi:10.1109/IECEC.1990.716551

Yingpeng Luo, Z. C. (2011). *A cascaded shunt active power filter with high performance for aircraft electric power system. In Energy Conversion Congress and Exposition (ECCE)* (pp. 1143–1149). IEEE.

Zerikat, M., & Chekroun, S. (2008). Adaptation Learning Speed Control for a High-Performance Induction Motor using Neural Networks. Proceedings of World Academy of Science, Engineering and Technology, 294-299.

Zhong Chen, Y. L., Yingpeng Luo, , & Miao Chen, . (2012). Control and Performance of a Cascaded Shunt Active Power Filter for Aircraft Electric Power System. *IEEE Transactions on Industrial Electronics, 59*(9), 3614–3623. doi:10.1109/TIE.2011.2166231

APPENDIX

The system parameters used are as follows:

- **Three-Phase Source Voltage:** 110V/50 Hz
- **Source Impedance:** R=0.1Ω, L=0.5 mH
- **Filter Inductor:** 2.5 mH
- **Filter Capacitor:** 30 uF,
- **DC Voltage Reference:** 600 V
- **DC Capacitor:** 3000 uF

Chapter 2
Swarm–Intelligence–Based Optimal Placement and Sizing of Distributed Generation in Distribution Network:
Swarm–Intelligence–Based Distributed Generation

Mahesh Kumar
Universiti Teknologi Petronas, Malaysia & Mehran University of Engineering and Technology, Pakistan

Perumal Nallagownden
Universiti Teknologi Petronas, Malaysia

Irraivan Elamvazuthi
Universiti Teknologi Petronas, Malaysia

Pandian Vasant
Universiti Teknologi Petronas, Malaysia

Luqman Hakim Rahman
Universiti Teknologi Petronas, Malaysia

ABSTRACT

In the distribution system, distributed generation (DG) are getting more important because of the electricity demands, fossil fuel depletion and environment concerns. The placement and sizing of DGs have greatly impact on the voltage stability and losses in the distribution network. In this chapter, a particle swarm optimization (PSO) algorithm has been proposed for optimal placement and sizing of DG to improve voltage stability index in the radial distribution system. The two i.e. active power and combination of active and reactive power types of DGs are proposed to realize the effect of DG integration. A specific analysis has been applied on IEEE 33 bus system radial distribution networks using MATLAB 2015a software.

DOI: 10.4018/978-1-5225-3129-6.ch002

INTRODUCTION

Nowadays, distributed generation has a very significant importance in electric power generation around the world due to its techno-economic advantages. DG can be defined as a smaller generating unit closer to the load consumption point (El-Fergany, 2015a; Moses, Mbuthia, & Odero, 2012). Typically, DG can be the renewable (non-conventional) i.e. small hydro, solar, wind, wave, tidal etc. or non-renewable (conventional) energy sources. Furthermore, these resources can be found naturally, depending on the geographical factor of the location. DGs are already implemented during the early days where the electricity was generated and supplied only to the neighborhood areas. As the time goes, centralized generation takes place and the power plant generates the electricity and transmits it through a transmission line to the far customers. This is because of the technological innovation where alternate current (AC) grid is invented, allowing the electricity to be transmitted over a long distance. Differs with the direct current (DC) grid during the early days, the transmission is only applied to a small area due to the limitation on a supply voltage (Pepermans, Driesen, Haeseldonckx, Belmans, & D'haeseleer, 2005). Later, DG was discovered to have more potential values than the existing centralized generation. By changing the way on how electric power system is being operated. It creates a new technology which is more efficient and clean for the future generation. DGs also provides continuity of electricity supplies to the customer and helps in reducing the electricity demand during the peak loads because of the installation of DG on the customer site of a meter (Ackermann, Andersson, & Söder, 2001). By integrating DG into the existing system, it will improve the performance of power system in term of voltage stability and voltage profile improvement and losses reduction. However, the distribution system is designed to operate in a one-way direction, integration of DG will transform the passive network to an active network, which eventually may increase the complexities (Mahesh, Nallagownden, & Elamvazuthi, 2015). The non-optimal placement and sizing of DG causes the instability of voltage and increase the losses in the distribution system. It may violate the value of the voltage profile lower than the permitted limit. Hence, the research on this subject has been focused more on determining and analyzing the optimum placement and sizing of the DG to improve the voltage stability and reduce the power losses in the distribution system. The proposed method has been tested on an IEEE 33-bus test system using MATLAB 2015a software package.

LITERATURE REVIEW

The maximum benefits from DG can only be obtainable if it is optimally placed with correct sizing. Hence, literature studies have shown that there are several methodologies that had been used to find the optimum placement and sizing of the DG. The methods are the analytical approaches, genetic algorithm, fuzzy-GA methods, linear and non-linear programming methods etc. But, the most of the authors have focused and kept power loss reduction as an objective function. For instance, author (Gözel & Hocaoglu, 2009) presented the loss sensitivity factor depends on the equivalent current injection by using two Bus-Injection to Branch-Current (BIBC) and Branch-Current to Bus-Voltage (BCBV) matrix to obtain the optimum size and location of the DG in the distribution system. The power loss reduction remains the main objective of the study. The optimal placement and sizing of distributed generation for power loss reduction using PSO optimization algorithm has been found in (Kansal, Kumar, & Tyagi, 2013). The author in (Viral & Khatod, 2015) presented an analytical approach for allocating the optimal placement and sizing of DG in the balanced radial distribution network aiming power loss reduction in the distribution system. The author Carmen et al. (Borges & Falcao, 2006) presented the combination of GA techniques to evaluate DG impacts in the distribution system. The reliability, losses and voltage profile remained the main parameters for optimization. The suggested analytical expressions are based on a power loss reduction correlated with the active and reactive component of branch currents by allocating the DG at different locations. The author in (Bahrami & Imari, 2014) has presented the Binary particle Swarm Optimization (BPSO) method for optimal placement of different types DG units. Reducing the long term total cost of the system was the objective of this research. In (Moradi & Abedini, 2012), the genetic algorithms (GA) is combined with PSO to locate the optimal location and capacity of DG, by considering the multi- objective limitation such as improved voltage regulations, voltage losses, and stability. The author in (Singh & Goswami, 2010) has proposed a new technique, depending on the nodal pricing to obtain the optimal placement of the distributed generation for reducing the cost, lost and also to improve the voltage rise phenomenon. The author in (Dharageshwari & Nayanatara, 2015) presented the operation of simulated annealing algorithm for obtaining the optimal sitting of multiple distributed generations in IEEE 33 bus radial distribution system. In this study, the multi-objective like voltage profile improvement and power losses reduction has been considered. Hasan et al. (Doagou-Mojarrad, Gharehpetian, Rastegar, & Olamaei, 2013) proposed the interactive fuzzy satisfying technique based on Hybrid Modified Shuffled Frog Leaping Algorithm for the Multi-objective optimal placement and sizing of DG. The objective of this problem is to reduce the total electrical energy cost, total electrical energy losses and total pollutant emissions produced. A simple search algorithm along with load flow study in Newton Raphson method is presented in (Ghosh, Ghoshal, & Ghosh, 2010) for optimal placement and sizing of DG, based on cost function and losses as the objectives of the research. This technique is simpler but consumes more time to identify the perfect location and size of the DG.

The above literature review presents that most of the work is highlighted with respect to power loss reduction, voltage profile improvement and integration of DG with cost analysis. Few studies like the author (El-Fergany, 2015a, 2015b) use the Backtracking search algorithm (BSA) and genetic algorithm (GA) for optimal placement and sizing of distributed generation to improve the voltage stability analysis. However, this chapter proposes the particle swarm optimization algorithm which improves the voltage stability index, associated with power loss reduction and voltage profile improvement. The proposed results are performed on standard IEEE 33 radial distribution system.

POWER FLOW STUDIES

The load-flow analysis is used to calculate the steady-state operating conditions of an electrical network. On the basis of the network topology with the impedances of all devices as well as with the in feeds and the consumers, the load-flow analysis can provide voltage profiles for all nodes and loading of network components, such as cables and transformers. The overall steps that need to be done during the load flow analysis in the MATLAB are:

1. Read the value of bus data, line resistance, and reactance data.
2. Read the value base MVA and base KV.
3. Calculate the load and impedance in the per unit value.
4. Identify the bus voltage, real power, and reactive power.

A forward-back sweep method is used in this experiment to solve the load flow problem of the distribution network. Forward sweep is used to determine the node-voltage in the system while the backward sweep is used to identify the power flow as presented in (Devi & Geethanjali, 2014).

PROBLEM FORMULATION

The main objective function of this chapter is to improve the voltages stability index (VSI) of the network. The (VSI) is an indicator, which shows the stability of distribution system (Chakravorty & Das, 2001; Mohandas, Balamurugan, & Lakshminarasimman, 2015; Sajjadi, Haghifam, & Salehi, 2013). This chapter is intended to observe the voltage stability of the system with the installation of different types of DGs. The Equation (1-6) are used to represent the VSI index of proposed model, which are derived from two bus radial distribution system as given in Figure 1. The details of these indices can be found in (Chakravorty & Das, 2001). In order to maintain the security and stability of distribution system, the VSI value should be greater than zero; otherwise, the distribution system is considered as a critical condition of instability.

From Figure 1, by applying basic Ohm's Law equation, $V=IR$ the current flows in the line and the total real and reactive power load supplied through the node m2 are obtained as below:

$$I\left(jj\right) = \frac{\left|V\left(m1\right)\right|\angle\delta\left(m1\right) - V(m2)\angle\delta\left(m2\right)}{r\left(jj\right) + jx(jj)} \tag{1}$$

$$P\left(m2\right) - jQ\left(m2\right) = V^*\left(m2\right)I(jj) \tag{2}$$

Equation (1) and (2) is combined with obtained the following equation

Figure 1. Electrical equivalent of 2 bus test system
where
jj = Number of branch
m1 = Sending-end node
m2 = Receiving-end node
I (jj) = Current at branch jj
V (m1) = Voltage at node m1
V (m2) = Voltage at node m
P (m2) = Total real power load supplied through node m2
Q (m2) = Total reactive power load supplied through node m2

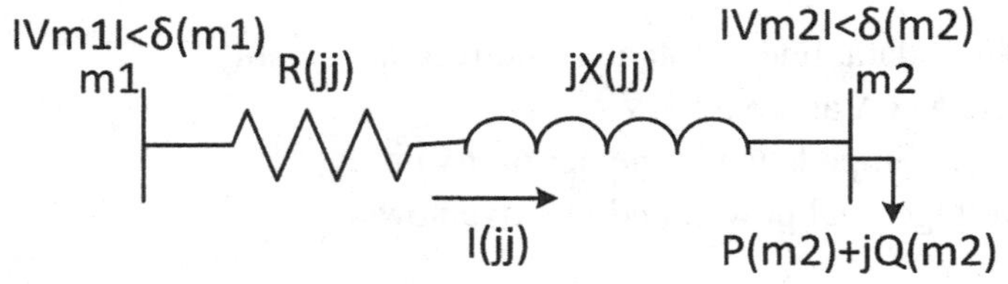

$$\frac{P\left(m2\right) - jQ\left(m2\right)}{V^*\left(m2\right)} = \frac{\left|V\left(m1\right)\right|\angle\delta\left(m1\right) - \left|V\left(m2\right)\right|\angle\delta\left(m2\right)}{r\left(jj\right) + jx(jj)} \tag{3}$$

After some multiplication:

$$\left|V\left(m1\right)\right|\left|V\left(m2\right)\right|\angle\delta\left(m1\right) - \delta\left(m2\right) - \left|V\left(m2\right)\right|^2 = \left[P\left(m2\right) - jQ\left(m2\right)\right]\left[r\left(jj\right) + jx(jj)\right] \tag{4}$$

After solving the above equation the Final equation will be given as:

$$\left|V\left(m1\right)\right|^4 - 4\left[P\left(m2\right)x\left(jj\right) - Q\left(m2\right)r(jj)\right]^2 - 4\left[P\left(m2\right)r\left(jj\right) + Q\left(m2\right)x\left(jj\right)\right]\left|V\left(m2\right)\right|^2 \geq 0 \tag{5}$$

Lets,

$$VSI(m2) = \left|V\left(m1\right)\right|^4 - 4\left[P\left(m2\right)x\left(jj\right) - Q\left(m2\right)r(jj)\right]^2$$
$$-4\left[P\left(m2\right)r\left(jj\right) + Q\left(m2\right)x\left(jj\right)\right]\left|V\left(m2\right)\right|^2 \tag{6}$$

where VSI is voltage stability index.

$$f_1 = \max \sum_{mi}^{Nb} VSI(mi) \tag{7}$$

where *VSI(m2)* is the VSI for bus *m2* and $\sum VSI(m2)$ is the VSI for whole system (*mi=2,3,4...Nb*); *Nb* is the total number of buses.

Constraints

There are two types of constraints, i.e. equability and non-equality constraints.

Equality Constraints

The equality constraints are a real and reactive power of DG injection at the specified bus. It means that real power injection by DG should be equal to the real power demand at that bus and real power losses of that branch. And same is for reactive power injection by DG should be equal to reactive power demand at that bus and reactive power losses of that branch. Mathematically real and reactive power injection by DG can be described as:

$$\sum P_{DG} = \sum P_{Loss} + \sum P_{Demand} \tag{8}$$

$$\sum Q_{DG} = \sum Q_{Loss} + \sum Q_{Demand} \tag{9}$$

where *PDG* and *QDG* are the real and reactive power injection by DG at the bus M. *PDemand* and *QDemand* are the total real and reactive power demand drawn from the bus M.

Inequality Constraints

Position of DG:

$$2 \leq DG\ position \leq nbuses \tag{10}$$

Voltage at load bus

$$V^{min} \leq V \leq V^{max}$$

V^{min} and V^{max} are the minimum and maximum voltage at specified bus.

PROPOSED METHODOLOGY

Particle Swarm Optimization (PSO)

PSO is an attractive stochastic optimization technique inspired by social behavior of living being such as birds flocking or fish schooling, introduced by Dr. Kennedy and Dr. Eberhart in 1995 (Kennedy J, 1995). The PSO algorithm is that population called swarm and consists of individuals called particles. The swarm is randomly generated in which particle changes their position (states) with time. In PSO each particle is moving in a multidimensional search space to adjust its position according to its own experience with the best solution it has achieved so for called *pbest* and the position tracked by its neighboring particle called *lbest*. When a particle takes all the swarm as its neighbors the best value (global best) will be called as *gbest*. Let us consider *v* and *i* are the velocity and position of particles in a search space respectively. Thus if i^{th} particle is shown as ($S_i = S_{i,1}, S_{i,2}, \ldots S_{i,d}$) where *d* is dimensional space. The best previous position for i^{th} particle will be *pbest*, where ($pbest_i = pbest_{i,1}, pbest_{i,2}, \ldots pbest_{i,d}$) the best particle among of all the particle will be *gbest* and the velocity of particle *i* will be represented by ($v_i = v_{i,1}, v_{i,2}, \ldots v_{i,d}$). The iteratively solved current velocity and position of each particle can be calculated by current velocity, previous velocity and previous position of that particle as shown in Equation 12, Equation 13.

$$v_{id}^{k+1} = \omega * v_{id}^{k} + c_1 * rand(\ ) * \left(pbest_{id} - v_{id}^{k}\right) + c_2 * rand(\ ) * \left(gbest_d - v_{id}^{k}\right) \tag{12}$$

$$S_{id}^{k+1} = S_{id}^{k} + v_{id}^{k+1}, i = 1, 2, \ldots . n, d = 1, 2 \ldots , m \qquad (13)$$

where n is the number of particle, m is number of members in particle, k is k^{th} iteration, ω is inertia weight factor, $c1$, $c2$ is acceleration constants, rand () is uniform random value in range (0, 1), v_{id}^{k}, S_{id}^{k} are velocity and position of particle I at k iteration. Shi and Eberhart in 1998 introduced a modified PSO with inertia weight, ω, parameter given in (Eberhart & Shi, 2000; Shi & Eberhart, 1998). Proper selection of ω gives a balance between global and local exploration and can be calculated by Equation 14.

$$\omega = \omega_{max} - \frac{\omega_{max} - \omega_{min}}{k_{max}} k \qquad (14)$$

where ω_{max} and ω_{min} are maximum a and minimum number of inertia weight that is designed to accelerate or decelerate the particle from its original path. The maximum value of the inertia weight helps in global search whereas minimum value helps in local exploration. Hence, in modified PSO it is recommended that reduce the inertia value from maximum to minimum with every iteration. This job can be done with linearly decreasing function provided in Equation 14 and the values of ω_{max} and ω_{min} are in range from $0 \le \omega_I \le 1.2$. In this chapter it is set as 0.9, and 0.4 respectively. The values of acceleration constants are range from $1.2 \le C_i \le 2.0$, in this chapter it is set as $c1$ and $c2$ are 2. The steps for optimal placement and sizing of distributed generation for voltage stability improvement are given in following steps. The complete flow chart is depicted in Figure 2.

PSO Implementation

Steps

- Inputs the system parameters i.e. resistance, reactance and load demand.
- Apply the base case load flow analysis and calculate the value of VSI.
- Set the PSO basic parameters.
- Set the value of minimum and the maximum amount of DG.
- Generate the random population of the swarm for optimal placement and sizing of DG.
- Start the generation and iterations.
- Apply the load flow analysis and calculate the value of VSI.
- Is value of VSI is greater than base case, if yes store it as pbest?
- Initiate the velocity and position of the swarm.
- Apply the load flow analysis and calculate the value of VSI.
- Is value of VSI greater than pbest, if yes store as global best i.e. gbest.
- Print the results.

Figure 2. Flow chart for optimal placement and sizing of DG with PSO optimization algorithm

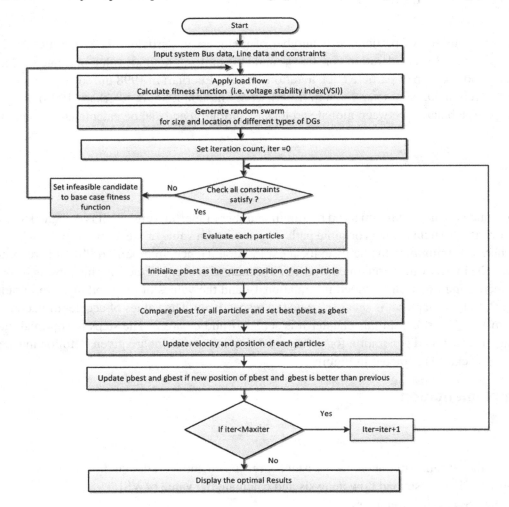

SIMULATION RESULTS AND DISCUSSION

The proposed method is implemented on IEEE 33 bus radial distribution network as shown in Figure 3. The base kV and base MVA of the system are 12.66 and 1 respectively. This radial distribution system has 33 nodes, 32 branches and a total of 3715 kW and 2300 kW active and reactive power loads respectively. The input resistance, reactance, and load data are given in Table 1 (Carreras-Sospedra, Vutukuru, Brouwer, & Dabdub, 2010; Kansal et al., 2013; Mahesh, Nallagownden, & Elamvazuthi, 2016). The backward-forward load flow is applied to observe the base case results. The Figure 4-5 shows the voltage profile and voltage stability index values at the base case when no DG is applied to this test system.

Based on Figure 4 and Figure 5, it can be observed that the highest voltage and VSI value are observed at bus 1, which is considered as substation bus and the value starts to reduce until bus 18. This is because the bus 1 receives the power input directly from the substation. The bus 18 is far from the substation, hence the voltage is dropped in subsequent buses until it reaches to bus 18. Hence, this bus has minimal VSI and voltage magnitude values. The voltage starts to rise again at bus 19 and start to reduce until bus

Table 1. IEEE 33 bus system data

Sending Node	Receiving Node	Active Power Rec. Node (kW)	Reactive Power Rec. Node (kVAR)	Resistance (ohms)	Reactance (ohms)
1	2	100	60	0.0922	0.0470
2	3	90	40	0.4930	0.2511
3	4	120	80	0.3660	0.1864
4	5	60	30	0.3811	0.1941
5	6	60	20	0.8190	0.7070
6	7	200	100	0.1872	0.6188
7	8	200	100	1.7114	1.2351
8	9	60	20	1.0300	0.7400
9	10	60	20	1.0440	0.7400
10	11	45	30	0.1966	0.0650
11	12	60	35	0.3744	0.1238
12	13	60	35	1.4680	1.1550
13	14	120	80	0.5416	0.7129
14	15	60	10	0.5910	0.5260
15	16	60	20	0.7463	0.5450
16	17	60	20	1.2890	1.7210
17	18	90	40	0.7320	0.5740
2	19	90	40	0.1640	0.1565
19	20	90	40	1.5042	1.3554
20	21	90	40	0.4095	0.4784
21	22	90	40	0.7089	0.9373
3	23	90	50	0.4512	0.3083
23	24	420	200	0.8980	0.7091
24	25	420	200	0.8960	0.7011
5	26	60	25	0.2030	0.1034
26	27	60	25	0.2842	0.1447
27	28	60	20	1.0590	0.9337
28	29	120	70	0.8042	0.7006
29	30	200	600	0.5075	0.2585
30	31	150	70	0.9744	0.9630
31	32	210	100	0.3105	0.3619
32	33	60	40	0.3410	0.5302
Total		3715	2300	21.5784	18.7843

Figure 3. IEEE 33 bus radial distribution system

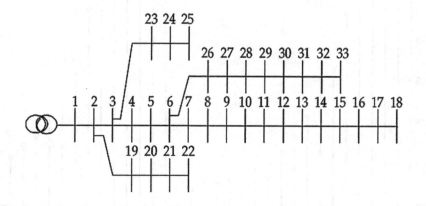

Figure 4. Voltage of 33 bus test system

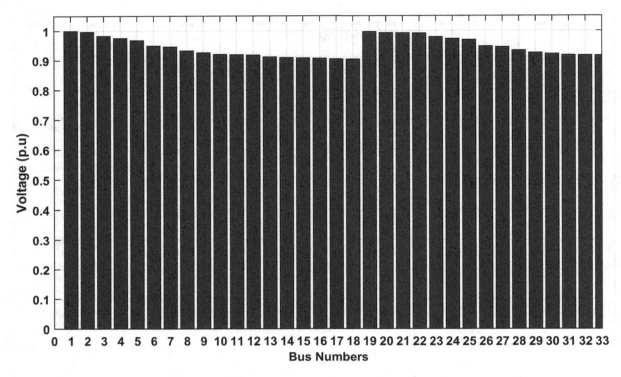

Figure 5. VSI value of 33 bus test system

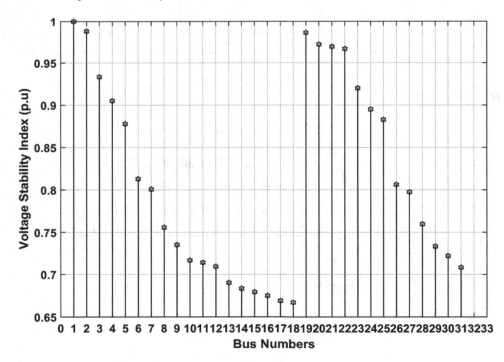

33 because the bus 19 is connected to bus 2, which is near to the substation bus. Therefore, this chapter proposes the two case studies i.e. case study 1, where the DGs of different sizes (only active power) are proposed at bus number 18, which is more sensitive to voltage stability. The case study 2 is proposed with PSO optimization algorithm to find the best DG size and location within the whole test system. The two types of DGs i.e., Type-1 (1 DG and 2 DG) and Type-3 (1 DG) are tested in this case study. The voltage stability index is kept as a basic objective function, whereas the power loss reduction and voltage profile improvement are also observed during the simulation.

For Case 1, different sizes of DG which are 80 kW, 100 kW, 120 kW and 140 kW will be placed at bus 18 because it has the lowest value of VSI value compared to other buses, which is more sensitive to voltage collapse.

Case Study 1

In this case study, the bus 18 is integrated with different sizes of DGs which are 80 kW, 100 kW, 120 kW, and 140 kW respectively. Table 2 shows the overall results of case study 1, whereas shows the value of voltage profile and voltage stability index values of whole test system respectively.

Based on Table 2, the busses with a minimum value of VSI is selected for DG integration. It is observed that as DG size is increased from 80 kW to 140 kW, the VSI values has improved. A similar effect has been observed for power losses which reduced from 211 kW base case to 167.50 kW when DG of 140 kW size is integrated at bus 18. The Table 3-4 shows the VSI and voltage profile values for the selected bus like substation bus, bus 18 and last bus 33 respectively.

It can be shown in Tables 3-4, that DG at bus 18 has significantly improved the values of VSI and voltage profile. However, a very minimal improvement has been observed at last bus, compared to the improvement in bus 18.

Table 2. The results of case study 1 in IEEE 33 distribution system

Test System	DG No's.	Power Loss		Base Case VSI	DG Size	DG Location	VSI (p.u)	Ploss kW
		kW	KVar	(p.u)	(kW)			
Active power DG	1	211	143	25.125	80	18	27.104	145.90
	1				100	18	27.568	147.40
	1				120	18	28.021	154.70
	1				140	18	28.46	167.50

Table 3. Data of Voltage in Case 1

Bus	Voltage (p.u) Base Case	Voltage (p.u) With DG (80kW)	Voltage (p.u) With DG (100kW)	Voltage (p.u) With DG (120kW)	Voltage (p.u) With DG (140kW)
1	1.0000	1.000	1.0000	1.0000	1.0000
18	0.9037	0.9675	0.9813	0.9944	1.0069
33	0.9164	0.9287	0.9314	0.9340	0.9365

Table 4. Data of VSI in Case 1

Bus	VSI (p.u) Base Case	VSI (p.u) With DG (80kW)	VSI (p.u) With DG (100kW)	VSI (p.u) With DG (120kW)	VSI (p.u) With DG (140kW)
1	1.0000	1.0000	1.0000	1.0000	1.0000
18	0.6670	0.8761	0.9273	0.9779	1.0278
31	0.7082	0.7470	0.7557	0.7641	0.7722

Case Study 2

In this case study, the PSO optimization algorithm is performed for optimal placement and sizing of distributed generation aiming to optimize the voltage stability index values. In this case study, the placement and sizing of DG are chosen from the random population and searched at many iterations. The optimization results for this case study are summarized in Table 5.

It can be seen that DG in distribution system has improved a significant amount of VSI. The results show that with Type-1 (1 and 2 DG), the value of VSI is improved upto 29.767 p.u and 32.067 p.u respectively from 25.125 p.u. whereas, with Type-3 (1 DG), the value of VSI is improved upto 32.974 from 25.125 p.u.

The similar study has been found in [19], However, for Type-1 (1 DG) and Type-3 (1 DG), the proposed method gives better results in voltage stability improvement as compared to backtracking search algorithm (BSA) presented in [19]. The power loss reduction is also improved from 211 kW to 179.4 kW, with the integration of distributed generation as highlighted in Table 5. The active and reactive power losses at each branch of proposed radial distribution system are presented in Table 6-7.

Moreover, the minimum and maximum voltage profile and voltage stability of the proposed method are also upfront. By giving priority to VSI as an objective function, the significant voltage profile and voltage stability improvement had been observed. The results of both parameters are depicted in Table 8-9.

It can be seen that with the installation of Type-1 (1 DG) and Type-1 (2 DG), the minimum voltage profile can be improved upto 0.9440 p.u and 0.9836 p.u respectively. Whereas, with the installation of Type-3 (1 DG) it can be improved upto 0.9629 p.u. Similarly, the installation of DG improves voltage stability as 0.7974 and 0.9360 with Type-1 (1 DG) and Type-1 (2 DG) respectively. The installation of Type-3 (1 DG) can improve the voltage stability upto 0.86303. It can be seen from Table 8-9 that the voltage profile and voltage stability of all buses satisfy the minimum voltage profile and voltage stability standard. However, Type-3 (1 DG) gave more improvement in results as compared to Type-1 DG.

Table 5. Optimal size, location, and percent of loss reduction in IEEE 33 distribution system.

Test System	DG No's.	Power Loss		Base Case VSI	DG Size		DG Location With P DG	DG Location With Q DG	VSI (p.u)	Ploss kW
		kW	KVar	(p.u)	MW	MVar				
Active power DG	DG1	211	143	25.125	1.999	---	16	---	29.767	194.9
	DG2				1.972	---	14	---	32.067	188.7
					1.860	---	30	---		
Active-Reactive power DG	DG1				1.956	2.0	15	10	32.974	179.4

Table 6. Active power losses at each branch for IEEE 33 distribution system

S. No.	Without DG	1 PDG	2 PDG	1 PQDG
1	12.30012	5.53708	3.424819	2.273089
2	52.07589	21.65675	15.60554	6.85527
3	20.05312	7.185731	11.4769	0.628407
4	18.84983	6.640245	12.17931	0.559901
5	38.56499	13.61571	26.67201	1.141845
6	1.946176	1.258042	1.168159	2.939379
7	11.87328	14.44845	13.53477	33.6134
8	4.265695	11.16064	10.51847	24.84513
9	3.63366	12.24037	11.54974	26.48762
10	0.565038	2.489398	2.351318	2.153463
11	0.89921	4.995312	4.722701	4.32696
12	2.721079	21.0227	19.89645	18.2398
13	0.744182	8.317213	7.878709	7.227669
14	0.364346	10.3973	0.277074	9.062293
15	0.287289	14.05282	0.218394	0.203809
16	0.256847	0.198408	0.19518	0.182131
17	5.42E-02	0.041892	0.04121	0.038454
18	0.160957	0.160579	0.160238	0.160395
19	0.832189	0.830234	0.828465	0.82928
20	0.10076	0.100523	0.100308	0.100407
21	4.36E-02	0.043532	0.04344	0.043482
22	3.181927	3.133575	3.090572	3.110439
23	5.144158	5.065835	4.996211	5.028397
24	1.287574	1.267902	1.250418	1.258502
25	2.601936	2.451259	2.237801	2.365184
26	3.330328	3.137019	3.246128	3.026672
27	11.30539	10.64728	12.57569	10.27251
28	7.836499	7.379658	10.00981	7.119788
29	3.897237	3.669751	6.82427	3.540392
30	1.594283	1.500742	1.329281	1.447589
31	0.213282	0.200759	0.177807	0.193643
32	1.32E-02	0.0124	0.010982	0.01196

CONCLUSION

In this chapter, the optimal placement and sizing of distributed generation are applied to ensure the stability of power system. The IEEE 33 bus radial distribution network has been used for applying the load flow study with and without the integration of DG in it. The two case studies are performed i.e. case study 1, where the selection of DGs are chosen randomly such as 80 kW-140 kW in four steps and applied on

Table 7. Reactive power losses of each branch for IEEE 33 distribution system

S. No.	Without DG	1 PDG	2 PDG	1 PQDG
1	6.2701	2.82259	1.745841	1.158733
2	26.5238	11.03045	7.948378	3.491599
3	10.2128	3.659618	5.845067	0.320041
4	9.6005	3.381978	6.203109	0.285166
5	33.2911	11.75373	23.02455	0.985695
6	6.4332	4.158528	3.861414	9.716281
7	8.5688	10.4273	9.767904	24.25845
8	3.0647	8.018325	7.556959	17.8499
9	2.5756	8.676125	8.186599	18.77475
10	0.1868	0.823046	0.777394	0.711979
11	0.2973	1.651762	1.56162	1.430763
12	2.1409	16.54034	15.65422	14.35079
13	0.9796	10.94782	10.37063	9.513673
14	0.3243	9.25377	0.246601	8.065594
15	0.2098	10.26234	0.159486	0.148835
16	0.3429	0.264903	0.260594	0.243172
17	0.0425	0.03285	0.032315	0.030154
18	0.1536	0.153236	0.15291	0.15306
19	0.7499	0.748104	0.746511	0.747245
20	0.1177	0.117436	0.117186	0.117301
21	0.0577	0.057558	0.057435	0.057492
22	2.1742	2.141137	2.111754	2.125329
23	4.0621	4.000205	3.945226	3.970642
24	1.0075	0.992105	0.978425	0.98475
25	1.3253	1.248572	1.139845	1.204729
26	1.6956	1.597209	1.652761	1.541026
27	9.9677	9.387502	11.08775	9.057072
28	6.827	6.428983	8.720311	6.202591
29	1.9851	1.869223	3.476007	1.803333
30	1.5756	1.483184	1.313729	1.430653
31	0.2486	0.233992	0.207241	0.225699
32	0.0205	0.01928	0.017075	0.018597

the most sensitive part of the system. In case study 2, the PSO optimization algorithm is proposed for optimal placement and sizing of distributed generation in the test system. To perform the experiment, the simulations are executed on MATLAB 2015a software package. It has been noticed that introduction of DG in the distribution system has a positive impact on voltage stability index. Among the voltage stability index, it also reduces the power loss reduction and improves the voltage profile of the system.

Table 8. Voltage profile of IEEE 33 distribution system.

S. No.	Without DG	1 PDG	2 PDG	1 PQDG
1	1	1	1	1
2	0.997025	0.9982	0.9992	0.9988
3	0.982892	0.9902	0.997	0.9939
4	0.975379	0.9873	0.9982	0.9932
5	0.967949	0.9846	0.9999	0.9929
6	0.949476	0.9764	1.001	0.9933
7	0.945953	0.9749	0.9996	0.9996
8	0.93229	0.982	1.0065	1.0212
9	0.925951	0.988	1.0123	1.036
10	0.920071	0.9946	1.0188	1.0513
11	0.919203	0.9961	1.0202	1.0527
12	0.917689	0.9991	1.0232	1.0557
13	0.911503	1.0102	1.034	1.0671
14	0.909202	1.0141	1.0377	1.0713
15	0.907769	1.0194	1.0365	1.0768
16	0.906383	1.0266	1.0353	1.0756
17	0.904321	1.0249	1.0336	1.0739
18	0.903706	1.0244	1.0331	1.0734
19	0.996497	0.9977	0.9987	0.9982
20	0.992919	0.9941	0.9951	0.9947
21	0.992214	0.9934	0.9944	0.994
22	0.991576	0.9927	0.9938	0.9933
23	0.979306	0.9867	0.9934	0.9903
24	0.972636	0.9801	0.9869	0.9837
25	0.96931	0.9768	0.9836	0.9804
26	0.947545	0.9745	1.0014	0.9914
27	0.944978	0.972	1.0022	0.989
28	0.933529	0.9608	1.0031	0.9781
29	0.925302	0.9528	1.0042	0.9703
30	0.921731	0.9493	1.0065	0.9669
31	0.91758	0.9453	1.0028	0.9629
32	0.916667	0.9445	1.002	0.9621
33	0.916384	0.9442	1.0018	0.9618

Table 9. Voltage stability for IEEE 33 distribution system

S. No.	Without DG	1 PDG	2 PDG	1 PQDG
1	1	1	1	1
2	0.988154	0.992756	0.99698	0.995034
3	0.933302	0.961547	0.987942	0.975716
4	0.905095	0.950193	0.992905	0.973055
5	0.87783	0.939957	0.999626	0.971795
6	0.812712	0.908766	1.00392	0.973397
7	0.800716	0.903447	0.998454	0.998237
8	0.755446	0.929839	1.026141	1.087678
9	0.735109	0.952834	1.050229	1.151793
10	0.716613	0.978573	1.077157	1.221341
11	0.713913	0.984559	1.083412	1.228281
12	0.709222	0.996554	1.095944	1.242147
13	0.690291	1.041559	1.142936	1.296699
14	0.683346	1.057452	1.159514	1.317216
15	0.679049	1.079936	1.154198	1.344431
16	0.674912	1.110868	1.148993	1.338631
17	0.668791	1.10355	1.141544	1.330071
18	0.666973	1.101291	1.139246	1.327515
19	0.986061	0.990659	0.994879	0.992933
20	0.971974	0.976542	0.980734	0.978795
21	0.969216	0.973779	0.977966	0.976027
22	0.966726	0.971283	0.975466	0.973527
23	0.91976	0.947811	0.974026	0.961863
24	0.894954	0.92265	0.948541	0.936474
25	0.882776	0.910296	0.936024	0.924007
26	0.80612	0.901766	1.005722	0.966224
27	0.797418	0.892521	1.008768	0.956753
28	0.759472	0.852332	1.012518	0.915271
29	0.73305	0.824284	1.017108	0.886315
30	0.721799	0.812262	1.026418	0.874005
31	0.708187	0.797908	1.010532	0.858976

ACKNOWLEDGMENT

The authors would like to acknowledge the Universiti Teknologi Petronas (UTP), Malaysia for the technical and financial support of this research.

REFERENCES

Ackermann, T., Andersson, G., & Söder, L. (2001). Distributed generation: A definition. *Electric Power Systems Research, 57*(3), 195–204. doi:10.1016/S0378-7796(01)00101-8

Bahrami, S., & Imari, A. (2014). Optimal placement of distributed generation units for constructing virtual power plant using binary particle swarm optimization algorithm. *Journal of Electrical & Electronics, 3*(2), 1.

Borges, C. L., & Falcao, D. M. (2006). Optimal distributed generation allocation for reliability, losses, and voltage improvement. *International Journal of Electrical Power & Energy Systems, 28*(6), 413–420. doi:10.1016/j.ijepes.2006.02.003

Carreras-Sospedra, M., Vutukuru, S., Brouwer, J., & Dabdub, D. (2010). Central power generation versus distributed generation–An air quality assessment in the South Coast Air Basin of California. *Atmospheric Environment, 44*(26), 3215–3223. doi:10.1016/j.atmosenv.2010.05.017

Chakravorty, M., & Das, D. (2001). Voltage stability analysis of radial distribution networks. *International Journal of Electrical Power & Energy Systems, 23*(2), 129–135. doi:10.1016/S0142-0615(00)00040-5

Devi, S., & Geethanjali, M. (2014). Optimal location and sizing determination of Distributed Generation and DSTATCOM using Particle Swarm Optimization algorithm. *International Journal of Electrical Power & Energy Systems, 62*, 562–570. doi:10.1016/j.ijepes.2014.05.015

Dharageshwari, K., & Nayanatara, C. (2015). *Multiobjective optimal placement of multiple distributed generations in IEEE 33 bus radial system using simulated annealing.* Paper presented at the Circuit, Power and Computing Technologies (ICCPCT), 2015 International Conference on.

Doagou-Mojarrad, H., Gharehpetian, G., Rastegar, H., & Olamaei, J. (2013). Optimal placement and sizing of DG (distributed generation) units in distribution networks by novel hybrid evolutionary algorithm. *Energy, 54*, 129–138. doi:10.1016/j.energy.2013.01.043

Eberhart, R. C., & Shi, Y. (2000). Comparing inertia weights and constriction factors in particle swarm optimization. *Proceedings of the 2000 Congress on Evolutionary Computation.* doi:10.1109/CEC.2000.870279

El-Fergany, A. (2015a). Multi-objective Allocation of Multi-type Distributed Generators along Distribution Networks Using Backtracking Search Algorithm and Fuzzy Expert Rules. *Electric Power Components and Systems*, 1-16.

El-Fergany, A. (2015b). Optimal allocation of multi-type distributed generators using backtracking search optimization algorithm. *International Journal of Electrical Power & Energy Systems, 64*, 1197–1205. doi:10.1016/j.ijepes.2014.09.020

Ghosh, S., Ghoshal, S. P., & Ghosh, S. (2010). Optimal sizing and placement of distributed generation in a network system. *International Journal of Electrical Power & Energy Systems, 32*(8), 849–856. doi:10.1016/j.ijepes.2010.01.029

Gözel, T., & Hocaoglu, M. H. (2009). An analytical method for the sizing and siting of distributed generators in radial systems. *Electric Power Systems Research, 79*(6), 912–918. doi:10.1016/j.epsr.2008.12.007

Kansal, S., Kumar, V., & Tyagi, B. (2013). Optimal placement of different type of DG sources in distribution networks. *International Journal of Electrical Power & Energy Systems, 53*, 752–760. doi:10.1016/j.ijepes.2013.05.040

Kennedy, J. E. R. (1995). *Particle swarm optimization*. Paper presented at the Particle Swarm Optim. doi:10.1109/ICNN.1995.488968

Mahesh, K., Nallagownden, P., & Elamvazuthi, I. (2016). Advanced Pareto Front Non-Dominated Sorting Multi-Objective Particle Swarm Optimization for Optimal Placement and Sizing of Distributed Generation. *Energies, 9*(12), 982. doi:10.3390/en9120982

Mahesh, K., Nallagownden, P. A., & Elamvazuthi, I. A. (2015). *Optimal placement and sizing of DG in distribution system using accelerated PSO for power loss minimization.* Paper presented at the 2015 IEEE Conference on Energy Conversion (CENCON). doi:10.1109/CENCON.2015.7409538

Mohandas, N., Balamurugan, R., & Lakshminarasimman, L. (2015). Optimal location and sizing of real power DG units to improve the voltage stability in the distribution system using ABC algorithm united with chaos. *International Journal of Electrical Power & Energy Systems, 66*, 41–52. doi:10.1016/j.ijepes.2014.10.033

Moradi, M. H., & Abedini, M. (2012). A combination of genetic algorithm and particle swarm optimization for optimal DG location and sizing in distribution systems. *International Journal of Electrical Power & Energy Systems, 34*(1), 66–74. doi:10.1016/j.ijepes.2011.08.023

Moses, P. M., Mbuthia, J., & Odero, N. A. (2012). *Reducing real and reactive power losses in the distribution system by DFIG placement and sizing using ordinary PSO and HGPSO: A comparison.* University of Nairobi.

Pepermans, G., Driesen, J., Haeseldonckx, D., Belmans, R., & Dhaeseleer, W. (2005). Distributed generation: Definition, benefits and issues. *Energy Policy, 33*(6), 787–798. doi:10.1016/j.enpol.2003.10.004

Sajjadi, S. M., Haghifam, M.-R., & Salehi, J. (2013). Simultaneous placement of distributed generation and capacitors in distribution networks considering voltage stability index. *International Journal of Electrical Power & Energy Systems, 46*, 366–375. doi:10.1016/j.ijepes.2012.10.027

Shi, Y., & Eberhart, R. (1998). A modified particle swarm optimizer. *Proceedings, 1998. IEEE World Congress on Computational Intelligence., The 1998 IEEE International Conference on.* doi:10.1109/ICEC.1998.699146

Singh, R., & Goswami, S. (2010). Optimum allocation of distributed generations based on nodal pricing for profit, loss reduction, and voltage improvement including voltage rise issue. *International Journal of Electrical Power & Energy Systems, 32*(6), 637–644. doi:10.1016/j.ijepes.2009.11.021

Viral, R., & Khatod, D. (2015). An analytical approach for sizing and siting of DGs in balanced radial distribution networks for loss minimization. *International Journal of Electrical Power & Energy Systems, 67*, 191–201. doi:10.1016/j.ijepes.2014.11.017

Yu, Z., & Lusan, D. (2004). Optimal placement of FACTs devices in deregulated systems considering line losses. *International Journal of Electrical Power & Energy Systems, 26*(10), 813–819. doi:10.1016/j.ijepes.2004.07.003

KEY TERMS AND DEFINITIONS

Algorithm: A rule or set of rules, specifying how to solve the problem.

Distributed Generation (DG): The distributed generation is the small source of power generation connected directly to the distribution system. There are the different types of distributed generation available nowadays, such as active power DGs, reactive power DGs and combination of active-reactive power DGs. The combination of active-reactive power DGs is further divided into two types of DGs, that it can be used to import active and reactive power to the distribution system and also it can be used to import active power and extract reactive power from the system.

Fuzzy Logic: It deals with reasoning that is approximately rather than fixed.

Optimization: The process of execution for an optimal value(s).

Particle Swarm Optimization (PSO): The particle swarm optimization algorithm is a computational technique, which is inspired by the bird and fish schooling. It works on the principle of the random population at the initial stage, later it modifies its position and velocity according to the experience gain by their particles. The individual in PSO called as a particle, the group of particles called as population or swarm. The robustness of the algorithm can be tested with the convergence of the algorithm.

Simulation: The process of modeling and tackling the problem.

Voltage Stability Index (VSI): The voltage stability index is the index, which is used to measure the ability of power system that how the system is stable. For instance, as the load is increasing in the distribution system, the voltage magnitudes and reactive power decreases and there a condition occur where the system is no more stable. Typically, the value of the VSI comes in a range of zero to one. One witnesses the stability of the system, whereas lesser than one indicates that system is instable.

APPENDIX: NOMENCLATURE

DG: Distributed generation.
GA: Genetic algorithm.
GHG: Greenhouse gas.
I2*R: Active power losses.
kW: Kilo watts.
KVar: Kilovolt amperes.
PSO: Particle Swarm Optimization.

Chapter 3
Genetic–Algorithm–Based Performance Optimization for Non–Linear MIMO System

Anitha Mary Xavier
Karunya University, India

ABSTRACT

Environmental regulations demand efficient and eco-friendly ways of power generation. Coal continues to play a vital role in power generation because of its availability in abundance. Power generation using coal leads to local pollution problems. Hence this conflicting situation demands a new technology - Integrated Gasification Combined Cycle (IGCC). Gasifier is one of the subsystems in IGCC. It is a multivariable system with four inputs and four outputs with higher degree of cross coupling between the input and output variables. ALSTOM – a multinational and Original Equipment Manufacturer (OEM) - developed a detailed nonlinear mathematical model, validated made this model available to the academic community and demanded different control strategies which will satisfy certain stringent performance criteria during specified disturbances. These demands of ALSTOM are well known as "ALSTOM Benchmark Challenges". The chapter is addressed to solve Alstom Benchmark Challenges using Proportional-Integral-Derivative-Filter (PIDF) controllers optimised by Genetic Algorithm.

INTRODUCTION

Electrical energy plays an important role in determining the quality of life in today's modern world. Coal, as a fuel, has been quite popular in power generation because of its availability in abundance. Unfortunately, it loses its ground due to the pollutants being produced and the stringent environmental regulations. The present day situation demands clean, climate-friendly and affordable energy. Although much efforts have been put on generating power through renewable sources such as solar energy, wind, geothermal, hydrogen and other green technologies, the contribution of energy from these sources continue to be minimal percentage compared to total requirement. At this juncture, the scientists have evolved new methods of combustion which will reduce or remove the unwanted pollutants from conventional

DOI: 10.4018/978-1-5225-3129-6.ch003

thermal power generation with the central idea of using cheap and plentiful coal. As one of the solutions to this problem, Integrated Gasification Combined Cycle (IGCC) is emerging as an attractive means of power generation due to very high efficiency (10% more than conventional power generation) coupled with significantly lower pollutants.

In the case of IGCC technology, the solid coal is converted into a gaseous fuel (Gasification process) and burnt in the gas turbine of the most popular combined cycle power generation scheme. In spite of IGCC being high efficient and clean source of power, the developmental efforts are sporadic and operating plants are a little in number because of its high capital cost. The notable IGCC plants are given in Table 1. It is worthwhile to mention a few significant advantages associated with IGCC technology. They are as follows:

- Environmentally acceptable and much lower atmospheric pollutants.
- Lower water consumption required for cooling purposes (an important consideration in areas of limited water resources).
- Less coal is used per megawatt - an hour of output (due to higher efficiency).

Schemes of IGCC

Two typical schemes of IGCC are shown in Figure 1 and Figure 2.

In Figure 1, Gasifier coupled with Conventional Combined Cycle Power plant while in Figure 2, the bedmass from the gas turbine are sent to Circulating Fluidized Bed Combustor (CFBC) for heat extraction.It is to be noted that the Gasifier serves as a fuel source for the gas turbine. Coal, steam, and air react with the gasifier and fuel gas (also known as syngas) is produced. This syngas becomes the fuel for the gas turbine and the pressure and temperature of syngas are to be maintained at specified values at the inlet of the gas turbine. Also, the pressure and temperature are to be controlled with minimal overshoot and undershoot during disturbances like load changes and changes in the calorific value of

Table 1. Notable IGCC plants across the world

S. No.	Name of the Plant	Country	Year of Commencement	Year of Delivering Power	Power Capacity (MW)
1	Wabash River Coal gasification plant	United States	1993	1995	262
2	Tampa Electric	United States	1996	2001	250
3	William Alexander	Beggenum, Netherlands	1994	1998	253
4	ELCOGAS	Puertollano, Spain	1998	1998	330
5	DUKE energy Edwardsport	Indiana	2008	2013	618
6	NOKOSO	Japan	2001	2007	250
7	Tianjin	China	2012	2012	250

Figure 1. Gasifier coupled with Conventional Combined Cycle Power Plant

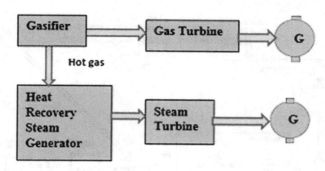

Figure 2. Gasifier coupled with CFBC Power Plant

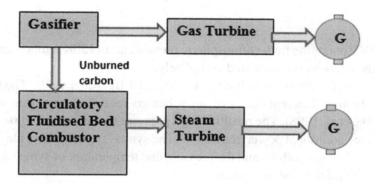

fuel fed into the gasifier. This calls for an efficient control strategy satisfying the specified performance criteria during disturbances.

AIR BLOWN GASIFICATION CYCLE

Even though a number of IGCC projects exist, the UK's Clean Coal Power Generation Group, ALSTOM has undertaken a detailed study on the development of a small-scale Prototype Integrated Plant (PIP), based on the Air Blown Gasification Cycle (ABGC) with 87 MW output (Pike et al. 1998). This type of prototype plant is useful in understanding the physics of the process, designing control systems and providing suitable protection schemes for integrated operation of the gasifier along with the combined cycle plant.

Figure 3 shows the block diagram of ABGC. Coal, steam, and air react within the gasifier operating at 22bar pressureand 1150K temperature conditions in order to produce fuel gas with low calorific value. Limestone is also added in order to remove sulphur. This fuel gas is burnt in a gas turbine coupled to a generator to produce electricity. Approximately 20% of carbon in the coal does not react in Gasifier which is extracted through ash removal system. This unburned carbon is fed to Circulating Fluidized

Figure 3. Block diagram of ABGC

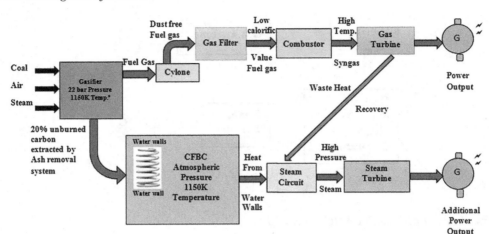

Bed Combustor (CFBC) operating under atmospheric pressure and 1150K temperature conditions. Here the remaining unburned carbon is combusted completely.

The water/steam (two phase mixture) absorbs heat from CFBC water walls. The steam separated by drum internals goes through different stages of super heaters receiving heat from exhaust gas coming from a gas turbine (Pike et al. 1998). The resulting high pressure steam is given to steam turbine coupled to a generator to produce additional power generation. The syngas from Gasifier plays an important role and becomes the fuel for the gas turbine and the pressure and temperature of syngas are to be maintained at specified values at the inlet of the gas turbine.

In this context, ALSTOM-a multinational and Original Equipment Manufacturer (OEM) developed a detailed nonlinear mathematical model and validated against the operational data obtained from a prototype of Gasifier of 87 MW capacity (Liu et al. 2000). Further, ALSTOM has made this model available to the academic community and demanded different control strategies which will satisfy certain stringent performance criteria during specified disturbances. The demands of Alstom are well known as "ALSTOM Benchmark Challenges I and II".

ALSTOM GASIFIER: INPUT AND OUTPUT VARIABLES

Alstom gasifier represents a difficult process for control because of its multivariable and non-linearity in nature with significant cross coupling between the input and output variables (Dixon 2006). Figure 4 shows the input and output variables of Gasifier.

The controllable input variables to the gasifier are

- **Char Off-Take (u1):** WCHR(Kg/s).
- **Air Flow Rate (u2):** WAIR(Kg/s).
- **Coal Flow Rate (u3):** WCOL (Kg/s).
- **Steam Flow Rate (u4):** WSTM(Kg/s).
- **Limestone Flow Rate (u5):** WLS(Kg/s).

Figure 4. Input and output variables of Coal Gasifier

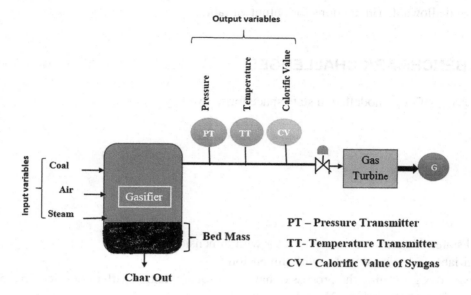

The Controlled output variables are:

- **Gas Calorific Value (y1):** CVGAS(J/Kg).
- **Bed Mass (y2):** MASS(Kg).
- **Fuel Gas Pressure (y3):** PGAS(N/m²).
- **Fuel Gas Temperature (y4):** TGAS(K).

One of the inputs, limestone mass (WLS) is used to absorb sulphur in the coal and its flow rate is set to a fixed ratio of 1:10 against another input coal flow rate (WCOL).This leaves effectively 4 degrees of freedom for the control design.

LOAD DEMAND ON GASIFIER

The flow rate of syngas to the gas turbine is controlled by a valve at the inlet of the turbine (also referred as controlled input disturbance to the gasifier). The pressure at the inlet of turbine called as PSink is the controlled variable. The control problem is to study the transient behaviour of gasifier process variables such as pressure, the temperature of the syngas for typical variations in gas flow drawing rate to gas turbine through appropriate changes in the throttle valve.

Any proposed control system should control the pressure and temperature of the syngas at the inlet of a gas turbine for any variation in gas turbine load – which in turn will affect throttle valve moment- without undue overshoots and undershoots. In fact, this particular aspect has been posed as a control challenge problem for gasifier by ALSTOM.

The input and output variables, allowable limits on output variables during load transients for three different loads (100%, 50% and no-load) as given by ALSTOM are reproduced for ready reference. Table

2 shows the steady state values for input variables for different operating loads. Table 3 shows the steady state values and allowable fluctuations for output variables.

ALSTOM BENCHMARK CHALLENGES

The ALSTOM gasifier is modelled in state space form given by

$$\dot{X} = Ax + Bu$$

$$Y = Cx + Du \tag{2.5}$$

where

x = Internal states of gasifier, a column vector with dimension 25x1
u = Input variables, a column vector with dimension 6x1
A = System matrix governing the process dynamics, a square matrix with dimension 25x25
B = Input matrix with dimension 25x6
Y = Output variables, a column vector with dimension 4x1
C = Observable matrix with dimension 4x25
D = disturbance matrix with dimension 4x6

Table 2. Input variables and their limits

Inputs	Description	Maximum Value	Rate	Steady State Values		
				100%	50%	0%
WCHR(Kg/s)	Char extraction flow rate	3.5	0.2 Kg/s^2	0.9	0.89	0.5
WAIR (Kg/s)	Air flow rate	20	1.0 Kg/s^2	17.42	10.89	4.34
WCOL(Kg/s)	Coal flow rate	10	0.2Kg/s^2	8.55	5.34	2.136
WSTM(Kg/s)	Steam flow rate	6.0	1.0Kg/s^2	2.70	1.69	0.676
WLS(Kg/s)	Limestone flow rate	1.0	0.02Kg/s^2	0.85	0.53	0.21

Table 3. Output variables and their limits

Outputs	Description	Allowed Fluctuations	Steady State Values			
			100%	50%	0%	
CVGAS(MJ/Kg)	Fuel gas calorific value	± 0.01	4.36	4.49	4.71	
MASS(Kg)	Bedmass	± 500	10000	10000	10000	
PGAS(N/m^2)	Fuel gas pressure	±1 x 10^4	2 x 10^6	1.55 x 10^6	1.12 x 10^6	
TGAS(K)	Fuel gas temperature	± 1.0	1223.2	1181.1	1115.1	

Towards this purpose, ALSTOM has made it available the following:

A, B, C, D for three different loads- 100%, 50% and no-load. A virtual gasifier mathematical model is made available with the above quantities (http://www.ieee.org/OnComms/PN/controlauto/benchmark.cf).

FIRST CHALLENGE (PIKE ET AL. 1998)

The first challenge involves the evaluation of control loop performances during disturbances occurring from load side. Towards this, the simulation test to be performed are:

Pressure Disturbance Test

Disturbance 1: A sudden disturbance of pressure change at throttle value with -0.2 bar, corresponding to a step change at 100% load.

Disturbance 2: A sudden disturbance of pressure change at throttle value with -0.2 bar, corresponding to a step change at 50% load

Disturbance 3: A sudden disturbance of pressure change at throttle value with -0.2 bar, corresponding to a step change in 0% load.

Disturbance 4: A disturbance of pressure change represented by A * Sin (ωt) with A= 0.2 bar and frequency ω = 0.04Hz at the throttle valve which corresponds to low frequency movements of inlet valve representing changes in grid frequency at 100% load.

Disturbance 5: A disturbance of pressure change represented by A * Sin (ωt) with amplitude A= 0.2 bar and frequency ω= 0.04Hz at the throttle valve which corresponds to low frequency movements of inlet valve representing changes in grid frequency at 50% load.

Disturbance 6: A disturbance of pressure change represented by A * Sin (ωt) with amplitude A= 0.2 bar and frequency ω =0.04Hz at the throttle valve which corresponds to low frequency movements of inlet valve representing changes in grid frequency at 0% load.

The following test case guideline should be followed

1. Initialize the plant (gasifier) model corresponding to desired operating point (say 100% Load).
2. Select the control strategy/algorithm and suitably incorporate the controller with the plant model.
3. Apply step disturbance of -0.2 bars at t=30 second and run the simulation for 300 seconds.
4. Calculate Maximum Absolute Error (MAE) during the transient period of gasifier output parameters such as calorific value (CVGAS), pressure (PGAS) and temperature (TGAS) of syngas and bed mass.
5. Evaluate the efficacy of the proposed control strategy based on the transient performance of the input /output process parameters examining the controlled output variable attains the specified set point.
   a. Overshoots and undershoots lie within the specified limits.
   b. The rate of variation of input variables lies within specified limits.
6. Repeat the steps 3 to 5 for all the six types of disturbances and for all operating conditions.

SECOND CHALLENGE

The second challenge consists of two test (Dixon and Pike 2006)

Load Change Test

Disturbance 7: Load transition: ramping up of the load from 50% to 100% operating point. This test facilitates the evaluation of controller performance across the full operating range of the plant. The plant model is initialized to represent 50% load and then increased continuously to 100% load at the rate of 5% per minute.

The proposed controller should ensure the following

1. Stability of the gasifier across the operating region.
2. Fluctuations of the input variables should lie within the limits.
3. The peak overshoots and undershoots at the end of the ramp input should meet the specified constraints.

Coal Quality Test

The investigation on the performance of the proposed controller during coupled disturbances, both from input and output sides of the gasifier constitute the second challenge. In other words, disturbances in PSink (output side of gasifier) and change in the calorific value of the coal (input side of gasifier) are to be simultaneously introduced to the plant model. Accordingly, the following types of pressure disturbance tests should be conducted along with a change in the calorific value of the fuel and any deviation from the desired performance is to be investigated.

Disturbance 8: A pressure disturbance represented by $A * Sin(\omega t)$ with amplitude $A = 0.2$ bar and frequency $\omega = 0.04$Hz at the throttle valve and simultaneously step change of 18% in calorific value over the designed calorific value of the fuel (coal) at 100% load.

Disturbance 9: A pressure disturbance represented by $A * Sin(\omega t)$ with amplitude $A = 0.2$ bar and frequency $\omega = 0.04$Hz at the throttle valve and simultaneously step change of 18% in calorific value over the designed calorific value of the fuel (coal) at 50% load.

Disturbance 10: A pressure disturbance represented by $A * Sin(\omega t)$ with amplitude $A = 0.2$ bar and frequency $\omega = 0.04$Hz at the throttle valve and simultaneously step change of 18% in calorific value over the designed calorific value of the fuel (coal) at 0% load.

Disturbance 11: A pressure disturbance represented by $A * Sin(\omega t)$ with amplitude $A = 0.2$ bar and frequency $\omega = 0.04$Hz at the throttle valve and simultaneously step change of 18%in calorific value under the designed calorific value of the fuel (coal) at 100% load.

Disturbance 12: A pressure disturbance represented by $A * Sin(\omega t)$ with amplitude $A = 0.2$ bar and frequency $\omega = 0.04$Hz at the throttle valve and simultaneously step change of 18%in calorific value under the designed calorific value of the fuel (coal) at 50% load.

Disturbance 13: A pressure disturbance represented by A* Sin (ωt) with amplitude A=0.2 bar and frequency ω= 0.04Hz at the throttle valve and simultaneously step change of 18%in calorific value under the designed calorific value of the fuel (coal) at 0% load.

Disturbance 14: A pressure disturbance of step change of -0.2 bar at the throttle valve and simultaneously step change of 18%in calorific value under the designed calorific value of the fuel (coal) at 100% load.

Disturbance 15: A pressure disturbance of step change of -0.2 bar at the throttle valve and simultaneously step change of 18%in calorific value over and above the designed calorific value of the fuel (coal) at 50% load.

Disturbance 16: A pressure disturbance of step change of -0.2 bar at the throttle valve and simultaneously step change of 18%in calorific value over and above the designed calorific value of the fuel (coal) at 0% load.

Disturbance 17: A pressure disturbance of step change of -0.2 bar at the throttle valve and simultaneously step change of 18%in calorific value under the designed calorific value of the fuel (coal) at 100% load.

Disturbance 18: A pressure disturbance of step change of -0.2 bar at the throttle valve and simultaneously step change of 18%in calorific value under the designed calorific value of the fuel (coal) at 50% load.

Disturbance 19: A pressure disturbance of step change of -0.2 bar at the throttle valve and simultaneously step change of 18%in calorific value under the designed calorific value of the fuel (coal) at 0% load.The maximum allowable limits for coal quality variations are $\pm$ 18% with respect to the original calorific value of the coal.

Figure 5 shows the closed loop representation of gasifier MIMO system and Table 4 shows the earlier Research attempt to solve Alstom challenge problems I & II. All the attempts of different investigators led to reasonable success in terms controlling the gasifier. However, the overall performance requirements stated in the challenges I and II have not been met fully and thus lending an opportunity to work on these challenge problems.

LOWER ORDER TRANSFER FUNCTION MODELS FOR ALSTOM GASIFIER

On analyzing the ALSTOM gasifier model, the model is found to be more complex and it contains very high cross-coupling between input and output (Dixon 2004). The state space equation is converted to transfer function using MATLAB comment

sys=ss (a, b, c, d) and [num,den]=ss2tf(a,b,c,d,1).

The transfer function of higher order model are given in equation (3.2)

Table 4. Earlier research attempt to solve Alstom challenge problems I and II

S. No.	Authors	Controller Methods	Disturbances for Which Control Requirements Have Been Met Are Indicated by √ While 'x' Indicates Partial Fulfilment of Control Requirements or These Disturbance Aspects Are Not Covered/Available for Comparison.																		
			D1	D2	D3	D4	D5	D6	D7	D8	D9	D10	D11	D12	D13	D14	D15	D16	D17	D18	D19
1	Liu et al., (2000)	Baseline PI controller (First Challenge)	√	√	√	√	√	x	x	x	x	x	x	x	x	x	x	x	x	x	x
2	Rice et al. (2000)	predictive control	√	√	√	√	√	x	x	x	x	x	x	x	x	x	x	x	x	x	x
3	Taylor et al. (2000)	Proportional integral plus (PIP)	√	√	√	√	√	x	x	x	x	x	x	x	x	x	x	x	x	x	x
4	Prempain et al. (2000)	H-infinity control	√	√	√	√	√	x	x	x	x	x	x	x	x	x	x	x	x	x	x
5	Griffin et al. (2000)	multi-objective Genetic algorithm (MOGA)	√	√	√	√	√	x	x	x	x	x	x	x	x	x	x	x	x	x	x
6	Sarah Gatley et.al., (2000)	H-infinity design approach	√	√	√	√	√	x	x	x	x	x	x	x	x	x	x	x	x	x	x
7	C S Chin and N Munro (2003)	LQG/LTR controller	√	x	x	√	x	√	x	x	x	x	x	x	x	x	x	x	x	x	x
8	Dixon et.al., (2006)	Base line PI controller (second challenge)	√	√	√	√	√	√	√	x	x	x	x	x	x	√	√	√	√	√	√
9	Adel Farag et.al., (2006)	Multiple PID controller design using GA	√	√	√	√	√	√	√	x	x	x	x	x	x	x	x	x	x	x	x
10	Rudy Agustriyanto and Zhang (2006)	Generalised relative disturbance gain analysis technique	√	√	√	√	√	√	x	x	x	x	x	x	x	x	x	x	x	x	x
11	Simm and Liu (2006)	Multi objective optimization approach	√	√	√	√	√	x	√	x	x	x	x	x	x	x	√	√	x	x	x
12	C J Taylor et.al (2006)	PIP controller	√	√	√	√	√	x	x	x	x	x	x	x	x	x	x	x	x	x	x
13	Al seyab and Cao (2006)	Non linear predictive controller	√	√	√	√	√	√	√	x	x	x	x	x	x	x	x	x	x	x	x
14	Wilson et.al., (2006)	state estimators to improve on the base line performance[45]	√	√	√	√	√	√	√	x	x	x	x	x	x	x	x	x	x	x	x
15	Amin Nobakhti (2008)	Self adaptive differential evolution	√	x	x	√	x	x	x	x	x	x	x	x	x	x	x	x	x	x	x
16	Yong Wang et.al., (2009)	Study on Fuzzy Gain-Scheduled Multiple Mode Predictive	√	√	√	√	√	x	x	x	√	x	x	x	x	x	x	x	x	x	x
17	Xue et.al. (2010)	Multi objective optimisation using NSGA II	√	√	√	√	√	√	√	x	x	x	x	x	x	x	√	√	x	x	x
18	W. Tan et.al., (2011)	Partially decentralized control	√	√	√	√	√	√	√	x	x	√	√	√	√	x	x	x	x	x	x
19	L Sivakumar and Kooteeswaran(2013)	PI with Fire Fly Algorithm	√	√	√	√	√	√	√	x	x	x	√	√	x	√	√	√	√	√	√
20	Kooteeswaran and L. Sivakumar (2013)	Bat algorithm based re-tuning of PI controller	√	√	√	√	√	√	√	x	x	x	x	x	x	√	√	√	√	√	√
21	Kooteeswaran and L. Sivakumar (2014)	PI with Cuckoo Algorithm	√	√	√	√	√	√	√	x	√	x	x	√	x	√	√	√	√	√	√
22	Kooteeswaran and L. Sivakumar (2014)	MOPSO algorithm	√	√	√	√	√	√	√	x	√	x	x	√	x	√	√	√	√	√	√

Figure 5. Closed loop representation of gasifier MIMO system

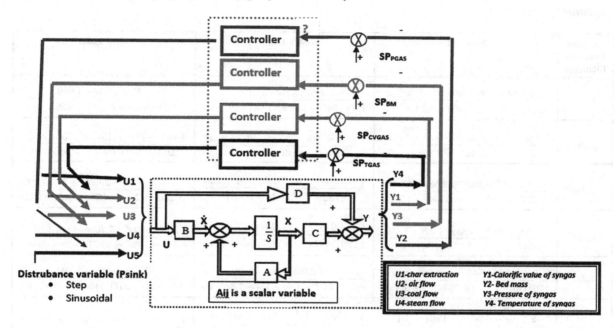

$$\begin{bmatrix} y_1(s) \\ y_2(s) \\ y_3(s) \\ y_4(s) \end{bmatrix} = \begin{bmatrix} G_{11}(s) & G_{12}(s) & G_{13}(s) & G_{14}(s) \\ G_{21}(s) & G_{22}(s) & G_{23}(s) & G_{24}(s) \\ G_{31}(s) & G_{32}(s) & G_{33}(s) & G_{34}(s) \\ G_{41}(s) & G_{42}(s) & G_{43}(s) & G_{44}(s) \end{bmatrix} \begin{bmatrix} u_1(s) \\ u_2(s) \\ u_3(s) \\ u_4(s) \end{bmatrix}$$

(3.2)

where

y_j = Output variables j $\in$ 1,2,3,4

j=1 Means calorific value of fuel gas; j=2 means bedmass;

j=3 Means pressure of the syngas;

j=4 Means temperature of the syngas.

ui = Manipulated variables with i$\in$ 1,2,3,4;

u_1 = Char extraction flow rate;

u_2= Air flow rate; u_3= coal flow rate and u_4 = steam flow rate

G_{ij} = Transfer characteristics with influence of jth output variable with

ith input variables with denominatoris of the 18th order and the numerator are of either the 16th or 15th order.

The gasifier is found to be operating under three operating loads namely 0% load, 50% load and 100% load. The lower order transfer function obtained using balanced realization for gasifier under different operating point are given in Table 5.

Table 5. Lower order transfer function obtained using balanced realization for gasifier under different operating point

Transfer Function Elements	0% Load	50% Load	100% Load
$g_{11}(s)$	$\dfrac{6412495.306104s + 59.515387}{81552.782s^2 + 14.789s + 8.741e-05}$	$\dfrac{82973.885s + 1.311}{1978.394s^2 + 1.308653s + 1.568e-05}$	$\dfrac{6.251e+04s + 1.059}{-2428.695s^2 + 2.256s + 3.204e-05}$
$g_{12}(s)$	$\dfrac{5.156e-6s^2 + 2.951e-4s + 3.342}{-3.343s^2 - 3.343s - 8.398e-05}$	$\dfrac{-4.151e-06s^2 + 0.182e-03s + 2.547}{-2.55s^2 - 2.549s - 0.915e-04}$	$\dfrac{4.704e-06s^2 - 1.648e-4s + 2.034}{2.036s^2 - 2.036s + 0.3505e-03}$
$g_{13}(s)$	$\dfrac{203764.66s^2 - 10907532.58s + 56.606}{-2370.734s^2 - 5009.316s + 0.0381}$	$\dfrac{727.803s^2 - 31191.578s + 1.266}{9.782s^2 - 7.184s + 0.0016}$	$\dfrac{-8.009e+2s^2 + 2.622e+2s + 1.022}{1.234e+2s^2 + 5.095e+2s + 0.002}$
$g_{14}(s)$	$\dfrac{8.872e+40s^2 - 4.859e+42s + 1.656}{-1.042e+42s^2 - 9.464e+40s + 0.032}$	$\dfrac{633.894s^2 - 26444.644s + 1.280}{11207.461s^2 - 350.714s + 0.216}$	$\dfrac{2.241e+2s^2 - 7.166e+2s + 1.018}{-5.648e+2s^2 - 4.927e+2s + 0.7002}$
$g_{21}(s)$	$\dfrac{-2.966e+10s + 114.021}{1762415.861s^2 - 382735.798s + 0.0009}$	$\dfrac{-7.638e+18s + 2.49}{6.3e+14s^2 + 4.9e+13s - 7.6e-05}$	$\dfrac{2.672e+07s + 1.992}{2892.89s^2 - 2371.445s - 5.438e-05}$
$g_{22}(s)$	$\dfrac{-2.216e-03s^2 + 0.126s + 3.475}{-41.366s^2 + 9.725s + 3.685e-04}$	$\dfrac{1.016e-04s^2 + 0.004s + 2.676}{-29.504s^2 + 3.382s - 10.282}$	$\dfrac{1.7e-04s^2 + 60.1e-04s + 2.16e-31}{22.909s^2 - 5.608s + 1.4004e-03}$
$g_{23}(s)$	$\dfrac{-1.783s^2 - 4.004e+09s + 2.152}{-392574.72s^2 - 671071.29s + 0.0003}$	$\dfrac{-150.691s^2 - 1.446e+12s + 1.682}{-1.409e+08s^2 + 4.81e+06s + 0.0001}$	$\dfrac{-0.0061s^2 - 1.891+08s + 1.366}{-18503.168s^2 - 14151.528s + 0.00011}$
$g_{24}(s)$	$\dfrac{-0.0003s^2 - 573649.04s + 1.69}{-81530.56s^2 - 7.775s + 0.028}$	$\dfrac{0.016s^2 + 1.19e+08s + 1.312}{2.249e+07s^2 + 4.007e+06s + 0.044}$	$\dfrac{524.578s^2 - 17801.672s + 1.0606}{267.915s^2 - 269.98s + 0.05}$
$g_{31}(s)$	$\dfrac{0334.30s + 3.27}{45.137s^2 - 1.79s - 8.741e-06}$	$\dfrac{-360120.42s + 2.506}{-44.47s^2 - 13.393s + 0.0001}$	$\dfrac{-6.107e+07s + 2.001}{-9296.79s^2 - 821.554s - 5.251e-05}$
$g_{32}(s)$	$\dfrac{2.1367e-07s^2 - 122.28e-07s + 3.34}{4.423s^2 + 4.802s + 3.116e-05}$	$\dfrac{3.716e-07s^2 - 160.82e-07s + 2.548}{3.47s^2 + 3.77s + 3.13e-04}$	$\dfrac{-7.57e-05s^2 - 2.654e-03s + 2.029}{2.892s^2 - 0.854s + 0.505e-03}$
$g_{33}(s)$	$\dfrac{67905.56s + 3.379}{407.551s^2 - 1891.87s - 0.007}$	$\dfrac{-3.106e+05s + 2.683}{-189.668s^2 - 551.803s + 0.005}$	$\dfrac{-9.86e+04s + 2.189}{-60.79s^2 - 97.577s + 0.0029}$
$g_{34}(s)$	$\dfrac{77345.24s + 1.937}{-472193.214s^2 - 1741.323s - 0.024}$	$\dfrac{59112.633s + 1.437}{-2.65e+05s^2 - 3511.145s - 0.053}$	$\dfrac{2.403e+04s + 1.155}{-103420.25s^2 - 2124.74s - 0.063}$
$g_{41}(s)$	$\dfrac{-1.664e+08s + 3.266}{10606.92s^2 + 1483.25s - 9.56e-06}$	$\dfrac{-2.72e+07s + 2.501}{2381.895s^2 + 740.758s - 2.58e-05}$	$\dfrac{-8042.924s + 1.995}{0.903s^2 - 0.362s - 4.907e-05}$
$g_{42}(s)$	$\dfrac{1.526e-03s^2 - 0.087s + 4.818}{-2490.99s^2 - 247081.25s - 15.27e-4}$	$\dfrac{2.011e-03s^2 - 0.087s + 3.708}{1304.88s^2 + 1.097e+05s - 3.36e-04}$	$\dfrac{2.605e-03s^2 - 0.0913s + 3.032}{932.662s^2 - 61593.894s - 4.105e-3}$
$g_{43}(s)$	$\dfrac{187977.32s + 4.505}{69.134s^2 + 119.112s + 0.001}$	$\dfrac{5.456e+04s + 3.632}{20.535s^2 + 20.261s + 0.0005}$	$\dfrac{2.913s + 3.0029}{11.256s^2 + 8.822s + 0.000387}$

continued on following page

Table 5. Continued

Transfer Function Elements	0% Load	50% Load	100% Load
$g_{44}(s)$	$\dfrac{58954.826s + 1.729}{-26761.155s^2 - 1437.956s - 0.014}$	$\dfrac{1.25e + 04s + 1.333}{-6380.258s^2 - 613.37s - 0.02}$	$\dfrac{5131.591s + 1.07958}{-2959.395s^2 - 377.795s - 0.0231}$

Proportional – Integral – Derivative- Filter Controller

A typical system/process with a PID controller is shown in Figure 6.

The control signal u(t) is the output of the PID controller and is given by:

$$u(t) = ke(t) + k_j \int_0^t e(t)dt + k_d \frac{de}{dt} \qquad (4.1)$$

where e(t) is the error signal obtained as the difference between the desired value, r(t) and actually measured value y(t). The reference value is also commonly called the set point. The control signal is thus a sum of three terms:

$u_p(t)$ = Error multiplied by K_p
$u_i(t)$ = Integral of the error multiplied by K_i
$u_d(t)$ = Derivative of the error multiplied by K_d.

However, one of the most common problems associated with PID is the synthesis of a derivative action. The ideal derivative has very high gain and is susceptible for noise accentuation (Desborough Honeywell, 2001). Hence the PIDF (Proportional–Integral-Derivative-Filter) controller are chosen, whose derivative action is represented as below:

$$Da = \frac{K_d s}{1 + sT_f} \qquad (1)$$

Figure 6. Closed loop representation of process with PID controller

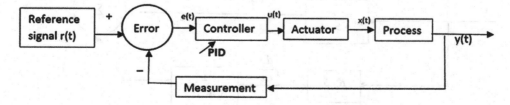

Here T_f is called filtering time and is chosen as $T_f = \dfrac{K_d / K_p}{x}$ where N is the filter coefficient and it can range between 2 to 100. The implementation of PIDF controller is schematically shown in Figure 7.

The transient response of a system depends upon the choice of K_p, K_i and K_d values. Usually, the control engineers will fix these parameters based on their experience or determined using tuning map concept. Basically, a tuning map concept involves trial and error method and labourers. Further, trial and error method will not necessarily lead to a successful determination of the required control parameters.

Hence this problem of obtaining suitable controller parameter has been conceived as an optimization problem wherein the stated constraints will become objective functions. The minimisation of objective functions through an iterative process leads to a successful set of optimal controller parameters. In this context, Genetic Algorithm – one of the soft computing techniques used for optimisation problems - is chosen to obtain the optimal controller parameters.

GENETIC ALGORITHMS

A genetic algorithm is one of the optimization technique that uses the principles of evolution, genetics from natural biological systems. It performs a parallel, stochastic but direct search method to evolve the fittest population. Genetic algorithms are highly used in the industrial process because of the following advantages (David E. Goldberg 2000).

1. It is simple, easy to understand and implement.
2. GA is a nonlinear process that it can be applied to most industrial Processes with good performance.
3. GA uses searching a population of points instead of searching a single solution.
4. GA needs to know the system information only for the fitness function.

The algorithm for the genetic algorithm are as follows:

Figure 7. Parallel realization of PIDF controller

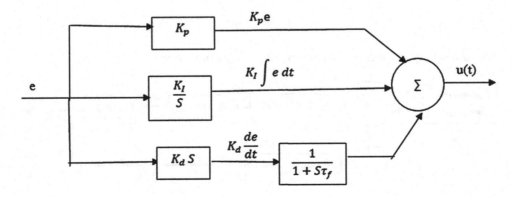

Step 1: Random population of n chromosomes are initialised (optimal solutions for the problem).

Step 2: The fitness f(x) of each chromosome x in the population are evaluated.

Step 3: A new population is created by repeating following steps until the new population is complete.

Step 4: Two parent chromosomes are selected from a population according to their fitness (the better fitness, the bigger chance to get selected).

Step 5: Cross over the parents with a crossover probability to form new offspring (children). If no crossover was performed, offspring is the exact copy of parents.

Step 6: Mutate new offspring with a mutation probability at each locus (position in chromosome).

Step 7: Place new offspring in the new population.

Step 8: Use newly generated population for a further sum of the algorithm.

Step 9: If the end condition is satisfied, stop and return the best solution in the current population.

Step 10: Go to step 2 for fitness evaluation.

GENETIC ALGORITHM BASED PID FILTER CONTROLLER FOR OPTIMALLY MEETING THE PERFORMANCE REQUIREMENTS OF ALSTOM GASIFIER CHALLENGE PROBLEMS

Any optimisation problem aims at achieving the objectives stated in the problem. Here the objectives are: For different disturbances (load changes, grid frequency changes and fuel calorific value changes), the controlled process parameters should reach the set points with overshoots and undershoots lying within the stated values. Further, the control signals should be such that the rate of variation of input signals also should not exceed the specified limits.

These objectives – quite often referred as *specified constraints* in the present thesis (in line with other researchers)- are to be met by proper tuning of PID controllers. Hence the optimization involved in the present study is to obtain proper Kp, Ki, and Kd coefficients which will ensure above stated objectives. PIDF controllers are mostly used in all industrial processes because of its well–known beneficial features like easy implementation, low cost, and its robustness.

In general, the performance of the system strongly depends on the controller's efficiency and hence tuning the PIDF parameters plays an important role in system behaviour. In this thesis, the PIDF parameters K_P, K_I K_D and N are tuned using a genetic algorithm.

Problem Formulation for Gasifier Control

PID tuning can be performed using techniques like empirical methods such as Zeigler Nicholas method (O'Dwyer 2009) analytical methods like root locus technique (Nise 2006) and optimisation methods such as Lopez and Ciancone methods (Ogata 2003). The PID values obtained through these methods can be applied to a system operating at a particular operating point. When the system is operating under different operating zones, Genetic algorithms can be used to tune PID parameters taking all non-linearity and process characteristics into account.

Objective Function for Pressure and Coal Quality Disturbance

For the proposed PID filter controller, step disturbance in PSink is applied to closed loop system and IAE (Integral Absolute errors) are calculated for over 300 seconds.

The objective functions for step and sine disturbance in Psink are given in equation (2) and (3).

$$f_1(x)_{step} = \sum_{j=1}^{3} \sum_{i=1}^{4} \int_0^{300} \left| y_{isp}^j(t) - y_i^j(t) \right| \tag{2}$$

$$f_2(x)_{sine} = \sum_{j=1}^{3} \sum_{i=1}^{4} \int_0^{300} \left| y_{isp}^j(t) - y_i^j(t) \right| \tag{3}$$

Similarly the objective function for coal quality change in equation in equation (4).

$$f_3(x)_{CV \, of \, coal} = \sum_{j=1}^{3} \sum_{i=1}^{4} \int_0^{300} \left| y_{isp}^j(t) - y_i^j(t) \right| \tag{4}$$

where

$f_1(x)_{step}$ is the objective function for step disturbance of -0.2 bar applied at Psink
$f_2(x)_{sine}$ is the objective function of sinusoidal disturbance of amplitude 0.2 bar and 0.04Hz frequency applied at Psink.
$f_3(x)_{cv \, of \, coal}$ is the objective function for disturbance at fuel fed-in.
$y_{isp}^j(t)$ is the steady state value for output number i at operating load.
i=1 Means CV of syngas; i=2 means bedmass output; i=3 means pressure output of the syngas; i=4 means temperature output for syngas; j=1 means 100% load;
j=2 Means 50% load and j=3 means 0% load.
$y_i^j(t)$ = Measured output value at the three operating loads.

Combining equations (2), (3) and (4), the fitness value D(x) can be obtained as given in equation (4.5)

$$D(x) = f_1(x)_{step} + f_2(x)_{sine} + f_3(x)_{CV \, ofcoal}. \tag{5}$$

It is necessary to minimise D(X).

Objective Function for Output Constraints

When the disturbances are applied, the controller must be tuned in such a way that output limits should not exceed. How well the controller meets the output constraints are given in equation (6) and (7)

$$C_{step} = \frac{\max\limits_{i} \max\limits_{j} \left\| y_i^j - y_{isp}^j \right\|}{D_i} \qquad (6)$$

$$C_{sine} = \frac{\max\limits_{i} \max\limits_{j} \left\| y_i^j - y_{isp}^j \right\|}{D_i} \qquad (7)$$

where

y_i^j = Measured variable for output i at operating point j

y_{isp}^j = Steady state valuefor output i at operating point j.

D_i = Allowable deviation of output i

Combining equation (6) and (7), the output objective function is given by

O = max $(C_{step,} C_{sine})$

Therefore, the overall objective function is to minimise D(x) if O <1.

The procedure for optimising PID filter controller with a genetic algorithm is given below:

Step 1: The PID tuning parameters (P, I, D) must be encoded in real numbers or vectors or binary strings

Step 2: Population size and limits are noted

Step 3: Normalised Geometric selection is applied to select any random values of parameters based on fitness value.

Step 4: Reproduce the selected parameters to get optimised solution.

Step 5: Arithmetic crossover and uniform mutation are performed to alter the parameters to optimised values.

Step 6: Calculate the fitness value D(x) for each iteration

Step 7: Repeat steps 8-10 for 'n' off springs

Step 8: Using fitness function, find the value of error in the Generation.

Step 9: The parameters with highest fitness value are chosen as the final parameter values.

Step 10: If the obtained values are not up to the mark, repeat step 2.

The flowchart for GA based PIDF Controller is given in Figure 8. Simulation results are performed in MATLAB. The number of the generations are chosen as 100. The parameter ranges of GA-PIDF controller are K_p ε [0 10],

K_i ε [0 0.1], K_d ε [0 0.01] and N ε [2 100]. The mutation range and cross over rate are taken as 0.5 and 0.8 respectively. The implementation of GA based PIDF controller for Gasifier control is shown in Figure 9.

As shown in Figures 8 and 9:

Figure 8. Flowchart representing optimization of PIDF controller using genetic algorithms for syngas pressure

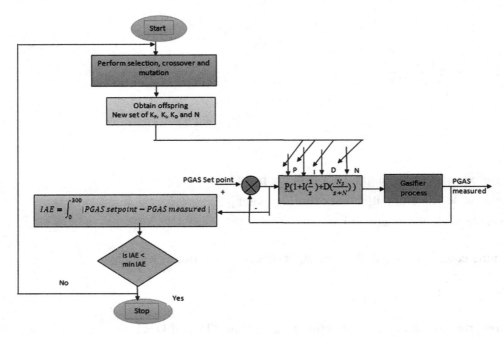

G11: Transfer function characteristics between char extraction flow rate and the calorific value of syngas.

G21: Transfer function characteristics between air flow rate and calorific value of syngas.

G31: Transfer function characteristics between coal flow rate and calorific value of syngas.

G41: Transfer function characteristics between steam flow rate and calorific value syngas.

G12: Transfer function characteristics between char extraction flow rate and bedmass.

G22: Transfer function characteristics between air flow rate and bedmass.

G32: Transfer function characteristics between coal flow rate and bedmass.

G42: Transfer function characteristics between steam flow rate and bedmass.

G13: Transfer function characteristics between char extraction flow rate and the pressure of syngas.

G23: Transfer function characteristics between air flow rate and pressure of syngas.

G33: Transfer function characteristics between coal flow rate and pressure of syngas.

G43: Transfer function characteristics between steam flow rate and pressure of syngas.

G14: Transfer function characteristics between char extraction flow rate and the temperature of syngas.

G24: Transfer function characteristics between air flow rate and temperature of syngas.

G34: Transfer function characteristics between coal flow rate and temperature of syngas.

G44: Transfer function characteristics between steam flow rate and temperature of syngas.

Also, adequate care has been taken to satisfy the input constraints by using a signal limiter and a signal rate limiter. Table 6 shows the PIDF parameter values optimized by GA for different control loops.

Figure 9. Closed loop structure for gasifier LOM with optimized PIDF control

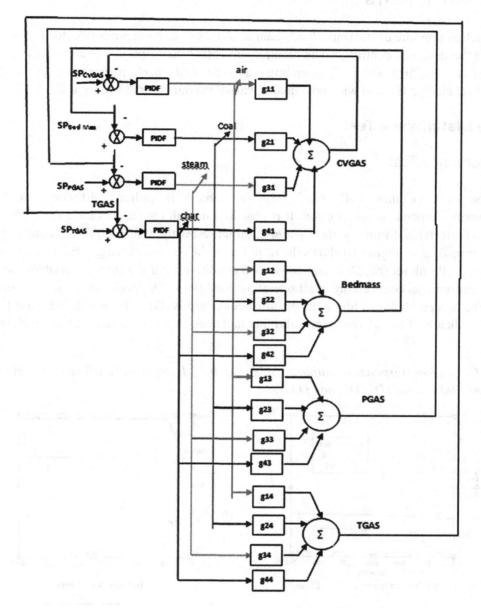

Table 6. Proportional-Integral-Derivative-Filter parameter values for different loops obtained through genetic algorithm

Output Variables	Kp	K_I	K_D	N
CVGAS	-0.002098	0.000362	0.01	100
MASS	0.000260	0.000147	0.2163021	100
PGAS	0.000189	0.000011	0.00001	0.03211
TGAS	1.724918	0.009927	0.151923	0.001574

PERFORMANCE TESTS

The tests such as pressure disturbance, load change, and coal variation are conducted to verify the performance of the designed controller. The requirement is that the response should meet the constraints (Table 2 and 3) at 0%, 50%, and 100% operating points during the performance tests, good output tracking during load change test and wide coal quality variations during coal quality test.

Pressure Disturbance Test

Step Disturbance Test

At 100% load, a step change of -0.2 bar in PSink disturbance is applied at 30 seconds to the gasifier and the dynamic response is investigated. It is observed that all the outputs meet the performance requirements comfortably. Similarly, the gasifier is initialised with 50% and 0% load conditions and the response is investigated. Figure 10 shows the response of the outputs of the gasifier respectively during a step change in PSink for 0%, 50%, and 100% load conditions. All the outputs variables meet the performance requirements comfortably at all operating conditions. The peak overshoots and undershoots are within the acceptable limits for all the disturbance scenarios (D1 to D3 tests). In Figure 10, the blue dashed line indicates 0% load, the green solid line indicates 50% operating load and black shaded line

Figure 10. Closed loop response of output variables (a, b, c, d) for step disturbance at load side during 0%, 50% and 100% loads (D1, D2, and D3 tests)

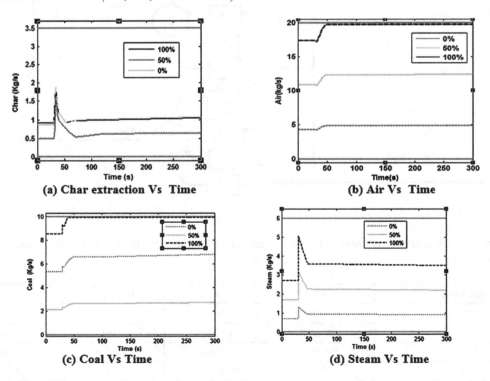

indicates 100% load. Figure 10, (a) represents the closed loop response of output variable – CVGAS- for step disturbance at load side during 0%, 50%, and 100% loads. (b) represents the closed loop response of output variable – Bedmass- for step disturbance at load side during 0%, 50%, and 100% loads. (c) represents the closed loop response of output variable – PGAS- for step disturbance at load side during 0%, 50%, and 100% loads. (d) represents the closed loop response of output variable – TGAS- for step disturbance at load side during 0%, 50%, and 100% loads.

Sinusoidal Disturbance

The above procedure is repeated for a sinusoidal PSink disturbance at all load conditions. Figure 11 shows the output response of gasifier at 0%. 50% and 100% loads during the sinusoidal PSink disturbance. All the output (Figure 11) satisfy the performance requirements. The peak overshoots and undershoots of all the outputs and input variables lies within the acceptable limits (D4 to D6 tests).

In Figure 11 (a) represents the closed loop response of output variable – CVGAS- for a sinusoidal disturbance at load side during 0%, 50%, and 100% loads. (b) represents the closed loop response of output variable – Bedmass- for a sinusoidal disturbance at load side during 0%, 50%, and 100% loads. (c) represents the closed loop response of output variable – PGAS- for a sinusoidal disturbance at load side during 0%, 50%, and 100% loads. (d) represents the closed loop response of output variable – TGAS- for a sinusoidal disturbance at load side during 0%, 50%, and 100% loads.

Figure 11. Closed loop response of output variables (a, b, c, d) for sinusoidal disturbance at load side during 0%, 50% and 100% loads (D4, D5, D6 tests)

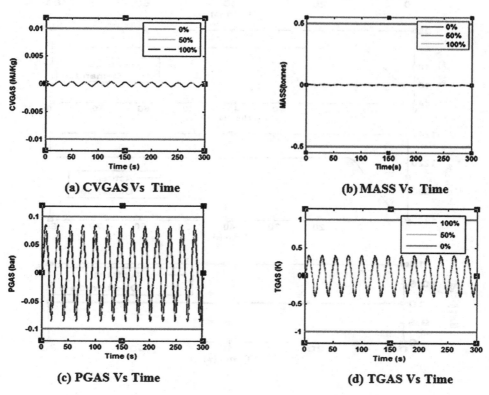

(a) CVGAS Vs Time   **(b) MASS Vs Time**

(c) PGAS Vs Time   **(d) TGAS Vs Time**

Load Change Test

Load change test is conducted to verify the stability of the Gasifier and controller function across the working range of the plant. The system is started at 50% load in steady state and ramped it to 100% over a period of 600 seconds (5% per minute) and the response is recorded for 80 minutes. Figure 12 shows the output response of the gasifier to load change from 50% to 100% respectively.

It is seen that the actual load, CVGAS, and PGAS track their demands quickly to set point while bedmass takes more time to reach its steady state, though manipulated inputs coal flow and char flow have reached their steady state immediately.

Coal Quality Variation Test

Carbon content and moisture content of the coal decides the quality of coal gas. Usually, the coal quality is not constant over a period of time and may vary by a considerable amount. The performance of

Figure 12. Closed loop response of output variables for Load ramping from 50% load to 100% load using LOM

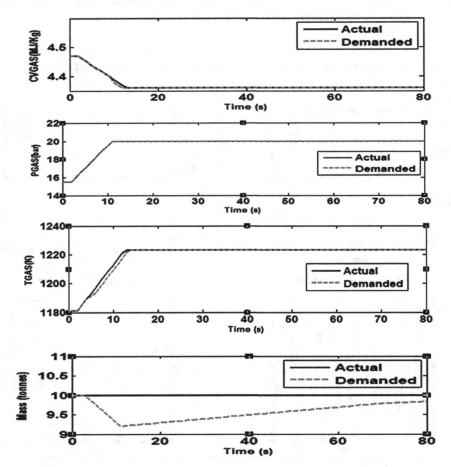

proposed PIDF controller during coupled disturbance in Psink (output side of gasifier) and change in the calorific value of coal (input side of Gasifier) are investigated.

For this purpose, the Gasifier is initialised with 100% load condition and subjected to a step change in PSink at 30 seconds. Then coal quality change (+18%) is introduced at 100 seconds. The response is observed for 300 seconds and any deviation from the desired performance is investigated. The same procedure is repeated for 100% with (-18%) changes in coal quality variations coupled with step disturbance.

Figure 13 shows the output responses of the coal gasifier at 100% during step disturbances in PSink coupled with ±18% of coal quality variations.

It is observed that all the output variables are within the tolerable limits and meet the performance requirements. In Figure 13, (a) represents the closed loop response of output variable –CVGAS, (b) represents the closed loop response of output variable - Bedmass, (c) represents the closed loop response of output variable- PGAS, (d) represents the closed loop response of output variable –TGAS for step disturbance at load side with ±18% CV of coal quality at 100% load.

Figure 13. Closed loop response of output response for step disturbance at load side coupled with ±18% CV of coal quality at 100% load

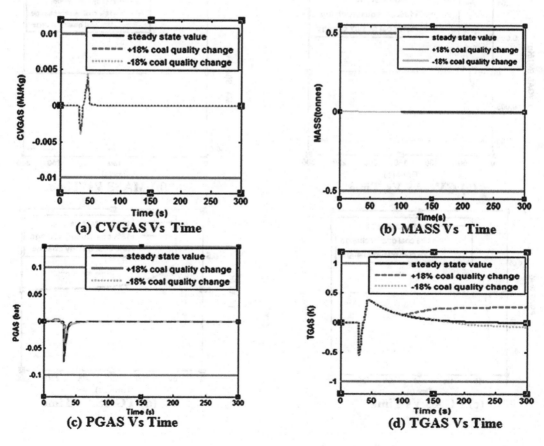

It is observed that all the output variables are within the tolerable limits and meet the performance requirements and the gasifier performs well even with maximum allowable coal quality variations.

Figure 14 and Figure 15 shows the response at 50% and 0% load respectively during a step change in PSink coupled with ±18% of coal quality variations. All the outputs meet the performance requirements without violating the constraints. The gasifier performs well even with maximum allowable coal quality variations.

Similarly, the Gasifier is tested with a sinusoidal disturbance at the output side. For this purpose, the Gasifier is initialised with 100% load condition and subjected to a sinusoidal change in PSink, then coal quality change (+18%) is introduced at 100 seconds. The response is observed for 300 seconds and any deviation from the desired performance is investigated. The same procedure is repeated for100% with -18% changes in coal quality variations.

Figure 14. Closed loop response of output response for step disturbance at load side coupled with ±18% CV of coal quality at 50% load

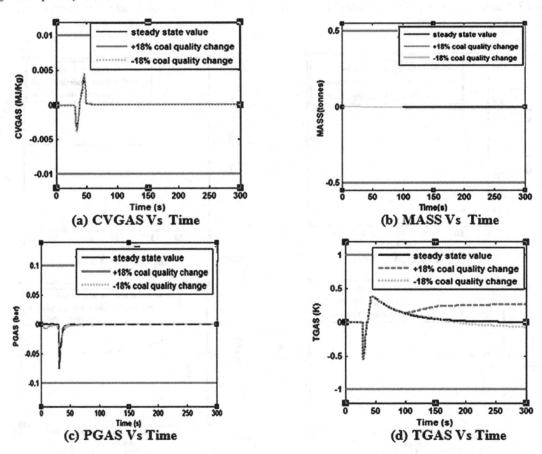

Figure 15. Closed loop response of output response for step disturbance at load side coupled with ±18% CV of coal quality at 0% load

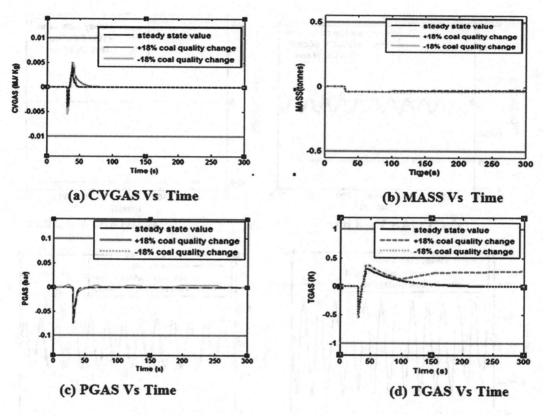

(a) CVGAS Vs Time   (b) MASS Vs Time

(c) PGAS Vs Time   (d) TGAS Vs Time

Figure 16 shows the output responses of the coal gasifier at 100% during sinusoidal disturbances in PSink coupled with ±18% of coal quality variations.It is observed that all the output variables are within the tolerable limits except TGAS reaches its allowable limit during -18%, which is considered as performance violation.

Similar tests are conducted for 50% and 0% operating loads. Figure 17 shows the output responses of the coal gasifier at 50% during sinusoidal disturbances in PSink coupled with ±18% of coal quality variations. It is observed that all the output variables are within the tolerable limits. Figure 18 shows the output responses of the coal gasifier at 0% during sinusoidal disturbances in PSink coupled with ±18% of coal quality variations.

It is observed that TGAS violate the limits under coal quality change for sinusoidal pressure disturbance and no output variable is found for step pressure disturbance.Table 7 shows the violation of the variables under positive (+18%) and negative change (-18%) in coal quality. Since input constraints are inbuilt in the actuator limits, output constraints are considered to be the actual violation.

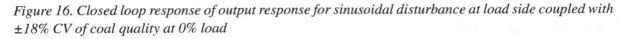

Figure 16. Closed loop response of output response for sinusoidal disturbance at load side coupled with ±18% CV of coal quality at 0% load

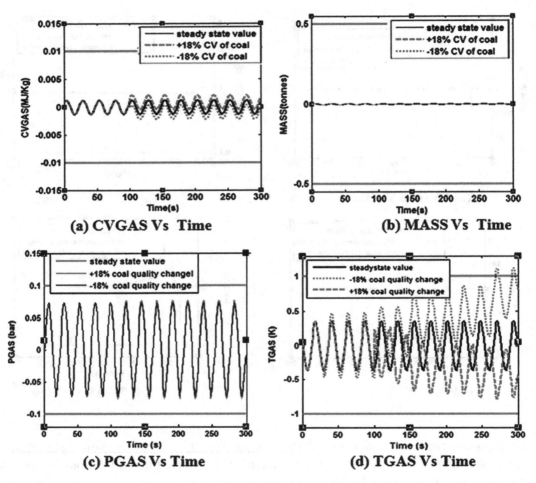

Table 7. Summary of input and output variables either meeting or not meeting the constraints in closed loop mode for different disturbances with LOM

S. No.	Variables	Disturbances for Which Control Requirements Have Been Met Are Indicated by √ While 'x' Indicates Partial Fulfilment of Control Requirements																		
		D1	D2	D3	D4	D5	D6	D7	D8	D9	D10	D11	D12	D13	D14	D15	D16	D17	D18	D19
1	CVGAS	√	√	√	√	√	√	√	√	√	√	√	√	√	√	√	√	√	√	√
2	MASS	√	√	√	√	√	√	√	√	√	√	√	√	√	√	√	√	√	√	√
3	PGAS	√	√	√	√	√	√	√	√	√	√	√	√	√	√	√	√	√	√	√
4	TGAS	√	√	√	√	√	√	√	√	√	√	x	√	x	√	√	√	√	√	√
5	WCHR	√	√	√	√	√	√	√	√	√	√	x	√	x	√	√	√	√	√	√
6	WAIR	√	√	√	√	√	√	√	√	√	√	√	√	√	√	√	√	√	√	√
7	WCOAL	√	√	√	√	√	√	√	√	√	√	√	√	√	√	√	√	√	√	√
8	WSTM	√	√	√	√	√	√	√	√	√	√	√	√	x	√	√	√	√	√	√

Figure 17. Closed loop response of output response for sinusoidal disturbance at load side coupled with ±18% CV of coal quality at 50% load

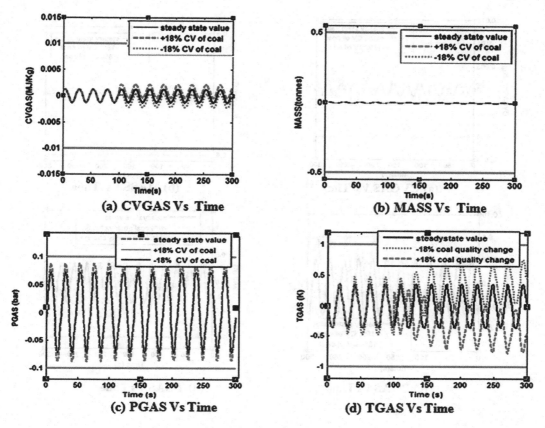

PERFORMANCE ANALYSIS OF OUTPUT VARIABLES DURING PRESSURE DISTURBANCE TEST

The transient performance analysis of gasifier output variables like CVGAS, Bedmass, PGAS and TGAS during load disturbances (D1 to D6) have been simulated using proposed PIDF controller. The maximum absolute error (MAE) observed during transient zone has been considered as reference and the results obtained by different control strategies- such as Linear Model Predictive control (Al Seyab and Cao 2006), Non-linear Model Predictive control (Al Seyab and Cao 2006), Baseline Proportional -Integral controller (Dixon and Pike et al. 2006), Proportional – Integral Controller optimised with genetic algorithms (PI with GA) (Simm and Liu 2006), Multiobjective PI with Cuckoo algorithm (Sivakumar and Kottesswaran 2014) and Bat optimization algorithms (Kotteeswaran and Sivakumar 2013) – have been compared and shown in Table 8 and Table 9. The values shown in bold represents the best value for a particular output variable during a particular disturbance test.

Figure 18. Closed loop response of output response for sinusoidal disturbance at load side coupled with ±18% CV of coal quality at 0% load

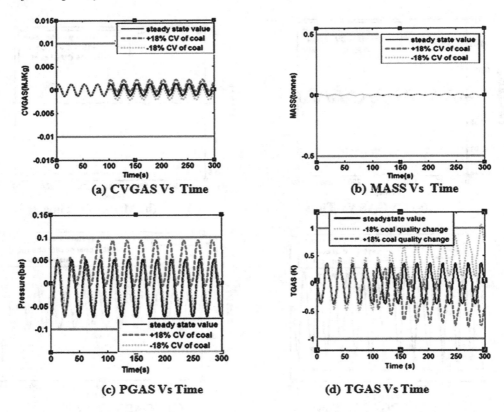

Figure 19. Performance of proposed controller during coal quality variations

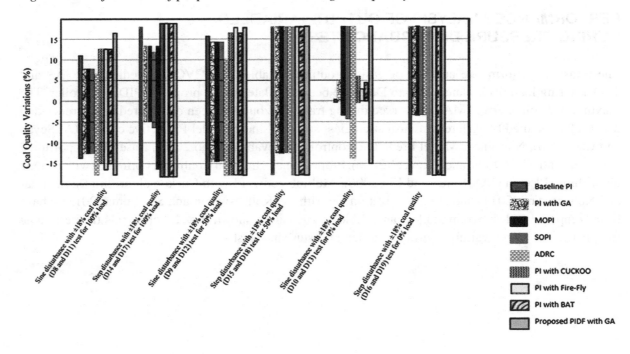

Table 8. Summary of Maximum Absolute Error analysis for output variables by different controllers

Disturbance	Output Variables	Linear Model Predictive Controller (Seyab and Cao 2006)	Non-Linear Model Predictive Controller (Seyab and Cao 2006)	Baseline (PI) Controller (Dixon and Pike 2006)	PI Optimised with Genetic Algorithm (Simm and Liu 2006)	PI Optimized with Bat Algorithm (Kotteeswaran and Sivakumar 2013)	PI Optimized with Cuckoo Based Algorithm (Sivakumar Kotteeswaran 2014)	Proposed PIDF Controller Optimized with GA
Step disturbance at PSink for 100% load (D1 test)	CVGAS (MJ/Kg)	0.00733	0.00669	0.00785	0.00625	0.006722	0.00797	**0.00622**
	Mass (kg)	16	10.613	6.9407	6.938	6.9382	6.9382	**5.88**
	PGAS (bar)	0.067	0.0735	0.0498	0.0513	**0.0425**	0.0609	0.076
	TGAS (K)	0.5194	0.5193	0.2395	0.2243	0.266	0.2787	**0.2221**
Step disturbance at PSink for 50% load (D2 test)	CVGAS (MJ/Kg)	0.00744	0.00623	0.00503	0.004599	0.00629	0.00672	**0.00405**
	Mass (kg)	12.42	4.054	8.4548	8.4548	8.454	8.454	**3.986**
	PGAS (bar)	0.076	0.0881	0.05768	0.05918	0.051	0.0496	**0.0489**
	TGAS (K)	0.611	0.542	0.266	0.2476	0.3024	0.3187	**0.2281**
Step disturbance at PSink for 0% load (D3 test)	CVGAS (MJ/Kg)	0.0089	0.00694	0.00589	0.0067	0.00724	0.008018	**0.00521**
	Mass (kg)	29.26	8.090	11.053	11.0529	11.053	11.053	7.65
	PGAS (bar)	0.0954	0.1006	0.0772	0.07854	0.0759	0.076	**0.0742**
	TGAS (K)	0.525	0.6005	0.3231	0.3018	0.818	0.4034	**0.2592**

Table 9. Summary of Maximum Absolute Error analysis for output variables by different controllers

Disturbance	Output Variables	Linear Model Predictive Controller (Seyab and Cao 2006)	Non-Linear Model Predictive Controller (Seyab and Cao 2006)	Baseline (PI) Controller (Dixon and Pike 2006)	PI Optimised with Genetic Algorithm (Simm and Liu 2006)	PI Optimized with Bat Algorithm (Kotteeswaran and Sivakumar 2013)	PI Optimized with Cuckoo Based Algorithm (Sivakumar and Kotteeswaran 2014)	Proposed PIDF Controller Optimized with GA
Sinusoidal disturbance at PSink for 100% load (D4 test)	CVGAS (MJ/Kg)	0.005065	0.005348	0.0041024	0.007406	0.003731	0.0037562	**0.00359**
	Mass (kg)	3.588	3.1789	10.858	10.173	10.718	10.756	**3.063**
	PGAS (bar)	**0.0315**	0.0354	0.04955	0.04049	0.0318	0.0591	0.0441
	TGAS (K)	0.302	0.321	0.3783	0.2806	0.3485	0.3523	**0.2498**
Sinusoidal disturbance at PSink for 50% load (D5 test)	CVGAS (MJ/Kg)	0.00431	0.00472	0.004712	0.004711	0.004257	0.0043039	**0.00407**
	Mass (kg)	6.663	6.191	12.852	11.991	12.664	12.719	**3.995**
	PGAS (bar)	**0.034**	0.04	0.0623	0.0494	0.0396	**0.0363**	0.0566
	TGAS (K)	**0.0349**	0.44	0.4226	**0.3106**	0.3862	0.03912	0.489
Sinusoidal disturbance at PSink for 0% load (D6 test)	CVGAS (MJ/Kg)	0.00807	0.003916	0.00585	**0.00348**	0.0061	0.0068	0.00432
	Mass (kg)	48.64	46.207	16.346	15.532	16.239	16.296	**14.339**
	PGAS (bar)	0.0774	0.099	0.1195	0.09041	0.0998	0.0991	**0.0567**
	TGAS (K)	0.7138	0.7705	0.479	**0.3656**	0.4747	0.5145	0.399

PERFORMANCE ANALYSIS OF GASIFIER DURING COAL QUALITY VARIATION TEST (D8 TO D19 TESTS)

One of the prime objective in challenge II problem is to investigate the performance of gasifier during pressure disturbance tests coupled with coal quality change. The philosophy behind these tests is to ascertain to what extent the variation in the calorific value of the coal could be met with the certain control strategy. Alstom Challenge problem envisages a variation of + 18% and − 18% step change in the calorific value of the coal fed into the gasifier. As on date, no control strategy ensured this requirement. According to published results, various control strategies met different % of variations in the calorific value of coal both in positive and negative directions.

The extent of % variation in the calorific value of coal which has been met by different control strategy is shown in Table 10 and graphically illustrated in Figure 19. Table 10 shows the comparison of allowed coal quality variations in % by different controllers such as Base PI controller (Dixon and Pike 2006),

Table 10. Comparison of allowed coal quality variations in % by different controllers

Controllers	Load Disturbance					
	100% Load		50% Load		0% Load	
	Sinusoidal Disturbance Coupled with ± 18% Coal Quality Change (D8 and D11 Test)	Step Disturbance Coupled with ± 18% Coal Quality Change (D14 and D17 Test)	Sinusoidal Disturbance Coupled with ± 18% Coal Quality Change (D9 and D12 Test)	Step Disturbance Coupled with ± 18% Coal Quality Change (D15 and D18 Test)	Sinusoidal Disturbance Coupled with ± 18% Coal Quality Change (D10 and D13 Test)	Step Disturbance Coupled with ± 18% Coal Quality Change (D16 and D19 Test)
Base line PI (Dixon and Pike 2006)	(-14,11)	(-18,18)	(-18,16)	(-18,18)	(0,0)	(-18,18)
PI with GA (Simm and Liu 2006)	(-13,8)	(-5,14)	(-14,14)	(-12,18)	(0.5)	(-8,18)
MOPI (Xue et al 2010)	(-13,8)	(-5,14)	(-14,14)	(-12,18)	(-3,18)	(-8,18)
ADRC (Huang et al. 2013)	(-18,6)	(-17,14)	(-18,10)	(-12,18)	(-18,18)	(-8,18)
PI with Bat algorithm (Kotteeswaran and Sivakumar 2013)	(-15,12)	(-18,18)	(-18,17)	(-18,18)	(0,4)	(-18,18)
PI with Firefly algorithm (Kotteewaran and Sivakumar 2013)	(-16,12)	(-18,18)	(-18,18)	(-18,18)	(0,3)	(-18,18)
PI with cuckoo algorithm (Sivakumar and Kotteeswaran 2014)	(-15,12)	(-18,18)	(- 18,17)	(-18,18)	(0,6)	(-18,18)
Proposed PIDF with GA	**(-16,18)**	**(-18,18)**	**(-18,18)**	**(-18,18)**	**(-15,18)**	**(-18,18)**

PI with GA (Simm and Liu 2006), Multi-Objective PI (Xue et al. 2010), Active disturbance rejection control (Huang et al. 2013), PI optimised with Bat algorithm (Kotteeswaran and Sivakumar 2013), PI optimised with cuckoo algorithm (Kotteeswaran and Sivakumar 2013), PI optimised with cuckoo algorithm (Sivakumar and Koteeswaran 2014) and Proposed PIDF optimised with GA(Kotteeswaran and Sivakumar 2016).

It is gratifying to note that the proposed PIDF controller accommodates a maximum range in coal quality variations from +18% to -18% during all disturbance (D8 to D19) tests sans D11 and D13.

After having compared the performance of gasifier (Closed loop gasifier performance) for different disturbance scenario by various control strategy, it is opined that the proposed PIDF controller optimized with Genetic Algorithms seems to be the best in the sense that the controller has holistically met most of the performance requirement of ALSTOM challenge I and II in comparison with other controllers.

CONCLUSION

After having compared the performance of gasifier (Closed loop gasifier performance) for different disturbance scenario by various control strategy, it is opined that the proposed PIDF controller optimized with Genetic Algorithms seems to be the best in the sense that the controller has holistically met most of the performance requirement of ALSTOM challenge I and II in comparison with other controllers.

REFERENCES

Agustriyanto, R., & Zhang, J. (2009). Control structure selection for the ALSTOM gasifier benchmark process using GRDG analysis. *International Journal of Modelling Identification and Control, 6*(2), 126–135. doi:10.1504/IJMIC.2009.024329

Al Seyab, R. K., & Cao, Y. (2006). Nonlinear model predictive control for the ALSTOM Gasifier. *Journal of Process Control, 16*(8), 795–808. doi:10.1016/j.jprocont.2006.03.003

Al Seyab, R. K., Cao, Y., & Yang, S. H. (2006). Predictive control for the ALSTOM gasifier problem. *IEEE Proceedings - Control Theory and Application, 153*(3), 293-301. doi:10.1049/ip-cta:20050049

Asmer, B. N., Jones, W. E., & Wilson, J. A. (2000). A process engineering approach to the ALSTOM gasifier problem. *Proceedings of the Institution of Mechanical Engineers. Part I, Journal of Systems and Control Engineering, 214*(6), 441–452. doi:10.1177/095965180021400601

Bansal, N. K., & Hake, J. (2000). Energy needs and supply option for developing countries. Proceedings of World Engineer's Convocation, 65-96.

Blasco, F. X. (1999). *Model based predictive control using heuristic optimization techniques: Application to non- linear multivariable processes* (Ph.D. thesis). Universidad Politecnica de Valencia, Valencia, Spain.

Chen-Ching, Y. (2007). *Auto tuning of PID controllers: A relay feedback approach* (2nd ed.). Springer Publication.

Chin, C. S., & Munro, N. (2003). Control of the ALSTOM Gasifier benchmark problem using H2 methodology. *Journal of Process Control, 13*(8), 759–768. doi:10.1016/S0959-1524(03)00008-8

Desborough & Honeywell. (2001). PID control. *Proceedings of the Sixth International Conference on Chemical Process Control.*

Dixon, R., & Pike, A. W. (2006). ALSTOM Benchmark Challenge II on Gasifier Control. *IEEE Proceedings. Control Theory and Applications, 153*(3), 254–261. doi:10.1049/ip-cta:20050062

Exadaktylos, V., Taylor, C. J., Wang, L., & Young, P. C. (2009). Forward path model predictive control using a non-minimal state-space form. *Proceedings of the Institution of Mechanical Engineers. Part I, Journal of Systems and Control Engineering, 223*(3), 353–369. doi:10.1243/09596518JSCE674

Goldberg, D. E. (2000). *Genetic Algorithms in search, optimization and machine learning.* New Delhi: Pearson Education Asia Ltd.

Griffin, I. A., Schroder, P., Chipperfield, A. J., & Fleming, P. J. (2000). Multi-objective optimization approach to the ALSTOM gasifier problem. *Proceedings of the Institution of Mechanical Engineers. Part I, Journal of Systems and Control Engineering, 214*(6), 453–469. doi:10.1243/0959651001540807

Haryanto, P., Siregar, D., Kurniadi, & Hong, K-S. (2008). Development of Integrated Alstom Gasification Simulator for Implementation Using DCS CS3000. *Proceedings of the 17th World Congress, the International Federation of Automatic Control,* 6-11.

Huang, Donghai, Li, & Xue. (2013). Active disturbance rejection control for the ALSTOM gasifier benchmark problem. *Control Engineering Practice, 21*(4), 556–564.

Kotteeswaran, R., & Sivakumar, L. (2013). Partial-retuning of decentralized PI Controller of nonlinear multivariable process using Firefly algorithm. *IEEE International Conference on Human Computer Interactions (ICHCI'13).*

Kotteeswaran, R., & Sivakumar, L. (2013). Normalized Normal Constraint algorithm based Multi- Objective optimal tuning of Decentralised PI controller of Nonlinear Multivariable Process – Coal gasifier, SEMCCO 2013. *Lecture Notes in Computer Science, 8297,* 333–344. doi:10.1007/978-3-319-03753-0_30

Kotteeswaran, R., & Sivakumar, L. (2013). Optimal Partial-retuning of decentralized PI controller of coal gasifier using Bat Algorithm, SEMCCO 2013. *Lecture Notes in Computer Science, 8297,* 750–761. doi:10.1007/978-3-319-03753-0_66

Kotteeswaran & Sivakumar. (2016). Coal Gasifier Control - A Heuristic Algorithm Based Optimization Approach. *Australian Journal of Basic and Applied Sciences, 10*(5), 161-167.

Liu, G. P., Dixon, R., & Daley, S. (2000). Multi-objective optimal-tuning proportional-integral controller design for the ALSTOM gasifier problem. *Proceedings of the Institution of Mechanical Engineers. Part I, Journal of Systems and Control Engineering, 214*(6), 395–404. doi:10.1243/0959651001540753

Munro, N., Edmunds, J. M., Kontogiannis, E., & Impram, I. M. (2000). A sequential loop closing approach to the ALSTOM gasifier problem. *Proceedings of the Institution of Mechanical Engineers. Part I, Journal of Systems and Control Engineering, 214*(6), 427–439. doi:10.1243/0959651001540780

Nise, N. S. (2006). *Control System Engineering* (3rd ed.). CECSA.

Nobakhti, A., & Wang, H. (2008). A simple self-adaptive Differential Evolution algorithm with application on the ALSTOM gasifier. *Applied Soft Computing*, *8*(1), 350–370. doi:10.1016/j.asoc.2006.12.005

O'Dwyer, A. (2009). Handbook of PI and PID Controller Tuning Rules (3rd ed.). Imperial College Press.

Ogata, K. (2003). *Modern Control Engineering* (4th ed.). Person Prentice Hall.

Phillips, J. (2006). Different types of gasifiers and their integration with gas turbines. In The Gas Turbine Handbook. U.S. Department of Energy, Office of Fossil energy, National Energy Technology Laboratory, DOE/NETL-2006-1230.

Pike, A. W., Donne, M. S., & Dixon, R. (1998). Dynamic modelling and simulation of the air blown gasification cycle prototype publication. *Proceedings of the International Conference on Simulation*, 354-361.

Ponnusamy, P., Sivakumar, L., & Sankaran, S. V. (1983). Low-order dynamic model of a complete thermal power plant loop. *Proceedings of the Power Plant Dynamics, Control and Testing Symposium*, 1.

Poongodi, P., & Victor, S. (2009). *Genetic algorithm based PID controller design for LTI system via reduced order model*. International Conference on Instrumentation, Control & Automation ICA2009, Bandung, Indonesia.

Prempain, P., Postlethwaite, I., & Sun, X. D. (2000). Robust control of the gasifier using a mixed-sensitivity H∞ approach. *Proceedings of the Institution of Mechanical Engineers Part I: Journal of Systems and Control Engineering*, *214*(6), 415-427.

Ramezan & Stiegel. (2006). Integrated coal gasification combined cycle. In *The gas turbine handbook*. Retrieved from http://www.netl.doe.gov/technologies/ coalpower/turbines/refshelf/handbok/1.2.pdf

Rice, M., Rosster, J., & Schurmans, J. (2000). An advanced predictive control approach to the Alstom gasifier problem. *Proceedings of the Institution of Mechanical Engineers Part I: Journal of Systems and Control Engineering*, *214*(6), 405-413.

Simm, A., & Liu, G. P. (2006). Improving the performance of the ALSTOM baseline controller using multiobjective optimisation. *IEEE Proceedings. Control Theory and Applications*, *153*(3), 286–292. doi:10.1049/ip-cta:20050131

Sivakumar, L., & Kotteeswaran, R. (2014). Soft computing based partial-retuning of decentralized PI Controller of nonlinear multivariable process. *ICT and Critical Infrastructure: Proceedings of the 48th Annual Convention of Computer Society of India*, 117-124.

Sivanandam, S.N., & Deepa, S.N. (2009). A Comparative Study Using Genetic Algorithm and Particle Swarm Optimization for Lower Order System Modelling. *International Journal of the Computer, the Internet and Management*, *17*(3), 1-10.

Tan, W., Lou, G., & Liang, L. (2011). Partially decentralized control for ALSTOM gasifier. *ISA Transactions*, *50*(3), 397–408. doi:10.1016/j.isatra.2011.01.008 PMID:21356534

Taylor, C. J., McCabe, A. P., Young, P. C., & Chotai, A. (2000). Proportional integral-plus (PIP) control of the ALSTOM gasifier problem. *Proceedings of the Institution of Mechanical Engineers. Part I, Journal of Systems and Control Engineering, 214*(6), 469–481. doi:10.1243/0959651001540816

Taylor, C. J., & Shaban, E. M. (2006). Multivariable proportional-integralplus (PIP) control of the ALSTOM nonlinear gasifier simulation. *IEEE Proceedings. Control Theory and Applications, 153*(3), 277–285. doi:10.1049/ip-cta:20050058

Wilson, J. A., Chew, M., & Jones, W. E. (2006). A state estimation based approach to gasifier control. *IEE Proceedings. Control Theory and Applications, 153*(3), 268–276. doi:10.1049/ip-cta:20050071

Xue, Y., Donghai, L., & Gao, F. (2010). Multi-objective optimization and selection for the PI control of ALSTOM gasifier problem. *Control Engineering Practice, 18*(1), 67-76.

Chapter 4
Metaheuristic– and Statistical– Based Sampling in Optimization

Yoel Tenne
Ariel University, Israel

ABSTRACT

Modern engineering often uses computer simulations as a partial substitute to real-world experiments. As such simulations are often computationally intensive, metamodels, which are numerical approximations of the simulation, are often used. Optimization frameworks which use metamodels require an initial sample of points to initiate the main optimization process. Two main approaches for generating the initial sample are the 'design of experiments' method which is statistically based, and the more recent metaheuristic-based sampling which uses a metaheuristic or a computational intelligence algorithm. Since the initial sample can have a strong impact on the overall optimization search and since the two sampling approaches operate based only widely different mechanisms this study analyzes the impact of these two approaches on the overall search effectiveness in an extensive set of numerical experiments which covers a wide variety of scenarios. A detailed analysis is then presented which highlights which method was the most beneficial to the search depending on the problem settings.

INTRODUCTION

Computer simulations, also termed in the literature as *computer experiments*, are used in engineering and science as a partial replacement to actual laboratory experiments. In this setup, candidate designs are represented as a vector of design variables and are sent to the computer simulation to evaluate how well they satisfy the design goals. This simulation-driven process results in an optimization problem with three distinct characteristics (Tenne & Goh, 2010a):

DOI: 10.4018/978-1-5225-3129-6.ch004

- The numerical simulation is often intricate, for example, involving the iterative solution of large sets of partial differential equations as commonly done in computational fluid mechanics (CFD) or computational structural mechanics (CSM). As such, there is no analytic relation which explains how an input vector is mapped to an output value, and thus the simulation is referred to in the literature as a *black-box* function. The lack of an analytic expression adds an optimization difficulty.

- Typically each run of the numerical simulation is computationally intensive, namely, requiring large computational resources, and hence only a small number of candidate designs can be directly evaluated with the simulation.

- The aforementioned 'black-box' function may have complicated features such as multiple local optima or discontinuities which are an outcome of either the underlying physics of engineering problem or result from the numerical simulation process itself. Regardless, such features render the task of locating an optimum even more difficult.

To circumvent these challenges optimization frameworks often use *metamodels* (also termed in the literature as *surrogates* or *response surfaces*), which are numerical approximations of the inputs-output mapping of the simulation but which are significantly cheaper to evaluate in terms of computational cost (Tenne & Goh, 2010a). Optimization frameworks which rely on such metamodels require an initial sample of vectors to generate a preliminary metamodel as a precursor step to the main optimization process. It follows that the initial sample can strongly impact the overall effectiveness of the optimization, which in turn motivates an analysis of this linkage.

Approaches for generating the initial sample include the statistical *design of experiments* (DOE) methodology in which the vectors are a-priori sampled to satisfy some optimality criterion (Chen et al., 2006; Queipo et al., 2005), and the more recent *metahueristic based sampling* (MHS) in which a metaheuristic optimization algorithm is used for a short duration and the vectors it generated are then used as the initial sample (Büche et al., 2005; Liang et al., 2000; R. Jin et al., 2005). Existing studies from the domain of metamodel-assisted optimization have focused mainly on the DOE methods, for example, as discussed by Queipo et al. (2005);

Chen et al. (2006); Sóbester et al. (2005); Forrester & Keane (2008); Wang & Shan (2007). However, the MHS approaches have received much less attention, in particular when their merits and demerits are compared to DOE methods. Accordingly, this chapter addresses this open question and extensively analyzes the impact of DOE and MHS sampling methods in the context of metamodel-assisted optimization. The analysis is performed through an extensive set of numerical experiments in which representative methods from each category were used in a wide range of optimization scenarios. Based on the results of these experiments a detailed analysis is presented as to which approach was preferable based on the settings of the problem which was being solved.

The remainder of this chapter is organized as follows: Section 2 provides the background information, Section 3 describes in detail the numerical experiments performed, Section 4 provides an extensive analysis and discussion, and lastly Section 5 concludes this chapter.

BACKGROUND

Black-Box Optimization Problems

Simulation-driven optimization is a common practice these days in engineering and science, and Figure 1 shows a typical layout. The optimization challenges described in Section 1 have motivated researchers to develop and apply heuristic and computational intelligence (CI) based optimization algorithms to such problems, as they are often able to better handle these challenges when compared to classical gradient-based methods. CI based algorithms typically use a population of candidate solutions and manipulate through various nature-inspired operators, and examples include evolutionary algorithms (EAs), particle swarm optimization (PSO) and simulated annealing (SA), to name a few (Tenne & Goh, 2010a,b).

Through their nature-inspired mechanisms, such algorithms drive the population to explore the function landscape and to cluster around good solutions of the objective functions. However, a demerit they exhibit is that they typically require a large number of function evaluations which makes them inapplicable per se in the realm of expensive optimization problems. To circumvent this issue several approaches can be used. First, the *order* (or *dimensionality*) of the problem might be reduced such that a simplified problem is obtained and which can be solved with a smaller number of function evaluations. Examples of this approach include the Principal Component Analysis (PCA) method (Lang et al. 2009), and the Sammon mapping technique (Figeroa, C. J., 2005), to name a few. Another established approach is that of using metamodels so that they would provide approximate objective values at a much lower computational cost. Variants of metamodels include artificial neural networks (ANN), Kriging/Bayesian Interpolation models, polynomials such as MARS and splines, and various radial basis functions (RBF) models (Queipo et al., 2005; Forrester & Keane, 2008). To show the layout of such frameworks Algorithm 1 gives a pseudocode of a typical metamodel-assisted framework. Metamodel-assisted optimization is an active research field and some recent examples include *ensembles* which aggregate the predictions of

Figure 1. The layout of a typical black-box optimization problem

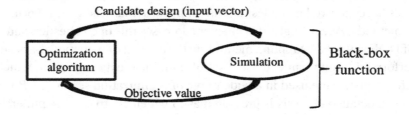

Algorithm 1. The micro-EA used in the MHS-EA method

```
Initialize a population of vectors and evaluate them;
Repeat
Select a group of vectors and designate them as parents;
Recombine the parents to create offspring;
Mutate some of the offspring;
Evaluate the offspring with the true expensive function;
Select the vectors which will comprise the next population;
  Until limit of evaluations reached;
```

several metamodels (Goel et al., 2007; Acar, 2010; Muller & Piché, 2011), *model selection* frameworks which online select the best metamodel variant during the search (Tenne & Armfield, 2009; Gorissen et al., 2009, 2010), and other involved implementations (Abramson et al., 2012; Regis & Shoemaker, 2013). It is noted that the above discussion considered problems which have a single objective, though engineering problems can require multi-objective optimization, and this has motivated the development of the application of dedicated techniques (Correia et. al, 2016, Huang et al., 2014).

Recent surveys are given by Queipo et al. (2005) and Forrester & Keane (2008), and a recent collection of studies is given by Tenne & Goh (2010a).

Sampling Methods

Sampling methods originated in the realm of designing real-world laboratory experiments and were therefore designed to produce a sample which minimizes the impact of noise or other uncertainties on the analysis. Examples of such methods include full and fractional factorial designs, central composite designs and the well-established Response Sufrace Methodology (RSM) (Chen et al., 2006; Wang & Shan, 2007). With the arrival of computer experiments and accordingly noise-free functions evaluations such considerations became irrelevant and hence new *design of experiments* (DOE) methods were introduced and whose goal is to generate a sample which is *space-filling*, namely, in which the sample vectors are well distributed over the entire search space to provide a better understanding of the behavior of the objective function. Examples in this class of methods include Latin hypercube (LH) designs, orthogonal arrays, and maximin/ minimax designs (Chen et al., 2006; Wang & Shan, 2007). Two main features of DOE methods are: i) the entire sample is often (but not always) generated prior to the main optimization search so the sample vectors can be evaluated in parallel to reduce the sample evaluation time (Sóbester et al., 2005), and ii) the black-box objective function does not influence which vectors are generated.

A more recent sampling approach is that of *metaheuristic based sampling* (MHS). Such methods use a metaheuristic or a CI based optimization algorithm for a short duration during which the latter directly calls the expensive black-box objective function directly. The vectors this optimization algorithm generated during its short run are then taken as the initial sample vectors. Examples of methods in this category include Büche et al. (2005) and Liang et al. (2000) which used EAs, and Jin et al (2005) which used a simmulated annealing algorithm. In contrast to the DOE methods, MHS methods have the following features: i) the sample vectors are generated gradually as the search progresses and so it is not possible to evaluate the full sample at once, and ii) since the metaheuristic optimization algorithm relies on the objective function the latter strongly affects which vectors are generated. To complete this discussion Table 1 summarizes the main features of the DOE and MHS approaches.

Related Studies

Various studies have examined the impact of sampling methods on the optimization search but in contexts completely different from that presented in this chapter. For example, Simpson et al. (2001) examined the interaction between five DOE methods and four metamodels variants and provided guidelines as to which combination had the highest prediction accuracy. Jin (2005) surveyed various sampling methods in relation to metamodel training and distinguished between offline training (generating the sample prior to the search) versus online training (generating the sample dynamically during the search). In another study, Sóbester et al. (2005) studied various problem settings which affect the initial sample and the optimization search. Also, Quttineh & Holmström (2009) compared how the search was affected by various sampling techniques which included Latin hypercube design (LHD) sampling, sampling at the edges (corners) of the search space, and sampling based on the expected improvement algorithm (Jones et al., 1998). Lastly, Laurenceau & Sagaut (2008) studied how several DOE methods compare to that of sampling based on the metamodel prediction error. Additional relevant studies include Chen et al. (2006); Wang & Shan (2007); Queipo et al. (2005); Forrester & Keane (2008).

NUMERICAL EXPERIMENTS

To evaluate the impact of DOE and MHS approaches on the effectiveness of the optimization search an extensive set of numerical experiments was formulated and performed, as follows. The experiments consisted of two stages: i) generating an initial sample by a sampling method (as described later), and ii) a full optimization search which was done by a metamodel-assisted algorithm. Following Myers & Montgomery (1995) the experiments included two main components:

Table 1. A comparison of the DOE and MHS sampling approaches

Feature	Approach	
	Design of Experiments (DOE)	**Metaheuristic Sampling (MHS)**
Sampling process	Sample vectors are generated by a statistical procedure	Sample vectors generated by a metaheuristic algorithm
Complete or gradual sample generation	The sample is typically (not always) generated in full prior to the main optimization search	The sample is generated incrementally as the search progresses
Impact of objective function on sample generation	None	Direct
Sample vectors are space-filling	Yes	Partially

Table 2. Settings of the numerical experiments

Component Type	Component Purpose	Experiments Values
Factor	Sampling method type	LHS, MHS-EA, MHS-Simplex
Control variable	Limit of evaluations of the true objective function	200, 2000
	Relative size of the initial sample from the limit of evaluations	10%, 25%
	Objective function type	Ackley, Griewank, Rastrigin, Rosenbrock, Schwefel 2.13, Weierstrass
	Objective function dimension	10, 50

1. A *factor* which is the main variable whose effect is being analyzed. In this study, the factor was the type of sampling method used to generate the initial sample: Latin hypercube sampling (LHS), MHS with an EA (MHS-EA), and MHS with a simplex optimization algorithm (MHS-Simplex), as described below.

2. The *control variables* which are the experiments settings which are kept fixed while different factor values (namely, sampling method type in this study) are been used. The experiments included four control variables: a) the size of the initial sample, b) the optimization budget, c) the function type, and d) the function dimension. Each control variable (except for *function dimension*) was assigned suitable 'low' and 'high' settings. This configuration defined 48 different *optimization scenarios*, namely, unique optimization problems where each has different settings, as presented in Table 2. Each sampling method was applied across all the 48 scenarios, and for an adequate statistical analysis 30 runs where repeated with each combination of sampling method and scenario, such that each sampling method was tested through 48x30=1440 optimization runs.

For the sampling methods, the following variants were used:

*   **Latin Hypercube Sampling (LHS):** A DOE method which aims to generate a sample which is space-filling so it covers the full search space adequately (McKay et al., 1979). The main steps in generating the sample are: i) if a sample of k vectors is needed then the range of each variable is divided into k equal intervals, and one point is drawn at random within each interval, ii) a sample point is selected at random and without replacement for each variable, and the latter are combined to produce a complete vector, iii) the procedure in steps i-ii is repeated for k times to generate the complete sample. Examples of applications of the LHS method include Mugunthan & Shoemaker (2006) and You et al. (2009).

*   **MHS-EA:** A sampling method from the MHS class which uses an evolutionary algorithm (EA) as the optimization algorithm. The EA is running for a short duration and the vectors it generated during its run are then taken as the initial sample. The underlying mechanics of an EA are based on the concepts of adaption and survival in organisms (de Jong, 2006). A typical EA setup is to start with an initial population of candidate solutions (namely, vectors), evaluate them with the objective function, and generate a new generation of solutions (offspring) based on recombination and mutation operators, namely, where parent vectors are combined to produce a new vector and where vector components are randomly perturbed. The resultant offspring are again evaluated and the fittest ones propagate to the next generation. Within the context of expensive optimization problems, the high cost of function evaluations dictates that the initial sample would be small and hence to avoid the scenario where the EA rapidly exhausts its optimization budget a *micro-EA* was used in the numerical experiments in this study. The latter differs from the standard EA formulation by using a much smaller population size (Krishnakumar, 1989; Liang et al., 2000; Senecal, 2000). For example, in this study, the micro-EA used a population of 5 solutions while a typical EA would use a population size of several tens or more solutions. Algorithm 2 gives micro-EA pseudocode and Table 3 gives its internal parameter settings.

Algorithm 2. The Nelder-Mead simplex algorithm used in the MHS-Simplex method

Initialize a set of d+1 vertex points and evaluate them;
Repeat
Order the vertices such that $f(x_1) \le f(x_2) \le \dots f(x_n)$;

Compute the centroid of the d best vertices: $\bar{x} = \dfrac{1}{d}\sum\limits_{i=1}^{d} x_i$;

    /*reflection step*/
    Compute the reflection vector $x_r = \bar{x} + \rho(\bar{x} - x_{d+1})$ and evaluate $f(x_r)$;
    If $f(x_1) \le f(x_r) \le f(x_n)$ then
            Accept x_r and terminate the iteration;
    /*expansion step*/
    If $f(x_r) < f(x_1)$ then
            Compute the expansion vector $x_e = \bar{x} + \chi(x_r - \bar{x})$ and evaluate
$f(x_e)$;
            If $f(x_e) < f(x_r)$ then
                    Accept x_e and terminate the iteration;
            Else
Accept x_r and terminate the iteration;
    /*contraction step*/
    If $f(x_r) \ge f(x_d)$ then
        /*outward expansion*/
        If $f(x_d) \le f(x_r) < f(x_{d+1})$ then
Compute the outward expansion vector $x_o = \bar{x} + \gamma(x_r - \bar{x})$ and evaluate $f(x_o)$;
        If $f(x_o) \le f(x_r)$ then
Accept x_o and terminate the iteration, else go to *shrinkage* step;
        /*inward contraction*/
        If $f(x_r) \ge f(x_{d+1})$ then
Compute the inward contraction vector $x_i = \bar{x} - \gamma(\bar{x} - x_{d+1})$ and evaluate $f(x_i)$;
        If $f(x_i) < f(x_{d+1})$ then
Accept x_i and terminate the iteration, else go to *shrinkage* step;
/*shrinkage step*/
        Compute the new vertices $v_i = x_1 + \sigma(x_i - x_1), i = 2 \dots d+1$ and evaluate
$f(v_i)$;

        Set the vertices of the new simplex to $x_1, v_2, \dots v_{d+1}$;
    Until *limit of evaluations reached*

Table 3. Parameter settings of the micro-EA used

Parameter	Settings
Population size	5
Selection operator	Stochastic Universal Selection (SUS)
Recombination operator	Intermediate, probability 0.7
Mutation operator	Breeder Genetic Algorithm. probability 0.1
Elitism	10%

- **MHS-Simplex:** A metaheuristic sampling method which uses the Nelder-Mead simplex algorithm as the metaheuristic optimization algorithm. The simplex algorithm uses a polytope consisting of $d + 1$ vertices (points), where d is the dimension of the objective function (Nelder & Mead, 1965; Powell, 1998). The initial vertex points are generated at random and are evaluated with the true objective function. The main loop of the simplex algorithm then begins in which the simplex shape is manipulated by operations such as reflection, contraction, extension, with the goal of having the simplex encompass a good solution of the objective function. Algorithm 3 gives the pseudocode of the simplex algorithm used in this study and Table 4 gives its internal parameters which are based on those suggested by Nelder & Mead (1965) and Powell (1998). Examples of applications of the algorithm include Caponio et al. (2007), Koshel (2005), and Zahara & Kao (2009). However, to the best of the author's knowledge, the simplex algorithm has not been used in the context of generating the initial sample as presented in this study.

As mentioned, after generating the initial sample a full optimization search was performed by a metamodel-assisted algorithm based on the concepts of Ratle (1999) and de Jong (2006). The main theme of this algorithm is to evaluate in each generation the best population members and to use these new values to update the metamodel, thereby improving its prediction accuracy and assisting the process to converge to a good solution of the true objective function. The algorithm implemented in this study uses a *hybrid approach* such that the population members are also refined by using a sequential

Algorithm 3. The hybrid metamodel-assisted optimization algorithm used

```
/*initial sampling*/
Generate an initial sample of vectors and evaluate them with the true objec-
tive function;
/*main search*/
While maximum number of analyses not reached do
Train a metamodel with the vectors evaluated so far;
Search for an optimum of the metamodel by using an EA followed by an SQP opti-
mization algorithm;
Evaluate with the true objective function the ten best population members
(vectors);
Return the best vector found;
```

Table 4. Parameter settings of the simplex algorithm used

Parameter	Settings
Reflection	1
Expansion	2
Contraction	0.5
Shrinkage	0.5

quadratic programming (SQP) algorithm, and the solution vector obtained at the end of SQP process then replaces the original solution vector in the EA population. The internal parameter settings of the EA were identical to those in Table 3, except for the population size which was increased to 100, and to complete its description Algorithm 4 gives the psuedocode of this hybrid metamodel-assisted algorithm.

With regards to the metamodel, the above algorithm used the well-established Kriging metamodel, also known as a *Bayesian interpolation* model (Forrester & Keane, 2008). It approximates the true expensive function by using a global 'drift' function which yields a coarse global approximation of the true objective function and adds to it a local refinement which is based on the correlation between the sampled vectors. Given a set of sampled vectors $x_i \in R^d, i = 1 \ldots n$, the metamodel performs a Lagrangian interpolation, namely, $m(x_i) = f(x_i)$, where $m(x)$ and $f(x)$ are the metamodel and true objective function outputs, respectively. With a constant drift function and a Gaussian correlation function the metamodel is then given by

$$m(x) = \hat{\beta} + r(x)^T R^{-1}(f - 1\hat{\beta}),$$

where

$$\hat{\beta} = \left(1^T R^{-1} 1\right)^{-1} 1^T R^{-1}$$

is the estimated drift coefficient, R is a symmetric matrix of the correlations between the vectors, f is the vector of objective function values, and 1 is a vector whose elements are all equal 1. Also, $r(x)$ is the vector of correlations between the new vector and the sampled ones such that

$$r(x)^T = \left[c(\theta, x, x_1), \ldots, c(\theta, x, x_n)\right]$$

and

$$c\left(\theta, \boldsymbol{x}, \boldsymbol{y}\right) = \prod_{i=1}^{d} \exp\left(-\theta\left(x_i - y_i\right)^2\right),$$

$$\hat{\sigma}^2 = \frac{1}{n}\left[\left(\boldsymbol{f} - 1\hat{\beta}\right)^T \boldsymbol{R}^{-1}\left(\boldsymbol{f} - 1\hat{\beta}\right)\right]$$

The correlation parameter θ is taken as the maximizer of the likelihood function

$$\psi\left(\theta\right) = \left|R\right|^{1/n} \hat{\sigma}^2 .$$

RESULTS AND DISCUSSION

Experiments with Mathematical Test Functions

The results of the numerical experiments were analyzed by using the following procedure:
In each optimization scenario every sampling methods were assigned two independent scores:

1. Based on the mean statistic: the method having the best final results was assigned a score of 2, the intermediate a score of 1, and the worst a score of 0, and
2. Based on the statistical significance of the results: every method was assigned a score which is the number of comparisons in which its corresponding results were better than those of the other sampling methods. The comparisons were performed with the nonparametric Mann–Whitney test (Sheskin, 2007, p.423–434) at the 0.05 significance level.

These two types of scores were used to allow analyzing the results both based on parametric statistics, where the statistical significance is based on a Gaussian distribution and also based on nonparametric statistics, in which that assumption is not made.

After calculating the above scores they were summed for each method across all the numerical experiments having the same settings of *function dimension*, *relative sample size*, and *optimization budget*, and across all the test functions. The resultant aggregated scores are referred to in the following discussion as the *cumulative scores*. It is highlighted that the MHS-Simplex method was inapplicable in scenarios which involved a high function dimension and a small sample size since then the initial sample size was too small to define a simplex with the required *d+1* vertices. Therefore in such instances, the entries corresponding to the MHS-Simplex method were given a null value.

The resultant scores from this analysis are summarized graphically in Figures 2 to 4 where the *x*-axis marks are *b* for optimization budget, *d* for function dimension, and *s* for sample size, and so each combination on the *x*-axis defines a set of optimization scenarios with the relevant control variable values. The right hand side y-axis shows the cumulative scores obtained based on the mean statistic (upper part) and based on statistical significance (lower part). Cumulative scores were calculated for different combinations of control variables (ranging from one to three variables) to study the impact of such various combinations on the search performance. The format of the plots in Figures 2-4 is such that in each combination of test settings the best performing method has the highest cumulative score, either based on the mean or on the statistical significance.

In the first analysis which is presented, Figure 2 shows the cumulative scores calculated based on three control variables, namely, scores were aggregated across all experiments in which the three control variables had the values indicated. It follows that the MHS-Simplex and MHS-EA methods performed best when the optimization budget was large (b=2000) or when the relative size of the initial sample was large (s=0.25). This was particularly pronounced in those scenarios as then the MHS methods had a pronounced advantage over the LHS method. In contrast, the LHS method dominated the scenarios with a small initial sample, namely, when either the total

optimization budget was small (b=200) or when the relative sample size was small (s=0.1). Its advantage was particularly pronounced in scenarios with a small optimization budget where it significantly outperformed the MHS methods. This advantage was highlighted also by the statistical significance scores.

Next, Figure 3 shows the cumulative scores which were calculated over combinations of two control variables. The results show that the MHS-Simplex method dominated the scenarios with a large optimization budget, as evident from both types of scores. It also performed well in scenarios with a small problem dimension (d=10). The MHS-EA did not excel in any of the parameter combinations but tended to perform better when either the optimization budget was small (b=200) or when the function dimension was high (d=50). Lastly, the LHS method performed well in scenarios with a small optimization budget (b=200) or when the relative sample size was small (s=0.1). In such scenarios, the LHS method did not perform well. In contrast, in scenarios with a small initial sample, namely with a small optimization budget

Figure 2. Cumulative scores based on three control variables

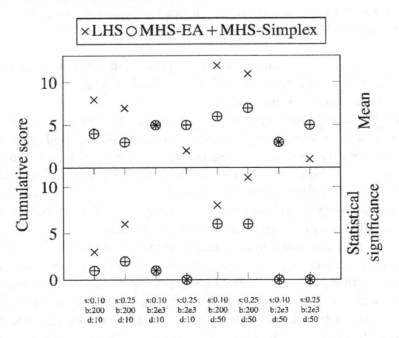

Figure 3. Cumulative scores based on two control variables

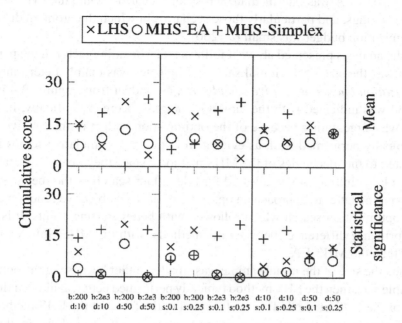

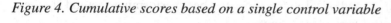

(b=200) or a small relative size (s=0.1) the LHS method performed well. These trends are also highlighted by the statistical significance scores.

To conclude the analysis in this section, Figure 4 shows the cumulative scores based on a single control variable. From these scores, it follows that the MHS-Simplex performed well when the optimization budget was large or when the relative sample size was large (*b*=2000, *s*=0.1), respectively. The

Figure 4. Cumulative scores based on a single control variable

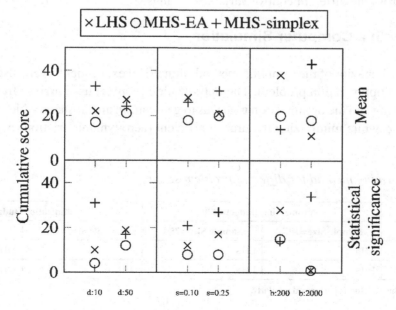

performance of the MHS-EA was intermediate across all scenarios, while the LHS method performed well across various settings, and particularly those scenarios in which the problem dimension was high (d=50) or the optimization budget was small (b=200).

Overall, from the analysis presented above it follows that a deciding factor in the performance of the sampling methods was the size of the initial sample. The latter was mainly determined by the control variables of *optimization budget* or *relative sample size,* as evident from Figures 2-4 in which the best performing method was indicated with the largest cumulative score. Specifically, in scenarios where the initial sample was large, either because of the optimization budget or the relative sample size, the MHS methods typically performed well, as evident from the high cumulative scores it obtained. This behavior is attributed to the mechanics of the MHS methods: since they invoke a metaheuristic optimization algorithm, a large initial sample allowed for a lengthier search of the metaheuristic algorithm. This, in turn, allowed the latter to approach an optimum of the true objective function and to, therefore, provide the main optimization search which followed with better starting points. It is noted that there were notable performance differences between the methods, with the MHS-Simplex method typically performing better than the MHS-EA.

In contrast, when the size of the initial sample was smaller, either because of the optimization budget or the relative sample size, then the LHS method typically performed better, again as indicated in Figures 2-4 by the scores of the LHS method. This is attributed to the fact that the LHS method distributes the sample vectors effectively over the entire search space, and when the sample is small this space-filling vectors provided information which is more beneficial to the optimization search than the solutions provided by the MHS methods. Specifically, due to the small size of the initial sample of MH algorithm was ran only for a short duration and hence was typically unable to approach an optimum of the true objective function. Consequently, the starting points it provided to the main optimization search were remote for an optimum of the true expensive function which degraded the search effectiveness. Overall, the results show that in such settings obtaining information on the global behavior of the objective function was a more effective approach than performing a short metaheuristic search. To summarize these performance trends of the three sampling methods Table 4 gives the best performing method (highest score achieved) across the different control variables settings.

Experiments with a Computer Simulation

To further study the behavior of the sampling methods numerical experiments were also performed with a simulation-driven optimization problem. The optimization problem used arrives from the domain of aerospace engineering and the optimization goal was to generate an airfoil shape which would maximize the lift coefficient c_l while minimizing the drag coefficient (aerodynamic friction) c_d at the prescribed

Table 5. Best performing method for different problem settings

	Optimization Budget=200		Optimization Budget=2000	
	Sample Size=10%	Sample Size=25%	Sample Size=10%	Sample Size=25%
Function dimension=10	LHS	LHS	All	MHS-Simplex/MHS-EA
Function dimension=50	LHS	LHS	All	MHS-Simplex/MHS-EA

"All" implies that all three methods performed similarly.

flight conditions. The latter consisted of the aircraft speed, altitude, and angle of attack (AOA) which is the angle between the aircraft velocity and the airfoil chord line. In the problem solved the prescribed flight conditions were an altitude of 30kft, a cruise speed of Mach 0.7 (70% of the sound speed), and an AOA of 5, which are representative flight settings. Figure 5 shows the formulation of the airfoil problem, namely, the physical quantities involved and the airfoil parameterization layout.

Candidate airfoils were represented by using the method of Hicks & Henne (1978) in which the upper and lower airfoil profiles were defined as

$$y = y_b + \sum_{i=1}^{h} \alpha_i \kappa_i \left(x \right), \kappa_i \left(x \right) = \left[\pi x^{\frac{\log(0.5)}{\log\left(\frac{i}{h+1}\right)}} \right]^4$$

where y_b is a baseline profile, which was taken in this study to be NACA0012 symmetric profile, $\kappa_i(x)$ are shape basis functions, h is the user-prescribed number of shape functions, and

$\alpha_i \in [-0.01, 0.01]$ are the basis functions weights to be determined, namely, these are the problem's design variables. The lift and drag coefficients were obtained with XFoil, a computer simulation for subsonic aerodynamics (Drela & Youngren, 2001). To obtain a structurally valid design the minimum airfoil thickness (t) between 0.2 to 0.8 of the chord line was required to be larger than a critical value $t^* = 0.1$. Accordingly, the objective function used was

$$f = -\frac{c_l}{c_d} + p, p = \begin{cases} \left| \frac{t^*}{t} \cdot \left| \frac{c_l}{c_d} \right| \right| & if \ t < t^* \\ 0 & otherwise \end{cases},$$

such that p is a penalty for violation of the thickness constraint.

Figure 5. Formulation of the airfoil problem

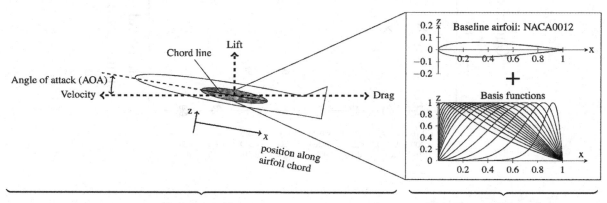

Physical quantities | Hicks-Henne airfoil parametrization

Following the analysis layout of the previous subsection, Figure 6 shows the resultant cumulative scores based on three control variables. From these results, it follows that the LHS method performed best when the optimization budget was small ($b = 200$ evaluations) while the MHS methods performed best when the budget was large ($b = 2000$). The results based on the statistical significance comparisons do not show a clear advantage to either approach.

Next, Figure 7 shows the cumulative scores based on two control variables. Based on these results it follows that the LHS method performed best in combinations of a small optimization budget and either a small or large relative sample size. In contrast, the MHS-Simplex method performed best when the optimization budget was large ($b = 2000$) across both settings of the small and large relative sample size.

As before, an analysis based on individual control variables was also preformed, and the resultant cumulative scores are shown in Figure 8. From this analysis, if follows that the LHS method performed well when the overall optimization budget was small ($b = 200$) while the MHS-Simplex method performed well when the budget was large ($b = 2000$). Another trend which is observed from this analysis is that the MHS-EA typically did not perform well except for the scenarios with a high dimension ($d = 50$).

Overall the trends observed with the airfoil problem are consistent with those observed with the mathematical test functions, and this agreement further validates the analysis presented. From the results and analysis presented both with the test functions and with the airfoil problem, it follows that when the overall optimization budget was small or when the relative initial sample size was small the

Figure 6. Cumulative scores for the airfoil problem, based on three control variables

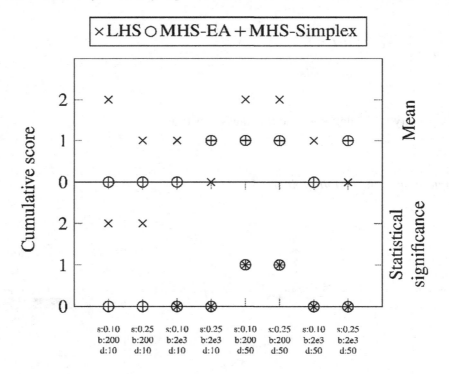

Figure 7. Cumulative scores for the airfoil problem, based on two control variables

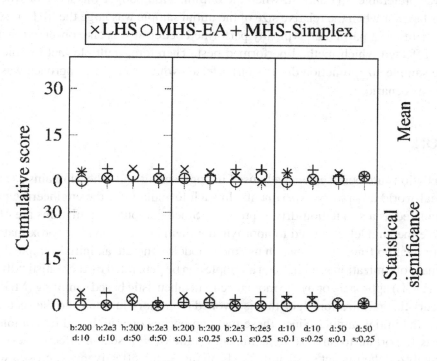

Figure 8. Cumulative scores for the airfoil problem, based on a single control variable

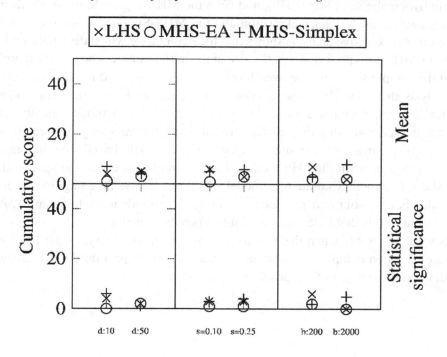

LHS method was preferable. In contrast, when the optimization budget was large or when the relative sample size was large or when the relative size of the initial sample was large the MHS methods, and the MHS-Simplex method, in particular, typically performed better. It was also observed that the problem dimension also affected which method performed best. Therefore, multiple factors (the optimization budget, relative sample size, function dimension) affected which sampling approach was preferable in each optimization scenario.

CONCLUSION

Numerical simulations are being extensively used in engineering and other domains as an efficient replacement to real-world laboratory experiments. In such formulations, the engineering product design process is formulated as a simulation-driven problem. Since computer simulations are often computationally-intensive metamodels are used to approximate them and to provide approximate values more efficiently. Optimization frameworks which use metamodels generate an initial sample of vectors prior to starting the main optimization search. Such a sample can be generated by the statistically-based design of experiments (DOE) approach, or by the more recent metaheuristic based sampling (MHS) approach in which a metaheuristic optimization algorithm is invoked for a short duration and the vectors it generated are then used as the initial sample. Since these two approaches operate based on completely different mechanisms it is important to analyze their impact on the overall search effectiveness. Accordingly, this study has analyzed the impact of such methods on the search effectiveness across a wide variety of scenarios and in an extensive set of numerical experiments. The sampling methods used were the DOE method of Latin hypercube sampling (LHS), and from the MHS approach, the methods used were the MHS-EA which uses an evolutionary algorithm and the MHS-Simplex which uses the Nelder-Mead simplex algorithm. An extensive analysis shows that the main factor which determines which sampling approach (DOE or MHS) was preferred was the size of the initial sample. The two main problem settings which affected the sample size were the overall optimization budget and the relative size of the initial sample. The analysis also showed that the function dimension also affected performance, but to a lesser extent. Specifically, when the initial sample size was large the MHS methods typically performed well as then the metaheuristic algorithm they employ was able to perform a lengthier search and to provide good starting points to the main optimization search which followed the initial sampling stage. In contrast, when the sample size was small the LHS method was preferable since then the space-filling sample it generated translated to a more accurate metamodel which in turn was able to guide the main search to better final results that the solutions provided by the MHS methods in such instances. Another trend which has been identified is that LHS was preferable when the function dimension was high, while the MHS methods were preferable when the dimension was low. In summary, as the DOE and MHS approaches operate based on completely different mechanics their impact on the overall search differed widely depending on the settings of the problem being solved.

REFERENCES

Abramson, M. A., Asaki, T. J., Dennis, J. E., Magallanez, R., & Sottile, M. (2012). An efficient class of direct search surrogate methods for solving expensive optimization problems with CPU-time-related functions. *Structural Optimization*, *45*(1), 53–64. doi:10.1007/s00158-011-0658-3

Acar, E. (2010). Various approaches for constructing an ensemble of metamodels using local measures. *Structural and Multidisciplinary Optimization*, *42*(6), 879–896. doi:10.1007/s00158-010-0520-z

Booker, A. J., Dennis, J. E. Jr, Frank, P. D., Serafini, D. B., Torczon, V., & Trosset, M. W. (1999). A rigorous framework for optimization of expensive functions by surrogates. *Structural Optimization*, *17*(1), 1–13. doi:10.1007/BF01197708

Büche, D., Schraudolph, N. N., & Koumoutsakos, P. (2005). Accelerating evolutionary algorithms with Gaussian process fitness function models. *IEEE Transactions on Systems, Man, and Cybernetics–Part C*, *35*(2), 183–194. doi:10.1109/TSMCC.2004.841917

Caponio, A., Cascella, G. L., Neri, F., Salvatore, N., & Sumner, M. (2007). A fast adaptive memetic algorithm for online and offline control design of PMSM drives. *IEEE Transactions on Systems, Man, and Cybernetics. Part B, Cybernetics*, *37*(1), 28–41. doi:10.1109/TSMCB.2006.883271 PMID:17278556

Chen, V. P., Barton, R. R., Meckesheimer, M., & Tsui, K.-L. (2006). A review on design, modeling, and applications of computer experiments. *IIE Transactions*, *38*(4), 273–291. doi:10.1080/07408170500232495

Chipperfield, A., Fleming, P., Pohlheim, H., & Fonseca, C. (1994). *Genetic algorithm toolbox for use with matlab, version 1.2 User's Guide*. Sheffield, UK: Academic Press.

Correia, V. M. F., Madeira, J. F. A., Aeaujo, A. L., & Soares, C. M. M. (n.d.). Multiobjective design optimization of laminated composite plates with piezoelectric layers. *Composite Structures*.

de Jong, K. A. (2006). *Evolutionary computation: A unified approach*. Cambridge, MA: MIT Press.

Drela, M., & Youngren, H. (2001). Xfoil 6.9 user primer [Computer software manual]. Cambridge, MA: Academic Press.

Figueroa, C. J., Estevez, R. A., & Hernandez, R. E. (2005). Nonlinear mappings based on particle swarm optimization. *Proceedings of the 2005 International Joint Conference on Neural Networks*.

Forrester, A. I. J., & Keane, A. J. (2008). Recent advances in surrogate-based optimization. *Progress in Aerospace Sciences*, *45*(1–3), 50–79.

Goel, T., Haftka, R. T., Shyy, W., & Queipo, N. V. (2007). Ensembles of surrogates. *Structural and Multidisciplinary Optimization*, *33*(3), 199–216. doi:10.1007/s00158-006-0051-9

Gorissen, D., Coukuyt, I., Demeester, P., & Dhaene, T. (2010). A surrogate modeling and adaptive sampling toolbox for computer based design. *Machine Learning*, *11*, 2051–2055.

Gorissen, D., Dhaene, T., & De Turck, F. (2009). Evolutionary model type selection for global surrogate modeling. *Journal of Machine Learning Research*, *10*, 2039–2078.

Hicks, R. M., & Henne, P. A. (1978). Wing design by numerical optimization. *Journal of Aircraft, 15*(7), 407–412. doi:10.2514/3.58379

Huang, W., Yang, J., & Yan, L. (2014, January). Multiobjective design optimization of the transverse gaseous jet in supersonic flows. *Acta Astronautica, 93*, 13–22. doi:10.1016/j.actaastro.2013.06.027

Jin, R., Chen, W., & Sudjianto, A. (2005). An efficient algorithm for constructing optimal design of computer experiments. *Journal of Statistical Planning and Inference, 134*(1), 268–287. doi:10.1016/j.jspi.2004.02.014

Jin, Y. (2005). A comprehensive survey of fitness approximation in evolutionary computation. *Journal of Soft Computing, 9*(1), 3–12. doi:10.1007/s00500-003-0328-5

Jones, D. R., Schonlau, M., & Welch, W. J. (1998). Efficient global optimization of expensive black-box functions. *Journal of Global Optimization, 13*(4), 455–492. doi:10.1023/A:1008306431147

Koshel, R. J. (2005). Simplex optimization method for illumination design. *Optics Letters, 30*(6), 649–651. doi:10.1364/OL.30.000649 PMID:15792005

Krishnakumar, K. (1989). Micro-genetic algorithms for stationary and nonstationary function optimization. In G. E. Rodriguez (Ed.), *Intelligent control and adaptive systems*. Bellingham, WA: SPIE.

Lang, Y., Malacina, A., Blegler, L. R., Munteanu, S., Madsen, J. L., & Zitney, S. E. (2009, March 19). lReduced Order Model Based on Principal Component Analyis for Process Simulation and Optimization. *Energy & Fuels, 23*(3), 1695–1706. doi:10.1021/ef800984v

Laurenceau, J., & Sagaut, P. (2008). Building efficient response surfaces of aerodynamic functions with Kriging and Cokriging. *AIAA Journal, 46*(2), 498–507. doi:10.2514/1.32308

Liang, K.-H., Yao, X., & Newton, C. (2000). Evolutionary search of approximated N-dimensional landscapes. *International Journal of Knowledge-Based Intelligent Engineering Systems, 4*(3), 172–183.

McKay, M. D., Beckman, R. J., & Conover, W. J. (1979). A comparison of three methods for selecting values of input variables in the analysis of output from a computer code. *Technometrics, 21*(2), 239–245.

Meckesheimer, M., Booker, A. J., Barton, R. R., & Simpson, T. W. (2002). Computationally inexpensive metamodel assessment strategies. *AIAA Journal, 40*(10), 2053–2060. doi:10.2514/2.1538

Mugunthan, P., & Shoemaker, C. A. (2006). Assessing the impacts of parameter uncertainty for computationally expensive groundwater models. *Water Resources Research, 42*(10). doi:10.1029/2005WR004640

Muller, J., & Piché, R. (2011). Mixture surrogate models based on Dempster-Shafer theory for global optimization problems. *Journal of Global Optimization, 51*(1), 79–104. doi:10.1007/s10898-010-9620-y

Myers, R. H., & Montgomery, D. C. (1995). *Response surface methodology: Process and product optimization using designed experiments*. New York: John Wiley and Sons.

Nelder, J. A., & Mead, R. (1965). A simplex method for function minimisation. *The Computer Journal, 7*(4), 308–313. doi:10.1093/comjnl/7.4.308

Parr, J. M., Holden, C. M. E., Forrester, A. I. J., & Keane, A. J. (2010). Review of efficient surrogate infill sampling criteria with constraint handling. In H. Rodrigues et al. (Eds.), *Second international conference on engineering optimization*. Academic Press.

Powell, M. J. D. (1998). Direct search algorithms for optimization calculations. *Acta Numerica, A*, 287–336.

Queipo, N. V., Haftka, R. T., Shyy, W., Goel, T., Vaidyanathan, R., & Tucker, K. P. (2005). Surrogate-based analysis and optimization. *Progress in Aerospace Sciences, 41*(1), 1–28. doi:10.1016/j.paerosci.2005.02.001

Quttineh, N.-H., & Holmström, K. (2009). The influence of experimental designs on the performance of surrogate model based costly global optimization solvers. *Studies in Informatics and Control, 18*(1), 87–95.

Ratle, A. (1999). Optimal sampling strategies for learning a fitness model. In *The 1999 IEEE congress on evolutionary computation–CEC 1999* (pp. 2078–2085). Piscataway, NJ: IEEE. doi:10.1109/CEC.1999.785531

Regis, R. G., & Shoemaker, C. A. (2013). A quasi-multistart framework for global optimization of expensive functions using response surface models. *Journal of Global Optimization, 56*(4), 1719–1753. doi:10.1007/s10898-012-9940-1

Sacks, J., Welch, W. J., Mitchell, T. J., & Wynn, H. P. (1989). Design and analysis of computer experiments. *Statistical Science, 4*(4), 409–435. doi:10.1214/ss/1177012413

Senecal, P. K. (2000). *Numerical optimization using the GEN4 micro-genetic algorithm code (Tech. Rep.)*. Engine Research Center, University Of Wisconsin-Madison.

Sheskin, D. J. (2007). *Handbook of parametric and nonparametric statistical procedures* (4th ed.). Boca Raton, FL: Chapman and Hall.

Simpson, T. W., Lin, D. K. J., & Chen, W. (2001). Sampling strategies for computer experiments: Design and analysis. *International Journal of Reliability and Applications, 2*(3), 209–240.

Sóbester, A., Leary, S. J., & Keane, A. J. (2005). On the design of optimization strategies based on global response surface approximation models. *Journal of Global Optimization, 33*(1), 31–59. doi:10.1007/s10898-004-6733-1

Tenne, Y., & Armfield, S. W. (2009). A framework for memetic optimization using variable global and local surrogate models. *Journal of Soft Computing, 13*(8), 781–793. doi:10.1007/s00500-008-0348-2

Tenne, Y., & Goh, C. K. (Eds.). (2010a). *Computational intelligence in expensive optimization problems* (Vol. 2). Berlin: Springer. doi:10.1007/978-3-642-10701-6

Tenne, Y., & Goh, C. K. (Eds.). (2010b). *Computational intelligence in optimization* (Vol. 7). Springer. doi:10.1007/978-3-642-12775-5

Toal, D. J. J., Bressloff, N. W., & Keane, A. J. (2008). Kriging hyperparameter tuning strategies. *AIAA Journal, 46*(5), 1240–1252. doi:10.2514/1.34822

Wang, G. G., & Shan, S. (2007). Review of metamodeling techniques in support of engineering design optimization. *Journal of Mechanical Design*, *129*(4), 370–380. doi:10.1115/1.2429697

You, H., Yang, M., Wang, D., & Jia, X. (2009). Kriging model combined with Latin hypercube sampling for surrogate modeling of analog integrated circuit performance. In *Proceedings of the tenth international symposium on quality electronic design–ISQED 2009* (pp. 554–558). Piscataway, NJ: IEEE. doi:10.1109/ISQED.2009.4810354

Zahara, E., & Kao, Y.-T. (2009). Hybrid Nelder-Mead simplex search and particle swarm optimization for constrained engineering design problems. *Expert Systems with Applications*, *36*(2), 3880–3886. doi:10.1016/j.eswa.2008.02.039

KEY TERMS AND DEFINITIONS

Black-Box Function: A common reference to an objective function whose output values are obtained from a computer simulation.

Evolutionary Algorithms: A class of metaheuristic methods whose operations are inspired by adaptation and survival of the fittest as observed in organisms.

Kriging: A metamodel which combines a global drift function (coarse approximation) with a local refinement function (fine approximation).

Latin Hypercube Sampling: A statistically-based sampling method which generates a space filling and ensures an adequate sampling of the complete range of each design variable.

Metaheuristic Optimization: An optimization process which relies on a set of operations which may be inspired by nature or other considerations, without necessarily having a mathematical justification.

Metamodel: A mathematical approximation of the computationally expensive black-box function. Also referred to in the literature as a *surrogate* or *response surface*.

Nelder-Mead Simplex Algorithm: A metaheuristic method which uses a polytope of $d+1$ vertices, where d is the function dimension. The method applies various geometric transformations to gradually have the polytope enclose an optimum of the objective function.

Sampling Method: A procedure to generate sample points (vectors) in the search.

Surrogate Model: A different term for a metamodel.

Chapter 5
A Study on Static Hand Gesture Recognition Using Type–1 Fuzzy Membership Function

Sriparna Saha
Jadavpur University, India

Amit Konar
Jadavpur University, India

ABSTRACT

The idea of this chapter is the use of Gaussian type-1 fuzzy membership functions based approach for automatic hand gesture recognition. The process has been carried out in five stages starting with the use of skin color segmentation for the isolation of the hand from the background. Then Sobel edge detection technique is employed to extract the contour of the hand. The next stage comprises of the calculation of eight spatial distances by locating the center point of the boundary and all distances are normalized with respect to the maximum distance value. Finally, matching based on Gaussian fuzzy membership function is used for the recognition of unknown hand gestures. This simple and effective procedure produces highest accuracy of 91.23% for Gaussian membership function and a time complexity of 2.01s using Matlab R2011b run on an Intel Pentium Dual Core Processor.

INTRODUCTION

This section presents the notion of gesture recognition as well as introduces the existing literature in this area of hand gesture recognition.

What Is Gesture Recognition?

Among all the modes of communication, gestures play a pivotal role (Bolt 1980; Capirci et al. 2005; McNeill 2000; Melinger and Levelt 2004). Gestures have always been used as a complementary way of expressing ideas. It is so much implanted in communication that gesturing is often used while speak-

DOI: 10.4018/978-1-5225-3129-6.ch005

ing. Recognition of meaningful gestures (Mitra and Acharya 2007) can be utilized to develop a suitable interface between machines and their users to achieve natural interaction with people.

What Is Its Utility in Day-to-Day Life?

Humans and computers have been known to interact with hardware devices like keyboard, mouse and other haptic devices (Clark and Mayer 2011; Gavrila 1999; Jaimes and Sebe 2007; Moeslund and Granum 2001; Rosenberg 2001). But these are not enough for human-computer interaction in some situations, like in the case of physically challenged people or to even in the manipulation of objects in a virtual environment. One of the ways for the elimination of the physical contact between operator and machine is automatic hand gesture recognition technology based on analyzing finger and hand movements for the operation of complex machines. The major areas of applications for hand gesture recognition are:

- Sign language detection (Liddell and Johnson 1989; Stokoe 1978).
- Interface between human and computer (Pavlovic, Sharma, and Huang 1997; Segen and Kumar 1998).
- Robot movement (Calinon and Billard 2007; Nickel and Stiefelhagen 2007).
- E-learning of dance (Kothari 1979, 1989).
- Clinical surgery (Graetzel et al. 2004; O'Hara et al. 2014).

Literature Survey

Some well-known hand gesture recognition techniques extract the hand region from the background using data glove. Fels and Hinton map of hand movements with speech using speech synthesizer using minor variations of the standard back propagation neural network (BPNN) (Fels and Hinton 1993). Wilson and Bobick use the Principal curve and dynamic time warping (DWT) for recognition of motion trajectories in various hand gestures in the limited background (A. F. Bobick and Wilson 1997). Starner *et al.* propose a technique to recognize of continuous ASL by the single camera using a color-based tracker (Starner, Weaver, and Pentland 1998). Black and Jepson model hand motions using temporal trajectories and match them using condensation algorithm by drawing random samples from the trajectories in an office environment (Black and Jepson 1998). Lien and Huang propose a vision based model using inverse kinematics to find a skeletal model for an input image by translating and rotating the hand model about x, y and z axes (Lien and Huang 1998). Lee and Kim extract the hand using skin color based segmentation and calculate likelihood threshold of an input pattern by thresholding (H.-K. Lee and Kim 1999). Recognition of known gestural patterns is done by hidden Markov model (HMM). In a similar study, Yoon *et al.* track hands in a gestural sequence by locating hand regions and connecting them for all frames (Yoon et al. 2001). Features are based on weighted position, angle, and velocity. Vogler and Metaxas break American Sign Language (ASL) into constituent phonemes and model them with parallel HMM (Vogler and Metaxas 2001). Yang *et al.* compute affine transformations to acquire pixel matches using multi-scale segmentation and obtain pixel-level motion trajectories using concatenation (M.-H. Yang, Ahuja, and Tabb 2002). Recognition is carried out using time delay neural network (TDNN). Ng and Ranganath represent hand shapes by Fourier descriptors, calculate pose likelihood vector by RBF network and classify pose using a combination of the recurrent neural network (RNN) (Ng and Ranganath 2002). Bretzner *et al.* propose a method to detect and track hand states for controlling consumer electronics using particle filtering (Bretzner, Laptev, and Lindeberg 2002). Chen *et al.* extract spatial features using Fourier descriptor and temporal by motion analysis (F.-S. Chen, Fu, and Huang 2003). Chen *et al.* recognize hand posture using Haar-like features and adaptive boosting (Adaboost) learning algorithm and hand gesture using stochastic context free grammar (Q. Chen, Georganas, and Petriu 2008). Stergiopoulou and Papamarkos extract palm morphologic features based on the output grid of neurons and recognize using self-growing and self-organized neural gas (SGONG) network (Stergiopoulou and Papamarkos 2009). Alon *et al.* recognize hand gestures in a complex background using DTW when foreground person performing the gesture (Alon et al. 2009). Suk *et al.* recognize continuous gestures for sign language recognition by the Dynamic Bayesian network (DBN) (Suk, Sin, and Lee 2010).

Proposed Work

The proposed chapter describes a five level system starting with color based segmentation for the extraction of the hand gesture from the background. After that, Sobel edge detection technique is used for the detection of the boundary of the hand. Center of the boundary is noted along with the calculation of eight spatial distances, which are 45 degrees apart from each other. The normalized values are found out by dividing the distances with the maximum distance value. The final stage comprises of the use of Gaussian membership function for the matching of unknown hand gesture with the known hand gesture primitives from the database. This system has the ability to deal with translation invariant hand gestures. The time required to recognize each unknown static image is 2.01s in Matlab R2011b with Intel Pentium Dual Core processor. The high accuracy rate of 91.23% is achieved when total twenty five hand gestures are taken into account.

PRE-PROCESSING OF HAND GESTURES

In this chapter, the authors are using a total of twenty five hand gesture from normal day-to-day life. The hand gestures can be processed mainly by two different methods; one is detecting the boundary of the hand gesture while the other one is applying morphological skeleton operation.

Boundary Extraction

Extracting the hand from the background is one of the most important pre-requisites for gesture recognition, as the background contains unnecessary information which in no way aids in the recognition procedure. The process of separation of hand gesture from the noisy background is done using segmentation. This segmentation technique is well-known in the field of image processing. It is used frequently to segment out human objects from their respective backgrounds. Varying illumination poses a major threat to the segmentation technique. Images generated in a scattered environment make it increasingly difficult to extract the required information from its background. Depending on the nature of the hand gesture this boundary extraction domain is mainly bifurcated into two parts: color and texture based segmentation.

Boundary Extraction Using Color Based Segmentation

Skin color segmentation is well-known in the field of image processing (Jones and Rehg 2002; Juang, Chiu, and Shiu 2007; Phung, Bouzerdoum Sr, and Chai Sr 2005; Sabeti and Wu 2007; Saha, Banerjee, et al. 2013; U. Yang, Kim, and Sohn 2009). It is used frequently to segment out human objects from their respective backgrounds. Varying illumination poses a major threat to the segmentation technique. Images generated in a colored environment make it increasingly difficult to extract the dancer from its background.

Here, the input images belong to the RGB color space, thereby inherently succumbs to the pitfalls of high correlation, non-uniformity, and mixing of chrominance and luminance. On the other hand, the YCbCr color space has the smallest overlap between the skin and non-skin pixels over various illumination conditions. Therefore, images in the RGB color space are converted into the YCbCr color space and this acts as the first pre-processing step of the segmentation procedure. Skin color is made up of a specific combination of Cb and Cr values. Here Y is known as luma, Cb is assigned value- blue minus luma (B-Y) and Cr is assigned value- red minus luma (R-Y). The conversion that takes place from the RGB color space to the YCbCr color space is linear in nature. The equations governing the conversion are as follows:

$$Y = 0.257R + 0.504G + 0.098B + 16 \,, \tag{1}$$

$$Cb = 0.148R - 0.291G + 0.439B + 128 \tag{2}$$

and

$$Cr = 0.439R - 0.368G - 0.071B + 128 \,. \tag{3}$$

Simultaneously, images in the RGB color space are also converted to the HSV color space. With the help of (4), the hue value of each pixel corresponding to its red green and blue parameters is calculated.

$$H = \arctan\left(\frac{\sqrt{3}\,(G - B)}{(R - G) + (R - B)}\right) \tag{4}$$

Figure 1 contains the block diagram illustrating the procedure employed to perform skin color segmentation.

Once the conversions are performed, the pixels corresponding to which $140 \leq Cb \leq 195$, $140 \leq Cr \leq 165$ and $0.01 \leq H \leq 0.1$ are considered as skin pixels and the rest are considered as background. In this case, the pre-determined range is obtained empirically. A new binary image of the performer is generated with the help of the procedure; where pixel value 1 corresponds to the skin segment and pixel value 0 corresponds to the background respectively. The segmented result may contain a rather noisy boundary that would also contain huge topological errors like holes. For this reason, morphological

Figure 1. Block diagram of skin color segmentation

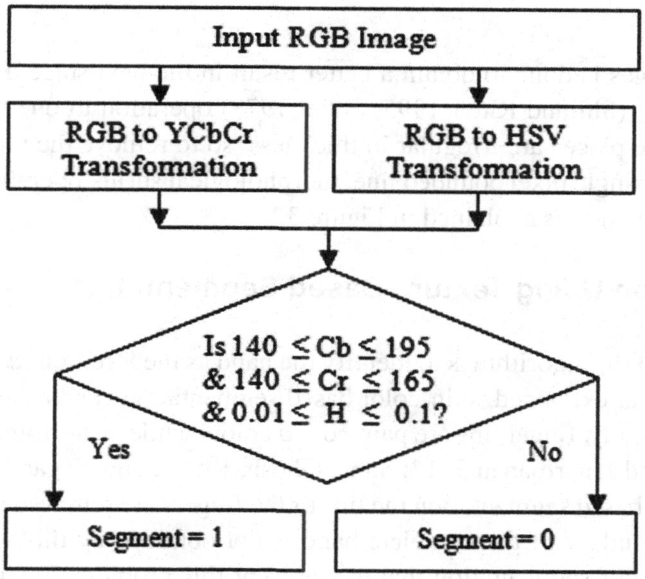

filling of holes is undertaken to capture actual patterns of the data, while leaving out noise. After filling the holes, Sobel edge detection technique is employed (Maini and Aggarwal 2009; Peli and Malah 1982; Senthilkumaran and Rajesh 2009; Ziou and Tabbone 1998). For this, a 3×3 neighborhood is taken into account as explained in Figure 2.

Partial derivatives are calculated by the following two equations

$$s_x = \left(a_2 + ca_3 + a_4\right) - \left(a_0 + ca_7 + a_6\right) \tag{5}$$

and

$$s_y = \left(a_0 + ca_1 + a_2\right) - \left(a_6 + ca_5 + a_4\right). \tag{6}$$

where c is a constant.

Magnitude, M is measured by (7).

Figure 2. Labeling of neighborhood pixels

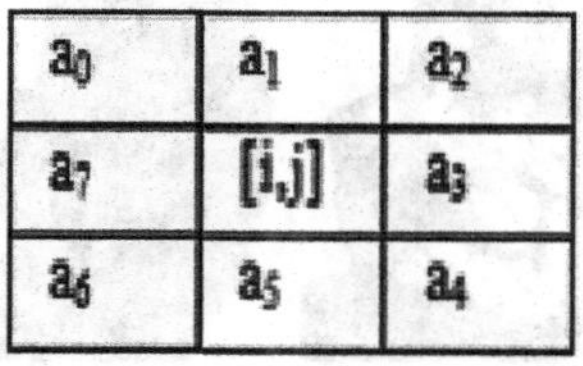

a_0	a_1	a_2
a_7	$[i,j]$	a_3
a_6	a_5	a_4

$$M = \sqrt{s_x^2 + s_y^2} \tag{7}$$

Smoothing of the edges is done to obtain a better result in the next stage. Here smoothing is done by morphological shrink (Shi and Ritter 1995; Sobel 1978) operation to one value. The boundary of the hand gesture in some places are irregular in thickness, so to remove the unwanted pixels from the boundary and produce a single pixel bounded line, morphological shrink operation is implemented. The total color based segmentation is explained in Figure 3.

Boundary Extraction Using Texture Based Segmentation

One of the major steps of the algorithm is to identify the hand as the foreground and segment it out from the background. As earlier explained, skin-color based segmentation can be used for this purpose. But there is a problem. Generally, finger tips are painted red colors while performing Indian classical dance (Saha, Ghosh, Konar, and Janarthanan 2013; Saha, Ghosh, Konar, and Nagar 2013; Saha, Konar, et al. 2014). Using skin-color based segmentation the tips of the fingers are removed as they are now no more skin-colored. So the boundary of the complete hand is not obtained by this segmentation algorithm. There is another method of segmentation that can prevent this problem. Texture based segmentation eliminates unnecessary information regarding the background.

The texture is a set of connected pixels that satisfies some gray-level property which occurs repeatedly in an image region. Hence, texture describes the gray-level distribution in the neighborhood. Texture based segmentation (Laws 1980; Nothdurft 1991; Pullen and Bregler 2002; Reed and Dubuf 1993; Silapasuphakornwong et al. 2010) automatically determines the boundaries between various textured regions from an image. When the texture primitive is small, it is called micro texture. On the other hand, when the size of the primitive is large, these are called macro texture. Statistical methods are generally applied for micro texture whereas for macro texture the shape and the properties of the basic primitive are first determined and then the rules of their placement are established.

As it becomes evident from the definition, texture is a spatial property and so, the one-dimensional histogram which does not capture the spatial information, cannot be used to characterize texture. Thus, a two-dimensional matrix called the gray-level co-occurrence matrix is widely in use from texture analysis.

For hand gesture recognition from Indian classical dance, the texture based segmentation is performed based on entropy calculation. This stage forms the pre-processing stage of the images for hand gesture

Figure 3. Images obtained after performing the experiments, namely (i) original RGB image, (ii) skin color segmented image, (iii) image after filling the holes and (v) edge detected image respectively

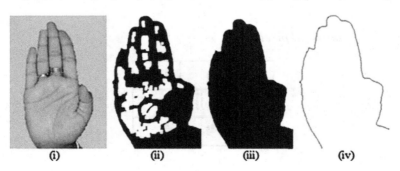

(i)   (ii)   (iii)   (iv)

recognition. For calculating local entropy a finite neighborhood is focused on processing. Here a 3×3 neighborhood is taken. At first, the gray-level co-occurrence matrix $G[i,j]$ is obtained. The displacement vector d that is used for this purpose is shown in Figure 4. Each element of the $G[i,j]$ matrix is the count of the number of pairs of pixels where gray level is separated from gray level j by the displacement vector d. Here d is specified as (1,1), which means one pixel to the right and one pixel below.

$$d = (dx, dy) = (1,1) \tag{8}$$

The gray-level co-occurrence matrix is not necessarily symmetric as the number of pixels having gray levels $[i,j]$ may not be equal to the number of pixels having gray levels $[j, i]$. Each element of the matrix is divided by a total number of pixel pairs to obtain a normalized value. For example, each entry of $G[i,j]$ is divided by 9. This normalized matrix $P[i,j]$ corresponds to the result of probability mass function. Based on this $P[i,j]$ values entropy is calculated.

$$Entropy = -\sum_i \sum_j P[i,j] \log P[i,j] \tag{9}$$

Entropy is chosen as the basis for segmentation due to the following reason. Suppose, if black pixels are randomly distributed without following a pattern, the $G[i,j]$ matrix will not show any preferred gray-level pairs i.e., the matrix will be uniformly populated. Entropy is a measure of the degree of randomness. Thus, entropy is a metric for randomness in gray-level distribution.

Other statistical measures that can be calculated from the gray-level co-occurrence matrix are energy, contrast, and homogeneity. The general approach is that the occurrence matrix is evaluated for several values of d and the one that maximizes a statistical measure computed from $P[i,j]$ is used.

$$Energy = \sum_i \sum_j P^2[i,j] \tag{10}$$

$$Contrast = \sum_i \sum_j (i-j)^2 P[i,j] \tag{11}$$

$$Homogeneity = \sum_i \sum_j \frac{P[i,j]}{1+|i-j|} \tag{12}$$

Figure 4. (i) 4×4 image, (ii) gray-level co-occurrence matrix for d=(1,1)

```
1 0 1 0
0 1 1 1     2 3
0 0 0 0     2 2
1 0 1 1
   (i)         (ii)
```

In the beginning, the input image is converted into a gray-scale image, where the pixel values are in the range of 0 (for black) to 255 (for white) representing the various intensity levels. Then from the gray-scale image, local entropy at every pixel is calculated. This gray-scale image is then transformed into a binary image (BW) based on a threshold value 0.7. The output image has 1 value for all the pixels which have entropies greater than 0.7. All the other pixels are assigned 0 value. This threshold value is chosen empirically.

$$BW = \begin{cases} 1 & if\ entropy > 0.7 \\ 0 & otherwise \end{cases} \tag{13}$$

Figure 5 summarizes the total process of texture based segmentation.

Depth Based Approach

The Kinect is an upcoming technology which captures gestures in terms of depth. It basically looks like a webcam as shown in Figure 6. It has the appearance of a long horizontal bar with a motorized base (Han et al. 2013; Henry et al. 2012; Hernandez-Lopez et al. 2012; Oszust and Wysocki 2013; Saha, Ghosh, Konar, and Nagar 2013; Saha, Konar, and Janarthanan 2015; Zhang 2012). It detects the three dimensional (3-D) image representation of an object. It tracks the skeleton of the person standing in front of within a finite amount of distance. It has a set of visible infrared (IR) and RGB cameras. The IR cameras are responsible for sensing the skeleton irrespective of the color of the performer's dress or distance from the camera. The Kinect sensor has the capability of capturing 3-D motion, facial gesture

Figure 5. 'Pathakam' hand gesture of Indian classical dance, (i) original RGB image, (ii) texture based segmented image, (iii) after filling of holes, (iv) extracted boundary after Sobel edge detection

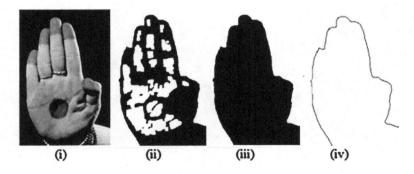

Figure 6. Microsoft's Kinect sensor

and voice gestures with the help of the RGB camera, the depth sensor or the IR camera and the multi-array microphone running proprietary software respectively.

Recognition of hand gesture can also be done using Microsoft's Kinect sensor (Ren et al. 2013). Several methods are already given to locating the hand gesture from the background. Super-pixel earth mover's distance (SP-EMD) can be carried out for scaling, translation as well as local distortions (Wang, Liu, and Chan 2015). Ren *et al.* implemented a system to apply hand gestures for arithmetic computation and rock-paper-scissors game using Finger-Earth Mover's distance (FEMD) (Ren et al. 2011). The two applications have 14 and 3 hand gestures respectively in the dataset.

Other depth based approach involves time-of-flight (TOF) camera as proposed by Xiang *et al.* (Xiang, Pan, and Tong 2011).

FEATURE EXTRACTION PROCEDURES

The following are the different feature extraction procedures already available in the literature.

Edge Orientation Histogram

Hariharan *et al.* (Hariharan, Acharya, and Mitra 2011) have designed a system for recognizing hand gestures of 'Bharatanatyam' Dance using orientation histogram (EOH) (Freeman and Roth 1995; Zhou, Lin, and Huang 2004) to recognize single hand gestures for Indian classical dance. Let the image I is filtered at θ orientation, then response of oriented filter is

$$R_1^\theta = \left(G_1^{0^0} * I\right)\cos\theta + \left(G_1^{90^0} * I\right)\sin\theta \tag{14}$$

where * represents convolution operator and G^θ_1 is one dimensional Gaussian steerable filter.

There are two major problems for which the algorithm is not applied on real time images. First of all, eight hand gestures are misclassified because connectivity graphs of nearly similar hand gestures are equal. To deal with these two problems, an algorithm is proposed in this chapter as the boundary of hand gesture is considered instead of the EOH.

Skeletonization

Another pre-processing method, skeletonization operation is applied to the hand gestures (Kotze and Van Schalkwyk 1992; Kresch and Malah 1998; Maragos and Schafer 1986, 1986; Tari, Shah, and Pien 1997). It primarily deals with removing boundary pixels from the object under consideration, ensuring the fact that the skeleton doesn't break the object. The procedure of skeletonization is also known as medial axis representation or representation with the help of stick figure diagrams. Skeletonization could be achieved with the help of the following procedures

1. By morphological opening
2. By hit-or-miss transform

The opening operation aids in skeleton formation. The morphological opening is nothing but a procedure where erosion precedes the dilation operation. Owing to the opening, all the pixel constructs, which are too small and are deemed unfit to be a part of the structuring element, are removed keeping the remaining part of the skeleton unaltered. Minkowski subtraction and addition are implemented to obtain erosion and dilation, the results of which when combined produces a morphological opening. The mathematical expressions pertaining to dilation and erosion are already mentioned. Opening of X by Y is denoted by

$$X \circ Y = (X \theta Y) \oplus X \tag{15}$$

Dilation is one of the primary morphological operations and is being used widely in the field of image processing. Dilation also knew as region growing or filling operation adds pixels in the boundary of the object. It adds pixels to the boundary of the object under consideration. The morphological operation governing dilation is based on Minkowski addition, which in turn is performed with the help of certain structuring elements (e.g. circle, square, etc.). The dilation operation is both commutative as well as associative in nature.

Suppose the object that needs to be dilated is represented by X and structuring element is represented by Y, then dilation of X by Y is given as

$$X \oplus Y = \left\{ z \in Z^2 \big| z = x + y \right\} \tag{16}$$

for some $x \in X$ and $y \in Y$.

$$X \oplus Y = \bigcup_{x \in X} Y_x \tag{17}$$

where $\bigcup$ represents the union.

$$X \oplus Y = \left\{ x \big| (Y')_x \cap X \neq \varphi \right\} \tag{18}$$

where Y' is the reflection of y about its origin, $(Y')_x$ is the shifting of Y' by x and is the null set.

Erosion is governed by Minkowski subtraction and a fundamental operation. The erosion of X by Y where X is an object and Y is the structuring element is given by

$$Y = \left\{ x \big| (Y)_x \leq X \right\} \tag{19}$$

where $(Y)_x$ is the translation of Y by x.

Let

$$nY = Y \oplus Y \oplus Y \oplus ... \oplus Y \text{ (n times, } n \geq 0).$$

The procedure of skeleton formation of object X with the help of structuring element Y is denoted as now the skeleton of X using Y is denoted a

$$S(X,Y) = \bigcup\nolimits_{n=0} S_n(X,Y) \tag{20}$$

where,

$$S_n(X,Y) = (X\theta n Y) - \left[(X\theta n Y) \circ Y\right]$$

and

$$n = Max\left[j \big| X \circ jY \geq \varphi\right].$$

The disadvantage of using skeletonization for hand gesture recognition is thoroughly described by Ren *et al.* (Ren et al. 2013). For a same gesture 'two' different skeletons are acquired which increases the ambiguity in the classification of gestures as provided in Figure 7.

Chain Code Generation

Saha *et al.* discusses a system where the main difficulty faced during segmentation of hand gesture is addressed (Saha, Konar, et al. 2014). This segmentation is achieved using hand texture properties. The boundary of the hand gesture is approximated depending on the slopes of the boundaries straight line approximation is done as shown in Figure 8.

For this approximation, a 10-sided regular polygon is used (also known as decagon) and a chain code is obtained. The sides 1 and 6, 2 and 7, 3 and 8, 4 and 9, 5 and 10 are parallel, having same slopes as shown in Figure 9. The corresponding polygon represented chain code is obtained as 33313333331444211333333332 for Figure 8 (iii). This algorithm for detecting hand gestures is translation invariant.

Figure 7. Two different skeleton structures are obtained for same hand gesture 'two', (i) original RGB image, (ii) skin color based segmented image, (iii) skeleton

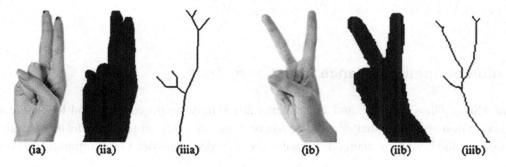

(ia)   (iia)   (iiia)   (ib)   (iib)   (iiib)

Figure 8. 'Hansapakshakam' hand gesture: (i) original Image, (ii) boundary extracted after Sobel edge detection, (iii) straight Line approximated boundary

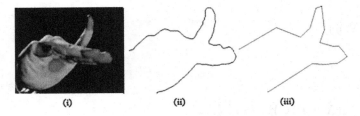

(i)   (ii)   (iii)

Figure 9. Decagon showing internal and external angles

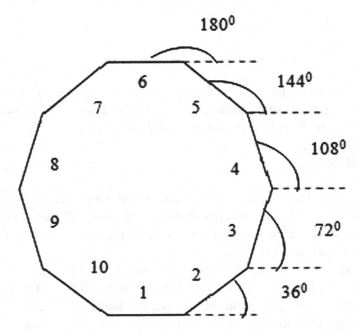

$$Code = \begin{cases} 1 & if\ 18 < slope \leq 54 & if \\ 2 & if\ 54 < slope \leq 90 & if \\ 3 & if\ 90 < slope \leq 126 & if \\ 4 & if\ 126 < slope \leq 152 & if \\ 5 & if\ 152 < slope \leq 180\ or\ 0 < slope \leq 18 & if \end{cases} \tag{21}$$

Calculation of Spatial Distance from Centre Point

Saha *et al.* (Saha, Ghosh, Konar, and Janarthanan 2013) have proposed a method for automatic hand gesture recognition of 'Bharatanatyam' dance where spatial distances are used for feature extraction. For this purpose, all the boundary pixel co-ordinates are recorded. Suppose (X, Y) represents a co-ordinate value for a boundary pixel. Then the minimum (X_{min}) and maximum values (X_{max}) of X axis are noted. Finally, the center point (X_c) calculation is done.

$$X_c = X_{min} + \frac{\left(X_{max} - X_{min}\right)}{2} \tag{22}$$

$$Y_c = Y_{min} + \frac{\left(Y_{max} - Y_{min}\right)}{2} \tag{23}$$

Once the center point of the image has been determined, the spatial distances between the center point and boundary co-ordinates are evaluated. Assume the co-ordinate of the center point pixel to be (i, j), which is shown in Figure 10. The horizontal and vertical axes are also given in the figure. The center point pixel at coordinate (i, j) has four horizontal and vertical neighbors whose coordinates are given by $(i+1, j)$, $(i-1, j)$, $(i, j+1)$, $(i, j-1)$. The four diagonal neighbors of the point have coordinates $(i+1, j+1)$, $(i+1, j-1)$, $(i-1, j+1)$, $(i-1, j-1)$.

Now the nearest neighbor of the center point along 0^0 angles is $(i+1, j)$. Proceeding further along 0^0 angles, co-ordinate $(i+2, j)$ is found which is the nearest neighbor of $(i+1, j)$. Thus, the looping continues until the boundary pixel along 0^0 angles is obtained. After that, the boundary pixel co-ordinate is noted and Euclidean distance between boundary co-ordinate and the center point is calculated as the spatial distance value along 0^0 angles. This same process is repeated for calculation of all the other spatial distances as depicted in Figure 11.

CLASSIFICATION METHODSTO DETECT HAND GESTURES

Numerous works have been proposed in the context of gesture recognition, while some deals with whole body gesture recognition and others focusing on hand of the subject only (Ahuja and Singh 2015; L. Chen et al. 2013; H. S. Hasan and Kareem 2012; M. M. Hasan and Mishra 2012; Mitra and Acharya 2007; Murthy and Jadon 2009; Suarez and Murphy 2012; Vijay et al. 2012).Several works have already been used to recognize hand gestures. Some of the procedures deal with static gestures and other with

Figure 10. 8-neighbors principle

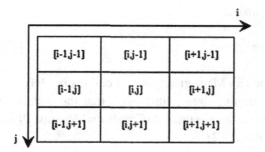

Figure 11. Eight spatial directions along with the 8 spatial distances obtained for Figure 3 (iv)

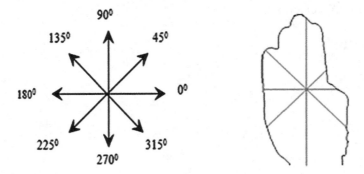

dynamic gestures (Mitra and Acharya 2007). Sign language detection is one of the application areas which deals with dynamic hand gesture recognition. For this purpose hidden Markov model is used explicitly (F.-S. Chen, Fu, and Huang 2003; Y. Lee and Jung 2009; Starner and Pentland 1997). The other most significant domain is robot control using hand movements (Ramamoorthy et al. 2003). Dynamic time warping (DTW) (Berndt and Clifford 1994) can also be executed instead of HMM. But here, this chapter is restricted to static hand gesture detection and for this purpose, the following techniques have substantial importance.

Distance Matching

Six standard gestures are recognized using Mahalanobis distance by Lin *et al.* (Lin and Ding 2013). A set A with mean and covariance matrix μ and C respectively, then the distance is defined by

$$D_M \left(A \right) = \sqrt{\left(A - \mu \right)^T C^{-1} \left(A - \mu \right)} \tag{24}$$

Sánchez-Nielsen *et al.* suggested to use Hausdorff distance to match 26 hand gestures (Sánchez-Nielsen, Antón-Canalís, and Hernández-Tejera 2004). Suppose two finite sets A $(=\{a_1,a_2,...,a_m\})$ and B $(=\{b_1,b_2,...,b_n\})$, then the Hausdorff distance is

$$H \left(A, B \right) = \max \left(h \left(A, B \right), h \left(B, A \right) \right) \tag{25}$$

where $h \left(A, B \right) = \max_{a \in A} \left(\min_{b \in B} \| a, b \| \right)$.

Support Vector Machine

Linear support vector machine (SVM) segregates two classes by defining a hyper plane, specified by 'support vectors', within the training data points, such that the distance margin between the support vectors, and hence the two classes is maximized (Cortes and Vapnik 1995; Mitchell 1999; Saha, Datta, et al. 2014; Sevakula and Verma 2012).

Let x_i be the feature vector of the training set. Here the values of range from 1, 2,…., N.

Assuming, these feature vectors belong to either of the two classes ω_1 and ω_2, which are linearly separable. The hyper plane function that classifies all the training vectors appropriately is represented by $g(x)$ in the following equation

$$g(x) = \omega^T x + \omega_0 = 0 \tag{26}$$

where, $\omega = \left[\omega_1, \omega_2, \omega_3 \ldots \omega_l\right]^T$ and it is called weight vector. ω_0 is called the threshold. Let x_1 and x_2 be two points on the decision hyper plane, then

$$0 = \omega^T x_1 + \omega_0 = \omega^T x_2 + \omega_0 \Rightarrow \omega^T (x_1 - x_2) = 0 . \tag{27}$$

However, linear SVM can be successfully used only where the data are linearly separable. This drawback can be overcome by mapping the data into a larger dimensional space using a kernel function. The RBF or Gaussian kernel with the width of the Gaussian as 1 has been used in the present work. For static gesture recognition, support vector machine (SVM) is applied by Trigueiros *et al.* (Trigueiros, Ribeiro, and Reis 2014).

Template Matching

A well-known recognition process is template matching (Ren et al. 2013; Wang, Liu, and Chan 2015) in image processing domain. This method involves searching and finding the position of an already given template image in a bigger image. One such method has been proposed by Davis and Bobick (A. Bobick and Davis 2001).

FUNDAMENTAL CONCEPTS ABOUT FUZZY SETS

Fuzzy Set

A Set is a well-defined collection of objects (Jech 2013). The constituents of a set are its elements or members, inclusions of which are governed by the characteristics that define the set. A set Z and the belongingness of an element b in it is denoted by the expression

$$b \in Z \tag{28}$$

The conditions defining the set boundaries in conventional sets are rigid and are discretely defined. In conventional set theory, members are either assigned membership value 0 or 1, based on which their belongingness in a particular set is decided. Elements having membership value 1 belong to the set whereas the ones with membership value 0 do not belong to it. The following connotations are used to describe the membership of an element b in a set Z.

$$\mu_b(Z) = 1 \tag{29}$$

$$\mu_b(Z) = 0 \tag{30}$$

Fuzzy sets follow a different principle, by virtue of which it assigns a spectrum of membership values in the interval [0,1] to its elements (Konar 1999, 2005; Saha, Banerjee, et al. 2013). Additionally, every element of the universal set is a member of a given set Z. Thus for every element $b \in U$,

$$0 \le \mu_b(Z) \le 1 \tag{31}$$

As all the members of the universal set U belong to fuzzy set Z, the boundary definitions of two fuzzy sets Z and X may overlap. A fuzzy set Z is a set of ordered pairs, given by

$$Z = \left\{ \left(b, \mu_z(b) \right) : b \in X \right\} \tag{32}$$

where X is a universal set of objects (also referred to as the universe of discourse) and $\mu_Z(b)$ is the grade of membership of the object b in Z. Usually, $\mu_Z(b)$ lies in the closed interval of [0,1].

It needs to be mentioned that sometimes the range of membership is relaxed from [0,1] to [0, R_{max}] where R_{max} is a positive finite real number. However one can easily convert [0, R_{max}] to [0,1] by dividing the membership values in the range [0, R_{max}] by R_{max}.

Membership Functions

The membership function $\mu_z(b)$ maps the object or its attribute b to positive real numbers in the interval [0,1]. A membership function $\mu_z(b)$ is denoted by the following mapping:

$$\mu_z(b) \Rightarrow [0,1], b \in X \tag{33}$$

where b describes an object or its attribute X is the universe of discourse and Z is a subset of X.

Continuous and Discrete Membership Functions

The universe of discourse of a fuzzy set exists in both the discrete and continuous spectrum. For example, the employee ids of the employees in an organization consist of a discrete universe. On the other hand, the weight of persons corresponds to a continuous universe. Data from the continuous domain is sampled at regular or irregular intervals in order to use it in the discrete universe.

γ Membership Function

The γ function has two parameters, α, and β and is formally defined as

$$\gamma(u;\alpha,\beta) = \begin{cases} 0 & if\ u \leq \alpha \\ \dfrac{u-\alpha}{\beta-\alpha} & if\ \alpha < u \leq \beta \\ 1 & if\ u > \beta \end{cases} \tag{34}$$

Figure 12 presents the graphical representation of the γ-function.

L Membership Function

The *L*-function is the converse of γ function and mathematically expressed as (Saha, Ghosh, Konar, and Janarthanan 2013)

$$L(u;\alpha,\beta) = \begin{cases} 1 & if\ u < \alpha \\ \dfrac{\beta-u}{\beta-\alpha} & if\ \alpha \leq u \leq \beta \\ 0 & if\ u > \beta \end{cases} \tag{35}$$

A typical L-function is illustrated in Figure 13. In general applications, L-functions are used to represent the fuzzy linguistic positive-small. Let us consider a fuzzy variable u, which should essentially have a positive value. Now the membership value of the variable should decrease as u increases.

Figure 12. Membership curve of the γ-function

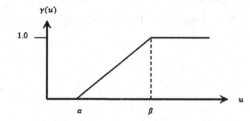

Figure 13. Membership curve of the L-function

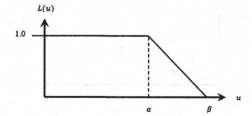

Triangular Membership Function

The triangular membership function also referred to as the bell-shaped function with straight lines, can be formally represented as follows

$$\Delta(u; \alpha, \beta, \gamma) = \begin{cases} 0 & if \ u \leq \alpha \\ \dfrac{u-\alpha}{\beta-\alpha} & if \ \alpha < u \leq \beta \\ \dfrac{\gamma-u}{\gamma-\beta} & if \ \beta < u \leq \gamma \\ 0 & if \ u > \gamma \end{cases} \tag{36}$$

One typical plot of the triangular membership function is given in Figure 14.

∏ Membership Function

The $\prod$- membership function can be formally defined as

$$\prod(u; \alpha, \beta, \gamma, \delta) = \begin{cases} 0 & if \ u \leq \alpha \\ \dfrac{u-\alpha}{\beta-\alpha} & if \ \alpha < u \leq \beta \\ 1 & if \ \beta < u \leq \gamma \\ \dfrac{\delta-u}{\delta-\gamma} & if \ \gamma < u \leq \delta \\ 0 & if \ u > \delta \end{cases} \tag{37}$$

A typical portrayal of the $\prod$- membership function is presented in Figure 15. The $\prod$- membership function is used to represent the fuzzy linguistic: neither so high nor so low.

Figure 14. Membership curve of the Δ -membership function

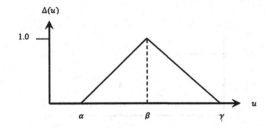

Figure 15. Membership curve of the $\prod$- membership function

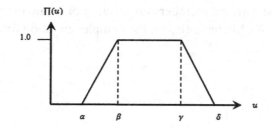

Gaussian Membership Function

A Gaussian membership function is defined as (Hameed 2011; Kreinovich, Quintana, and Reznik 1992)

$$G\left(u;m,\sigma\right)=\exp\left[-\left\{\left(u-m\right)/\sqrt{2}\sigma\right\}^{2}\right] \tag{38}$$

where the parameters m and σ control the center and width of the membership function. A plot of the Gaussian membership function is presented in Figure 16. The Gaussian membership function has extensive applications in literature dealing with fuzzy sets and systems.

Operations on Fuzzy Sets

For any two fuzzy sets A and B defined with respect to a common universe of discourse X, the intersection of the fuzzy sets, characterized by a T-norm operator, is represented as

$$\mu_{A\cap B}\left(x\right)=T\left(\mu_{A}\left(x\right),\mu_{B}\left(x\right)\right) \tag{39}$$

For any two fuzzy sets A and B defined with respect to a common universe of discourse X, the intersection of the fuzzy sets, characterized by an S-norm operator, is represented as

$$\mu_{A\cup B}\left(x\right)=S\left(\mu_{A}\left(x\right),\mu_{B}\left(x\right)\right) \tag{40}$$

Figure 16. Membership curve of the Gaussian-membership function

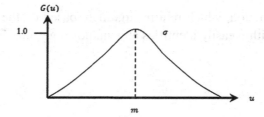

Given a fuzzy set A defined with respect to a universe of discourse X, fuzzy complementation over a set A is a mapping that transforms the membership function of A into the membership function of the complement of A, denoted by A^c. Mathematically, the complementation function c can be defined as

$$c\left[\mu_A\left(x\right)\right] = \mu_A^c\left(x\right) \tag{41}$$

PROPOSED WORK FOR MATCHING OF HAND GESTURES USING GAUSSIN MEMBERSHIP FUNCTION

The algorithm takes an RGB image of hand gesture as an input. The input image is then processed through five different stages. In the first stage, the hand gesture from the background is isolated using skin color segmentation and then the contour of the hand is extracted by using Sobel edge detection technique. In the next stage, the center point of the boundary is located and based on this, eight spatial distances are calculated. These distances are normalized by dividing the maximum distance value. In a later stage, fuzzy Gaussian Membership values are calculated for each distance and matching of an unknown hand gesture is done with the known hand gestures from the database based on Gaussian fuzzy membership function.

Based on fuzzy Gaussian membership values, matching of unknown hand gesture with respect to the 25 known primitives are done in this stage. Fuzzy Gaussian membership curve is described in the following Figure 16. Using (Gaussian equation), $G\left(u; m, \sigma\right)$ the value is calculated. For matching of unknown hand gesture with respect to 25 hand primitives, 25 set of different membership values (μunknown) is obtained when comparing normalized distances of unknown and known hand gestures using (42). For matching with each known primitive 8 membership values are produced for 8 spatial distances. These 8 membership values are summed and total 25 summations of membership values are obtained. The result is that known hand gesture for which maximum membership value summation is obtained using (43).

$$Sum_{unknown} = \sum_{1}^{8} \mu_{unknown} \tag{42}$$

$$SF = \arg\max \bigvee_{p=25} \left[Sum_{unknown}\right] \tag{43}$$

where SF is the similarity function, which returns argument based on the summation of membership values. So the proposed algorithm easily identifies any unknown gesture. Figure 17 shows each step of the proposed algorithm.

Figure 17. Block diagram of the proposed algorithm

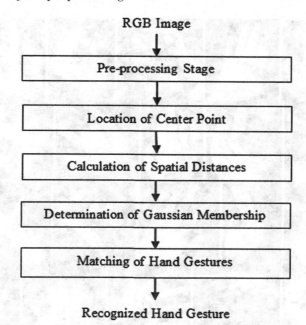

RESULTS AND DISCUSSIONS

The proposed approach is applied on hand gestures made by people in indoor environments. In this section results obtained from the use of the above algorithm on hand gestures in a setup that is typical for human robot, interaction applications are presented.

Hand Gestures Under Consideration

Figure 18 depicts the hand gestures which are processed by the algorithm.

Dataset Preparation

A dataset is prepared after taking RGB images from several websites, where each specific hand gesture is acquired 50 times. For the training purpose, 80% of the total dataset is taken, i.e., 40 images from each gesture are processed. The remaining gestures are used for testing purpose.

Creation of Type-1 Gaussian Membership Function

For the unknown gesture provided in Figure 3, there is 40 total known gestures. From each known gesture, 8 spatial distances are measured. For sake of simplicity, the designing of type-1 Gaussian membership function for 0^0 angle is explained in Table 1.

Figure 18. Twenty five hand gestures

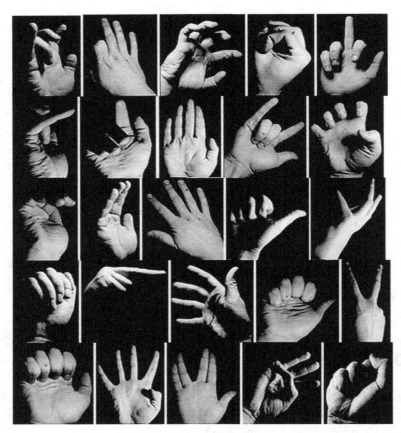

Results Obtained

Figure 3 depicts various intermediate results obtained at different stages of the approach. A frame of the test sequence is shown in Figure 3(i). Figure 3(ii) depicts the result of the skin color segmentation. Here, skin color segmentation is used as the pre-processing step to separate the hand gesture from the background and remove unwanted information in the background. Skin color segmentation is based on the process of discrimination between the skin and non-skin pixels i.e., the value of the pixel. Detection using skin color is fast and robust to minimize the processing time. Therefore, in this application, skin color segmentation approaches are used as the detection scheme. In order to achieve real-time performance, edge detection is then done in conjunction with hole filling to recognize and segment objects with well-defined boundaries as picturized in Figure 3(iii). Figure3(iv) depicts that after application of edge detection technique, exact boundary of hand is obtained. Actual eight spatial distances and the normalized values (i.e., dividing by maximum distance value) for Figure 12 are [30, 39, 53, 16, 25, 43, 52, 37] and [0.5660, 0.7358, 1.0000, 0.3019, 0.4717, 0.8113, 0.9811, 0.6981]. Table 2elaborately explains the matching method for the unknown gesture.

Table 1. Construction of type-1 Gaussian membership function for 40 known gestures for 0^0 angle

Serial No.	Spatial Distances	Mean	Standard Deviation	Type-1 Gaussian Membership Curve
1	0.54	0.52	0.04	
2	0.55			
3	0.54			
4	0.59			
5	0.48			
6	0.45			
7	0.46			
8	0.46			
9	0.59			
10	0. 48			
11	0.52			
12	0.55			
13	0.53			
14	0.54			
15	0.53			
16	0.54			
17	0.52			
18	0.54			
19	0.46			
20	0.59			
21	0.49			
22	0.48			
23	0.58			
24	0.53			
25	0.54			
26	0.53			
27	0.48			
28	0.57			
29	0.55			
30	0.54			
31	0.46			
32	0.54			
33	0.51			
34	0.51			
35	0.54			
36	0.51			
37	0.57			
38	0.56			
39	0.48			
40	0.50			

Table 2 gives all the membership values obtained for 8 different angles for 25 known gestures Gaussian membership curves. The maximum value of $Sum_{unknown}$ is calculated as 6.80, which is for 8-th known gesture. *SF* returns the argument as 8. Thus the correct hand gesture is recognized using our proposed work.

PERFORMANCE ANALYSIS

The performance metrics include 9 parameters. For a binary confusion matrix if the True Positive, True Negative, False Positive and False Negative samples are denoted by *TP*, *TN*, *FP* and *FN* respectively.

Table 2. Procedure for unknown hand gesture recognition using type-1 Gaussian membership function

Gesture No.	Angle Direction								$Sum_{unknown}$	Max-imum	SF
	0^0	45^0	90^0	135^0	180^0	225^0	270^0	315^0			
1	0.35	0.43	0.48	0.23	0.37	0.34	0.20	0.30	2.70	**6.80**	**8**
2	0.83	0.72	0.60	0.68	0.63	0.48	0.55	0.50	4.99		
3	0.60	0.85	0.61	0.50	0.80	0.62	0.55	0.63	5.16		
4	0.53	0.55	0.63	0.47	0.85	0.87	0.67	0.67	5.24		
5	0.83	0.75	0.82	0.85	0.86	0.79	0.79	0.94	6.63		
6	0.49	0.50	0.87	0.88	0.70	0.47	0.55	0.60	5.06		
7	0.70	0.92	0.89	0.92	0.72	0.76	0.78	0.86	6.55		
8	**0.72**	**0.95**	**0.84**	**0.74**	**0.98**	**0.90**	**0.84**	**0.83**	**6.80**		
9	0.81	0.74	0.77	0.74	0.52	0.46	0.45	0.65	5.14		
10	0.73	0.88	0.72	0.86	0.82	0.89	0.87	0.92	6.69		
11	0.71	0.61	0.79	0.57	0.77	0.57	0.64	0.75	5.41		
12	0.73	0.76	0.73	0.78	0.67	0.72	0.86	0.61	5.86		
13	0.72	0.63	0.86	0.62	0.63	0.61	0.63	0.71	5.41		
14	0.92	0.78	0.87	0.74	0.70	0.88	0.82	0.82	6.53		
15	0.67	0.89	0.87	0.75	0.78	0.76	0.62	0.66	6.00		
16	0.92	0.85	0.85	0.91	0.90	0.84	0.74	0.76	6.77		
17	0.90	0.84	0.78	0.80	0.71	0.77	0.91	0.79	6.50		
18	0.50	0.52	0.43	0.32	0.36	0.57	0.34	0.54	3.58		
19	0.68	0.73	0.79	0.68	0.79	0.82	0.67	0.63	5.79		
20	0.46	0.59	0.32	0.43	0.33	0.58	0.30	0.53	3.54		
21	0.72	0.72	0.83	0.82	0.77	0.68	0.83	0.73	6.10		
22	0.41	0.44	0.40	0.39	0.65	0.55	0.54	0.40	3.78		
23	0.69	0.89	0.73	0.65	0.88	0.91	0.74	0.63	6.12		
24	0.55	0.56	0.37	0.44	0.41	0.55	0.45	0.57	3.90		
25	0.81	0.53	0.87	0.81	0.69	0.67	0.67	0.62	5.67		

$$PPV = \frac{TP}{TP + FP} \tag{44}$$

$$PPV = \frac{TP}{TP + FP} \tag{45}$$

$$Sensitivity = \frac{TP}{TP + FN} \tag{46}$$

$$Specificity = \frac{TN}{TN + FP} \tag{47}$$

$$PLR = \frac{Sensitivity}{1 - Specificity} \tag{48}$$

$$NLR = \frac{1 - Sensitivity}{Specificity} \tag{49}$$

$$Accuracy = \frac{TP + TN}{TP + TN + FP + FN} \tag{50}$$

$$Error\ Rate = \frac{FP + FN}{TP + TN + FP + FN} \tag{51}$$

$$F1\_Score = 2\frac{Precision \times Recall}{Precision + Recall} \tag{52}$$

Here, *PPV*, *NPV*, *PLR* and *NLP* stands for precision/ positive predicted value, negative predicted value, positive likelihood ratio and negative likelihood ratio correspondingly. The time required to detect an unknown gesture is also taken as a parameter for comparison.

Comparative Framework

The comparative framework includes 6 existing algorithms (namely Trigueiros *et al.* (Trigueiros, Ribeiro, and Reis 2014), Saha *et al.* (Saha, Ghosh, Konar, and Janarthanan 2013), Saha et al. (Saha, Konar, et al. 2014), Hariharan *et al.* (Hariharan, Acharya, and Mitra 2011), Sánchez-Nielsen *et al.*(Sánchez-Nielsen, Antón-Canalís, and Hernández-Tejera 2004) and Lin *et al.* (Lin and Ding 2013)) along with the proposed work.

Results of Performance Metrics

The mean and the standard deviation (within parenthesis) values of the performance metrics are provided in Table 3 for 40 independent runs. Here '+' indicates that the proposed algorithm is producing a better result than all the other algorithms for that particular performance metric and vice versa for '−'. From Table 3, it is clearly identified that the proposed method is the best for recognition of hand gestures.

Figure 19 depicts the region of convergence (ROC) curves for 7 concerned algorithms. These curves are drawn by taking sensitivity along the *y*-axis and (1 − specificity) along the *x*-axis.

McNemar's Statistical Test

Let f_A and f_B be two classifiers achieved by algorithms A and B, when both the algorithms have a common training set R. Let n_{01} be the number of examples misclassified by f_A but not by $f_{B,}$ and n_{10} be the number of examples misclassified by f_B but not by f_A (Dieterich 1998).

$$Z = \frac{\left(\left|n_{01} - n_{10}\right| - 1\right)^2}{n_{01} + n_{10}} \tag{53}$$

Figure 19. ROC curves for 7 concerned algorithms

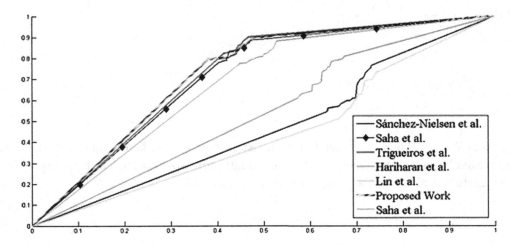

Table 3. Comparison of different algorithms with proposed work for 40 independent runs

Performance Metrics	Proposed Work	Trigueiros *et al.*	Saha *et al.*	Saha *et al.*	Hariharan *et al.*	Sánchez-Nielsen *et al.*	Lin *et al.*	Significance
PPV	**0.86** **(0.11)**	0.83 (0.19)	0.85 (0.02)	0.77 (0.09)	0.79 (0.03)	0.75 (0.03)	0.65 (0.05)	+
NPV	**0.89** **(0.16)**	0.88 (0.17)	0.87 (0.01)	0.85 (0.15)	0.79 (0.19)	0.70 (0.16)	0.74 (0.18)	+
Sensitivity	0.83 (0.09)	**0.87** **(0.17)**	0.85 (0.12)	0.85 (0.11)	0.78 (0.03)	0.69 (0.17)	0.64 (0.12)	+
Specificity	**0.89** **(0.03)**	0.82 (0.10)	0.85 (0.05)	0.88 (0.18)	0.82 (0.18)	0.70 (0.10)	0.64 (0.07)	+
PLR	**7.55** **(0.18)**	4.83 (0.04)	5.67 (0.01)	7.08 (0.08)	4.33 (0.18)	2.30 (0.08)	1.78 (0.15)	+
NLR	0.19 (0.03)	**0.16** **(0.07)**	0.18 (0.04)	0.17 (0.03)	0.27 (0.08)	0.44 (0.10)	0.56 (0.01)	−
Accuracy	**0.91** **(0.06)**	0.88 (0.04)	0.85 (0.16)	0.80 (0.13)	0.81 (0.14)	0.73 (0.09)	0.68 (0.18)	+
Error Rate	**0.11** **(0.04)**	0.12 (0.02)	0.21 (0.19)	0.14 (0.11)	0.29 (0.05)	0.26 (0.01)	0.34 (0.07)	+
F1_score	**0.91** **(0.16)**	0.89 (0.09)	0.84 (0.14)	0.77 (0.04)	0.70 (0.13)	0.68 (0.01)	0.79 (0.09)	+
Time Taken (s)	2.01 (0.07)	3.98 (0.11)	1.98 (0.08)	2.33 (0.16)	1.93 (0.03)	1.64 (0.02)	**1.25** **(0.04)**	−

Let A be the proposed work and B is one of the other six algorithms. Here the suffix i refers to the algorithm in row number i of Table 4. In Table 4 the null hypothesis has been rejected, if $Z_i > \chi^2_{1,\alpha=0.05} = 3.84$, where $\chi^2_{1,\alpha=0.05} = 3.84$ is the critical value of the chi-square distribution for 1 degree of freedom at an error probability of 0.05 (Bickel and Li 1977).

Table 4. McNemar's statistical test

Competitor Algorithm = B	Control Algorithm A = Proposed Work			
	n_{01}	n_{10}	Z_i	Comment
Trigueiros *et al.*	7	5	0.08	Accept
Saha *et al.*	0	8	6.16	Reject
Saha *et al.*	1	8	4.00	Reject
Hariharan *et al.*	0	6	4.17	Reject
Sánchez-Nielsen *et al.*	14	2	7.56	Reject
Lin *et al.*	10	2	4.08	Reject

Friedman Statistical Test

Let r_i^j be the ranking of the observed *Accuracy* obtained by the *i*-th algorithm for the *j*-th database (García et al. 2009). The best of all the *k* algorithms, i.e., $i = [1, k]$, is assigned a rank of 1 and the worst is assigned the ranking *k*. Then the average ranking acquired by the *i*-th algorithm over all $j = [1, N]$ algorithms is defined as follows.

$$R_i = \frac{1}{N} \sum_{j=1}^{N} r_i^j \tag{54}$$

Then χ_F^2 distribution with degree of freedom equals to $k - 1$ (García et al. 2009) is measured.

$$\chi_F^2 = \frac{12N}{k(k+1)} \left[\sum_{i=1}^{k} R_i^2 - \frac{k(k+1)^2}{4} \right] \tag{55}$$

In this chapter, for each hand gesture, 50 images are acquired. Now, these 50 images are divided into 5 groups. For each group, 4 images are used for training and 1 is kept for the testing purpose. Here, N = number of databases considered = 5 and k = number of competitor algorithms = 7. In Table 5, it is shown that the null hypothesis has been rejected, as $\chi_F^2 = 18.02$ is greater than $\chi_{6, \alpha=0.05}^2 = 12.592$, where $\chi_{6, \alpha=0.05}^2 = 12.592$ is the critical value of the χ_F^2 distribution for $k - 1 = 6$ degrees of freedom at an error probability of 0.05 (Zar 1999). In Table 5, 2nd, 3rd and 4th column represent the ranks of those datasets belonging to the 5 different groups for which the results are calculated.

CONCLUSION AND FUTURE WORK

In this chapter, the authors have focused on type-1 fuzzy Gaussian membership function based recognition of 25 hand gestures. The hand gesture recognition algorithm builds on a framework that allows the utilization of multiple information cues to efficiently detect image regions that belong to human hands. Additionally, in this chapter, the authors have presented a novel gesture recognition system intended

Table 5. Friedman statistical test

Algorithm	r_i^1	r_i^2	r_i^3	r_i^4	r_i^5	R_i	χ_F^2	Comment
Proposed Work	2	1	1	2	1	1.4	18.02	Reject
Trigueiros *et al.*	1	2	2	1	2	1.6		
Saha *et al.*	3	3	4	4	3	3.4		
Saha *et al.*	4	4	3	3	4	3.6		
Hariharan *et al.*	5	5	5	6	5	5.2		
Sánchez-Nielsen *et al.*	6	6	7	5	7	6.2		
Lin *et al.*	7	7	6	7	6	6.6		

for natural interaction with autonomous robots. Experimental results presented in this chapter, confirm the effectiveness and the efficiency of the proposed approach, meeting the run-time requirements of the task at hand. Moreover, the overall accuracy rate of 91.23% is achieved with a very small computation time 2.01s in an Intel Pentium Dual Core Processor running Matlab R2011b.

However, this proposed algorithm also has some limitations. This algorithm is suitable for an image possessing in a simple background; it should be improved for an image having a complex background. Here as the authors have used the simple background for hand gesture recognition, an accuracy rate of 91.23% is achieved easily.

Another problem lies in the use of cropped images, whether in reality, most of the images are taken by a static camera containing the whole body as an input. These shortcomings can be overcome by using practical filtering approach for detection of hand region in a video. Thus, modeling of a fully automatic hand posture recognition system still remains a challenging work. Our final goal is to build such a system.

REFERENCES

Ahuja, M. K., & Singh, A. (2015). A Survey of Hand Gesture Recognition. *International Journal (Toronto, Ont.), 3*(5).

Alon, J., Athitsos, V., Yuan, Q., & Sclaroff, S. (2009). A Unified Framework for Gesture Recognition and Spatiotemporal Gesture Segmentation. *IEEE Transactions on Pattern Analysis and Machine Intelligence, 31*(9), 1685–1699. doi:10.1109/TPAMI.2008.203 PMID:19574627

Berndt, D. J., & Clifford, J. (1994). Using Dynamic Time Warping to Find Patterns in Time Series. *KDD Workshop*, 359–70.

Bickel, P. J., & Li, B. (1977). Mathematical Statistics. Test. Citeseer.

Black, M. J., & Jepson, A. D. (1998). A Probabilistic Framework for Matching Temporal Trajectories: Condensation-Based Recognition of Gestures and Expressions. *European Conference on Computer Vision*, 909–24. doi:10.1007/BFb0055712

Bobick, A., & Davis, J. (2001). The Representation and Recognition of Action Using Temporal Activities. *IEEE Transactions on Pattern Analysis and Machine Intelligence, 23*(3), 257–267. doi:10.1109/34.910878

Bobick, A. F., & Wilson, A. D. (1997). A State-Based Approach to the Representation and Recognition of Gesture. *IEEE Transactions on Pattern Analysis and Machine Intelligence, 19*(12), 1325–1337. doi:10.1109/34.643892

Bolt, R. A. (1980). *14 "Put-That-There": Voice and Gesture at the Graphics Interface*. ACM.

Bretzner, L., Laptev, I., & Lindeberg, T. (2002). Hand Gesture Recognition Using Multi-Scale Colour Features, Hierarchical Models, and Particle Filtering. *Automatic Face and Gesture Recognition, 2002. Proceedings. Fifth IEEE International Conference on*, 423–28. doi:10.1109/AFGR.2002.1004190

Calinon, S., & Billard, A. (2007). Incremental Learning of Gestures by Imitation in a Humanoid Robot. *Proceedings of the ACM/IEEE International Conference on Human-Robot Interaction*, 255–62. doi:10.1145/1228716.1228751

Capirci, O., Contaldo, A., Caselli, M. C., & Volterra, V. (2005). From Action to Language through Gesture: A Longitudinal Perspective. *Gesture*, *5*(1–2), 155–177. doi:10.1075/gest.5.1-2.12cap

Chen, F.-S., Fu, C.-M., & Huang, C.-L. (2003). Hand Gesture Recognition Using a Real-Time Tracking Method and Hidden Markov Models. *Image and Vision Computing*, *21*(8), 745–758. doi:10.1016/S0262-8856(03)00070-2

Chen, L., Wang, F., Deng, H., & Ji, K. (2013). A Survey on Hand Gesture Recognition. *Computer Sciences and Applications (CSA), 2013 International Conference on*, 313–16. doi:10.1109/CSA.2013.79

Chen, Q. (2008). Hand Gesture Recognition Using Haar-like Features and a Stochastic Context-Free Grammar. *IEEE Transactions on Instrumentation and Measurement*, *57*(8), 1562–1571. doi:10.1109/TIM.2008.922070

Clark, R. C., & Mayer, R. E. (2011). *E-Learning and the Science of Instruction: Proven Guidelines for Consumers and Designers of Multimedia Learning*. Wiley.com.

Cortes, C., & Vapnik, V. (1995). Support Vector Machine. *Machine Learning*, *20*(3), 273–297. doi:10.1007/BF00994018

Dietterich, T. G. (1998). Approximate Statistical Tests for Comparing Supervised Classification Learning Algorithms. *Neural Computation*, *10*(7), 1895–1923. doi:10.1162/089976698300017197 PMID:9744903

Fels, S., & Hinton, G. E. (1993). Glove-Talk: A Neural Network Interface between a Data-Glove and a Speech Synthesizer. *IEEE Transactions on Neural Networks*, *4*(1), 2–8. doi:10.1109/72.182690 PMID:18267698

Freeman, W. T., & Roth, M. (1995). Orientation Histograms for Hand Gesture Recognition. *International Workshop on Automatic Face and Gesture Recognition*, 296–301.

García, S., Molina, D., Lozano, M., & Herrera, F. (2009). A Study on the Use of Non-Parametric Tests for Analyzing the Evolutionary Algorithms' Behaviour: A Case Study on the CEC'2005 Special Session on Real Parameter Optimization. *Journal of Heuristics*, *15*(6), 617–644.

Gavrila, D. M. (1999). The Visual Analysis of Human Movement: A Survey. *Computer Vision and Image Understanding*, *73*(1), 82–98. doi:10.1006/cviu.1998.0716

Graetzel, Fong, Grange, & Baur. (2004). A Non-Contact Mouse for Surgeon-Computer Interaction. *Technology and Health Care, 12.*

Hameed, I. A. (2011). Using Gaussian Membership Functions for Improving the Reliability and Robustness of Students Evaluation Systems. *Expert Systems with Applications*, *38*(6), 7135–7142. doi:10.1016/j.eswa.2010.12.048

Han, J., Shao, L., Xu, D., & Shotton, J. (2013). Enhanced Computer Vision With Microsoft Kinect Sensor: A Review. *Cybernetics, IEEE Transactions on*, *43*(5), 1318–1334. doi:10.1109/TCYB.2013.2265378 PMID:23807480

Hariharan, D., Acharya, T., & Mitra, S. (2011). Recognizing Hand Gestures of a Dancer. In *Pattern Recognition and Machine Intelligence* (pp. 186–192). Springer. doi:10.1007/978-3-642-21786-9_32

Hasan & , Mishra. (2012). Hand Gesture Modeling and Recognition Using Geometric Features: A Review. *Canadian Journal of Image Processing and Computer Vision, 3*(1), 12–26.

Hasan, H. S., & Abdul Kareem, S. (2012). Human Computer Interaction for Vision Based Hand Gesture Recognition: A Survey. *Advanced Computer Science Applications and Technologies (ACSAT), 2012 International Conference on*, 55–60. doi:10.1109/ACSAT.2012.37

Henry, P., Krainin, M., Herbst, E., Ren, X., & Fox, D. (2012). RGB-D Mapping: Using Kinect-Style Depth Cameras for Dense 3D Modeling of Indoor Environments. *The International Journal of Robotics Research, 31*(5), 647–663. doi:10.1177/0278364911434148

Hernandez-Lopez, J.-J., Quintanilla-Olvera, A.-L., López-Ramírez, J.-L., Rangel-Butanda, F.-J., Ibarra-Manzano, M.-A., & Almanza-Ojeda, D.-L. (2012). Detecting Objects Using Color and Depth Segmentation with Kinect Sensor. *Procedia Technology, 3*, 196–204. doi:10.1016/j.protcy.2012.03.021

Jaimes, A., & Sebe, N. (2007). Multimodal Human–computer Interaction: A Survey. *Computer Vision and Image Understanding, 108*(1), 116–134. doi:10.1016/j.cviu.2006.10.019

Jech, T. (2013). *Set Theory*. Springer Science & Business Media.

Jones, M. J., & Rehg, J. M. (2002). Statistical Color Models with Application to Skin Detection. *International Journal of Computer Vision, 46*(1), 81–96. doi:10.1023/A:1013200319198

Juang, C.-F., Chiu, S.-H., & Shiu, S.-J. (2007). Fuzzy System Learned through Fuzzy Clustering and Support Vector Machine for Human Skin Color Segmentation. *Systems, Man and Cybernetics, Part A: Systems and Humans, IEEE Transactions on, 37*(6), 1077–1087. doi:10.1109/TSMCA.2007.904579

Konar, A. (1999). *Artificial Intelligence and Soft Computing: Behavioral and Cognitive Modeling of the Human Brain*. CRC Press. doi:10.1201/9781420049138

Konar, A. (2005). *Computational Intelligence: Principles, Techniques, and Applications*. Springer. doi:10.1007/b138935

Kothari, S. (1979). *Bharata Natyam: Indian Classical Dance Art*. Marg Publications.

Kothari, S. (1989). *Kathak, Indian Classical Dance Art*. Abhinav Publications.

Kotze, J. J., & Van Schalkwyk, J. J. D. (1992). Image Coding through Skeletonization. *Communications and Signal Processing, 1992. COMSIG'92., Proceedings of the 1992 South African Symposium on*, 87–90. doi:10.1109/COMSIG.1992.274306

Kreinovich, V., Quintana, Ch., & Reznik, L. (1992). Gaussian Membership Functions Are Most Adequate in Representing Uncertainty in Measurements. *Proceedings of NAFIPS*, 15–17.

Kresch, R., & Malah, D. (1998). Skeleton-Based Morphological Coding of Binary Images. *Image Processing, IEEE Transactions on, 7*(10), 1387–1399. doi:10.1109/83.718480 PMID:18276206

Laws, K. I. (1980). *Textured Image Segmentation*. DTIC Document.

Lee, H.-K., & Kim, J.-H. (1999). An HMM-Based Threshold Model Approach for Gesture Recognition. *IEEE Transactions on Pattern Analysis and Machine Intelligence, 21*(10), 961–973. doi:10.1109/34.799904

Lee, Y., & Jung, K. (2009). Non-Temporal Mutliple Silhouettes in Hidden Markov Model for View Independent Posture Recognition. *Computer Engineering and Technology, 2009. ICCET'09. International Conference on*, 466–70. doi:10.1109/ICCET.2009.113

Liddell, S. K., & Johnson, R. E. (1989). American Sign Language: The Phonological Base. *Sign Language Studies*, *64*(1), 195–277. doi:10.1353/sls.1989.0027

Lien, C.-C., & Huang, C.-L. (1998). Model-Based Articulated Hand Motion Tracking for Gesture Recognition. *Image and Vision Computing*, *16*(2), 121–134. doi:10.1016/S0262-8856(97)00041-3

Lin, J., & Ding, Y. (2013). A Temporal Hand Gesture Recognition System Based on Hog and Motion Trajectory. *Optik-International Journal for Light and Electron Optics*, *124*(24), 6795–6798. doi:10.1016/j.ijleo.2013.05.097

Maini, R., & Aggarwal, H. (2009). Study and Comparison of Various Image Edge Detection Techniques. *International Journal of Image Processing*, *3*(1), 1–11.

Maragos, P., & Schafer, R. (1986). Morphological Skeleton Representation and Coding of Binary Images. *Acoustics, Speech and Signal Processing, IEEE Transactions on*, *34*(5), 1228–1244. doi:10.1109/TASSP.1986.1164959

McNeill, D. (2000). *Language and Gesture*. Cambridge University Press. doi:10.1017/CBO9780511620850

Melinger, A., & Levelt, W. J. M. (2004). Gesture and the Communicative Intention of the Speaker. *Gesture*, *4*(2), 119–141. doi:10.1075/gest.4.2.02mel

Mitchell, T. M. (1999). Machine Learning and Data Mining. *Communications of the ACM*, *42*(11), 30–36. doi:10.1145/319382.319388

Mitra, S., & Acharya, T. (2007). Gesture Recognition: A Survey. *Systems, Man, and Cybernetics, Part C: Applications and Reviews, IEEE Transactions on*, *37*(3), 311–324. doi:10.1109/TSMCC.2007.893280

Moeslund, T. B., & Granum, E. (2001). A Survey of Computer Vision-Based Human Motion Capture. *Computer Vision and Image Understanding*, *81*(3), 231–268. doi:10.1006/cviu.2000.0897

Murthy, G. R. S., & Jadon, R. S. (2009). A Review of Vision Based Hand Gestures Recognition. *International Journal of Information Technology and Knowledge Management*, *2*(2), 405–410.

Ng, C. W., & Ranganath, S. (2002). Real-Time Gesture Recognition System and Application. *Image and Vision Computing*, *20*(13), 993–1007. doi:10.1016/S0262-8856(02)00113-0

Nickel, K., & Stiefelhagen, R. (2007). Visual Recognition of Pointing Gestures for Human–robot Interaction. *Image and Vision Computing*, *25*(12), 1875–1884. doi:10.1016/j.imavis.2005.12.020

Nothdurft, H. C. (1991). Texture Segmentation and Pop-out from Orientation Contrast. *Vision Research*, *31*(6), 1073–1078. doi:10.1016/0042-6989(91)90211-M PMID:1858322

OHara, K., Dastur, N., Carrell, T., Gonzalez, G., Sellen, A., Penney, G., & Rouncefield, M. et al. (2014). Touchless Interaction in Surgery. *Communications of the ACM*, *57*(1), 70–77. doi:10.1145/2541883.2541899

Oszust, M., & Wysocki, M. (2013). Recognition of Signed Expressions Observed by Kinect Sensor. *Advanced Video and Signal Based Surveillance (AVSS), 2013 10th IEEE International Conference on,* 220–25. doi:10.1109/AVSS.2013.6636643

Pavlovic, Sharma, & Huang. (1997). Visual Interpretation of Hand Gestures for Human-Computer Interaction: A Review. *Pattern Analysis and Machine Intelligence, IEEE Transactions on, 19*(7), 677–95.

Peli, T., & Malah, D. (1982). A Study of Edge Detection Algorithms. *Computer Graphics and Image Processing, 20*(1), 1–21. doi:10.1016/0146-664X(82)90070-3

Phung, Bouzerdoum, & Chai. (2005). Skin Segmentation Using Color Pixel Classification: Analysis and Comparison. *Pattern Analysis and Machine Intelligence, IEEE Transactions on, 27*(1), 148–54.

Pullen, K., & Bregler, C. (2002). Motion Capture Assisted Animation: Texturing and Synthesis. In *ACM Transactions on Graphics (TOG)* (pp. 501–508). ACM. doi:10.1145/566570.566608

Ramamoorthy, A., Vaswani, N., Chaudhury, S., & Banerjee, S. (2003). Recognition of Dynamic Hand Gestures. *Pattern Recognition, 36*(9), 2069–2081. doi:10.1016/S0031-3203(03)00042-6

Reed, T. R., & Hans Dubuf, J. M. (1993). A Review of Recent Texture Segmentation and Feature Extraction Techniques. *CVGIP. Image Understanding, 57*(3), 359–372. doi:10.1006/ciun.1993.1024

Ren, Z., Meng, J., Yuan, J., & Zhang, Z. (2011). Robust Hand Gesture Recognition with Kinect Sensor. *Proceedings of the 19th ACM International Conference on Multimedia,* 759–60. doi:10.1145/2072298.2072443

Ren, Z., Yuan, J., Meng, J., & Zhang, Z. (2013). Robust Part-Based Hand Gesture Recognition Using Kinect Sensor. *Multimedia, IEEE Transactions on, 15*(5), 1110–1120. doi:10.1109/TMM.2013.2246148

Rosenberg, M. J. (2001). *E-Learning: Strategies for Delivering Knowledge in the Digital Age.* McGraw-Hill New York.

Sabeti, L., & Jonathan Wu, Q. M. (2007). High-Speed Skin Color Segmentation for Real-Time Human Tracking. *Systems, Man, and Cybernetics, 2007. ISIC. IEEE International Conference on,* 2378–82. doi:10.1109/ICSMC.2007.4413744

Saha, Ghosh, Konar, & Nagar. (2013). Gesture Recognition from Indian Classical Dance Using Kinect Sensor. *Computational Intelligence, Communication Systems and Networks (CICSyN), 2013 Fifth International Conference on,* 3–8.

Saha, S., & Banerjee, A. (2013). Fuzzy Image Matching for Posture Recognition in Ballet Dance. *Fuzzy Systems (FUZZ), 2013 IEEE International Conference on,* 1–8. doi:10.1109/FUZZ-IEEE.2013.6622401

Saha, S., Datta, S., Konar, A., & Janarthanan, R. (2014). A Study on Emotion Recognition from Body Gestures Using Kinect Sensor. *Communications and Signal Processing (ICCSP), 2014 International Conference on,* 56–60. doi:10.1109/ICCSP.2014.6949798

Saha, S., Ghosh, L., Konar, A., & Janarthanan, R. (2013). Fuzzy L Membership Function Based Hand Gesture Recognition for Bharatanatyam Dance. *Computational Intelligence and Communication Networks (CICN), 2013 5th International Conference on,* 331–35. doi:10.1109/CICN.2013.75

Saha, S., & Konar, A. (2014). Bharatanatyam Hand Gesture Recognition Using Polygon Representation. *Control, Instrumentation, Energy, and Communication (CIEC), 2014 International Conference on*, 563–67. doi:10.1109/CIEC.2014.6959152

Saha, S., Konar, A., & Janarthanan, R. (2015). Two Person Interaction Detection Using Kinect Sensor. In *Facets of Uncertainties and Applications* (pp. 167–176). Springer. doi:10.1007/978-81-322-2301-6_13

Sánchez-Nielsen, Antón-Canalís, & Hernández-Tejera. (2004). *Hand Gesture Recognition for Human-Machine Interaction*. Academic Press.

Segen, J., & Kumar, S. (1998). Human-Computer Interaction Using Gesture Recognition and 3D Hand Tracking. *Image Processing, 1998. ICIP 98. Proceedings. 1998 International Conference on*, 188–92. doi:10.1109/ICIP.1998.727164

Senthilkumaran, N., & Rajesh, R. (2009). Edge Detection Techniques for Image Segmentation–a Survey of Soft Computing Approaches. *International Journal of Recent Trends in Engineering*, *1*(2), 250–254.

Sevakula & Verma. (2012). Support Vector Machine for Large Databases as Classifier. In *Swarm, Evolutionary, and Memetic Computing*. Springer.

Shi & Ritter. (1995). A New Parallel Binary Image Shrinking Algorithm. *Image Processing, IEEE Transactions on*, *4*(2), 224–26.

Silapasuphakornwong, Phimoltares, Lursinsap, & Hansuebsai. (2010). Posture Recognition Invariant to Background, Cloth Textures, Body Size, and Camera Distance Using Morphological Geometry. *Machine Learning and Cybernetics (ICMLC), 2010 International Conference on*, 1130–35.

Sobel, I. (1978). Neighborhood Coding of Binary Images for Fast Contour Following and General Binary Array Processing. *Computer Graphics and Image Processing*, *8*(1), 127–135. doi:10.1016/S0146-664X(78)80020-3

Starner, T., & Pentland, A. (1997). Real-Time American Sign Language Recognition from Video Using Hidden Markov Models. In *Motion-Based Recognition* (pp. 227–243). Springer. doi:10.1007/978-94-015-8935-2_10

Starner, T., Weaver, J., & Pentland, A. (1998). Real-Time American Sign Language Recognition Using Desk and Wearable Computer Based Video. *Pattern Analysis and Machine Intelligence, IEEE Transactions on*, *20*(12), 1371–1375. doi:10.1109/34.735811

Stergiopoulou, E., & Papamarkos, N. (2009). Hand Gesture Recognition Using a Neural Network Shape Fitting Technique. *Engineering Applications of Artificial Intelligence*, *22*(8), 1141–1158. doi:10.1016/j.engappai.2009.03.008

Stokoe, W. C. (1978). *Sign Language Structure*. Academic Press.

Suarez & Murphy. (2012). Hand Gesture Recognition with Depth Images: A Review. *RO-MAN, 2012 IEEE*, 411–17.

Suk, H.-I., Sin, B.-K., & Lee, S.-W. (2010). Hand Gesture Recognition Based on Dynamic Bayesian Network Framework. *Pattern Recognition*, *43*(9), 3059–3072. doi:10.1016/j.patcog.2010.03.016

Tari, Z., Shah, J., & Pien, H. (1997). Extraction of Shape Skeletons from Grayscale Images. *Computer Vision and Image Understanding*, 66(2), 133–146. doi:10.1006/cviu.1997.0612

Trigueiros, Ribeiro, & Reis. (2014). Generic System for Human-Computer Gesture Interaction. *Autonomous Robot Systems and Competitions (ICARSC), 2014 IEEE International Conference on*, 175–80.

Vijay, P. K., Suhas, N. N., Chandrashekhar, C. S., & Dhananjay, D. K. (2012). Recent Developments in Sign Language Recognition: A Review. *Int J Adv Comput Eng Commun Technol*, 1, 21–26.

Vogler, C., & Metaxas, D. (2001). A Framework for Recognizing the Simultaneous Aspects of American Sign Language. *Computer Vision and Image Understanding*, 81(3), 358–384. doi:10.1006/cviu.2000.0895

Wang, C., Liu, Z., & Chan, S.-C. (2015). Superpixel-Based Hand Gesture Recognition With Kinect Depth Camera. *Multimedia, IEEE Transactions on*, 17(1), 29–39. doi:10.1109/TMM.2014.2374357

Xiang, Pan, & Tong. (2011). Depth Camera in Computer Vision and Computer Graphics: An Overview. *Jisuanji Kexue yu Tansuo, 5*(6), 481–92.

Yang, M.-H., Ahuja, N., & Tabb, M. (2002). Extraction of 2d Motion Trajectories and Its Application to Hand Gesture Recognition. *Pattern Analysis and Machine Intelligence, IEEE Transactions on*, 24(8), 1061–1074. doi:10.1109/TPAMI.2002.1023803

Yang, U., Kim, B., & Sohn, K. (2009). Illumination Invariant Skin Color Segmentation. *Industrial Electronics and Applications, 2009. ICIEA 2009. 4th IEEE Conference on*, 636–41.

Yoon, H.-S., Soh, J., Bae, Y. J., & Seung Yang, H. (2001). Hand Gesture Recognition Using Combined Features of Location, Angle, and Velocity. *Pattern Recognition*, 34(7), 1491–1501. doi:10.1016/S0031-3203(00)00096-0

Zar, J. H. (1999). *Biostatistical Analysis*. Pearson Education India.

Zhang, Z. (2012). Microsoft Kinect Sensor and Its Effect. *Multimedia, IEEE, 19*(2), 4–10. doi:10.1109/MMUL.2012.24

Zhou, Lin, & Huang. (2004). Static Hand Gesture Recognition Based on Local Orientation Histogram Feature Distribution Model. *Computer Vision and Pattern Recognition Workshop, 2004. CVPRW'04. Conference on*, 161.

Ziou & Tabbone. (1998). Edge Detection Techniques-an Overview. *Pattern Recognition and Image Analysis, 8*, 537–59.

KEY TERMS AND DEFINITIONS

Color-Based Segmentation: Detecting the requisite partition from a larger image based on the color of that partition is known as color based segmentation.

Edge Detection: In edge detection procedure, the boundary of the required information is calculated based on an abrupt change in brightness.

Euclidean Distance: The straight line distance between two points is known as Euclidean distance.

Fuzzy Membership Function: Contrary to traditional method, the fuzzy membership function associates element in the interval of [0,1].

Gaussian Curve: Named after mathematician Carl Friedrich Gauss, the Gaussian curve is also known as symmetric "bell curve" shape. It is characterized by mean and standard deviation values in a set of elements.

Gesture: Gesture represents a static or dynamic orientation of the structural components of a human being, aimed at communicating a certain message to others.

Normalization: Several techniques can be adopted for normalization, whereas the most common are to divide the data by the maximum value obtained.

Similarity Function: The function which quantifies the matching between known and unknown gestures.

Texture-Based Segmentation: Texture is a set of connected pixels that satisfies some gray-level property and based on same gray-level property, an image can be segregated.

Chapter 6
Robust Stability Self–Tuning Fuzzy PID Digital Controller

Ginalber Serra
Federal Institute of Education, Science, and Technology, Brazil

Edson B. M. Costa
IFMA, Brazil

ABSTRACT

A self-tuning fuzzy control methodology via particle swarm optimization based on robust stability criterion, is proposed. The plant to be controlled is modeled considering a Takagi-Sugeno (TS) fuzzy structure from input-output experimental data, by using the fuzzy C-Means clustering algorithm (antecedent parameters estimation) and weighted recursive least squares (WRLS) algorithm (consequent parameters estimation), respectively. An adaptation mechanism based on particle swarm optimization is used to tune recursively the parameters of a fuzzy PID controller, from the gain and phase margins specifications. Computational results for adaptive fuzzy control of a thermal plant with time varying delay is presented to illustrate the efficiency and applicability of the proposed methodology.

INTRODUCTION

In general, the most practical control loop is characterized by changes in the plant to be controlled due to uncertainty, nonlinearity, stochastic disturbances, change in the nature of the input, propagation of disturbances along the chain of unit processes, varying time pure delay, etc. In all such situations, a conventional controller presents limitations to maintain the performance of the control loop at acceptable levels. Therefore, to overcome this problem, there is a need for an adaptive control, which can automatically sense these unforeseen variations in the plant behavior and be able to correct itself so guarantee the desired performance of the control loop. Adaptive control was first proposed in 1951 by (Draper & Li, 1951) to optimize the performance of an internal combustion engine in the presence of uncertainties, in which an optimal control law was automatically designed according to the operating point. The next major step in adaptive control was taken by Whitaker et al. (1958) when they considered adaptive aircraft flight control systems, employing a reference model to obtain error signals between the actual

DOI: 10.4018/978-1-5225-3129-6.ch006

and desired behavior, which were used to modify the controller parameters to attain ideal behavior to the extent possible in spite of uncertain and time varying dynamic behavior.

In fact, the adaptive control has proved its viability with important current and potential applications (Nair et al., 2015; Masumpoor et al., 2015; Mendes & Neto, 2015; Niu et al., 2014; Fuhrhop et al., 2013). Although has reached a considerable degree of maturity with respect to significant theoretical and algorithmic advances, adaptive control is still an open field for the proposal of new methodologies. In this context, a self-tuning adaptive fuzzy control methodology based on robust stability criterion via particle swarm optimization is proposed. The plant to be controlled is identified by a TS fuzzy inference structure from input-output experimental data, by using the fuzzy C-Means clustering algorithm and WRLS algorithm for antecedent and consequent parameters estimation, respectively. An adaptation mechanism based on particle swarm optimization is used to tune the fuzzy PID controller parameters, via Parallel Distributed Compensation (PDC) strategy (Wang et al., 1995), based on gain and phase margins specifications, recursively, according to identified fuzzy model parameters of the plant to be controlled. Computational results for adaptive fuzzy control of a thermal plant with time varying delay is presented to illustrate the efficiency and applicability of the proposed methodology.

BACKGROUND

The pioneer researches in adaptive control occurred in the early 1950s motivated mainly by the design of autopilots for high-performance aircraft. The main complexities in such projects are the wide range of speeds and altitudes that the aircraft operates, nonlinear dynamics and time varying characteristics. Primary results on adaptive flight control are given in Gregory (1959), Mishkin and Braun (1961) and Whitaker et al. (1958). Although these works were successful, the lack of concise theoretical framework and a disaster in a flight test diminished the interest in the area (Taylor and Adkins, 1965).

However, the interest in adaptive control increased again in the 1970s due to many contributions to control theory in the 1960s (Astrom, 1983). State space techniques, stochastic control and stability theory based on Lyapunov were introduced. Dynamic programming introduced by Bellman (1957) and dual control theory introduced by Feldbaum (1960-1961), increased the understanding of the adaptive process. Tsypkin (1971), who showed that many schemes for learning and adaptive control could be described in a common framework as recursive equations of the stochastic approximation type, also made fundamentals contributions. There were also important developments in systems identification and in parameters estimation (Astrom and Eykhoff, 1971).

The adaptive control theory has matured since contributions mentioned above, and have emerged in three main adaptive control schemes: *Gain scheduling, model reference adaptive systems and self-tuning controllers*. Gain scheduling approach is used when it is possible to find measurable variables, called scheduling variables, which correlate well with changes in the process dynamics in various operations points. These variables are normally obtained based on knowledge of the physics of the system. The controller parameters are determined for each operating point and stored into a look-up table. The gain scheduler consists of an adjustment mechanism, which detects the system operating point through the scheduling variables and selects the corresponding values of the controller parameters in the look-up table. In the model reference adaptive control approach, some reference model is defined to specify the desired performance of the control system. The parameters of the controller are adjusted by an adjustment mechanism, in such a way that the error between the model output and the process output becomes small. The self-tuning control approach is composed of a recursive parameters estimator based on input/output data and a controller tuning mechanism based on the identified model.

In parallel to the adaptive control theory development, several nature-inspired computational techniques were being developed, giving rise to the field called Computational Intelligence. This techniques and their inspiration from nature are Fuzzy Logic (language processing), Artificial Neural Networks (biological neurons), Swarm Intelligence (social behavior of organisms living in swarms or colonies), Evolutionary Computation (biological evolution), and Artificial Immune Systems (biological immune system). The application of intelligent systems in engineering problems led to several advantages in approaches that traditional methods are ineffective or infeasible. The theory of fuzzy systems has been widely used in adaptive control field applications, giving origin to the field of study known as adaptive fuzzy control.

The first adaptive fuzzy controller called the linguistic self-organizing controller (SOC) was introduced in Procyk & Mamdani (1979). Since then, several other adaptive fuzzy control techniques have been proposed, in which some topics of interest include improved adaptive fuzzy control schemes with smaller number of tuning parameters or better performance (Gao et al., 2015), robust adaptive fuzzy controller with various kinds of performance with respect to external disturbances (Li et al., 2014), fuzzy model reference adaptive control (Amrane et al., 2013), fuzzy sliding mode controller (Do et al., 2014) and self-organizing schemes to tune fuzzy membership functions (Lian, 2014). Recently, new adaptive fuzzy control strategies have been developed with the use of other computational intelligence techniques, such as genetic algorithms (Hajebi & AlModarresi, 2013), particle swarm optimization (Chiou et al., 2012), simulated annealing algorithm (Hosovsky et al., 2014) and artificial neural networks (Hajebi & AlModarresi, 2013). In this context, a self-tuning adaptive fuzzy control methodology based on robust stability criterion via particle swarm optimization is proposed.

SELF-TUNING CONTROL METHODOLOGY

The block diagram of the adaptive fuzzy control methodology based on robust stability criterion is depicted in Figure 1. The plant to be controlled is identified by WRLS algorithm and an adaptation mechanism based on particle swarm optimization is used to modify a fuzzy PID controller based on gain and phase margins specifications, so guarantee the robustness to variations in the plant behavior and the tracking of the reference signal.

In this chapter, the plant to be controlled is described by the following TS fuzzy model:

$$R^i : IF \ x_1 \ is \ F_1^i \ AND \cdots AND \ x_q \ is \ F_p^i \ THEN \ G_p^i(z) = \frac{b_0^i + b_1^i z^{-1} + \cdots + b_{n_u}^i z^{-n_u}}{1 + a_1^i z^{-1} + a_2^i z^{-2} + \cdots + a_{n_y}^i z^{-n_y}} z^{-\tau_d^i/T}$$

where τ_d^i is the time delay for i-th inference rule R^i, l is the number of rules, n_u and n_y are the orders of the numerator and denominator of the transfer function with $a_{1,2,\cdots,n_y}^i$ and $b_{1,2,\cdots,n_u}^i$ its parameters, respectively. The variable x_j belongs to a fuzzy set F_j^i with a truth-value given by a membership function $\mu_{F_j}^i : \mathbb{R} \rightarrow [0,1]$.

Figure 1. Robust stability adaptive fuzzy control scheme

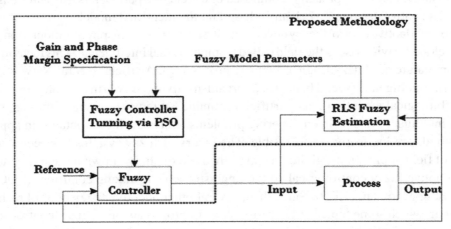

The TS fuzzy PID controller, to be designed based on gain and phase margins specifications according to PDC strategy, in the $i\,|^{i=1,2,...,l}$-th rule, without loss of generality, is given by:

$$R^i : IF\ x_1\ is\ F_1^i\ AND\cdots AND\ x_q\ is\ F_p^i\ THEN\ G_c^i(z) = \frac{\alpha^i z^2 + \beta^i z + \gamma^i}{z^2 - z}$$

with:

$$\alpha^i = K_P^i + \frac{K_I^i T}{2} + \frac{K_D^i}{T}$$

$$\beta^i = \frac{K_I^i T}{2} - K_P^i - \frac{2K_D^i}{T}$$

$$\gamma^i = \frac{K_D^i}{T}$$

where K_P^i, K_I^i and K_D^i are proportional, integral, and derivative fuzzy controller gains of the i-th inference rule, and T are the sample time, respectively (Jacquot, 1995).

From equations (1.1) and (1.2), the gain and phase margins of the fuzzy control system, are given by:

$$arg\left[\sum_{i=1}^{l} \mu^i G_c^i\left(z, e^{j\omega_p}\right) G_P^i\left(z, e^{j\omega_p}\right)\right] = -\pi$$

$$GM = \cfrac{1}{\left| \sum_{i=1}^{l} \mu^i G_c^i \left(z, e^{j\omega_p} \right) G_P^i \left(z, e^{j\omega_p} \right) \right|}$$

$$\left| \sum_{i=1}^{l} \mu^i G_c^i \left(z, e^{j\omega_g} \right) G_P^i \left(z, e^{j\omega_g} \right) \right| = 1$$

$$PM = arg \left[\sum_{i=1}^{l} \mu^i G_c^i \left(z, e^{j\omega_g} \right) G_P^i \left(z, e^{j\omega_g} \right) \right] + \pi$$

where the gain margin is given by equations (1.6) and (1.7), and the phase margin is given by equations (1.8) and (1.9), respectively. The ω_p is called phase crossover frequency and ω_g is called gain crossover frequency.

The optimal parameters of the fuzzy PID controller are tuned, recursively, based on the fuzzy model parameters estimated by WRLS estimator ($\hat{\theta}^i(k)$), from the gain and phase margin specifications (GMs and PMs) and the degree of activation of each rule (μ^i). Considering l rules and p particles, a $3l$-Dimensional swarm is initially generated to define the search space around the controller parameters, as given by:

$$\alpha_p^i(0) \sim U \left(\alpha^i - \alpha_{min}, \alpha^i + \alpha_{max} \right)$$

$$\beta_p^i(0) \sim U \left(\beta^i - \beta_{min}, \beta^i + \beta_{max} \right)$$

$$\gamma_p^i(0) \sim U \left(\gamma^i - \gamma_{min}, \gamma^i + \gamma_{max} \right)$$

where α_{max}, α_{min}, β_{max}, β_{min}, γ_{max}, γ_{min} are defined by an expert; α^i, β^i and γ^i are the controller parameters of the $i \left|^{i=1,2,\cdots,l} \right|$-th rule. The recursive particle swarm adaptation mechanism is implemented as shown in Algorithm 1.

COMPUTATIONAL RESULTS

The computational results are based on experimental data from a thermal plant. Virtual instrumentation environment, data acquisition hardware, sensor, and actuator, as shown in Fig. 2 compose the data acquisition platform. The thermal plant operating range is from $25°C$ to $200°C$.

The virtual instrumentation environment (Human Machine Interface) is based on LabVIEW software (LABoratory Virtual Instrument Engineering Workbench) which allows the designer to view, storage and process the acquired data. The data acquisition hardware performs the interface between sensors/

Algorithm 1. Adaptation Mechanism Algorithm

```
Repeat
    for each particle  p ∈ 1,...,N  do
        Compute the Gain and Phase Margin:
```

$$arg\left[\sum_{i=1}^{l}\mu^i G_c^i\left(z,e^{j\omega_p}\right)G_P^i\left(z,e^{j\omega_p}\right)\right]=-\pi$$

$$GMc(k)=\frac{1}{\left|\sum_{i=1}^{l}\mu^i G_c^i\left(z,e^{j\omega_p}\right)G_P^i\left(z,e^{j\omega_p}\right)\right|}$$

$$\left|\sum_{i=1}^{l}\mu^i G_c^i\left(z,e^{j\omega_p}\right)G_P^i\left(z,e^{j\omega_p}\right)\right|=1$$

$$PMc(k)=arg\left[\sum_{i=1}^{l}\mu^i G_c^i\left(z,e^{j\omega_p}\right)G_P^i\left(z,e^{j\omega_p}\right)\right]+\pi$$

```
        if   (GMc(k) < GMs or PMc(k) < PMs)    then
            for each fuzzy rule  i ∈ 1,...,l  do
```
$$\alpha_p^i(k)=\alpha_p^i(k-1)$$
$$\beta_p^i(k)=\beta_p^i(k-1)$$
$$\gamma_p^i(k)=\gamma_p^i(k-1)$$
```
            end
        end
        else
            Evaluate the fitness of the  p -th particle  f_p
```
$$f_p=\delta_1(GMc(k)-GMs)^2+\delta_2(PMc(k)-PMs)^2$$
```
        end
        Update local best position
        if  f_(local)<f_p  then
    for each fuzzy rule  i ∈ 1,...,l  do
```
$$\alpha_{p(local)}^i(k)=\alpha_p^i(k)$$
$$\beta_{p(local)}^i(k)=\beta_p^i(k)$$
$$\gamma_{p(local)}^i(k)=\gamma_p^i(k)$$
```
    end
        end
    end
        Update global best position
        if  f_(global) < f_(local)   then
            for each fuzzy rule   i ∈ 1,...,l.  do
```
$$\alpha_{p(global)}^i(k)=\alpha_{p(local)}^i(k)$$

continued on following page

Algorithm 1. Continued

$$\beta^i_{p(global)}(k) = \beta^i_{p(local)}(k)$$

$$\gamma^i_{p(global)}(k) = \gamma^i_{p(local)}(k)$$

end

    end

    Apply velocity update $\mathbf{v}_p(k+1)$

    for each fuzzy rule $i \in 1,...,l.$ **do**

$$v^{[\alpha^i_p]}_p(k+1) = \omega v^{3i-2}_p(k) + c_1 r^{[\alpha^i_p]}_1(k)\Big[\alpha^i_{p(local)}(k) - \alpha^i_p(k)\Big] + c_2 r^{[\alpha^i_p]}_2(k)\Big[\alpha^i_{p(global)}(k) - \alpha^i_p(k)\Big]$$

$$v^{[\beta^i_p]}_p(k+1) = \omega v^{3i-1}_p(k) + c_1 r^{[\beta^i_p]}_1(k)\Big[\beta^i_{p(local)}(k) - \beta^i_p(k)\Big] + c_2 r^{[\beta^i_p]}_2(k)\Big[\beta^i_{p(global)}(k) - \beta^i_p(k)\Big]$$

$$v^{[\gamma^i_p]}_p(k+1) = \omega v^{3i}_p(k) + c_1 r^{[\gamma^i_p]}_1(k)\Big[\gamma^i_{p(local)}(k) - \gamma^i_p(k)\Big] + c_2 r^{[\gamma^i_p]}_2(k)\Big[\gamma^i_{p(global)}(k) - \gamma^i_p(k)\Big]$$

    end

    Apply position update $\mathbf{x}_p(k+1)$

    for each fuzzy rule $i \in 1,...,l.$ **do**

$$\alpha^i_p(k+1) = \alpha^i_p(k) + v[\alpha^i_p]_p(k+1)$$

$$\beta^i_p(k+1) = \beta^i_p(k) + v^{[\beta^i_p]}_p(k+1)$$

$$\gamma^i_p(k+1) = \gamma^i_p(k) + v^{[\gamma^i_p]}_p(k+1)$$

    end

$k = k+1$

until iterations number of PSO;

Figure 2. Data acquisition platform based on virtual instrumentation

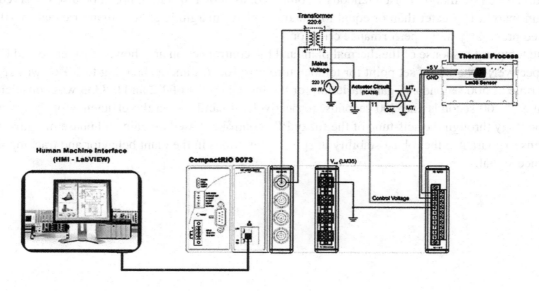

actuators and the virtual instrumentation environment, and it is composed by NI cRIO-9073 integrated system, the NI 9219 analog input module and the NI 9263 analog output module. The temperature sensor was the LM35, and the actuator is based on TCA 785 (Serra, 2012).

For recursive estimation of the consequent parameters of the Takagi-Sugeno fuzzy model, the input signal (RMS Voltage, in Volts) applied to thermal plant and the corresponding response (temperature, degree Celsius) were used as experimental data. A batch identification procedure was considered to obtain the initial conditions for implementation of the self-tuning fuzzy control system. The antecedent membership functions of the Takagi-Sugeno fuzzy model (with two rules) were obtained using FCM (Fuzzy C-Means clustering) algorithm. The time delay was estimated by computing the cross-correlation function between input and output signals of the thermal plant, resulting in a time delay of 130 and 266 samples, corresponding to $\tau_d^1 = 2.210$ seconds and $\tau_d^2 = 4.522$ seconds to a sample time of $T = 17 ms$, for the second order transfer functions in first and second rules, respectively. The parameters of the transfer functions were $b_0^1(0) = 0.0007$, $b_1^1(0) = -0.0001$, $a_1^1(0) = -0.5643$, $a_2^1(0) = -0.4352$, $b_0^2(0) = 0.0290$, $b_1^2(0) = -0.0284$, $a_1^2(0) = -0.5510$, $a_2^2(0) = -0.4490$ for the second order transfer functions in first and second rules, respectively. The forgetting factor adopted was of $\lambda^1 = \lambda^2 = 0.999$ and the initial covariance matrix was of $P^i(0) = 10^{-5} I_4$. The gain and phase margins specified were 5 - 70°, and from a multi-objective particle swarm optimization algorithm, the initial parameters of the fuzzy PID controller were: $\alpha^1 = 2.6710$, $\beta^1 = -2.6738$, $\gamma^1 = 0.0039$, $\alpha^2 = 3.2719$, $\beta^2 = -3.3553$, $\gamma^2 = 0.0839$, and the gain and phase margins obtained were $5 - 72,37^\circ$ and $5,064 - 70,73^\circ$, in the first and second rules, respectively. The results for TS fuzzy model parameters recursive estimation of the thermal plant are shown in Figure 3.

The recursive particle swarm adaptation of the fuzzy PID controller parameters is shown in Fig. 4. In this implementation of the particle swarm adaptation mechanism, the following conditions were adopted: $\alpha_{max} = \alpha_{min} = \beta_{max} = \beta_{min} = 1.0$, $\gamma_{max} = \gamma_{min} = 0.01$, $GMs = 5.0$, $PMs = 70.0$, $\delta_1 = 0.96$, $\delta_2 = 0.04$, $p = 5$ (number of particles) and $numiter = 7$ (number of iterations). It can be seen that according to variations in the parameters of the plant, as shown in Fig. 3, the corresponding parameters of the controller, as shown in Fig. 4, were satisfactorily estimated to guarantee the robust stability from the gain and phase margins instantaneously computed, as shown in Fig.5. It can be also observed that the gain margin is greater than or equal to 5 and the phase margin is greater than or equal to 70°, as required previously in the performance criterion.

The temporal response of the thermal plant and the control action are shown in Figure 6 and Figure 7, respectively. The initial set point for temperature was $100^\circ C$, and a changing to $80^\circ C$ was applied at the time of 500 seconds. A gain variation for the thermal plant of 1.2 and 0.8333 was considered at the time of 200 seconds and 700 seconds, respectively. It can be seen the efficiency of the proposed methodology through the self-tune of the fuzzy PID controller based on gain and phase margins specifications to guarantee the robust stability in spite of variations in the plant behavior and tracking of the reference signal.

Figure 3. Recursive parametric estimation: (a)-(d) consequent parameters of the first rule, (e)-(h) consequent parameters of the second rule

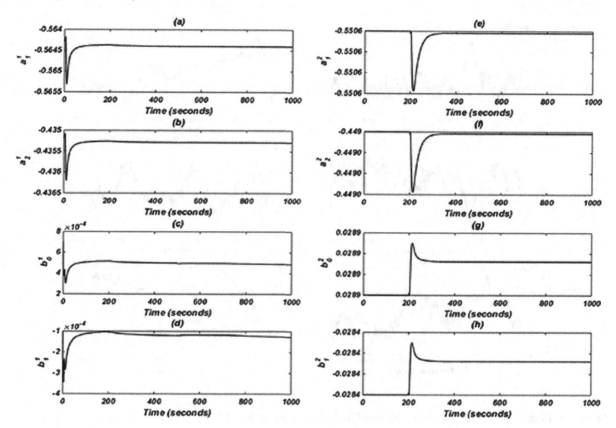

FUTURE RESEARCH DIRECTIONS

The use of PSO algorithm as adjustment mechanism in self-tuning adaptive fuzzy control loop proved to be efficient in the sense that it is not necessary to establish a direct mathematical equation that relates the fuzzy PID controller parameters with the gain and phase margin specifications. Likewise, many other applications where there are no well-defined analytical mathematical formulas to the problem can be developed using the proposed methodology. From this point of start, the development of an "evolving fuzzy controller" and its development for MIMO systems are of particular interest.

CONCLUSION

In this chapter, an adaptive fuzzy control methodology based on gain and phase margins specifications has been proposed. The use of multi-objective particle swarm optimization proved to be efficient due to its simplicity of implementation, having only a few parameters to be setted, and it is effective in global search, requiring a small number of particles and iterations. The robust stability was satisfied via particle

Figure 4. Recursive estimation fuzzy PID controller parameters: (a)-(c) consequent parameters of the first rule, (d)-(f) consequent parameters of the second rule

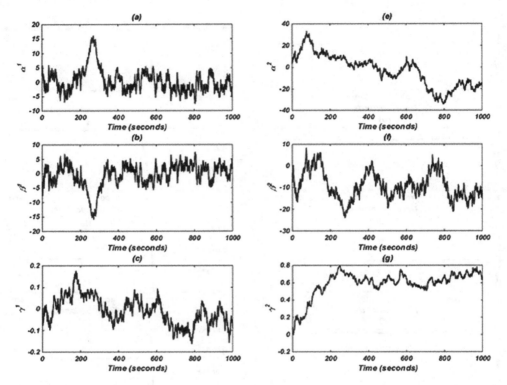

Figure 5. Gain and phase margin obtained for the thermal plant

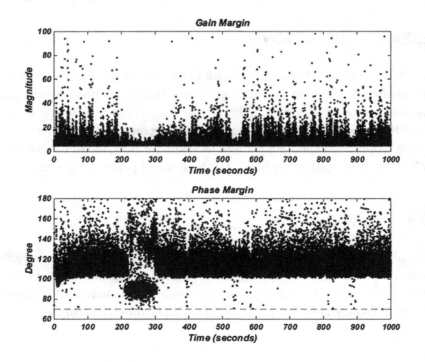

Figure 6. Temporal response of the adaptive fuzzy PID control system

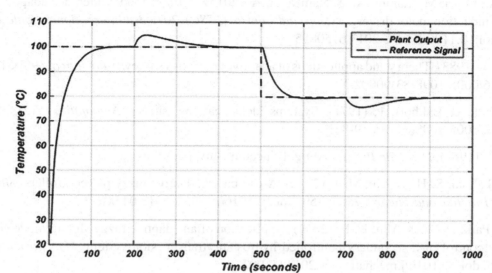

Figure 7. Control action of the adaptive fuzzy PID controller

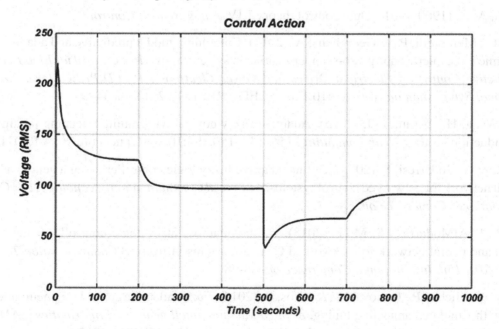

swarm adaptation mechanism developed to tune the fuzzy PID controller parameters, guaranteeing good tracking of the reference trajectory for self-tuning fuzzy control of a thermal plant with time varying delay and disturbance.

REFERENCES

Amrane, A., Louri, M., Larabi, A., & Hamzaoui, A. (2013). A fuzzy model reference adaptive system control for induction motor drives. *Systems and Control (ICSC), 2013 3rd International Conference on*, 177-182. doi:10.1109/ICoSC.2013.6750855

Astrom, K. J. (1983). Theory and applications of adaptive control: A survey. *Automatica, 19*(5), 471–486. doi:10.1016/0005-1098(83)90002-X

Astrom, K. J., & Eykhoff, P. (1971). Systems identification-a survey. *Automatica, 7*(2), 123–162. doi:10.1016/0005-1098(71)90059-8

Bellman, R. (1957). *Dynamic Programming*. Princeton University Press.

Chiou, J.-S., Tsai, S.-H., & Liu, M.-T. (2012). A pso-based adaptive fuzzy pid-controllers. *Simulation Modelling Practice and Theory, 26*, 49–59. doi:10.1016/j.simpat.2012.04.001

Do, H. T., Park, H. G., & Ahn, K. K. (2014). Application of an adaptive fuzzy sliding mode controller in velocity control of a secondary controlled hydrostatic transmission system. *Mechatronics, 24*(8), 1157–1165. doi:10.1016/j.mechatronics.2014.09.003

Draper, C., & Li, Y. (1951). *Principles of optimizalizing control systems and an application to the internal combustion engine*. ASME Publication.

Feldbaum, A. A. (1960-1961). Dual control theory I-IV. *Aut & Remote Control*.

Fuhrhop, C., Mercorelli, P., & Georgiadis, A. (2013). Combining model predictive and adaptive control for an atomic force microscope piezo-scanner-cantilever system. *Sensorless Control for Electrical Drives and Predictive Control of Electrical Drives and Power Electronics (SLED/PRECEDE), 2013 IEEE International Symposium on*, 1–6. doi:10.1109/SLED-PRECEDE.2013.6684499

Gao, Y., Wang, H., & Liu, Y.-J. (2015). Adaptive fuzzy control with minimal leaning parameters for electric induction motors. *Neurocomputing, 156*, 143–150. doi:10.1016/j.neucom.2014.12.071

Hajebi, P., & AlModarresi, S. (2013). Online adaptive fuzzy logic controller using a genetic algorithm and neural network for networked control systems. *Advanced Communication Technology (ICACT), 2013 15th International Conference on*, 88–98.

Hajebi, P., & AlModarresi, S. M. T. (2013). Online adaptive fuzzy logic controller using a genetic algorithm and neural network for Networked Control Systems. *Advanced Communication Technology (ICACT), 2013 15th International Conference on*, 88-98.

Hosovsky, A., Michal, P., Tothova, M., & Biros, O. (2014). Fuzzy adaptive control for pneumatic muscle actuator with simulated annealing tuning. *Applied Machine Intelligence and Informatics (SAMI), 2014 IEEE 12th International Symposium on*, 205–209. doi:10.1109/SAMI.2014.6822408

Jacquot, R. (1995). *Modern Digital Control Systems*. Marcel Dekker.

Li, Y., Tong, S., Liu, Y., & Li, T. (2014). Adaptive Fuzzy Robust Output Feedback Control of Nonlinear Systems With Unknown Dead Zones Based on a Small-Gain Approach. *Fuzzy Systems. IEEE Transactions on*, *22*(1), 164–176.

Lian, R. J. (2014, March). Adaptive Self-Organizing Fuzzy Sliding-Mode Radial Basis-Function Neural-Network Controller for Robotic Systems. *Industrial Electronics. IEEE Transactions on*, *61*(3), 1493–1503.

Masumpoor, S., Yaghobi, H., & Khanesar, M. A. (2015). Adaptive sliding mode type-2 neuro-fuzzy control of an induction motor. *Expert Systems with Applications*, *42*(19), 6635–6647. doi:10.1016/j.eswa.2015.04.046

Mendes, N., & Neto, P. (2015). Indirect adaptive fuzzy control for industrial robots: A solution for contact applications. *Expert Systems with Applications*, *42*(22), 8929–8935. doi:10.1016/j.eswa.2015.07.047

Nair, R.R. & Behera, L. & Kumar, V. & Jamshidi, M. (2015). Multisatellite Formation Control for Remote Sensing Applications Using Artificial Potential Field and Adaptive Fuzzy Sliding Mode Control. *Systems Journal, IEEE, 9*(2), 508-518.

Niu, Y., Li, X., Lin, Z., & Li, M. (2014). Adaptive decentralized-coordinated neural control of hybrid wind-thermal power system. Innovative Smart Grid Technologies Conference Europe (ISGT-Europe), 2014 IEEE PES, 1–6. doi:10.1109/ISGTEurope.2014.7028981

Procyk, T., & Mamdani, E. (1979). A linguistic self-organizing process controller. *Automatica*, *15*(1), 15–30. doi:10.1016/0005-1098(79)90084-0

Serra, G. L. O. (Ed.). (2012). *Highlighted Aspects From Black Box Fuzzy Modeling For Advanced Control Systems Design, Frontiers in Advanced Control Systems*. InTech; doi:10.5772/45717

Tsypkin, Ya. Z. (1971). *Adaptation and Learning in Automatic Systems*. New York: Academic Press.

Wang, H., Tanaka, K., & Griffin, M. (1995). Parallel distributed compensation of nonlinear systems by takagi-sugeno fuzzy model. *Fuzzy Systems. International Joint Conference of the Fourth IEEE International Conference on Fuzzy Systems and The Second International Fuzzy Engineering Symposium., Proceedings of 1995 IEEE Int*, 2, 531–538. doi:10.1109/FUZZY.1995.409737

Whitaker, H., Yamron, J., & Kezer, A. (1958). *Design of model reference adaptive control systems for aircraft. Reporter No. R-164. Instrumentation Lab*. MIT.

KEY TERMS AND DEFINITIONS

Adaptive Control: Control method used by a controller which must adapt to a controlled system with parameters which vary, or are initially uncertain.

Digital PID Control: Control action by controller type PID (with proportional, integral and derivative gains), in the discrete time domain.

Fuzzy C-Means Clustering: Fuzzy c-means (FCM) is a method of clustering which allows one piece of data to belong to two or more clusters so that items in the same class are as similar as possible, and items in different classes are as dissimilar as possible.

Fuzzy Control: Control based on fuzzy rules. The control action is performed from membership degrees of each controller of the rule base.

Gain Margin: Corresponds to reciprocal of the magnitude of the system, at the phase crossover frequency, i.e., the frequency where the phase angle is -180°. It is an important measure of robustness because it is related to the stability of a closed loop system.

Multi-Objective Optimization: Multi-objective optimization involves mathematical optimization problems that contain more than one objective function to be optimized simultaneously.

Parallel Distributed Control (PDC): In the PDC strategy, the fuzzy controller shares the same existing fuzzy sets in the antecedent of the fuzzy model rules. In the controller fuzzy system, each rule's consequent is a control law designed to control the linear system in the corresponding consequent of the model fuzzy system.

Particle Swarm Optimization (PSO): PSO is a population-based stochastic optimization algorithm that mimics the social behavior of bird flocking or fish schooling. In a PSO system, a swarm of individuals (called particles) flies through the n-dimensional search space where the position of each particle is adjusted according to its own experience (cognitive component) and that of its neighbors (social component), and each particle represents a candidate solution to the optimization problem.

Phase Margin: The difference between the phase of the system and -180° at the gain crossover frequency, i.e., the frequency where the module of the open loop transfer function is unitary. It is an important measure of robustness because it is related to the stability of a closed loop system.

Robust Control: A control action designed to track a reference trajectory and keep stability, despite uncertainties of the process to be controlled.

Takagi-Sugeno Fuzzy System: TS rules use functions of input variables as the rule consequent. This system is based on using a set of fuzzy rules to describe global nonlinear systems in terms of a set of local linear models which are smoothly connected by fuzzy membership functions.

Weighted Recursive Least Squares (WRLS): An Adaptive filter which recursively finds the coefficients that minimize a weighted linear least squares cost function relating to the input signals.

Chapter 7
Detection of Music-Induced Emotion Changes by Functional Brain Networks

Reshma Kar
Jadavpur University, India

Amit Konar
Jadavpur University, India

Aruna Chakraborty
St. Thomas' College of Engineering and Technology, India

ABSTRACT

This chapter discusses emotions induced by music and attempts to detect emotional states based on regional interactions within the brain. The brain network theory largely attributes statistical measures of interdependence as indicators of brain region interactions/connectivity. In this paper, the authors studied two bivariate models of brain connectivity and employed thresholding based on relative values among electrode pairs, in order to give a multivariate flavor to these models. The experimental results suggest that thresholding the brain connectivity measures based on their relative strength increase classification accuracy by approximately 10% and 8% in time domain and frequency domain respectively. The results are based on emotion recognition accuracy obtained by decision tree based linear support vector machines, considering the thresholded connectivity measures as features. The emotions were categorized as fear, happiness, sadness, and relaxation.

INTRODUCTION

The ease with which the brain completes seemingly complex tasks like pattern recognition and reasoning with words has fascinated scientists. Researchers have consistently argued that a thorough understanding of how the brain organizes computation is a necessary prerequisite of building systems which can rival brain-like computation (Körner et al., 2002, Martinez et al., 2013). This covers many aspects including synthesis and recognition of emotions.

DOI: 10.4018/978-1-5225-3129-6.ch007

There has been widespread research aiming at emotion recognition from different modalities such as gestures, facial expressions, and voice (Konar et al., 2012, Kar et al., 2013). Unfortunately, these modalities cannot correctly detect the emotion of subjects as the subjects might pretend by voluntarily controlling their emotions. EEG signals contain the instantaneous electrical signature of the brain function, and carry sufficient information to recognize the true emotion of the subjects. There has been a lot of work in deciphering emotion from EEG signals (Kar et al., 2014, Petrantonakis et al., 2016), as well as to determine the dependency of brain region activities on emotional states of a person (Kroupi et al., 2011). However, deciphering neural signatures for different emotions has remained a difficult task, primarily because emotions result as a chain of interactions in the brain rather than just isolated activities of different brain regions (Horlings et al., 2008). Similarity measures of various types have been proposed to understand the relations between EEG electrode signals (Golińska, 2011, Xu et al., 2008) but most were lacking in the fundamental requirement that brain signals exhibit not only pairwise but simultaneous interdependence (Baccalá et al., 2009).

According to Davison's motivational model, the left brain is associated with positive emotions, while the right brain with negative emotions (Müller et al., 1999). However, there is not much agreement about this according to all researchers (Dennis et al., 2010, Körner et al., 2002). While earlier brain theories attempted regional mapping of different brain areas to different aspects of cognition, the more recent brain theories suggest that cognitive computation is facilitated by interaction/connectivity between different parts of the brain. The presented approach to decipher neural signatures of brain activity during emotion arousal tries to capture the multivariate nature of brain interactions. In this chapter, the authors described two techniques of decoding the neural signaling structure and outlined a simple way of extending the presented two techniques. The experiments performed by the authors suggest that considering relativity between the considered brain connectivity measures increases accuracy in classifying the emotional state of a subject. These measures are dependent on linear correlation/coherence among brain signals and are more robust than other dependency measures, primarily because both consider multiple signal relationships. The authors have compared the proposed methods with well-known similarity measures like linear correlation, correntropy (Xu et al., 2008), coherence (Golińska, 2011), and Itakuara distance (Kong et al., 1995). The proposed methods of similarity measurement have outperformed all the other four similarity measures in the domain of emotion recognition.

The first task in any physiological experiment is the design of appropriate stimuli. In this work, the authors have chosen to study the influence of music on the emotional state of a person. In order to avoid any subjective bias towards a particular language, the authors selected instrumental music as stimuli.

During stimuli selection, volunteers were asked to identify emotions carried by different instrumental music pieces. The music pieces which mostly evoked emotions of a particular class were selected as stimuli to inducing emotions of that class only. After careful stimuli selection, a new set of volunteers were asked to listen to the selected music during which their EEG was recorded. Connectivity estimates among the EEG signals were used to construct brain networks. SVM was used to classify these brain networks as representative of the following categories of emotions a) fear b) happiness c) sadness d) relaxation. Different connectivity measures were tested on their ability to indicate emotions. It was seen that considering relative values enhanced the accuracy of emotion recognition.

PRELIMINARIES OF BRAIN-COMPUTER INTERFACING

Brain Lobes and Their Functionalities

The brain is an integral part of the central nervous system and is basically a controlling unit which dictate the communication patterns within the entire nervous system and hence brings about desired bodily changes. A brain is a multifunctional unit which controls physiological processes such as heartbeat and eye blinking as well as psychological processes like thinking and emotion, with the help of the central and peripheral nervous system. The peripheral nervous system is primarily controlled by 12 pairs of peripheral nerves connected to our spinal cord. On the other hand, complex decision making, planning, learning, arithmetic logical computing and the like are performed by the central nervous system with the brain as the key element. There exists an interrelationship between physiological processes, involving motor control, sensory functionalities with psychological aspects of the brain including emotion, rationality, and judgment.

Structurally, the brain can be identified as a conglomeration of two symmetric, vertically separated halves, known as the left-hemisphere and right-hemisphere. Each of these hemispheres can be divided into four different lobes (Figure 1) believed to be unique in their functionalities. These lobes are listed as follows.

- **Frontal Lobe:** Located at the frontal section of the brain and the largest among all the human brain lobes. It plays a central role in working memory and works in close association with other brain areas to facilitate learning memory, attention, and motivation (Tamminga et al., 2005). The frontal lobe is primarily associated with cognitive aspects like memory, emotion, olfaction, goal directed behavior and executive control (Miller & Cohen, 2001; Fuster, 1988; Hornak et al., 1996).
- **Parietal Lobe:** The parietal lobe is located behind the frontal lobe and is primarily associated with tasks like thinking and planning. A study conducted on monkeys revealed that the parietal lobe plays a role in action organization and understanding intentions of agents present in the environment (Fogassi et al., 2005). Parietal lobe has also been found to play a role in episodic memory (Wagner et al., 2005). Further, the posterior parietal cortex is believed to be a part of motor systems and plays a role in visuomotor transformations (Fogassi & Luppino, 2005).

Figure 1. The brain and its lobes

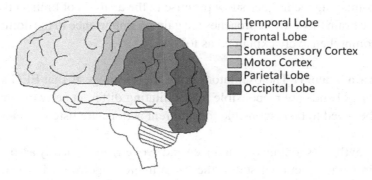

☐ Temporal Lobe
☐ Frontal Lobe
☐ Somatosensory Cortex
☐ Motor Cortex
☐ Parietal Lobe
☐ Occipital Lobe

- **Motor-Cortex:** The motor cortex is divided into three areas, namely primary motor cortex Karni*et. al,* 1988) pre-motor cortex (Rizzolatti et al., 1996) and supplementary motor area (Roland et al., 1980). It is located behind the parietal lobe and is influential in motor planning and execution. For example, different types of finger movement are associated with different patterns of motor cortex activation (Kim et al., 1993). Further, the motor cortex is involved in complex voluntary movements (Purves et. al., 2001) and smart movement planning (Gentili et al., 2007).
- **Occipital Lobe:** Visual perception is facilitated through extensive communication between the occipital and other lobes of the brain. Stimulation of the occipital region triggers visual sensations. The occipital lobe is mostly responsible for vision and is located at the rear of the brain. The lateral occipital lobe is believed to play a fundamental in the processing of visually presented objects (Basar et al., 1999).
- **Temporal Lobe:** The temporal lobes are located beside the ears and are believed to be responsible for sound perception as well as storage of short-term memory and the formation of long term memory (Zatorre et al., 1988, Squire et al., 1991). The medial temporal lobe shows larger activation to support cognitive actions of patients with mild cognitive impairments (Kuipers et al., 2006).

As illustrated above, the brain demonstrates plasticity (Kuipers et al., 2006) (a mechanism by which working parts of the brain complete tasks of other brain parts). Previously, the only possible means of evaluating brain's mechanism of action was by dissection or by the study of lesion induced ailments. Fortunately, new avenues of brain computer interfaces provide non-invasive means of interaction between brain and computer.

Popular Brain-Computer Interfacing Theories

Typical human-computer interfaces are based on communication through a hand held devices such as a mouse, touchpad, and remote. Currently, an alternative means of human-computer interaction is developing which allows humans to perform thought driven control and communication. This kind of an interaction is supported by brain imaging technologies and hence called brain-computer interfacing (BCI). Brain imaging technologies can be both invasive and non-invasive. While invasive technologies like Electrocorticogram (ECoG) are more accurate, the precision of non-invasive brain imaging technologies like EEG and fNIRS have demonstrated considerable improvement after the inclusion of improvised computational techniques (Wolpaw et al.,1991, Ayaz et al., 2009). Thus, fortunately, present non–invasive bio-imaging techniques show promise in the analysis of brain activities. In the area of BCI, two fundamental brain theoretic approaches are gaining importance in the domain of EEG analysis. These theories are comprehensively explained as follows.

- **Oscillatory Brain Theory:** The oscillatory brain theory suggests that EEG signals belonging to different frequency bands are responsible for facilitating different activities in the brain. The frequency bands believed to be responsible for different actions are listed as shown in Table 1.

Oscillatory brain rhythms (spontaneous, induced and evoked) are typically associated with the above different roles, but in some functional states, they also interchange roles. For example, event related potential (ERPs) of the mid gamma band (35-45 Hz) and higher gamma band (46-65 Hz) were seen to

Table 1. Frequency oscillations/ bands and their frequent associations

Frequency Band	Approximate Range	Associations
Delta (δ)	0-4 Hz	Sleep
Theta (θ)	4-8 Hz	Meditation, Concentration
Alpha (α)	8-16 Hz	Emotion
Beta (β)	16-30 Hz	Motor activities
Gamma (γ)	30-80Hz	Cognition

be associated with negative and positive emotions respectively (Keil *et.al*, 2001). Similarly, evoked delta response is observed in processing sensory information (Basar et al., 1999).

- **Brain Network Theory:** Brain network theory states that different cognitive activities of the brain are supported by the formation of unique brain networks. The latter is said to describe the communication pattern taking place in the brain. Researchers have focused on two different categories of brain networks, namely functional and effective brain networks. While the former attempts to examine undirected connectivity, the later attempts to examine directed connectivity. A traditional approach to recognizing cognitive states by evaluating brain networks involves estimation of connectivity by statistical techniques and then recognition of these connectivity patterns by computational techniques (Achard et al., 2006, Van Den Heuvel et al., 2010, Bullmore et al., 2012 and De Schotten et al., 2011). Examples of undirected connectivity measures are correlation and coherence (Lee Rodgers et al., 1988 Litovitz et al., 1991). Examples of undirected brain network creation models are Granger causality and dynamic causal modeling (Kar et al., 2015, Friston et al., 2011). An excellent review of brain network creation techniques has been performed by Sakkalis (2011).

The Study of Emotions in EEG Based BCI Literature

A Brief Comparison Among EEG Studies Involving Different Emotion Induction Modalities

In this section, a few publications on emotion recognition by EEG analysis will be reviewed. As discussed earlier an emotion can be induced in a subject by stimulating the various senses of the subject, such as touch, smell, vision, hearing, and taste, or a combination of any of the above. Further subjects can be asked to imagine emotions and corresponding physiological changes may be monitored. For example, in Table 2, four emotion recognition schemes associated with unique modalities of emotion induction are summarized in a table. The same publications are then briefly discussed. It can be seen that Support Vector Machines (SVM), remained a popular choice of researchers and was associated with high accuracy

Petrantonakis and Hadjileontiadis (2010), studied the influence of emotionally expressive facial images on healthy subjects. They recorded EEG from 3 channels namely Fp1, Fp2 and a bipolar channel of F3-F4 according to the 10-20 electrode system. They proposed an EEG feature referred to as higher order crossings (HOC). In order to compute the HOC, the EEG signals were subjected to backward differencing and then thresholding. This resulted in a binary array corresponding to each EEG signal. The

Table 2. Brief representative literature of emotion induction modalities

Ref.	Emotion Induction Modality	No. of Channels and Brain Area Distribution	EEG Features	Classifier	Classification Accuracy
Petrantonakis & Hadjileontiadis, 2010.	Emotionally Expressive Facial Images (Visual Stimuli)	4 channels, frontal and prefrontal areas	Hybrid Adaptive Filtering-Higher Order Crossings	SVM	85.17%
Lin et. al, 2011	Emotional Music (Audio Stimuli)	32 channels; whole brain	Power Spectral Density, Power difference at symmetric electrode pair	SVM	93.57%
Bradley, 1995	Movies (Audio-Visual Stimuli)	62 channels; whole brain	Log band energy of Fourier Transform, combined with feature selection and smoothing	SVM	89.22%
Min *et. al*, 2005	Emotional Memories	2 channels; Frontal and Parietal lobe, other Physiological Signals	Relationship between α and β power	Manual	———

HOC was then calculated as the sum of the squared differences among the previously obtained binary signals. The frequency band considered was 0.5-30 Hz. The HOC signals were classified as indicating Ekman's six basic emotions namely happiness, sadness, fear, anger, and surprise. Four different classifiers namely Support Vector Machines, QDA, k-nearest neighbor and Mahalanobis distance was applied for emotion recognition from HOC features. Among them, the first classifier outperformed all the others by a significant margin.

Recently, Lin et al. (2011), demonstrated an emotion recognition scheme in which emotions were induced during music listening. One of the fundamental contributions of the chapter was the systematic comparison of the performance of four feature extraction techniques in the emotion recognition problem using SVM. They also employed a feature selection technique using the customary philosophy of minimizing intra-class scatter/spread of features while maximizing their inter-class scatter. The features that they employed were a) average power spectral density of 30 EEG electrodes in the delta, alpha, beta, theta and gamma bands and a combination of all the five bands (the entire range covering delta to gamma), b) average power spectral density of 24 electrodes in all the aforementioned bands, c) Difference of 12 symmetric electrode pairs' signals d) Ratio of 12 symmetric electrode pairs' signals. For all frequency bands except gamma band, feature (c) was the winning feature, while for gamma band feature (a) was the winning feature. This system considers music as an emotion induction modality and reports a high classification accuracy with 32 electrodes, in comparison, the technique presented in this chapter is of acceptable classification accuracy, but uses only 21 electrodes.

An interesting work presenting EEG based emotion recognition during watching movies was presented in [49]. Six healthy subjects were presented several kinds of movie clips in random order. Each of the subjects was asked to rate the movies on the three affective dimensions according to the self-assessment manikin (Bradley, 1995). The self-assessment manikin is a collection of a set of 5 figures for each of the 3 affective dimensions. The figures are arranged as follows. The first row expresses valence (pleasure induced by the stimulus) in increasing order by five consecutive figures. In a similar manner, the second and third rows contain five figures each indicating arousal (excitement induced by the stimulus) and valence (degree of control exerted by the stimulus) respectively, in increasing order.

The subjects were asked to check three figures which most appropriately describe their valence, arousal, and dominance respectively, after watching each movie clip. The data for the experimental purpose was selected based on dominance scores, as only those data which were related to high dominance (indicated by 4th or 5th position figure representing dominance) were employed for emotion recognition. The data was collected by placing a 62-channel electrode cap on the scalp of the subjects. In the feature extraction step, the log band energy of each sample belonging to the FFT of the signal in the five bands (delta, alpha, beta, theta, and gamma) was computed. The signals thus obtained were smoothed by employing linear dynamical system (Shi and Lu, 2010) to remove noise.

In the classification phase, they divided the training and testing data respectively in the ratio of 7:3. The aforementioned five bands and a combination of all the features obtained from the five bands were separately employed for classification. Linear SVM was used for classification and the most appropriate parameters of the linear kernel of the SVM were selected by 10-fold cross validation. They also performed feature selection by ranking features such that features with the highest correlation with the target labels were given highest preference. The top 10 subject-independent features among all the features were considered for classification. Each time this processes was repeated by considering 10 more features as compared to the previous feature set. In this way, features were incrementally added to the set of considered features, till the classification accuracy stabilizes. Finally, the trajectory of emotion changes was calculated by reducing the entire feature set into one dimension by manifold learning (Tenenbaum et al., 2000). A consistent interrelationship was found between the calculated emotion feature and the emotion labels which were in the range (-1, 1), where the labels specified the valance of the subjects from low (-1) to high (1).

Min. et al. (2005), studied the effect of imagination on different physiological signals like EEG, Electro-cardiogram (ECG), Galvanic Skin Response (GSR), skin temperature (SKT) and respiration (RSP). The subjects were asked to imagine four different emotional states namely pleasantness, unpleasantness, arousal and relaxation. EEG data collected from the Fz and Cz regions. EEG signals were filtered in the alpha (α) and beta (β) band. The values of $\alpha/(\alpha+\beta)$ and $\beta/(\alpha+\beta)$, were found significant to detect emotional changes, along with average RSP interval.

Music as an Important Emotion Induction Modality

It is well known that emotions can be influenced by external events. These external events include everything a subject can perceive about the environment. Thus if the subject's environment is positive, it is expected that the subject will be positively influenced. The same holds true for a negative environment. Emotion related experiments are mostly carried out in a controlled environment where subjects are presented with stimuli which are emotion evoking. Many modalities can be employed for evoking emotions, for example, touch (Hertenstein et al., 2009), smell (Zald et al., 1997), audio (De Silva et al., 200), visual (Schuller et al., 2012), or a combination of any of them. The positive influence of music on emotions has led to the development of music therapy which is an established mode of providing emotional support (Can, 2011, Hertenstein et al., 2009) in the presented experiments the authors chose music as external stimuli, because it is easier to present music to patients who may not prefer seeing video, or being touched.

Multiple experiments from different groups have confirmed that music has the capacity to influence emotional state of a person (Koelsch et al., 2010, Hayakawa et al., 2000). Determination of emotions portrayed by music is popularly known as music emotion recognition (MER). MER may be performed by analysis of the acoustic and lyrical components of a music piece as well as a combination of both (Kim, 2010; Patra, 2015; Patra, 2013). Another approach is to perform brain image analysis of subjects listening to a music piece. Hayakawa *et al.*, 2000 studied the effect of music on the mental state of subjects during exercise. Their experiments revealed that the subjects, who listened to music during exercising, experienced significantly less fatigue as compared to those who did not listen to music while exercising. Koelsch et al. (2010), the author described music perception from a biological perspective. They emphasized that music perception has the potential to influence emotions, autonomic nervous system, hormone and immune system, and (pre) motor representations.

Although there has been significant research on the positive influence of music on emotion (Bailey, 1984, Koelsch et al., 2010), much lesser attempts have been made in the study of music in inducing negative emotions like fear and sadness. In the presented experiments, the authors study the effect of music in inducing four different emotions a) Fear b) Sadness c) Happiness and d) Relaxation. It was seen that all music belonging to the aforementioned four categories have computationally differentiable brain network patterns.

TOOLS AND TECHNIQUES USED

In the presented experiments, the authors attempt to study the influence of music on the signaling pathways in the brain. To find out if the different brain regions are interdependent (exchanging signals), the correlation/coherence among the different EEG signals specific to the considered brain regions were analyzed. It is known that both correlation and coherence measure the similarity between a pair of signals. Further, coherence is a frequency domain counterpart of correlation. In previous experiments, the authors observed that considering relative values of correlation improved the classification accuracy in an emotion recognition problem, where visual stimuli were used for inducing emotions (Kar et al., 2015). In this experiment, the authors avoid ocular artifacts by restricting the stimuli to instrumental music. Since taking relative values in the time domain (correlation), improved classification accuracy, it was natural to enquire if the same holds true for the frequency domain (coherence). The experiments in this chapter are an attempt to reveal the answer to this fundamental question. Unlike our last work, this work considers music as stimuli and is more applicable for administration to subjects who are emotionally disturbed and would not want to see the video.

To overcome the problems associated with pairwise dependency measures, the authors outline two measures namely relative correlation and relative coherence. The relative correlation/coherence (RC) is a matrix of binary indices in which 1 indicates that an EEG signal from an electrode position is relatively more connected to another, and 0 indicates the opposite. Our next task is to classify emotion from the RC matrices obtained from an unknown subject. The RC matrices maybe viewed as adjacency matrices such that brain region connectivity and may be used to create brain connectivity graph.

Traditional Functional Connectivity Estimates

- **Analyzing Linear Interdependencies in Time Domain:** In order to identify the mutual interrelationship between brain signals of different regions, the authors employed the well-known linear dependency measure known as Pearson's correlation coefficient. The correlation between any two pairs of electrode signals called cross-correlation. Thus for the set of 21 electrode channels, one obtains a 21×21 matrix in which each (i, j)th element is the Pearson's correlation coefficient between the signals obtained from the ith and jth electrode. The Pearson's correlation coefficient is evaluated as follows (Lee Rodgers, 1988).

$$R_{x,y} = \frac{n \sum_{i=1}^{n} (x_i - \overline{x})(y_i - \overline{y})}{\sqrt{\sum_{i=1}^{n} (x_i - \overline{x})^2 (y_i - \overline{y})^2}} \tag{1}$$

Here, $R_{x,y}$ is the Pearson's correlation coefficient, which indicates linear dependence between signals x and y. $\overline{x}$ is the average value of signal x, $\overline{y}$ is the average value of the signal y, n is the number of samples of the signal that considered, x_i is the ith sample of the signal x and y_i is the ith sample of signal y. It may be noted here that the correlation matrix obtained will be symmetric because the linear correlation between any two signals is bi-directionally same. For instance, the sample correlation between four electrode signals for the emotion fear is given in Table 3.

- **Analyzing Linear Interdependencies in Frequency Domain:** In order to identify the frequency coupling between brain signals, one may use the well-known similarity measure known as magnitude squared coherence (Golińska *et. al*, 2011) calculated as follows.

$$C(\omega) = \frac{\left| Pxy(\omega) \right|^2}{P_{xx}(\omega) P_{yy}(\omega)} \tag{2}$$

Here P_{xy} indicates cross-power spectral density between signals x and y. P_{yy} and P_{xx} are power spectral densities of signals x and y respectively. For each considered normalized frequency ω one obtains

Table 3. Correlation/Mean Coherence Matrix R

	ch1	ch2	ch3	ch4
ch1	0	0.99986	0.99971	0.9987
ch2	0.99986	0	0.9887	0.9624
ch3	0.99971	0.9887	0	0.9512
ch4	0.9987	0.9624	0.9512	0

a 21×21 coupling matrix known as $C(\omega)$; as 21 channels are considered in our experiments. Finally, the authors considered the average coherence matrix obtained for each of the normalized frequency samples belonging to the alpha band. Coherence is also known as the frequency domain counterpart of correlation.

Hierarchial Linear SVM

The linear support vector machine (SVM) employs a linear decision function to separate patterns represented by data-point vectors into different classes. This linear decision function, representing the separating hyperplane, is designed with the help of support vectors lying at the boundary of the two classes of data points on either side of the separating hyperplane (Schölkopf&Smola, 2002). SVM attempts to minimize the margin of separation of the support vectors with the separating hyperplane. The above optimization problem is formulated using Lagarange's multiplier approach with an aim to determine the parameters of the hyperplane. Linear SVM provides satisfactory results with acceptable classification accuracy for most of the linearly separable 2-class classification problem. When the number of classes exceeds 2, a hierarchical extension of fundamental SVM is performed, where at each level of the hierarchy, we classify the data points into one specific class (say class-A) and non-class (i.e., not class A). The non-class A includes all other classes. At the next level, the data points lying in non-class-A may again be classified into two classes: B and non-B, where non-B includes all classes excluding class A and B. The process of hierarchical classification continues until all classes appear at leaves of the hierarchical structure (tree). In this chapter, we use linear SVM to separate multi- class data points.

PROPOSED EXTENSION OF FUNCTIONAL CONNECTIVITY ESTIMATES

Traditional functional connectivity measures, generally take into account, the bivariate relationship among different brain regions. These inter-electrode connectivity patterns may be represented as matrices, such that, the $(i, j)^{th}$ element of the matrix represents the connection strengths between the ith and j^{th} electrodes. Thus, each element of the matrix represents the exclusive relationship between two electrodes. As brain-network theory suggests that the brain simultaneously inter-networks among its various regions, the study of only bivariate connectivity may not be very rewarding. In this chapter, the authors attempted to study the multivariate relationship among brain regions by employing a novel scheme which is illustrated as follows. Let us consider a densely connected brain network. Here each brain region is assumed to exchange signals with multiple other regions. Thus it is natural for each brain region to prioritize their connections with those regions which maximize communication. Following this philosophy, the authors ranked connections of each brain region (here considered row-wise), and thresholded these connections based on their strengths to form a binary matrix. The resultant binary matrix was superior in classification performance to the traditional bivariate connectivity estimates. An illustrative example of this kind of thresholding based on relative values is illustrated next.

- **Illustrative Example:** Let us suppose, that the authors analyzed the cross-correlation/mean coherence among the EEG signals generated by each any four electrode channels: ch1, ch2, ch3 and ch4 and recorded them as in Table 3. The relative correlation adjacency matrix (Table 3) is simply formed by creating another table in which the highest two (upper ceiling of 50% of the channels considered) cross-correlations in each row (of Table 3) is marked as 1 and rest are marked as 0. The RC matrix named r' thus created stores the relatively stronger connections among all possible electrode connections. Similarly, for, a table containing cross-coherence among any number of electrode positions, one may choose to represent the 50% strongest cross-coherence as 1 and rest as 0. While calculating relative correlation/coherence, the authors made the diagonal elements 0 they represent auto-correlation and auto-coherence values. The resultant of calculations performed on Table 3 are stored in Table 4 and the overall scheme is presented in Figure 2.

EXPERIMENTS

Experiment 1: Stimulus Selection

The first task in any physiological experiment is the design of appropriate stimuli. In this work, the authors have chosen to study the influence of music on the emotional state of a person. In order to avoid any subjective bias towards a particular language, the authors selected instrumental music as stimuli. In

Table 4. Relative Correlation/ Coherence Adjacency Matrix R'

	ch1	ch2	ch3	ch4
ch1	0	1	1	0
ch2	1	0	1	0
ch3	1	1	0	0
ch4	1	1	0	0

Figure 2. Proposed Computation of Relative Correlation/Coherence Matrix; deeper colors indicated higher values. a) Matrix obtained by Traditional Techniques, b) Intermediate Step c) RC matrix

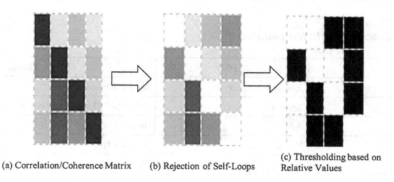

(a) Correlation/Coherence Matrix   (b) Rejection of Self-Loops   (c) Thresholding based on Relative Values

the first step, brief 20-30 second clips of 40 pieces of instrumental music were selected to create a music database, from clips of full music songs listed in a tabular manner below. The music was selected in sets, such that each set of 10 music stimuli was capable of inducing one of the four emotions namely a) relaxation b) fear c) sadness and d) happiness. In the second phase of stimuli selection, five volunteers were asked to identify emotions which they felt after listening to the selected instrumental music pieces. They were also asked to rate the each music piece on a scale of 1 (low) to 10 (high) depicting how much the music influenced them to feel a particular emotion. For the same music piece, the score is set to zero for other emotions. Finally, the average of all scores attained by the music piece for inducing each emotion was calculated. The music pieces obtaining the top 5 scores for inducing an emotion e is selected as the stimuli for inducing emotion e. Finally, a total of 5 music clips for each of the four emotions were selected as stimuli. The music pieces from which stimuli were selected are given below in Tables 5 to 8.

Experiment 2: Emotion Induction by Musical Stimuli

A set of 10 graduate students (not involved in rating the stimuli) were asked to listen to the selected stimuli. The stimuli were organized in the following manner. Instrumentals were arranged such that the presentation induced happiness, sadness, fear and relaxation in the mentioned order. Between each pair of music pieces, there was a gap of 10 seconds to avoid the influence of the previous stimuli. After the presentation of one such set was complete, a gap of few minutes was given to the subject and then the same order of presentation was repeated for different music set. This procedure was repeated 5 times. The EEG data were collected in a controlled environment, and the subjects were asked to listen to the music with eyes closed. Our data set consists of the data obtained from 10 subjects for 5 emotions induced 5 times each. Thus the authors have a total of 10×4×5 instances where each database for each of the 4 emotion has a total of 10×5 sets of labeled data. The volunteers were asked that if they felt the desired

Table 5. Music extracts for happy emotion

Title	Artist	Album
Inside Views	La Verue	Riez Noir
O Pindo	PELdeNOZ	Ensaio 16 de abril de 2008
Habanera	Manuzik	Ouverture
Modal Jazz	Music Delta	n/a
Chinese Jiang Nan	Music Delta	n/a

Table 6. Music extracts for relaxed emotion

Title	Artist	Album
happy child singing	Ruediger Kramer	Japanese blues
Homecoming	BeatRaider	A Journey Through My World
La note en cage	AdHoc	Toutes directions
Lights	You Me Tree	You Me Tree
LA	Podington Bear	Background

Table 7. Music extracts for sad emotion

Title	Artist	Album
Interlude	Tom La Meche	Blog
Lonely Fool	Steve.e!	SUN LP
Jazzy Mode	Behrang Shegarfkar	Wasted Time
Definition	Joel Helander	n/a
Flutter	Molloy And His Bike	Rex Is For Records - 5 Years Compilation Vol.2

Table 8. Music extracts for fear emotion

Title	Artist	Album
Neon	ADC LEVEL	Subway Stories
Impressions of Saturn	Matthew Entwistle	n/a
Corona Radiata	Nine Inch Nails	The Slip
Track 12	The Wire Orchestra	CordinRidin.
First Loser	The New Mellow Edwards	Big Choantza

emotion when they listened to the music. 90% of the listeners agreed that they felt the desired emotions. The data of the volunteers who actually felt the desired emotion were employed for the classification experiment. Synchronization between EEG and music listening to avoid surprising the subjects was ensured by letting the considering readings after a 10 second delay after the music started.

Experiment 3: Classification of Emotion Induced by Music.

- **Data Acquisition and Filtering:** The subjects (same as experiment 2) were presented the selected and organized music stimuli in a noise-free environment. Special seating arrangement is made for the subject with cushion and armrests. The subject received music stimuli from a laptop equipped with high quality headphones. The experiment was conducted on 10 subjects: 5 male and 5 female in the age group 24±5. The data was acquired using 21 EEG channels Nihon Kohden's EEG 1200 device (Saha et al., 2013). Alpha band is found to have significance in emotional feelings of a person (Petrantonakis & Hadjileontiadis, 2010; Soleymani, 2012). Hence the authors designed a band-pass Chebyshev filter of order 10 to filter the alpha band. The authors then used the filtered raw signals for further analysis. For construction of relative correlation/coherence adjacency matrix the authors considered the relative correlation/coherence of all the 21channels (F3, Fz, F4, P4, P3, O1, O2, C3, Cz, C4, F7, F8, T3, T4, T5, T6, Fp1, Fp2, T2, T1, Pz) with each other. Thus 21×21 matrices containing relative correlation/coherence values were obtained.
- **Feature Extraction and Classification:** Let us consider m number of experimental subjects. Each subject was shown n videos which would induce the subject with a specific emotion, say fear. For each of the video clip, one can construct two types of RC matrices (one obtained by considering correlation and another obtained by calculating coherence). Let us first consider the correlation based connectivity matrix. As each of the m emotions is induced in a subject n times, one can ob-

tain the n×m number of correlation based RC matrices for each emotion. Thus if one considers k emotions, one will obtain the n×m×k number of RC matrices. With this data leave-one out cross-validation was performed, such that each time, the data of all but one subject would be employed for training and the remaining data of one subject would be employed for testing. The training and testing procedure is listed as follows. In order to classify the unknown emotion indicated by the RC matrices obtained, Support Vector Machine (SVM) classifier was trained with the RC matrices of all the k emotions (here k=4) (Fear, Happiness, Sadness, Relaxation). Here each RC matrix is a p×p adjacency matrix which indicates connectivity among the p EEG channels. Each data point in SVM is represented by a row matrix of r elements indicating r-dimensional data. In the performed experiments, each data point is a linearly rearranged adjacency matrix obtained from RC matrix. Thus one needs to reshape the RC matrix into a row vector. This reshaping was done by placing all rows sequentially in the new row vector of (1×p.p) dimension. The SVM classifier was first trained to separate data of fear and non-fear categories. In the testing phase, SVM was employed to categorize the unknown data into one of the two training classes. In a similar manner, the non-fear category was categorized into relaxation and non-relaxation. This kind of binary categorization was continued till all the emotions have been separated.

The same process listed in the above paragraph is repeated for RC matrices obtained from coherence. Finally, the classification accuracies for both the techniques were obtained and compared with the traditional techniques in Table 11.

- **Time Domain Approach:** After data acquisition and filtering, the authors constructed a matrix containing absolute values of cross correlation, with the elements indicating connection strength, ranging between zero and one. The matrix was sorted row-wise. The cells corresponding to the highest absolute cross-correlation values in each row were marked as 1, while the others were marked as zero. This resulted in the formation of RC matrix which was binary. Sample plots for relative correlation are indicated in Figure 3. In the following plots, the X-axis and Y-axis represent channels 1 to 21 in the following order (F3, Fz, F4, P4, P3, O1, O2, C3, Cz, C4, F7, F8, T3, T4, T5, T6, Fp1, Fp2, T2, T1, Pz). The cells in the graphs are color shaded as white (low) or black (high). Final classification results obtained for traditional and described brain network calculation techniques are listed in Table 9. Sample RC matrices are plotted in Figure 3.
- **Frequency Domain Approach:** In the frequency domain approach, the authors followed the same philosophy as the time domain approach. The only difference here is that coherence values are considered instead of correlation. Figure 4 indicates the relative coherence matrices for dif-

Table 9. Classification accuracy of the correlation based technique

Emotion	Classification Accuracy
Fear	93.33%
Happy	86.67%
Sad	86.67%
Relax	62%
Average Accuracy	82.16%

Figure 3. Sample relative correlation matrices obtained for a) happiness b) anger c) sadness and d) fear

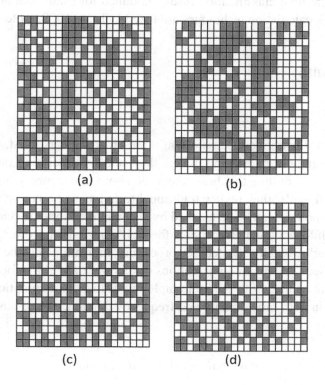

Figure 4. Sample relative coherence matrices obtained for a) happiness b) anger c) sadness and d) fear

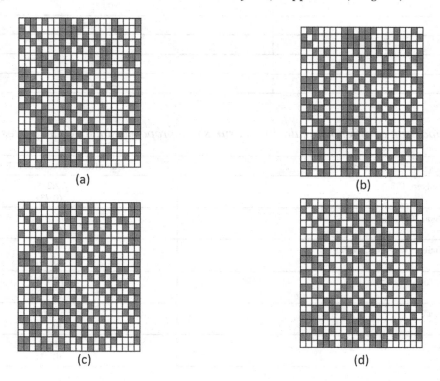

ferent emotions. The final classification results obtained for traditional and described coherence based brain network calculation techniques are listed in Table 10. Sample RC matrices are plotted in Figure 4.

Classification Results

CONCLUSION

This chapter provides an illustrative discussion on three broad aspects. First, the authors discuss the preliminaries of brain-computer interfacing, where they start by describing the functions of different brain lobes, and then briefly outline two brain theoretic approaches namely brain network theory and oscillatory brain theory. Finally, they review traditional techniques of emotion recognition while demonstrating the fact that emotions can be influenced by different modalities including music. Second, the authors describe their philosophy which accounts for their contributions towards the effective creation of functional brain networks. Finally, the detailed procedure, indicating how the authors completed their experiments was discussed. The major contributions of this work are a) the formulation of a technique to determine multivariate connectivity without employing statistical assumptions, b) the validation of the proposed technique in both time domain and frequency domain, c) a discussion of brain computer

Table 10. Classification accuracy of the coherence based technique

Emotion	Classification Accuracy
Fear	93.33%
Happy	89.67%
Sad	86.67%
Relax	70%
Average Accuracy	84.91%

Table 11. Comparison of different similarity measures and proposed similarity measures

Emotion	Classification Accuracy (F Score)
Correlation(Lee Rodgers 1988)	72.21% (0.73)
Coherence (Golińska, 2011)	76.58% (0.77)
Correntropy coefficient (Xu *et. al,* 2008)	75.33% (0.76)
Itakuara Distance(Kong *et. al,* 1995)	79.75% (0.80)
Relative Correlation	82.16% (0.83)
Relative Coherence	84.91% (0.85)

interfacing techniques and philosophies, and d) a review of different approaches to emotionally influence subjects and analyze their emotions through brain-computer interfacing.

The proposed technique of detecting functional brain networks is computationally inexpensive. The underlying philosophy proposed is that, instead of considering absolute values of pairwise connectivity measures, one may consider the relative values, which mean that multiple channel interactions will be considered, and hence the accuracy of classification into different cognitive states will increase. This philosophy was tested on an emotion recognition problem, by considering functional brain networks based on correlation and coherence. The results indicate that considering relative values have a positive influence on classification accuracy. There is still scope to establish in a similar fashion, the relative Itakuara distance and relative crosscorrentropy, which are expected to further better the results of emotion recognition. However, correlation/coherence are the simplest and most trusted measures of linear dependence in time- and frequency-domains respectively.

ACKNOWLEDGMENT

The work reported in this chapter is supported by a grant from the UPE-II funding of University Grants Commission (UGC).

REFERENCES

Achard, S., Salvador, R., Whitcher, B., Suckling, J., & Bullmore, E. D. (2006). A resilient, low-frequency, small-world human brain functional network with highly connected association cortical hubs. *The Journal of Neuroscience*, 26(1), 63–72. doi:10.1523/JNEUROSCI.3874-05.2006 PMID:16399673

Ayaz, H., Shewokis, P. A., Bunce, S., Schultheis, M., & Onaral, B. (2009). Assessment of cognitive neural correlates for a functional near infrared-based brain computer interface system. In Foundations of Augmented Cognition. Neuroergonomics and Operational Neuroscience (pp. 699-708). Springer Berlin Heidelberg. doi:10.1007/978-3-642-02812-0_79

Baccalá, L. A., & Sameshima, K. (2001). Overcoming the limitations of correlation analysis for many simultaneously processed neural structures. *Progress in Brain Research*, 130, 33–47. doi:10.1016/S0079-6123(01)30004-3 PMID:11480285

Basar, E., Basar-Eroglu, C., Karakas, S., & Schürmann, M. (1999). Oscillatory brain theory: A new trend in neuroscience. *Engineering in Medicine and Biology Magazine, IEEE*, 18(3), 56–66. doi:10.1109/51.765190 PMID:10337564

Dennis, T. A., & Solomon, B. (2010). Frontal EEG and emotion regulation: Electrocortical activity in response to emotional film clips is associated with reduced mood induction and attention interference effects. *Biological Psychology*, 85(3), 456–464. doi:10.1016/j.biopsycho.2010.09.008 PMID:20863872

Dickerson, B. C., Salat, D. H., Bates, J. F., Atiya, M., Killiany, R. J., Greve, D. N., & Sperling, R. A. (2004). Medial temporal lobe function and structure in mild cognitive impairment. *Annals of Neurology*, 56(1), 27–35. doi:10.1002/ana.20163 PMID:15236399

Fogassi, L., Ferrari, P. F., Gesierich, B., Rozzi, S., Chersi, F., & Rizzolatti, G. (2005). Parietal lobe: From action organization to intention understanding. *Science*, *308*(5722), 662–667. doi:10.1126/science.1106138 PMID:15860620

Fogassi, L., & Luppino, G. (2005). Motor functions of the parietal lobe. *Current Opinion in Neurobiology*, *15*(6), 626–631. doi:10.1016/j.conb.2005.10.015 PMID:16271458

Fuster, J. M. (1988). *Prefrontal cortex. In Comparative neuroscience and neurobiology* (pp. 107–109). Birkhäuser Boston. doi:10.1007/978-1-4899-6776-3_43

Gentili, R., Cahouet, V., & Papaxanthis, C. (2007). Motor planning of arm movements is direction-dependent in the gravity field. *Neuroscience*, *145*(1), 20–32. doi:10.1016/j.neuroscience.2006.11.035 PMID:17224242

Golińska, A. K. (2011). Coherence function in biomedical signal processing: A short review of applications in Neurology, Cardiology, and Gynecology. *Studies in Logic, Grammar, and Rhetoric*, *25*(38), 73–82.

Horlings, R., Datcu, D., & Rothkrantz, L. J. (2008, June). Emotion recognition using brain activity. In Proceedings of the 9th international conference on computer systems and technologies and workshop for Ph.D. students in computing (p. 6). ACM. doi:10.1007/978-3-642-24571-8_58

Hornak, J., Rolls, E. T., & Wade, D. (1996). Face and voice expression identification in patients with emotional and behavioural changes following ventral frontal lobe damage. *Neuropsychologia*, *34*(4), 247–261. doi:10.1016/0028-3932(95)00106-9 PMID:8657356

Kar, R., Chakraborty, A., Konar, A., & Janarthanan, R. (2013). Emotion recognition system by gesture analysis using fuzzy sets. In *International Conference on Swarm, Evolutionary, and Memetic Computing* (pp. 354-363). Springer International Publishing. doi:10.1007/978-3-319-03756-1_32

Kar, R., Konar, A., Chakraborty, A., & Nagar, A. K. (2014). Detection of signaling pathways in the human brain during arousal of a specific emotion. In *Neural Networks (IJCNN), 2014 International Joint Conference on* (pp. 3950-3957). IEEE. doi:10.1109/IJCNN.2014.6889939

Karni, A., Meyer, G., Rey-Hipolito, C., Jezzard, P., Adams, M. M., Turner, R., & Ungerleider, L. G. (1998). The acquisition of skilled motor performance: Fast and slow experience-driven changes in primary motor cortex. *Proceedings of the National Academy of Sciences of the United States of America*, *95*(3), 861–868. doi:10.1073/pnas.95.3.861 PMID:9448252

Keil, A., Müller, M. M., Gruber, T., Wienbruch, C., Stolarova, M., & Elbert, T. (2001). Effects of emotional arousal in the cerebral hemispheres: A study of oscillatory brain activity and event-related potentials. [Chicago.]. *Clinical Neurophysiology*, *112*(11), 2057–2068. doi:10.1016/S1388-2457(01)00654-X PMID:11682344

Kim, S. G., Ashe, J., Hendrich, K., Ellermann, J. M., Merkle, H., Ugurbil, K., & Georgopoulos, A. P. (1993). Functional magnetic resonance imaging of motor cortex: Hemispheric asymmetry and handedness. *Science*, *261*(5121), 615–617. doi:10.1126/science.8342027 PMID:8342027

Konar, A., Chakraborty, A., Halder, A., Mandal, R., & Janarthanan, R. (2012). Interval type-2 fuzzy model for emotion recognition from facial expression. In *Perception and Machine Intelligence* (pp. 114–121). Springer Berlin Heidelberg. doi:10.1007/978-3-642-27387-2_15

Kong, X., Thakor, N., & Goel, V. (1995, September). Characterization of EEG signal changes via Itakura distance. In *Engineering in Medicine and Biology Society, 1995., IEEE 17th Annual Conference* (Vol. 2, pp. 873-874). IEEE. doi:10.1109/IEMBS.1995.579247

Körner, E., & Matsumoto, G. (2002). Cortical architecture and self-referential control for brain-like computation. *Engineering in Medicine and Biology Magazine, IEEE, 21*(5), 121–133. doi:10.1109/MEMB.2002.1044182 PMID:12405066

Kroupi, E., Yazdani, A., & Ebrahimi, T. (2011). EEG correlates of different emotional states elicited during watching music videos. In *Affective Computing and Intelligent Interaction* (pp. 457–466). Springer Berlin Heidelberg.

Kuipers, S. D., & Bramham, C. R. (2006). Brain-derived neurotrophic factor mechanisms and function in adult synaptic plasticity: New insights and implications for therapy. *Current Opinion in Drug Discovery & Development, 9*(5), 580–586. PMID:17002218

Martinez, H. P., Bengio, Y., & Yannakakis, G. N. (2013). Learning deep physiological models of affect. *IEEE Computational Intelligence Magazine, 8*(2), 20–33. doi:10.1109/MCI.2013.2247823

Miller, E. K., & Cohen, J. D. (2001). An integrative theory of prefrontal cortex function. *Annual Review of Neuroscience, 24*(1), 167–202. doi:10.1146/annurev.neuro.24.1.167 PMID:11283309

Müller, M. M., Keil, A., Gruber, T., & Elbert, T. (1999). Processing of affective pictures modulates right-hemispheric gamma band EEG activity. *Clinical Neurophysiology, 110*(11), 1913–1920. doi:10.1016/S1388-2457(99)00151-0 PMID:10576487

Petrantonakis, P. C., & Hadjileontiadis, L. J. (2010). Emotion recognition from EEG using higher order crossings. *IEEE Transactions on Information Technology in Biomedicine, 14*(2), 186–197. doi:10.1109/TITB.2009.2034649 PMID:19858033

Petrantonakis, P. C., & Hadjileontiadis, L. J. (2012). Adaptive emotional information retrieval from EEG signals in the time-frequency domain. *IEEE Transactions on Signal Processing, 60*(5), 2604–2616. doi:10.1109/TSP.2012.2187647

Purves, D., Augustine, G. J., Fitzpatrick, D., Katz, L. C., LaMantia, A. S., McNamara, J. O., & Williams, S. M. (2001). *The Primary Motor Cortex: Upper Motor Neurons That Initiate Complex Voluntary Movements*. Academic Press.

Rizzolatti, G., Fadiga, L., Gallese, V., & Fogassi, L. (1996). Premotor cortex and the recognition of motor actions. *Brain Research. Cognitive Brain Research, 3*(2), 131–141. doi:10.1016/0926-6410(95)00038-0 PMID:8713554

Roland, P. E., Larsen, B., Lassen, N. A., & Skinhoj, E. (1980). Supplementary motor area and other cortical areas in organization of voluntary movements in man. *Journal of Neurophysiology, 43*(1), 118–136. PMID:7351547

Soleymani, M., Lichtenauer, J., Pun, T., & Pantic, M. (2012). A multimodal database for affect recognition and implicit tagging. *IEEE Transactions on Affective Computing*, *3*(1), 42–55. doi:10.1109/T-AFFC.2011.25

Squire, L. R., & Zola-Morgan, S. (1991). The medial temporal lobe memory system. *Science*, *253*(5026), 1380–1386. doi:10.1126/science.1896849 PMID:1896849

Tamminga, C. A., & Buchsbaum, M. S. (2004). Frontal cortex function. *The American Journal of Psychiatry*, *161*(12), 2178. doi:10.1176/appi.ajp.161.12.2178 PMID:15569885

Wagner, A. D., Shannon, B. J., Kahn, I., & Buckner, R. L. (2005). Parietal lobe contributions to episodic memory retrieval. [Chicago.]. *Trends in Cognitive Sciences*, *9*(9), 445–453. doi:10.1016/j.tics.2005.07.001 PMID:16054861

Wolpaw, J. R., McFarland, D. J., Neat, G. W., & Forneris, C. A. (1991). An EEG-based brain-computer interface for cursor control. *Electroencephalography and Clinical Neurophysiology*, *78*(3), 252–259. doi:10.1016/0013-4694(91)90040-B PMID:1707798

Xu, J. W., Bakardjian, H., Cichocki, A., & Principe, J. C. (2008). A new nonlinear similarity measure for multichannel signals. *Neural Networks*, *21*(2), 222–231. doi:10.1016/j.neunet.2007.12.039 PMID:18272331

Zatorre, R. J. (1988). Pitch perception of complex tones and human temporal-lobe function. *The Journal of the Acoustical Society of America*, *84*(2), 566–572. doi:10.1121/1.396834 PMID:3170948

Van Den Heuvel, M. P., & Pol, H. E. H. (2010). Exploring the brain network: A review on resting-state fMRI functional connectivity. [PubMed]. *European Neuropsychopharmacology*, *20*(8), 519–534.

Bailey, L. M. (1984). The use of songs in music therapy with cancer patients and their families. *Music Therapy*, *4*(1), 5–17. doi:10.1093/mt/4.1.5

Bradley, M. M., & Lang, P. J. (1994). Measuring emotion: The self-assessment manikin and the semantic differential. *Journal of Behavior Therapy and Experimental Psychiatry*, *25*(1), 49–59. doi:10.1016/0005-7916(94)90063-9 PMID:7962581

Bullmore, E., & Sporns, O. (2012). The economy of brain network organization. *Nature Reviews. Neuroscience*, *13*(5), 336–349. PMID:22498897

Can, M. T. (2011). *What is music therapy?*. Academic Press.

De Schotten, M. T., DellAcqua, F., Forkel, S. J., Simmons, A., Vergani, F., Murphy, D. G., & Catani, M. (2011). A lateralized brain network for visuospatial attention. *Nature Neuroscience*, *14*(10), 1245–1246. doi:10.1038/nn.2905 PMID:21926985

De Silva, L. C., & Ng, P. C. (2000). Bimodal emotion recognition. In *Automatic Face and Gesture Recognition, 2000. Proceedings. Fourth IEEE International Conference on* (pp. 332-335). IEEE. doi:10.1109/AFGR.2000.840655

Friston, K. J., Harrison, L., & Penny, W. (2003). Dynamic causal modeling. *NeuroImage*, *19*(4), 1273–1302. doi:10.1016/S1053-8119(03)00202-7 PMID:12948688

Hayakawa, Y., Miki, H., Takada, K., & Tanaka, K. (2000). Effects of music on mood during bench stepping exercise. *Perceptual and Motor Skills*, *90*(1), 307–311. doi:10.2466/pms.2000.90.1.307 PMID:10769915

Hertenstein, M. J., Holmes, R., McCullough, M., & Keltner, D. (2009). The communication of emotion via touch. *Emotion (Washington, D.C.)*, *9*(4), 566–573. doi:10.1037/a0016108 PMID:19653781

http://www.nihonkohden.com/products/products_en/type/eeg/eeg1200.html

Kar, R., Konar, A., Chakraborty, A., Sen Bhattacharya, B., & Nagar, A. (2015). EEG Source Localization by Memory Network Analysis of Subjects Engaged in Perceiving Emotions from Facial Expressions, International Joint Conference on Neural Networks. In *Neural Networks (IJCNN)*, 2015 *International Joint Conference on*. IEEE.

Kim, Y. E., Schmidt, E. M., Migneco, R., Morton, B. G., Richardson, P., Scott, J., & Turnbull, D. et al. (2010, August). Music emotion recognition: A state of the art review. *Proc. ISMIR*, 255-266.

Koelsch, S. (2010). Towards a neural basis of music-evoked emotions. *Trends in Cognitive Sciences*, *14*(3), 131–137. doi:10.1016/j.tics.2010.01.002 PMID:20153242

Lee Rodgers, J., & Nicewander, W. A. (1988). Thirteen ways to look at the correlation coefficient. *The American Statistician*, *42*(1), 59–66. doi:10.1080/00031305.1988.10475524

Lin, Y. P., Wang, C. H., Jung, T. P., Wu, T. L., Jeng, S. K., Duann, J. R., & Chen, J. H. (2010). EEG-based emotion recognition in music listening. *Biomedical Engineering. IEEE Transactions on*, *57*(7), 1798–1806.

Litovitz, T. A., Krause, D., & Mullins, J. M. (1991). Effect of coherence time of the applied magnetic field on ornithine decarboxylase activity. *Biochemical and Biophysical Research Communications*, *178*(3), 862–865. doi:10.1016/0006-291X(91)90970-I PMID:1872866

Min, Y. K., Chung, S. C., & Min, B. C. (2005). Physiological evaluation of emotional change induced by imagination. *Applied Psychophysiology and Biofeedback*, *30*(2), 137–150. doi:10.1007/s10484-005-4310-0 PMID:16013786

Nie, D., Wang, X. W., Shi, L. C., & Lu, B. L. (2011, April). EEG-based emotion recognition during watching movies. In *Neural Engineering (NER), 2011 5th International IEEE/EMBS Conference on* (pp. 667-670). IEEE. doi:10.1109/NER.2011.5910636

Patra, B. G., Das, D., & Bandyopadhyay, S. (2013). Automatic Music Mood Classification of Hindi Songs. *Sixth International Joint Conference on Natural Language Processing*, 24.

Patra, B. G., Maitra, P., Das, D., & Bandyopadhyay, S. (2015). MediaEval 2015: Feed-Forward Neural Network based Music Emotion Recognition. *MediaEval 2015 Workshop*.

Petrantonakis, P. C., & Hadjileontiadis, L. J. (2010). Emotion recognition from brain signals using hybrid adaptive filtering and higher order crossings analysis. *Affective Computing. IEEE Transactions on*, *1*(2), 81–97.

Saha, A., Konar, A., Rakshit, P., Ralescu, A. L., & Nagar, A. K. (2013, August). Olfaction recognition by EEG analysis using differential evolution induced Hopfield neural net. In *Neural Networks (IJCNN), The 2013 International Joint Conference on* (pp. 1-8). IEEE.

Sakkalis, V. (2011). Review of advanced techniques for the estimation of brain connectivity measured with EEG/MEG. *Computers in Biology and Medicine, 41*(12), 1110–1117. doi:10.1016/j.compbiomed.2011.06.020 PMID:21794851

Schölkopf, B., & Smola, A. J. (2002). *Learning with kernels: Support vector machines, regularization, optimization, and beyond.* MIT Press.

Schuller, B., Valster, M., Eyben, F., Cowie, R., & Pantic, M. (2012, October). Avec 2012: the continuous audio/visual emotion challenge. In *Proceedings of the 14th ACM international conference on Multimodal interaction* (pp. 449-456). ACM. doi:10.1145/2388676.2388776

Shi, L. C., & Lu, B. L. (2010, August). Off-line and on-line vigilance estimation based on linear dynamical system and manifold learning. In *Engineering in Medicine and Biology Society (EMBC), 2010 Annual International Conference of the IEEE* (pp. 6587-6590). IEEE.

Tenenbaum, J. B., De Silva, V., & Langford, J. C. (2000). A global geometric framework for nonlinear dimensionality reduction. *Science, 290*(5500), 2319–2323. doi:10.1126/science.290.5500.2319 PMID:11125149

Zald, D. H., & Pardo, J. V. (1997). Emotion, olfaction, and the human amygdala: Amygdala activation during aversive olfactory stimulation. *Proceedings of the National Academy of Sciences of the United States of America, 94*(8), 4119–4124. doi:10.1073/pnas.94.8.4119 PMID:9108115

KEY TERMS AND DEFINITIONS

Affective Dimensions: Some researchers are of the view that, emotions are part of a continuum expressed in terms of affective dimensions. These affective dimensions include arousal, valence, and dominance.

Arousal: The tendency of a subject to be relaxed (low arousal) or excited (high arousal).

Bipolar EEG Channel: Generally an EEG amplifier is supplied with two inputs, namely Input 1 and Input 2. The output is the amplified version of Input 1 minus Input 2. Input 2 is often considered as a reference channel like A1 or A2 (placed on the earlobes), depending on whether right hemisphere or left hemisphere electrode is considered respectively. In a bipolar channel, two electrode channels placed on the scalp of the subject are supplied as Input 1 and Input 2 to the amplifier.

Continuous Model of Emotion Nomenclature: In a continuous model of emotion nomenclature, emotions are categorized by a continuum specified by affective dimensions. The Russel's Circumplex Model is one of the oldest and most popular examples of such a model. In this model, emotions are categorized as points on a 2 dimensional plane where the X-axis represents valance and the Y-axis represents arousal.

Discrete Emotion Theory: It views emotions as a set few discrete entities. For example, Paul Ekman's categorization of emotions into six different classes namely fear, happiness, sadness, anger, disgust and surprise, is an example of such a model.

Dominance: The extent to which an emotion is felt from low (low dominance) to high (high dominance)

Electroencephalogram (EEG): It is an amplified recording of the electrical activities of the brain. EEG signals are generated when neurons/ groups of neurons in the brain communicate by generating charged positive/ negative ions. When the push/ pull generated by these charged ions reach the scalp, they can either push or pull the negatively charged ions of the electrode. The difference in the push or pull voltages of any two electrodes can be measured by a voltmeter. This gives rise to the EEG reading. The time varying amplitude of these potentials are continuous and of the order of micro-volts and hence these need to be amplified (to the order of milli-volts) and digitized before these can be considered for computation.

Evoked Brain Rhythms: The electrical activities in the brain which occur after an event and are both times -locked and phase-locked to the event. An example of an event producing evoked potential is odd-ball stimuli (stimuli significant different from naturally occurring stimuli). This is also known as event related potential.

Induced Brain Rhythms: The electrical activities in the brain which occur after an event and may or may not be time-locked (occurring at an approximately same time after the event) but are not phase-locked (occurring at approximately same phase lag after the event). An example of an event producing induced potential is motor imagination. These induced oscillations cannot be extracted by averaging across trials but may be extracted by frequency domain analysis. This is also known as event related synchronization/desynchronisation.

K-Fold Cross Validation: It is a means of generalizing the performance of a statistical test on a given problem. In k-fold cross validation, the labeled data is divided into k sections, among these, k-1 partitions are employed for training and the remaining partition is employed for training. This process is repeated k times, till all the combinations of training and testing data have been tried. A special type of k-fold cross validation is the leave-one-out cross validation, in which the n number of labeled data points are partitioned for n-fold cross validation.

Oscillatory Brain Rhythms: Oscillatory brain rhythms indicate the activity of brain in specific frequency bands (say alpha, beta and so on).

Spontaneous Brain Rhythms: The natural electrical activities which are not related to external stimulations. For example, spontaneous brain rhythms can be recorded during sleep.

Valance: The tendency of a subject to be happy (low arousal) or sad (high arousal).

Chapter 8
EEG Analysis to Decode Tactile Sensory Perception Using Neural Techniques

Anuradha Saha
Jadavpur University, India

Amit Konar
Jadavpur University, India

ABSTRACT

This chapter introduces a novel approach to examine the scope of tactile sensory perception as a possible modality of treatment of patients suffering from certain mental disorder using a Support Vector Machines with kernelized neural network. Experiments are designed to understand the perceptual difference of schizophrenic patients from normal and healthy subjects with respect to three different touch classes, including soft touch, rubbing, massaging and embracing and their three typical subjective responses. Experiments undertaken indicate that for normal subjects and schizophrenic patients, the average percentage accuracy in classification of all the three classes: pleasant/acceptable/unpleasant is comparable with their respective oral responses. In addition, for schizophrenic patients, the percentage accuracy for acceptable class is very poor of the order of below 12%, which for normal subjects is quite high (42%). Performance analysis reveals that the proposed classifier outperforms its competitors with respect to classification accuracy in all the above three classes.

INTRODUCTION

Touch refers to physical contact of a person's skin with any non-living substance or living organisms. Perceiving touch usually depends largely on the subjective experience of people. For example, a baby of two months old can recognize his mother by the way she holds the baby. In this way, touch perception can be considered as one of the most important modality during his development stages (Essick et

DOI: 10.4018/978-1-5225-3129-6.ch008

al., 2010; Gallace & Spence, 2010; McGlone, 2014). The sense of touch is perceived by various tactile receptors, which in general, utilizes *A-beta* fibers to transmit tactile information with extremely rapid speed. In addition, relatively slower *A-delta* and even slower *C* fibers are also used for signal transmission by free nerve endings (Schore, 2005). Receptors gather tactile information during various touch nourishments including soft touch, rubbing or massaging from a relatively larger area of the skin, which causes ambiguity in locating the source of the stimulus. Tactile information (sensation) for each touch nourishments are fed to the spine from the receptors by the nerve endings and then ascend to the brain using the spino-thalamic pathway.

This chapter aims at classifying distinctive touch patterns commonly used in hospitals/health centers to treat physio- and psycho-therapeutic patients from their acquired electro-encephalographic (EEG) signals. It refers to the electrical response of the brain to external stimuli or memory based incidental thought/activity. EEG is usually acquired by specialized electrodes placed on the scalp of human subjects/animals. The acquired signals are pre-processed, filtered and analyzed to decode/classify cognitive tasks undertaken by the subjects. Pre-processing refers to filtering and artifact (noise) removal technique for electroencephalographic (EEG) signals that require a suitable band-pass filter and computational strategies. Artifacts are unwanted spurious pick-ups in signal amplitude, especially due to un-volunteered movements of eye-blinking and/or muscle activation, which appears as noise in the main signal.

Experiments have been performed with both normal (healthy) subjects and schizophrenic patients to determine their level of pleasure in three different types of (non-sexual) touch-nourishments offered by nurses or inmates of the subjects from their cortical responses. The cortical response also shows the variation in blood concentration near the active regions for different types of touch nourishment. Later the degree of nourishment perceived is matched with the oral response of the subject to test the validity of the experimental results obtained from cortical responses.

The fundamental contribution of the present work lies in developing a data-point as well as feature selection algorithm by determining skewness of a hyperplane-based neural network (NN) classifier to classify detected touch modality into levels of pleasure (unpleasant, acceptable and pleasant). Since, like any other patterns, an EEG signal too is described by its features, feature extraction and selection, therefore are considered as the important steps in touch perception. Here, authors select well-known EEG features such as time- (Hjorth parameters (Vourkas et al., 2000), Adaptive autoregressive parameters (Schlögl et al., 1997), frequency- (Power spectral density, or in short PSD (Stoica & Moses, 1997), and time-frequency (Discrete wavelet transform, or in short DWT (Panda et al., 2010). Approximate entropy (Srinivasan et al., 2007) domain to extract features from acquired EEG signal depending on the touch nourishments provided. It is important to mention here that classifying tactile information has always been a serious pattern classification problem, and sometimes, computationally complex feature generates a very high dimensional feature space which may contain both relevant and redundant features. The presence of redundant features adversely affects the performance of the classifier in terms of accuracy and time complexity. Feature selection hence aims at reducing the dimension of the feature set by retaining only the most relevant features and rejecting the rest.

Besides classifier, other important coverage of the chapter includes defining *degree of pleasure perceived* (DPP) (Saha et al., 2015) by a subject based on the EEG feature estimates, and comparing the measured DPP with subjective assignments by the patients. Moreover, DPP measure for pleasant touch, as perceived by the subjects, is used to select the best-performing and hence most appropriate nurse to serve the patient. Lastly, authors compare the classification accuracy of the proposed classifier with the listed classifiers after application of touch therapy and observe that the proposed classifier correctly classifies the touch as pleasant/acceptable/unpleasant.

The rest of the chapter is organized as follows. In section 2, authors present preliminaries of certain standard techniques that are useful in understanding the rest of the chapter. Section 3 provides a literature survey of recent advancement in touch perception. In section 4, authors provide physiological interfaces required for touch classification. Section 5 offers techniques for feature extraction. In section 6, authors provide techniques for data-point selection, feature selection, and feature ranking. Section 7 presents a brief discussion about decoding of tactile perception. In section 8, authors propose the relationship between the degree of pleasure perceived and its ranking as pleasant/acceptable/unpleasant. Experimental results obtained are presented in section 9. Future research direction is provided in section 10 and conclusions are listed in section 11.

Literature Survey

The existing researches that motivated the authors to classify touch-nourishments and metric-design are listed below:

- **M. Peltoranta and G. Pfurtscheller, 1994:** This paper reports the classification accuracy of EEG responses, as collected one second prior to movement of the right or left index finger. The performance of various well-known classifiers including self-organising feature map, learning vector quantizer, K-mean and the back-propagation neural net is compared, where, concatenated spatial and temporal information from EEG electrodes and time incidents respectively during hand imagery are considered as feature vectors for classification. In addition, power values within the extended alpha-band (5-16 Hz) are extracted using autoregressive model and are used as EEG features, which provide around 85-90% classification accuracies, when used the aforesaid classifiers.
- **T. Nakamura, Y. Tomita, S. I. Ito, and Y. Mitsukura, 2010:** This paper deals with the classification of touch-sensation from human EEG signals, when a person touches objects. Fast Fourier transform (FFT) is used to extract significant features from the acquired EEG signals, whereas factor analysis and artificial neural network (ANN) are utilized for multiclass classification and rating of touch sensation. The fast determination of weight and bias of the ANN is performed by particle swarm optimization(PSO) algorithm.
- **H. Singh, M. Bauer, W. Chowanski, Y. Sui, D. Atkinson, S. Baurley, M. Fry, J. Evans and N. Bianchi-Berthouze, 2014:** This paper explores the relation between the degree of pleasantness perceived from touch sensation and the EEG power from the significant brain regions. Experiments are performed to determine electrophysiological correlates of affective sensation during tactile caressing of the right forearm using pleasant and unpleasant textile fabrics. Later, it has been experimentally found that the degree of pleasantness has a positive correlation with the beta power increase in the parietal, temporal and frontal regions. There is significant discrimination in beta power around somatosensory cortex of the right hemisphere during pleasant and unpleasant stimulations when using single trial classification technique.

- **M. Bauer, R. Oostenveld, M. Peeters and P. Fries, 2006:** This paper deals with brain-activities primarily in the somatosensory cortex during tactile stimulation. The experiment reveals that after tactile stimulation, there exists significant increase in high-frequency gamma band power around primary somatosensory cortex, whereas suppression in alpha and beta band power around parieto-occipital cortex.

- **M. Feurra, W. Paulus, V. Walsh and R. Kanai, 2011:** In this paper, the association between mu-band power suppression and tactile stimulation over the somatosensory cortex is observed. In order to do so, experiments are performed to check whether transcranial alternating current stimulation around the primary somatosensory cortex could elicit frequency-dependent tactile sensations in humans. Experiments reveal that stimulation in alpha and high gamma band produces stronger tactile sensation in the contralateral hand, whereas beta stimulation produces the much weaker effect. These findings motivated the authors to study the role of transcranial alternating current stimulation as a powerful online stimulation technique to reveal the causal roles of oscillatory brain activities.

- **C. E. Chapman, 1994:** This paper is based on discrimination of perceptual-abilities for active and passive tactile sensations. In general, active and passive touch, which are associated respectively with and without voluntary movement on the part of the human subject, can be described by tactile discriminations depending on relative differences in inputs. This paper determines the perceptual equivalence for active and passive touch by examining several factors such as reducing the degree of gating, optimally bringing the most sensitive skin areas into contact with the target object, and activating central influences during voluntary movement to enhance performance during active touch.

- **M. Ploner, J. Gross, L. Timmermann and A. Schnitzler, 2002:** This paper deals with the direct comparison between first and second pain-related cortical responses to cutaneous laser stimuli in humans. In general, the first and second pain sensations are two successive and qualitatively distinct sensations evoked by single painful stimuli and sensed by Adelta and C fibers. Experiments reveal that first pain is chiefly related to activation of primary somatosensory cortex, whereas second pain is mainly related to activation of anterior cingulate cortex. In addition, significant observation has been made on the fact that first pain signals carries specific sensory information for an instant withdrawal, whereas second pain involves long-lasting attention, which influences behavioral responses to limit further injury and optimize recovery.

- **E. G. Reed-Geaghan and S. M. Maricich, 2011:** This paper provides a review on the cadre of genes that control specification and differentiation of mechanosensitive neurons and support cells of the skin that mediate different aspects of the sense of touch.

- **F. van Ede, F. de Lange, O. Jensen and E. Maris, 2011:** This paper deals with tactile anticipation in association with the spatial and temporal orientation of attention. There exists past evidence of spatially specific modulations of ongoing oscillations within sensory cortex for spatial orienting of attention. This paper examines the modulating nature of sensorimotor oscillations during tactile anticipation. From experimental findings, a spatially specific contralateral suppression of alpha- and beta-band oscillations is observed within sensorimotor cortex during an upcoming tactile event.

- **S. Chen, C. F. Cowan and P. M. Grant,2009:** This paper deals with an alternative learning procedure for radial basis function neural network based on the orthogonal least-squares method instead of well-known singular-value decomposition technique. This method provides an efficient means for fitting the neural networks, which is later validated for two different signal processing applications.

- **M. Guo, Y. Yu, J. Yang and J. Wu, 2012:** This paper provides a review on crossmodal information processing between visual and tactile sensory systems since there already exists previous studies regarding the mutual effects between visual and tactile perception. This paper highlights the two stages of the integration, such as combination and integration.

- **Q. Wu, C. Li, S. Takahashi, and J. Wu, 2012:** This paper deals with a review of neural networks involved in attention-related tasks, mainly visual and tactile attention-related brain networks. Two types of attention-related brain structure are discussed in this paper; one is the top-down structure that includes intraparietal sulcus/superior parietal lobe- ventral frontal cortex. The other is the bottom-up structure that includes temporoparietal junction-ventral frontal cortex. It is found that both visual and tactile attention-related brain networks are similar to each other.

KEY TERMS

Following is the list of terms that has been used in the subsequent sections of this chapter.

- **Power Spectral Density-Power Spectral Density (PSD):** One of the most popular features extraction methods, called PSD, may be defined as a mode of describing the power distribution contained in the signal. PSD evaluates the power density for filtered EEG recordings. Mathematically, PSD is defined as a Fourier Transform of the autocorrelation sequence of the time series, which is given in (1).

$$EEg(f) = \int_{t_1}^{t_2} eeg(t)e^{-2\pi ft}dt \qquad (1)$$

$$PSD(f) = 2\frac{\left\|EEG(f)\right\|^2}{(t_2 - t_1)}$$

- **Discrete Wavelet Transform (DWT):** In this chapter, authors have employed the use of wavelet transform as one of the feature extraction methods from their EEG signals. Wavelet Transform (WT) has its obvious advantages over techniques based on time-domain (like Time Domain Parameters (TDP)) or frequency-domain (like Fourier transforms (FT)). Standard Frequency based techniques lack the ability to deal with non-stationary signals because of their inability to deal with non-stationary signals. TDP are unable to quantify frequency related information and

FT is unable to quantify time related information. Also, FT misses local changes in high frequency components since it considers the whole time domain. These drawbacks are overcome by using wavelet transforms (WT) by providing localized frequency related information at a given time. The discrete wavelet transforms (DWT) analyzes the signals at different resolutions by decomposing the signal into coarse approximation and detail information. Each level includes two digital filters and two down-samplers by 2. The down-sampled outputs of the first high-pass and low-pass filters provide the detail D1 and approximation A1, respectively. The first approximation is further decomposed and the process is continued until the desired level of decomposition is obtained.

- **Adaptive Autoregressive Model:** The time-varying characteristics of autoregressive (AR) parameter can be classically estimated with the help of segmentation based approach. In this approach, the information is divided into short segments and the AR parameters are predicted from each segment. The accuracy and resolution time of estimated parameters are determined by their segment length. For AR model, the shorter the segment length, the higher is the time resolution although this can increase error of the AR estimates. On the other hand, the adaptive autoregressive (AAR) algorithm is used to execute the computation with a very less effort. This technique is concurrent to the data acquisition, where buffering is not required and the model has the following form given in (2).

$$y_k = a_{1,k}y_k + \ldots + a_{p,k}y_{k-p} + \varepsilon_k \tag{2}$$

where y_k is EEG time series and $a_{1,k}$, $\ldots\ldots\ldots a_{p,k}$ are time-variant autoregressive parameters. For AAR estimation, the least mean squares (LMS) approach and the recursive least squares (RLS) approaches have been effectively applied for online analysis due to the advantages of AAR model.

- **Hjorth Parameters:** The parameters introduced by Hjorth (1970) are time domain parameters which have three features defined as follows:

$$Activity = \text{var}(x(t)), the\ signal\ power \tag{3}$$

$$Mobility = \sqrt{\frac{Activity\left(\dfrac{dx(t)}{dt}\right)}{Activity(x(t))}}, the\ mean\ frequency \tag{4}$$

$$Complexity = \frac{Mobility\left(\dfrac{dx(t)}{dt}\right)}{Mobility(x(t))} \tag{5}$$

Hjorth parameters are advantageous for checking whether a different number of derivatives of the signal can enhance the classification performance, and hence, the number of derivatives calculated, *p* is needed as a parameter of p_i.

$$p_i(t) = \mathrm{var}\left(\frac{d^i x(t)}{dt^i}\right), i = 0, \ldots, p \qquad (6)$$

- **Approximate Entropy-Approximate Entropy (ApEn):** ApEn is a well-known feature extraction technique based on a statistical method. ApEn measures the unpredictability of fluctuations in a time series and thus can be used to classify complex problems. The advantage of ApEn is that it is robust or insensitive to artifacts. ApEn was initially designed to handle short and noisy time series data and it can detect changes in the underlying episodic behavior which is otherwise not reflected in peak occurrences or amplitudes. The more complex the sequence of data, the larger the value of the corresponding ApEn is.
- **Skewness:** A moment is a precise quantitative measure of the shape of the distribution of a set of data points. The third central moment is skewness which is a measure of lopsideness of the distribution. In probability theory and statistics, skewness (Doane & Seward, 2011; Saha et al., 2015b) is a measure of the asymmetry of the probability distribution of a real-valued random variable about its mean. Let, there are N number of data points $\{x_1, x_2, \ldots, x_n\}$, mean of these data points is μ and the standard deviation is σ, then the skewness for these data points *sk* can be calculated using equation (7).

$$sk = \frac{1}{N}\sum_{i=1}^{N}\left[\frac{x_i - \mu}{\sigma}\right]^3 \qquad (7)$$

There are two types of skewness depending on the density of the data points around its mean, *positive skew* and *negative skew*.

- **Differential Evolution:** Differential Evolution (DE) (Storn & Price, 1997; Das et al., 2009) has gained enough popularity in the last decades because of its simplicity and efficiency. It is the most widely used evolutionary algorithm due to its inherent merits of low computational overhead, requirement of fewer control parameters and above all its high accuracy. The stages of DE, initialization, mutation, crossover, selection, are discussed in brief.

Let, differential evolution (DE) be used to optimize the value of *(a₃, b₃)* by using F_k as the fitness function. The optimized values of (a₃, b₃) are selected when F_k reaches local minima for a given stopping criteria. The parameters selection in the DE algorithm for this study are as follows: scaling factor (F) = 10, population size (NP) = 50, crossover ratio (Cr) = 0.8, maximum number of generations = 10000, stopping criteria = same fitness over 20 generations.

DE starts with a population of *NP* *D*-dimensional parameter vectors representing the candidate solutions which in this case are a set of different trajectories. Let us denote the subsequent generations in DE by $G = 0, 1, ..., G_{max}$. Then, authors can represent the ith vector of the population at the current generation as $\vec{X}_{i,G} = \left[x_{1,i,G}, x_{2,i,G}, ..., x_{D,i,G} \right]$.

Initialization

The initial population (at *G=0*) covers the entire search space by uniformly randomizing individuals within the search space controlled by the prescribed minimum and maximum bounds:

$$\vec{X}_{min} = \left[x_{1,min}, x_{2,min}, ..., x_{D,min} \right], and$$
$$\vec{X}_{max} = \left[x_{1,max}, x_{2,max}, ..., x_{D,max} \right] \tag{8}$$

Hence the jth component of the ith vector is initialized as

$$x_{j,i,0} = x_{j,min} + rand_{i,j}\left(0,1\right).\left(x_{j,max} - x_{j,min}\right) \tag{9}$$

where $rand_{i,j}\left(0,1\right)$ is a uniformly distributed random number lying between 0 and 1 and is independent of each component of the ith vector. The following steps are taken next: mutation, crossover, and selection (in that order), which are discussed below.

Mutation

After initialization, DE creates a donor vector $\vec{V}_{i,G}$ corresponding to each population member $\vec{X}_{i,G}$ in the current generation through mutation "DE/rand/1" technique, which is defined as

$$\vec{V}_{i,G} = \vec{X}_{r_1^i,G} + F.\left(\vec{X}_{r_2^i,G} - \vec{X}_{r_3^i,G}\right) \tag{10}$$

The indices r_1^i, r_2^i and r_3^i are mutually exclusive integers randomly chosen from the range [1, *NP*], and all are different from the base index *i* and $\vec{X}_{best,G}$ is the vector with the best fitness in the population at generation *G*.

Crossover

The donor vector interchanges its components with the target vector $\vec{X}_{i,G}$ under this operation using a binomial crossover. In this operation, the exchange is performed $\vec{X}_{i,G}$ for each of the *D* variables whenever a randomly picked number between 0 and 1 is less than or equal to the *Cr* value. The scheme may be outlined as

$$u_{j,i,G} = \begin{cases} v_{j,i,G}, & if\ rand_{i,j}\left(0,1\right) \leq Cr\ or\ j = j_{rand} \\ x_{j,i,G}, & otherwise \end{cases} \qquad (11)$$

where $rand_{i,j}\left(0,1\right) \in \left[0,1\right]$ is a uniformly distributed random number lying between 0 and 1 and is independent for each jth component of the ith vector. $j_{rand} \in \left[1,2,...,D\right]$ is a randomly chosen index, which guarantees that $\vec{U}_{i,G}$ gets at least one component from $\vec{V}_{i,G}$.

Selection

The next step of the algorithm determines whether the target or the trial vector survives to the next generation i.e., at $G = G + 1$. This step keeps the population size constant over subsequent generations. This selection operation is described as follows:

$$u_{j,i,G} = \begin{cases} \vec{U}_{i,G}, & if\ f\left(\vec{U}_{i,G}\right) \leq f\left(\vec{X}_{i,G}\right) \\ \vec{X}_{i,G}, & if\ f\left(\vec{U}_{i,G}\right) > f\left(\vec{X}_{i,G}\right) \end{cases} \qquad (12)$$

where, $f\left(\vec{X}\right)$ is the function to be minimized. Now, if the new trial vector yields an equal or lower value of the fitness function, it replaces the corresponding target vector in the next generation or else the target is retained in the population. Thus, the population either gets better or remains the same but it never deteriorates.

The above processes are repeated until a maximum number of generations is reached.

PHYSIOLOGICAL INTERFACE

This section introduces the basic scheme for touch classification from the acquired EEG signals of the subject.

System Overview

Figure 1 provides an overview of touch perception by EEG-analysis. Here, a person (subject) experiences one out of four touch nourishments (i.e., massaging) from a nurse while her brain signal is recorded using a stand-alone EEG system, manufactured by Nihon Cohden. After perceiving the touch nourishment, EEG signals are first pre-processed (filtered) to keep it free from artifacts due to eye-blinking and spurious pick-ups of line noise. The filtered data are sent for feature extraction (FE) to extract the basic primitives of the original signal. After FE, it has been found that all the trial instances and the samples for a particular touch stimulus are not equally essential. To identify the right data-point and samples useful for subsequent classification, authors here employ skewness for performing the first data-point selection and then feature selection (FS).

Figure 1. An overview of touch perception by EEG analysis
FE: Feature extraction, DPS: Data-point selection, FS: Feature selection

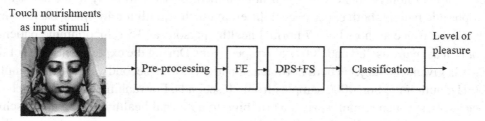

In general, data-point selection refers to the process of deriving a unique set of features from a set of data-points for a particular class *k,* by identifying the commonality among the feature vectors, (hereafter called data-points) obtained over multiple experimental trials of the same subject with the same stimulus. On the other hand, FS refers to the process of removing irrelevant and redundant features and selecting a small set of informative features that are necessary and sufficient for good classification. It is one of the key factors affecting the success of a classification algorithm. Here, at first, it selects the most useful features from the ideal class-representative. This is performed by maximizing inter-class variance and minimizing intra-class variance. It means, for an ideal class-representative, only those features are retained which have high discrimination value among different touch nourishments. Here, Differential evolution (DE) has been applied to optimally select fewer, i.e., *d* out of *D* (where *d<<D*) a number of significant tactile features that correctly classify the different touch nourishments. Second, an optimal number of EEG feature types (such as power spectral density, discrete wavelet transform and so on) is selected among the different feature extraction techniques for reduced EEG feature sets. Finally, the selected feature vector for each class is applied for classification using radial basis function (RBF) induced back propagation neural network (BPNN). A brief description of each building block is presented in the following sections.

EEG Signal Acquisitions

EEG signals are acquired from both normal subjects and schizophrenic patients with alpha-power asymmetry. These patients are selected based on the level of their asymmetry, detected by functional Near Infrared Spectroscopy (f-NIRS) machines in a different experiment. The details of this experiment are dropped here to avoid discussing issues out of the main context.

The experimental framework includes a 21 channel EEG machine (manufactured by Nihon Kohden), 5 nurses and 12 subjects (7 normal healthy subjects and 5 schizophrenic patients) in the age group of 20-32. Out of 21 channels, authors use channels F_3, F_4, F_7, F_8, P_3, P_4, P_z, C_3 and C_4 channels from frontal, parietal and somato-sensory cortex of the subject's scalp in conventional 10-20 EEG electrode-placement system. The parietal electrodes offer a good resolution in a textural pattern of the touched surface. Prefrontal and frontal electrodes are responsible for "the emotional (feeling component)" of touch. The somato-sensory cortex electrodes offer the tactile sensation as a measure of mu-suppression and beta-band power while touching the subject's skin (Crone et al., 1998; Cheyne et al., 2003).

The EEG system has a sampling rate of 200 Hz with a signal resolution of 100µV. Four distinct touch nourishments, including soft touch, rubbing, embracing and massaging are applied as the stimuli of touch nourishment for the experimental subjects. An experiment comprises 4 trials, where each trial refers to one specific touch nourishment. For touch nourishment classification by a normal healthy person and a schizophrenic patient, both experience 4 different touch stimuli for 40 times, each stimulus being given for 10 times. Since authors have 7 normal healthy persons and 5 schizophrenic patients; authors altogether obtain as many as 280 and 200 trials respectively. During the experiment, each of three touch nourishments is given to a subject (both normal and patient) for 20 seconds. Being the sampling rate of EEG of 200 Hz, authors obtain 4000 samples from 20 seconds. For ranking of nurses, each of 5 nurses provides one specific touch stimulus, such as rubbing to a normal healthy person and a schizophrenic patient both for 10 times, i.e., for all touch nourishments given by a single nurse, total number of input stimuli is 40 for both normal healthy person and a schizophrenic patient.

EEG Signal Preprocessing

After data acquisition, pre-processing is the next primary concern for classification of different touch nourishments. Pre-processing of a signal is required to improve the signal to noise ratio (SNR) with the help of filtering and artifact removals, which simplifies detection and classifying tasks. In order to perform this, filtering of EEG signal within the suitable frequency bands is necessary. The aim of this experiment is two-fold. First is the selection of appropriate filter to clean the raw EEG signal; and second is the selection of pass-band frequency of the chosen filter. The first problem has been taken care by designing four common infinite impulse response (IIR) filter realizations including Butterworth, Chebyshev type-1 and type-2, and elliptic. Authors here consider four competitive filters: Butterworth of order 6, Chebyshev type-1 and type-2 of order 4, and elliptic filter of order 4 and finally select the last one based on its merit and authors' previous knowledge of using it (Saha et al., 2014; Saha et al., 2015a). It has already been observed that among the above four IIR filters, elliptic filter obtains the sharpest roll-off and good attenuation in stop band ripples for varied filter order.

The second problem has been solved by filtering the acquired EEG signals by the selected elliptic band pass filter having a suitable band pass frequencies. Since the present problem itself has the novelty; authors decide to observe the frequency response of the acquired EEG signal from 0.5 to 30 Hz comprising delta (0.5-3 Hz), theta (3-7 Hz), alpha (7-13 Hz) and beta (13-30 Hz). Figure 2(a) presents raw EEG signals for two touch nourishments: massage and rubbing, and Figure 2(b) provides the filtered EEG response for the above two touch nourishments. It is observed from Figure 2(b) that filtered EEG signal response possesses its higher magnitude in the frequency range of 3-18 Hz. Hence, authors can confirm that the prominent features of touch nourishment are present in the EEG signals within the range of 3-18 Hz.

FEATURE EXTRACTION

Features of a pattern are best defined by its basic primitives that represent the original pattern in time-, frequency- and/or time-frequency domain. In the present chapter, frequency domain features including power spectral density (PSD) offer information about the power spectrum of an EEG signal during various kinds of touch stimuli. Besides PSD, time-domain features including adaptive autoregressive parameters (AAR), time-frequency analysis such as discrete wavelet transform (DWT), Hjorth parameter and approximate entropy (ApEn) provide both temporal and spatial information of EEG signals during the experiment.

Figure 2a. Raw EEG signals for two touch nourishments: massage and rubbing

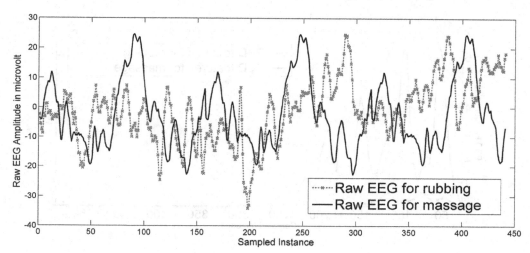

Figure 2b. Filtered EEG response for two touch nourishments: massage and rubbing

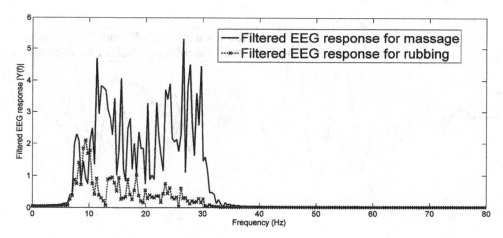

After feature extraction, authors obtain 513 PSD features, 2004 wavelet coefficients (approximate coefficient), 3 Hjorth parameters, 99 AAR parameters and 1 ApEn coefficient.

Figure 3 shows a plot of PSD features and Figure 4 presents a plot of DWT features respectively extracted from a patient for altogether for 50 trials for two touch nourishments: massage and rubbing. From Figure 4, it is confirmed that few out of 513 PSD features, such as 5th, 12th, 55th and 58th provide prominent feature level discrimination.

In the case of Figure 4, feature level discriminations seem to be difficult only by observing the extracted approximate coefficient, since the dimension of the features is very high, i.e., 2004. To deal with the problem, authors need to select only significant features from the high dimensional feature sets. Moreover, to obtain one single data-point as a representative of one specific touch nourishment class and to reduce computational complexity, authors perform reduction in data-points (experimental trials). A combined strategy for data-point and feature selection is described in next section.

Figure 3. PSD features extracted for two distinct touch nourishments: massage and rubbing

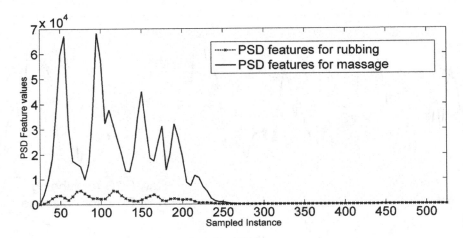

Figure 4. Approximate wavelet coefficient features extracted for two distinct touch nourishments: massage and rubbing

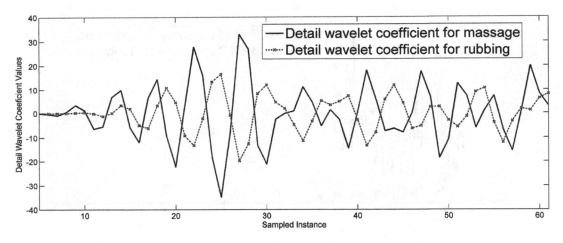

DATA-POINT AND FEATURE SELECTION STRATEGY

This section addresses a novel approach of data-point reduction and feature selection, and ranking of features to classify motor imagery signals. Here, the method is two-fold. First is to determine the skewness sk of the hyper-plane-based neural network for selecting one unique class-representative (data-point) from each type of extracted EEG feature set for which the hyper-plane carries wider margin. The skewness of each feature vector for a class is considered as the objective function of Differential evolution (DE) algorithm, where each feature vector represents a chromosome. The optimal solution of DE provides a feature vector, from which d- the number of features lying closer to the mean has been selected. Second is to rank all the different feature types and after ranking, feature values of each feature type are updated by multiplying them with the rank of that corresponding feature type.

Combined Strategy for Data-Point Selection and Feature Selection

Data point selection/reduction is an important issue in EEG based classification problem in order to select one unique class-representative from a large set of data points (trials). Here, authors too attempt to determine one unique representative for each touch-nourishment class by determining skewness for classification of different touch stimuli using different types of EEG features. EEG signals, being non-deterministic by nature, does not offer the unique features extracted from several trials of the EEG signals captured from the same subject for the same stimulus. Therefore, authors need to identify the ideal class representative of each data point representing a feature vector of fixed dimension. Let, for each touch stimulus, a set $A_k = \left\{ \vec{X}_{i,j}, \vec{X}_{i,j}, ..., \vec{X}_{i,j} \right\}$ is obtained for each type of EEG feature set, where, $i = \{1, 2, \cdots, N\}$ be data-points and $j = \{1, 2, \cdots, D\}$ be the features. Let there be K number of classes, i.e., k lies in $[1, K]$. Here by determining skewness, authors reduce A_k by identifying the representative data point $\vec{}_{,k}$ of dimension $1 \times D$ for each class $k = 1$ to K. Determining skewness for all features of all the classes results in an increase in the margin of the hyperplane. A DE algorithm is used to maximize the skew value for Class$_1$ while minimizing the skew value for Class$_2$.

After obtaining a reduced feature vector (data-point) $\vec{X}_i^N$ of dimension $1 \times D$, d out of D a number of features, which are closest to the mean of $\vec{X}_i^N$, are selected from $\vec{X}_i^N$. The selection is based on determining the Euclidean distance $\vec{d}_i$ of feature values corresponding to ideal data point $\vec{X}_i^N$ from its mean.

Feature Ranking

Let there are m number of different types of EEG features. There is a priority vector $\vec{P}$ of length m where $\{p_1, p_2, ... p_m\}$ are the data elements of the vector $\vec{P}$. These data elements $p_1, p_2, ... p_m$ are the rank/priority of each EEG feature types. The selected feature values of each feature type are scaled by the rank of that feature type and these scaled features will be fed to the classifier for training and testing. Let the length of the test data set is n_t. Then the objective function, as given in (13) is to be minimized (Saha et al., 2015b). Ranking of the feature types is confirmed when the difference between fitness values of current trial and the pervious trial has very small value of 0.0001.

$$fit = \sum_{i=1}^{n_t} \left| Actual\ Class(\vec{X}_i) - Obtained\ Class(\vec{X}_i) \right| \tag{13}$$

DECODING OF TACTILE SENSORY PERCEPTION

Tactile perception, as introduced in this chapter, requires designing a suitable classifier capable of classifying touch stimuli into multiple classes with a good level of accuracy. The quality of touch being detrimental to the texture of the contact-surface, movement frequency of the touching organ and temperature-rise of the contact area, is an important issue to influence classifier-performance. In addition,

Algorithm 1. Pseudo code for feature ranking algorithm

Input: Selected feature m number of selected EEG features for all classes (here, Class$_1$ and Class$_2$).

Output: Rank or priority vector of the m EEG feature types.

Step 1: Read values of the control parameters of DE: scale factor F, crossover rate Cr, and the population size NP from the user.

Step 2: Set the generation number $t=0$ and randomly initialize a population of NP chromosome $X_t = \left\{ \vec{P}_1(t), \vec{P}_2(t), \ldots\ldots, \vec{P}_{NP}(t) \right\}$

with

$$\vec{P}_i(t) = \left\{ p_{i,1}(t), p_{i,2}(t), \ldots\ldots, p_{i,m}(t) \right\}$$

for $i = [1, NP]$ individual uniformly distributed in the range, where

$$\vec{P}_{min} = \left[\vec{P}_{min-1}, \vec{P}_{min-2}, \ldots\ldots\ldots, \vec{P}_{min-m} \right]$$

and

$$\vec{P}_{max} = \left[\vec{P}_{max-1}, \vec{P}_{max-2}, \ldots\ldots\ldots, \vec{P}_{max-m} \right].$$

Evaluate $fit(\vec{P}_i(t))$ for chromosome $\vec{P}_i(t)$, $i = [1, NP]$.

Step 3: WHILE the stopping criterion is not satisfied

        DO

                FOR i = 1 to NP //do for each individual sequentially

        Step 3.1 – Mutation: Generate a donor vector $\vec{V}_{i,G} = \left\{ v_{1,i,G}, \ldots, v_{m,i,G} \right\}$ corresponding to the ith target vector $\vec{P}_{i,G}$ via the differential mutation scheme of DE as:

$$\vec{V}_{i,G} = \vec{P}_{r_1^i, G} + F \cdot \left(\vec{P}_{r_2^i, G} - \vec{P}_{r_3^i, G} \right)$$

where r_1^i, r_2^i and r_3^i are three random number between 1 to NP satisfying the condition $r_1^i \neq r_2^i \neq r_3^i$

        Step 3.2 – Crossover: Generate a trial vector $\vec{U}_{i,G} = \left\{ u_{1,i,G}, \ldots, u_{m,i,G} \right\}$

for the ith target vector $\vec{P}_{i,G}$ through binomial crossover in the following way:

$$u_{j,i,G} = \begin{array}{l} v_{j,i,G}, \quad if \left(rand_{i,j}[0,1] \right) \leq Cr \ or \ j = j_{rand} \\ u_{j,i,G}, \quad otherwise \end{array}$$

        Step 3.3 – Selection: Evaluate the trial vector $\vec{U}_{i,G}$

Calculate its fitness value fit ($\vec{U}_{i,G}$) using (7);

        IF $fit(\vec{U}_{i,G}) \leq fit(\vec{P}_{i,G})$

          THEN $\vec{P}_{i,G+1} = \vec{U}_{i,G}$

  ELSE $\vec{P}_{i,G+1} = \vec{P}_{i,G}$.

        END IF

        END FOR

        Step 3.4: Increase the Generation Count G = G + 1 END WHILE

physiological parameters of the subject in contact, the personality, and relation to the person touching the subject also sometimes influence his/her the cortical responses. Designing a suitable classifier capable of classifying touch into three class labels: unpleasant, acceptable, and pleasant, is an important concern for the present application. In order to accomplish this, authors implement well-known support vector machine (SVM) classifier and its different variants for proven performance in two class classification problems and their low computational overhead. The use of kernel function along with SVM is important to design non-linear SVM classifier so that the resulting algorithm fits the maximum-margin hyper-plane in a transformed feature space.

An SVM classifier is the most widely used classifier in BCI research (Lin et al., 2008; Zhong et al., 2008; Li et al., 2011; Costantini et al., 2009; Saha et al., 2015b). Here, along with the construction of an optimized hyperplane, two separate margins are constructed on both sides of the hyperplane from the nearest training points (known as support vectors). Maximizing this margin increase the generalization capability of the classifier and a regularization parameter accommodates outliers and allows error on the training set. Normally, a linear decision boundary enables the SVM to perform classification and it has shown to provide good performance while decoding mental states in BCI problem. Kernelized SVM (KSVM) is employed when we do not have knowledge about the linear separable nature of the data points of two classes. The KSVM attempts to minimize the following cost functional to find an optimal choice of the weight vector **w**. It is given in (14).

$$\Phi(w, \xi, \xi') = \frac{1}{2} w^T w + C \sum_{i=1}^{N} (\xi_i + \xi_i') \tag{14}$$

where for $i=1$ to N the following constraints should hold.

$$d_i - w^T \Phi(x_i) \leq \varepsilon + \xi_i,$$

$$w^T \Phi(x_i) - d_i \leq \varepsilon + \xi_i',$$

$$\xi_i \geq 0 \text{ and } \xi_i' \geq 0,$$

In the above formulation, $\{(\mathbf{x}_i, d_i)\}$ for $i=1,2,\ldots N$ are the training samples with x_i being the input pattern for the i-th example and d_i is the target class label +1 or -1. Slack variable ξ_i and ξ_i' represent ε-insensitive loss function (Hykin & Lippmann, 1994) and

$$\Phi(x_i) = \left[\Phi_0(x_i) \Phi_1(x_i) \Phi_{m_1}(x_i) \right],$$

whose $\{ \Phi_j(x_i) \}$ for j=0 to m_1 denote a set of non-linear basis function. Estimation of ε-insensitive loss function is important to enable SVM to overcome the over-fitting problem of BPNN. w is the

m_1-dimensional unknown weight vector, and C is a user-defined positive parameter. Here, $K(\boldsymbol{x}, \boldsymbol{x}_i) = \boldsymbol{\Phi}^T(\boldsymbol{x})\boldsymbol{\Phi}(\boldsymbol{x}_i)$ is an inner product kernel.

Since the proposed method is applicable for all hyper-plane based neural network, LSVM and SVM along with four popular kernel functions (Schölkopf, B. & Smola, 2002) including linear, Gaussian radial basis function (Labate et al., 2013), homogeneous polynomial and hyperbolic tangent (Cristianini & Shawe-Taylor, 2000) are selected for decoding of tactile perception. Eq. (15)-(18) present the kernel functions of SVM used in this chapter.

1.   1. Linear function:

$$K(\boldsymbol{x}, \boldsymbol{x}_i) = (1 + \boldsymbol{x}^T \boldsymbol{x}_i) \tag{15}$$

2.   2. Gaussian radial basis function:

$$K(\boldsymbol{x}, \boldsymbol{x}_i) = \exp\left(-\gamma \left\| \boldsymbol{x} - \boldsymbol{x}_i \right\|^2 / 2\sigma^2\right) for \ \gamma > 0, \sigma = 0.75 \ and \ C = 1 \tag{16}$$

3.   3. Homogeneous polynomial function:

$$K(\boldsymbol{x}, \boldsymbol{x}_i) = (1 + \boldsymbol{x}^T \boldsymbol{x}_i)^l, \ \text{where, } l = number\ of\ polynomials\ (here=2), \tag{17}$$

4.   4. Hyperbolic tangent:

$$K(\boldsymbol{x}, \boldsymbol{x}_i) = \tanh\left(K\boldsymbol{x} \cdot \boldsymbol{x}_i + C\right) \in K < 0 \ and \ C > 0 \tag{18}$$

FOR DEGREE OF PLEASURE PERCEIVED

This section provides a method of calculating the degree of pleasure perceived (*DPP*) by a patient in presence of particular touch nourishment to him/her. The degree of pleasure perceived by k-th patient due to nourishment provided by j-th nurse is presented in (19).

$$Deviation^{j,k} = \sum_{\forall i} \sum_{\forall F_i^j} \left| F_i^j - F_i^{best} \right|^k \tag{19}$$

Here, i denotes a particular type of touch and F_i^{best} is the best feature for a given class of touch nourishment provided to a subject irrespective of any nurses.

The percentage measure of the normalized degree of pleasure perceived by k-th patient due to nourishment provided by j-th nurse is given by (20).

$$DPP = \left(1 - \frac{Deviation^{j,k}}{\sum\limits_{\forall i} \sum\limits_{\forall features} F_i^{best}}\right) \times 100\% \tag{20}$$

Now, the degree of pleasure perceived is utilized to set fuzzy membership variables for three distinct pleasure labels, Pleasant, Acceptable and Unpleasant. Here, we consider triangular membership functions and define fuzzy sets for the above three pleasure labels as follows:

$$D_{PLEASANT}(pleasure\,; 60, 80, 100)\,,$$

$$D_{ACCEPTABLE}(pleasure\,; 30, 45, 60)\,, \text{ and}$$

$$D_{UNPLEASANT}(pleasure\,; 0, 15, 30)\,.$$

EXPERIMENTAL RESULTS

This section provides the experimental findings by performing a number of experiments as described in the following sections.

Using the Proposed Data-Point and Feature Selection Algorithm

This section presents a comparative study of classifier performance usingthe proposed data-point and feature selection strategy and that by using well-known Principal component analysis (PCA) (Smith, 2002). The confusion matrices of average classification accuracies of different touch nourishments using the above techniques are presented in Table 1. It is clear from Table 1 that the proposed data-point and feature selection technique altogether provides better classification accuracies (more than 88%) as compared to that of PCA for all touch nourishment stimuli.

Table 1. Confusion matrices of touch nourishment classification using the proposed data-point and feature selection technique and Principal Component Analysis

		Predicted Class Using Proposed Technique				Predicted Class Using PCA			
		Soft Touch	Rubbing	Massaging	Embracing	Soft Touch	Rubbing	Massaging	Embracing
Actual Class	**Soft Touch**	**92.77**	1.11	1.66	2.77	**80.77**	6.11	4.66	8.77
	Rubbing	1.11	**90.55**	4.33	5.00	7.33	**82.5**	5.33	4.77
	Massaging	2.00	5.33	**88.00**	4.55	10.33	4.77	**78.33**	6.77
	Embracing	3.88	5.22	1.22	**90.00**	8.88	4.22	7.22	**80.00**

Ranking of EEG Features

This section provides the ranking for all EEG feature types for tactile sensory perception. After initializing with a random ranking for all feature types, DE has automatically updated their ranking as the classification accuracies have been found better for *NP* number of populations offered for all given trials (here, 30). The final rank has been obtained if the fitness function, i.e., the classification accuracy of classifiers is optimized. An EEG feature type is selected if it has been found to possess higher ranking in the rank vector for optimized classification accuracy obtained from a particular classifier. Table 2 presents EEG feature type selection through ranking, as the average classification accuracies for different touch nourishment stimuli using LSVM) is given in column 7of Table 2. Table 2 reveals that for each touch nourishment, PSD and DWT features hold the top two rank values, and hence these two are selected as the most promising EEG features for decoding touch nourishment during tactile perception.

Classifier Performance

This section provides the classification accuracies of four standard neural network classifier including LSVM, SVM-RBF, SVM-polynomial and SVM-hyperbolic after data-point and feature selection. The classification accuracies are obtained after performing 10-fold classification, where, 9 out of 10 fold is used for training and the remaining fold is applied for validation. Table 3 lists the average classification accuracies for all four classifiers during testing of four touch nourishments: Soft touch, Rubbing, Massaging and Embracing, where the highest average classification accuracy for DWT and SVM-RBF as the best feature-classifier pair is marked in bold.

Table 2. Selection of EEG features from their rank values to obtain optimal classification accuracy

Touch Nourishments	Rank of Features					Average Classification Accuracy (%)
	PSD	DWT	Hjorth	ApEn	AAR	
Soft Touch	**0.49**	**0.37**	0.03	0.08	0.03	88.00%
Rubbing	**0.53**	**0.33**	0.02	0.07	0.05	87.53%
Massaging	**0.48**	**0.32**	0.04	0.09	0.07	90.03%
Embracing	**0.55**	**0.31**	0.03	0.07	0.04	89.07%

Validation of Subject-Defined Class Label

This section provides the validation of the subject-defined class labels (unpleasant, acceptable and pleasant) with feature vectors obtained for that class label from multiple experimental instances. This is undertaken by computing the similarity in the patterns of the same class, measured by the Euclidean norm of each feature vector with respect to the class mean, obtained by component-wise averaging of the feature vectors in each class. If the Euclidean norm of the furthest feature vector with respect to the mean is very small (of the order of 0.001 or less), authors accept that the class labels have parity with the observed feature distributions.

Table 3. Average classification accuracies of testing data for four touch nourishments using PSD and DWT features and variants of neural network classifiers

Touch Nourishments	EEG Features	Classifiers			
		LSVM	SVM-Hyperbolic	SVM-Polynomial	SVM-RBF
Soft Touch	PSD	64.83 (0.041435)	73.15 (0.039964)	84.57 (0.025303)	90.48 (0.012898)
	DWT	60.45 (0.057424)	70.44 (0.031111)	80.36 (0.022429)	**93.05 (0.014978)**
Rubbing	PSD	66.11 (0.049244)	75.00 (0.035146)	89.55 (0.017868)	90.44 (0.013721)
	DWT	62.74 (0.045524)	72.22 (0.07289)	86.33 (0.011079)	**93.11 (0.013281)**
Massaging	PSD	71.77 (0.055172)	73.44 (0.042126)	84.77 (0.033340)	90.55 (0.011700)
	DWT	65.44 (0.068212)	76.22 (0.05946)	80.55 (0.018120)	**92.77 (0.012549)**
Embracing	PSD	72.22 (0.056788)	78.00 (0.041941)	86.55 (0.036689)	90.33 (0.013261)
	DWT	71.22 (0.062178)	77.33 (0.055521)	83.11 (0.042959)	**93.55 (0.012931)**

To determine the percentage accuracies of touch nourishments according to the *DPP* (pleasant/acceptable/unpleasant) from both subjective oral and EEG responses of healthy persons and schizophrenic patients, first, we determine the DPP in percentage for each of four touch nourishments: Soft Touch, Rubbing, Massaging and Embracing; and depending on the estimated DPP, the class labels are confirmed. For example, if DPP for a given touch nourishment lies between 0-30%, the class of that touch nourishment is labeled as UNPLEASANT and so on, as the fuzzy membership grades of each class are defined in section 8. Next, we accumulate all the responses (oral and EEG) from the healthy person and the patient for all four kinds of touch nourishments. It has been observed that percentage of accuracy for classifying all touch nourishments from 5 nurses as pleasant/acceptable is quite high for healthy persons, in comparison to the patients. Table 4 provides the percentage classification accuracy of the realization made by a healthy person and a patient when all 4 touch nourishments are provided by 5 nurses.

After a careful analysis from Table 4, it is observed that unlike healthy person, for patient, most of the touch nourishments are classified as pleasant/unpleasant, thus realizing the fact that the degree of membership for these two feelings is quite higher than that of acceptable class. For schizophrenic patients, the percentage accuracy for the acceptable class is very poor of the order of below 12%, which for normal subjects is quite high (42%). On the contrary, for schizophrenic patients, the percentage accuracy for the unpleasant class is higher and having the order of below 26%, in comparison to the normal subjects (of the order 6%). It is also confirmed that the average percentage accuracy in classification of all the three classes: pleasant/acceptable/unpleasant is comparable with their respective oral responses.

Table 4. Touch nourishment classification in accordance to %DPP by averaging over 5 nurses

Subject	Type of Nourishments	Average Percentage (%) Accuracy of Nourishment Subclass					
		Pleasant		Acceptable		Unpleasant	
		From Oral Response	From EEG	From Oral Response	From EEG	From Oral Response	From EEG
One healthy (normal)	Soft Touch/ Massaging/ Rubbing/ Embracing	47%	53%	43%	42%	10%	5%
One schizophrenic patient	Soft Touch/ Massaging/ Rubbing/ Embracing	68%	64%	8%	12%	26%	24%

Ranking of Nurses from EEG Responses of Patients

This experiment attempts to select the best-performing nurse for the psychotherapeutic (schizophrenic) patients when the patients perceive pleasant touch from any subject. The rank of a nurse is computed from the DPP measure, averaged over all subjects by the pleasant touch (Saha et al., 2015a).

During this experiment, each nurse is advised to provide all three kinds of pleasant touch nourishments to all schizophrenic patients and F_i^{best} for a given class of touch, nourishment has been calculated irrespective of any nurses. Based on the deviation of the features extracted from the k-th patient for the nourishments given by j-th nurse, the degree of pleasure perceived by the patient k, (DPP^k) is obtained. Table 5 presents deviation, DPP^k measure, and ranking of five nurses for a given subject S_k. To compute a rank, authors sorted two entries of Table 5: nurse number, and DPP^k measure, and sort the list of entries in descending order of the DPP^k measure. The last column in Table 5 provides the computed rank of individual nurse. The best-performing nurse with rank 1 is given in bold.

Decoding of Tactile Perception (Pleasant/Acceptable and Unpleasant) Based on Classifier Performance

In this section, the performance of all classifiers is compared for decoding the tactile perception i.e., Pleasant/Unpleasant and Acceptable for all touch nourishment stimuli, when applied in presence of PSD

Table 5. Ranking of nurses based on degree of pleasure perceived from pleasant touch nourishment

Nurse	F_i^{best}	$Deviation^k$	DPP^k (%)	Rank
1	7.3256	0.5920	91.34	3
2		0.2148	**96.94**	**1**
3		0.3915	94.71	2
4		0.8594	87.28	5
5		0.7227	90.23	4

and DWT features. For offline training, a ten-fold cross-validation technique has been implemented using 480 trials over healthy and schizophrenic patients, where nine-folds are used for training, and the remaining fold is used for validation purpose. The result of the online testing is tabulated in Table 6, where SVM-RBF outperforms the rest in presence of both feature sets.

Classifier Validation Using Mc'Nemar Test

McNemar's Test (McKetta, 1976) has been applied to determine the performance of two classification algorithms for correct classification of the feature vectors. Here, authors define a null hypothesis suggesting that the two algorithms A and B should have a same error rate, i.e., $n_{01} = n_{10}$, where n_{01} be the number of examples misclassified by A but not by B and n_{10} be the number of examples misclassified by B but not by A (vide Table 7). Let f_A and f_B are classifiers' output obtained by algorithms A and B respectively when both the algorithms run on a common training dataset. Authors now define a statistic as χ^2 with 1 degree of freedom, called Z scores, which is given by (21).

$$Z = \frac{\left(\left|n_{01} - n_{10}\right| - 1\right)^2}{n_{01} + n_{10}} \tag{21}$$

Table 6. Mean classifier accuracy and statistical significance of testing data along with feature sets

Features	Pleasure Level	Percentage Classifier Accuracy (in %) for				Statistical Significance
		LSVM	SVM-Hyperbolic	SVM-Polynomial	SVM-RBF	
PSD	Pleasant	77.4	76.2	85.48	**90.45**	t=51.4890 standard error of difference=0.002
	Acceptable	78.64	81.08	86.56	**92.29**	
	Unpleasant	82.52	81.12	87.52	**94.04**	
DWT	Pleasant	77.44	82.08	86.20	**90.92**	t = 9.9720 standard error of difference=0.007
	Acceptable	82.08	83.76	87.56	**94.08**	
	Unpleasant	83.04	84.56	89.92	**96.98**	

Table 7. Statistical comparison of classifiers using McNemar's Test

Reference Algorithm: SVM-RBF				
Classifier Algorithm Used for Comparison Using Desired Features d=50	Parameters Used for McNemar Test		Z	p
	n_{01}	n_{10}		
LSVM	210	354	36.2570	p< 0.00001
SVM-Hyperbolic	196	277	13.5306	p< 0.00001
SVM-Polynomial	180	254	12.2788	p< 0.00001

At the end of the test, the Z scores will indicate whether the null hypothesis is accepted and the alternative hypothesis is rejected or vice-versa.

Authors evaluate Z which denotes the comparator statistic of misclassification between the DE-hybridized recurrent network-based classification algorithm (Algorithm: A) and any one of the competitor algorithms (Algorithm: B) for the Indian dataset for the desired number of features equal to 20. The hypothesis is rejected if $Z > \chi^2_{1,0.95} = 3.841459$, which indicates that the probability of the null hypothesis is correct only to a level of 5% of error for two-tailed chi-square test and so, authors reject it. It is apparent from Table 7 that SVM-RBF classifier outperforms all its competitors with a wider margin.

FUTURE RESEARCH DIRECTIONS

This chapter indeed provides a significant study on tactile perception, which is an extension of existing research work (Saha et al., 2015-a). However, authors believe that the arousal of feelings during touch nourishments (pleasant/acceptable/unpleasant) is associated with the deeper cortical region in the frontal lobe. This motivated the authors to decode tactile perception by using far-near infrared spectroscopy (fNIRs), which will provide the information of subjective feeling during different touch nourishments from their oxy-hemoglobin blood concentration. Therefore, the future research direction would be the study of brain signals as well-as brain maps by using EEG and fNIRs altogether to obtain both temporal and spatial information of schizophrenic patients.

CONCLUSION

This study offers two interesting outcomes for future researchers in brain/cognitive sciences interested in pursuing research on touch perception on patients suffering from schizophrenia. A thorough investigation undertaken reveals one most fundamental aspect of the present research. For normal subjects and schizophrenic patients, the average percentage accuracy in classification of all the three classes: pleasant/acceptable/unpleasant is comparable with their respective oral responses. In addition, for schizophrenic patients, the percentage accuracy for the acceptable class is very poor of the order of below 12%, which for normal subjects is quite high (42%). The second inference authors derive from Table 5 is that nurse selection for schizophrenic patients becomes easier by ranking the degree of pleasure perceived by the patients due to touch nourishments delivered by the nurse.

REFERENCES

Bauer, M., Oostenveld, R., Peeters, M., & Fries, P. (2006). Tactile spatial attention enhances gamma-band activity in somatosensory cortex and reduces low-frequency activity in parieto-occipital areas. *The Journal of Neuroscience*, 26(2), 490–501. doi:10.1523/JNEUROSCI.5228-04.2006 PMID:16407546

Chapman, C. E. (1994). Active versus passive touch: Factors influencing the transmission of somatosensory signals to primary somatosensory cortex. *Canadian Journal of Physiology and Pharmacology*, 72(5), 558–570. doi:10.1139/y94-080 PMID:7954086

Chen, S., Cowan, C. F., & Grant, P. M. (1991). Orthogonal least squares learning algorithm for radial basis function networks. *IEEE Transactions on Neural Networks*, 2(2), 302–309. doi:10.1109/72.80341 PMID:18276384

Cheyne, D., Gaetz, W., Garnero, L., Lachaux, J. P., Ducorps, A., Schwartz, D., & Varela, F. J. (2003). Neuromagnetic imaging of cortical oscillations accompanying tactile stimulation. *Brain Research. Cognitive Brain Research*, 17(3), 599–611. doi:10.1016/S0926-6410(03)00173-3 PMID:14561448

Costantini, G., Todisco, M., Casali, D., Carota, M., Saggio, G., Bianchi, L., & Quitadamo, L. et al. (2009, July).SVM Classification of EEG Signals for Brain Computer Interface. *2009 conference on Neural Nets WIRN09: Proceedings of the 19th Italian Workshop on Neural Nets*, 229-233.

Cristianini, N., & Shawe-Taylor, J. (2000). *An introduction to support vector machines and other kernel-based learning methods*. Cambridge University Press. doi:10.1017/CBO9780511801389

Crone, N. E., Miglioretti, D. L., Gordon, B., Sieracki, J. M., Wilson, M. T., Uematsu, S., & Lesser, R. P. (1998). Functional mapping of human sensorimotor cortex with electrocorticographic spectral analysis. *Brain*, 121(Pt 12), 2271–2299. doi:10.1093/brain/121.12.2271 PMID:9874480

Das, S., Abraham, A., Chakraborty, U. K., & Konar, A. (2009). Differential evolution using a neighborhood-based mutation operator. *IEEE Transactions on Evolutionary Computation*, 13(3), 526–553. doi:10.1109/TEVC.2008.2009457

Doane, D. P., & Seward, L. E. (2011). Measuring skewness: A forgotten statistic. *Journal of Statistics Education*, 19(2), 1–18.

Essick, G. K., McGlone, F., Dancer, C., Fabricant, D., Ragin, Y., Phillips, N., & Guest, S. et al. (2010). Quantitative assessment of pleasant touch. *Neuroscience and Biobehavioral Reviews*, 34(2), 192–203. doi:10.1016/j.neubiorev.2009.02.003 PMID:19896001

Feurra, M., Paulus, W., Walsh, V., & Kanai, R. (2011). Frequency specific modulation of human somatosensory cortex. *Frontiers in Psychology*, 2. PMID:21713181

Gallace, A., & Spence, C. (2010). The science of interpersonal touch: An overview. *Neuroscience and Biobehavioral Reviews*, 34(2), 246–259. doi:10.1016/j.neubiorev.2008.10.004 PMID:18992276

Guo, M., Yu, Y., Yang, J., & Wu, J. (2012). The Crossmodal between the Visual and Tactile for Motion Perception. *Biomedical Engineering and Cognitive Neuroscience for Healthcare: Interdisciplinary Applications: Interdisciplinary Applications*, 99.

Haykin, S., & Lippmann, R. (1994). Neural networks, a comprehensive foundation. *International Journal of Neural Systems*, 5(4), 363–364. doi:10.1142/S0129065794000372

Labate, D., Palamara, I., Mammone, N., Morabito, G., La Foresta, F., & Morabito, F. C. (2013, August). SVM classification of epileptic EEG recordings through multiscalepermutation entropy. *Proceedings of the 2013 International Joint Conference on Neural Networks (IJCNN)*, (pp. 1-5). IEEE. doi:10.1109/IJCNN.2013.6706869

Li, S., Zhou, W., Cai, D., Liu, K., & Zhao, J. (2011). EEG signal classification based on EMD and SVM. *Journal of Biomedical Engineering*, 28(5), 891–894. PMID:22097250

Lin, Y. P., Wang, C. H., Wu, T. L., Jeng, S. K., & Chen, J. H. (2008, October). Support vector machine for EEG signal classification during listening to emotional music. *10th Workshop on Multimedia Signal Processing*, (pp. 127-130). IEEE. doi:10.1109/MMSP.2008.4665061

McKetta, J. J., Jr. (1976). Encyclopedia of Chemical Processing and Design: Volume 1-Abrasives to Acrylonitrile. CRC Press.

Nakamura, T., Tomita, Y., Ito, S. I., &Mitsukura, Y. (2010, September). A method of obtaining sense of touch by using EEG. In *RO-MAN*, (pp. 276-281). IEEE.

Panda, R., Khobragade, P. S., Jambhule, P. D., Jengthe, S. N., Pal, P. R., & Gandhi, T. K. (2010, December). Classification of EEG signal using wavelet transform and support vector machine for epileptic seizure diction. *Proceedings of International Conference on Systems in Medicine and Biology (ICSMB)*, (pp. 405-408). IEEE. doi:10.1109/ICSMB.2010.5735413

Peltoranta, M., & Pfurtscheller, G. (1994). Neural network based classification of non-averaged event-related EEG responses. *Medical & Biological Engineering & Computing*, *32*(2), 189–196. doi:10.1007/BF02518917 PMID:8022216

Ploner, M., Gross, J., Timmermann, L., & Schnitzler, A. (2002). Cortical representation of first and second pain sensation in humans. *Proceedings of the National Academy of Sciences of the United States of America*, *99*(19), 12444–12448. doi:10.1073/pnas.182272899 PMID:12209003

Reed-Geaghan, E. G., & Maricich, S. M. (2011). Peripheral somatosensation: A touch of genetics. *Current Opinion in Genetics & Development*, *21*(3), 240–248. doi:10.1016/j.gde.2010.12.009 PMID:21277195

Saha, A., Konar, A., Chatterjee, A., Ralescu, A., & Nagar, A. K. (2014). EEG analysis for olfactory perceptual-ability measurement using a recurrent neural classifier. *IEEE Transactions on Human-Machine Systems*, *44*(6), 717–730. doi:10.1109/THMS.2014.2344003

Saha, A., Konar, A., Das, P., Sen Bhattacharya, B., & Nagar, A. (2015b). Data-point and Feature Selection of Motor Imagery EEG Signals for Neural Classification of Cognitive Tasks in Car-Driving. *Proceedings of International Joint Conference on Neural Networks (IJCNN)*, (pp. 1-8). IEEE.

Saha, A., Konar, A., Sen Bhattacharya, B., & Nagar, A. (2015a). EEG Classification to Determine the Degree of Pleasure Levels in TouchPerception of Human Subjects. *Proceedings of International Joint Conference on Neural Networks (IJCNN)*, (pp. 1-8). IEEE.

Schlögl, A., Lugger, K., & Pfurtscheller, G. (1997, November). Using adaptive autoregressive parameters for a brain-computer-interface experiment. *Proceedings of 19th International Conference IEEE Engineering in Medicine and Biology Society (IEEE/EMBS)*, (pp. 1533-1535). IEEE. doi:10.1109/IEMBS.1997.757002

Schölkopf, B., & Smola, A. J. (2002). *Learning with kernels: Support vector machines, regularization, optimization, and beyond*. MIT Press.

Schore, A. N. (2005). A neuropsychoanalytic viewpoint: Commentary on paper by Steven H. Knoblauch. *Psychoanalytic Dialogues*, *15*(6), 829–854. doi:10.2513/s10481885pd1506_3

Singh, H., Bauer, M., Chowanski, W., Sui, Y., Atkinson, D., Baurley, S., & Bianchi-Berthouze, N. et al. (2014). The brain's response to pleasant touch: An EEG investigation of tactile caressing. *Frontiers in Human Neuroscience*, 8. PMID:25426047

Smith, L. I. (2002). A tutorial on principal components analysis. *Cornell University, USA, 51*, 52.

Srinivasan, V., Eswaran, C., & Sriraam, N. (2007). Approximate entropy-based epileptic EEG detection using artificial neural networks. *IEEE Transactions on Information Technology in Biomedicine, 11*(3), 288–295. doi:10.1109/TITB.2006.884369 PMID:17521078

Stoica, P., & Moses, R. L. (1997). *Introduction to spectral analysis*. Upper Saddle River, NJ: Prentice Hall.

Storn, R., & Price, K. (1997). Differential evolution–a simple and efficient heuristic for global optimization over continuous spaces. *Journal of Global Optimization, 11*(4), 341–359. doi:10.1023/A:1008202821328

Van Ede, F., de Lange, F., Jensen, O., & Maris, E. (2011). Orienting attention to an upcoming tactile event involves a spatially and temporally specific modulation of sensorimotor alpha-and beta-band oscillations. *The Journal of Neuroscience, 31*(6), 2016–2024. doi:10.1523/JNEUROSCI.5630-10.2011 PMID:21307240

Vourkas, M., Micheloyannis, S., & Papadourakis, G. (2000). Use of ann and hjorth parameters in mental-task discrimination. *First International Conference on Advances in Medical Signal and Information Processing*, (pp. 327-332). IET. doi:10.1049/cp:20000356

Wu, Q., Li, C., Takahashi, S., & Wu, J. (2012). Visual-Tactile Bottom-Up and Top-Down Attention. *Biomedical Engineering and Cognitive Neuroscience for Healthcare: Interdisciplinary Applications: Interdisciplinary Applications*, 183.

Zhong, M., Lotte, F., Girolami, M., & Lécuyer, A. (2008). Classifying EEG for brain computer interfaces using Gaussian processes. *Pattern Recognition Letters, 29*(3), 354–359. doi:10.1016/j.patrec.2007.10.009

Chapter 9

An Ant–Colony–Based Meta–Heuristic Approach for Load Balancing in Cloud Computing

Santanu Dam
Future Institute of Engineering and Management, India

Gopa Mandal
Kalyani Government Engineering College, India

Kousik Dasgupta
Kalyani Government Engineering College, India

Parmartha Dutta
Visva-Bharati University, India

ABSTRACT

This book chapter proposes use of Ant Colony Optimization (ACO), a novel computational intelligence technique for balancing loads of virtual machine in cloud computing. Computational intelligence(CI), includes study of designing bio-inspired artificial agents for finding out probable optimal solution. So the central goal of CI can be said as, basic understanding of the principal, which helps to mimic intelligent behavior from the nature for artifact systems. Basic strands of ACO is to design an intelligent multi-agent systems imputed by the collective behavior of ants. From the perspective of operation research, it's a meta-heuristic. Cloud computing is a one of the emerging technology. It's enables applications to run on virtualized resources over the distributed environment. Despite these still some problems need to be take care, which includes load balancing. The proposed algorithm tries to balance loads and optimize the response time by distributing dynamic workload in to the entire system evenly.

INTRODUCTION

Cloud computing is an entirely internet-based approach where all the applications and files are hosted on a cloud, it thrives application and services. Cloud computing is one of the most emerging technologies that provides standard for large scale distributed and parallel computing. It's a framework for enabling

DOI: 10.4018/978-1-5225-3129-6.ch009

applications to run on virtualized resources and accessed by common network protocol and standards. It provides computing and infrastructural resource and services in a very flexible manner that can be scaled up or down according to demand of the end user. Due to exponential growth of Internet in last decade cloud computing got solid platform to spread its era by providing virtualized hardware and software infrastructure over the Internet. Cloud uses high speed internet to disperse jobs from local or private PC to remote PC or Data Center. Computing service provided by cloud service provider may be used by individual or industry from anywhere of the world. Cloud's on demand service coupled with pay as-you go model has attracted more and more user for better utility computing. Another reason that companies and end users are getting attracted is provisioning and deprovisioning, which reduce capital cost. Ensuring the QoS (ensuring better and fast service in stipulated time) and meeting the demand of the end users for resources in proper time is one of the main challenges of cloud service provider. Gartner defines cloud computing as: "A style of computing where massively scalable IT-related capabilities are provided as a service across the Internet to multiple external customers using internet technologies "("Gartner Highlights Five Attributes of Cloud Computing" [on13 Dec 2013])

As per Prerakmody ("Cloud Computing" on-line (on 9 Jan 2014)) Cloud computing caters to the following needs:

1. **Dynamism:** Cloud computing provides dynamism, facilitating scaling up and down demand of the resources as and when required according to our needs.
2. **Abstraction:** Cloud computing provides abstraction to the end users. The end users do not need to take care for the OS, the plug-ins, web security or the software platform.
3. **Resource Sharing:** Cloud computing provides resource sharing which allows optimum utilisation of resources in the cloud.

Any cloud service provider (CSP) makes available these services as computing, software and hardware as service. It is the sole responsibility of CSP to ensure QoS. If the above mentioned feature are maintained properly then it can be said that in coming decades cloud computing has a glorious future. But there are many problems that still need to be resolved; load balancing is one of them. Load balancing can be said to distribute dynamic workload across multiple nodes evenly in a distributed environment. Load balancing also needs to take into account for two major issues one is resource provisioning or allocation and other is task scheduling.

Load balancing is an essential task in cloud computing environment to achieve the maximum utilization of resources. Load balancing algorithm may be static or dynamic, centralized or distributed with their pros and cons. Static load balancing scheme are easy to implement and monitor but fails to model heterogeneous environment of the cloud. On the contrary dynamic algorithms are difficult to implement but best fitted in heterogeneous environment. Unlike centralized algorithm where all the allocation and scheduling decision are made by a single node. In distributed approach the load balancing algorithm are executed together by the all nodes present in the system. These nodes are interacting continuously among themselves to achieve load balancing. The advantage of distributed algorithm is that it provides better fault tolerance but needs higher degree of replication. Distributed load balancing can be of two forms co-operative and non-cooperative.

Load balancing also helps in scheduling task over different nodes of cloud environment. Moreover, load balancing is also an optimization technique. It ensures distribution of the total workload evenly in the entire system, such that each resources does approximately equal amount of works at any point of time. Whenever a certain node becomes overloaded it should be neutralized by some under loaded node. Hence by adapting load balancing algorithms service providers can manage their resources and maintains the QoS helping to increase throughput and minimize the response time.

In this chapter we are trying to portray a novel ant colony based load balancing technique by searching least loaded node in entire cloud environment. Our experimental result for typical sample applications of the proposed technique is really encouraging. The results show significant optimization in response time of the user jobs. Divergently it also outperformed the some traditional approaches.

BACKGROUND

Availability of high speed internet access has helped to extend cloud by using large data centers and powerful servers that host web applications and services. Today anyone with a internet connection and a browser can attach itself to access cloud enabled services. In the following section the characteristics of cloud computing are detailed with respect to their traditional counterpart are discussed.

Cloud Computing Characteristics

Cloud Computing enticed by various industries and academia across the world today, so it has become more important to know it's essential characteristics in particular. According to National Institute of Standards and Technology, Cloud computing is a model for enabling ubiquitous, convenient, on-demand network access to a shared pool of configurable computing resources (e.g., networks, servers, storage, applications, and services). It can be rapidly provisioned and released with minimal management effort or service provider interaction (Mell, P., & Grance, T. (2009)). Figure 1 shows the essential characteristics for any cloud enabled model.

Figure 1. Five essential characteristics of cloud computing

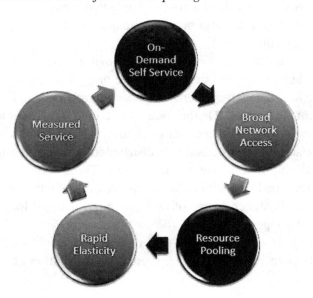

Figure 2. Cloud computing model

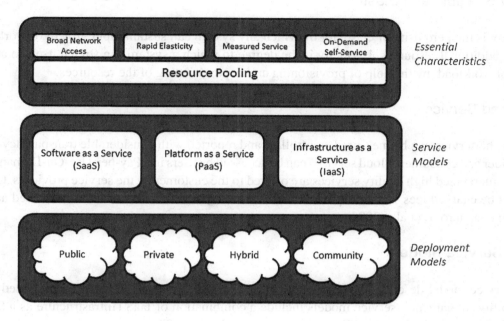

This cloud model is comprising of five essential characteristics, three service models, and four deployment models. For this reason it's important to clearly articulate its essential characteristics as a software offering.

On-Demand Self Service

The system should provide on-demand self service so that a consumer can unilaterally provision computing capabilities such as server time and network storage, CPU etc., as needed automatically without requiring interaction of human with each service's provider "Gartner Highlights Five Attributes of Cloud Computing" [on 13 Dec 2013]).

Broad Network Access

Cloud service should be available through standard Internet-enable devices. So that it can be accessed any time anywhere. It promotes heterogeneity through thin or thick client's platforms such as mobile phones, laptops and PDAs.

Resource Pooling

The provider's computing resources are pooled to serve multiple consumers using a multitenant model with no particular resource assigned to any individual user. Basically resources are dynamically provisioned based on the demand of end users.

Rapidly Scalable and Elastic

Scalability is the perquisite of elasticity by which any system can sustain rapid growth of workload by enabling additional resources. Elasticity is the degree to which a system can stretch itself to adapt the change of workload, by the help of provisioning and deprovisioning of the resources.

Measured Service

Usage of the service can be measured, controlled, and reported with considerable transparency for both the provider and consumer. Cloud services can be accessed by users in a Pay-per-Use-On-Demand model in which guaranteed high quality services are offered to the customer by the service providers. Consumers could be charged fees which may be in terms of hours, data transfers or other use-based attributes delivered (Vaquero, L et al., (2008)).

Cloud Service Models

Cloud service model describes how service will be available by cloud for their users. Based on type of capability fundamental service models include a combination of IaaS (Infrastructure as a Service), PaaS (Platform as a Service), and SaaS (Software as a Service). These three service models synergies between each other or they may interact interdependently.

Cloud Infrastructure as a Service (IaaS)

The IaaS model provides infrastructure components to clients. These components may include the following virtual machines (Vm), storage, networks, firewalls, load balancers, and so on. The lowest level software stack can be made available or intractable by the clients by the help of IaaS. With ensuring Quality of Service (QoS), these parameters are established through a Service Level Agreement (SLA) between the customer and the service provider. Thus end user has total control over the virtualized hardware instances and customized them according to their need. Amazon Web Services is one of largest IaaS providers.

Features and parts of IaaS include:

- Utility computing service and billing model.
- Automation of administrative tasks.
- Dynamic scaling.
- Desktop virtualization.
- Policy-based services.

Cloud Platform as a Service (PaaS)

The PaaS model delivers a pre-built application platform to the client. Depending upon the current demand of the backend, PaaS automatically scales and provisions the required infrastructure components. Typically, a set of function includes by PaaS solutions which provide an API that helps to programmatic platform management and solution development. Two well known PaaS provider are Google App Engine and Amazon Web Services.

Cloud Software as a Service (SaaS)

SaaSis a deployment model of software. It provides software as a service according to the demand of the user. Under the traditional SaaS model, the datacenter is responsible to reside data and application. The end users access remotely the data via web browser. The provider of the SaaS software has complete control over application software. SaaS application examples include online mail, project-management systems, CRMs, and social media platforms. The main difference between SaaS and PaaS is that PaaS normally represents a platform for application development, while SaaS provides online applications that are already developed. Examples of SaaS are Salesforce.com and Clarizen.com, which respectively provide online Customer Relationship Management (CRM) and project management services.

Cloud Deployment Models

A cloud deployment model represents a specific type of cloud environment, primarily distinguished by ownership, size, and access. Based on this different types and different category of end users, the National Institute of Standards and Technology (NIST) have recommended these models (retrieved from http://whatiscloud.com/cloud_deployment_models (2015, August 1)).

Public Cloud

A public cloud provides an environment that is publicly accessible by any one. It is owned by a third-party cloud service provider. The IT resources on public clouds are usually provisioned via the cloud service models and are generally offered to cloud consumers or are commercialized via other avenues (such as advertisement).

The service provider is responsible for the creation and maintenance of the public cloud and its resources.

Private Cloud

A dedicated particular organization may be an owner of a private cloud enable an organization to use cloud computing technology. This helps to create the centralizing access to IT resources from different parts, locations or departments of the organization. Due to centralizing access in comparison of public cloud, private cloud exists as a controlled environment which reduces the risk of data security and integrity. It can be hosted internally or externally.

There are two variations of private clouds.

On-Premise Private Cloud

This type of cloud is hosted within an organization's own facility. A businesses IT department would incur the capital and operational costs for the physical resources with this model. On-Premise hosted internally has complete control and configurability of the infrastructure and security.

Externally Hosted Private Cloud

Externally hosted private clouds are used exclusively by one organization, but are hosted by a specialized third party service provider facilitates by providing cloud infrastructure. The service provider ensures full guarantee of privacy.

Community Clouds

A community cloud is very similar to private cloud but its access is restrained to a particular community for whom the service it's providing. Community cloud can be jointly owned by the community and the third party service providers. More precisely we can say it's a public cloud with a limited access.

Hybrid Clouds

Hybrid clouds are comprised of more than one cloud deployment model, or a mix. For example, users of hybrid cloud separate their service regarding sensitive data in private cloud and less sensitive data service provided through public cloud.

Virtualization

Virtualization is a framework or methodology by which we can virtually divide the resources of a computer into multiple execution environments, using concepts or technologies such as time-sharing, partial or complete machine simulation, hardware and software partitioning etc.. It is basically a software implementation of real hardware that helps to execute different programs like a real machine. Virtualization is also related to cloud, because using virtualization technique the user facilitates with the different services of a cloud via datacenter.

There are two types of virtualization in cloud computing full virtualization and para virtualization (see Figure 3).

Full Virtualization

In full virtualization the underlying hardware is make physically available through simulation. Virtualization makes the physical machine available to unmodified guests such that they can virtually run their application on physical machines. It allows the flexibility to move entire virtual machines from one host

Figure 3. Full virtualization and para-virtualization

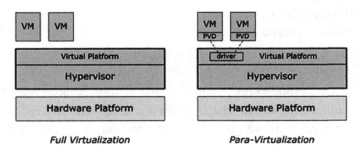

to another host very easily. Migration of the virtual machine from one host to other though adds to extra cost and performance overhead. Here the remote datacenter delivers the services in a fully virtualized manner. Full virtualization has been successful in application such as:

1. Sharing a computer system among multiple users
2. Isolating users from each other and from the control program
3. Emulating hardware on another machine

Para Virtualization

In para virtualization, the hardware allows multiple operating systems to run on single machine by efficient use of system resources such as memory and processor. It builds communication between the guest OS and the hypervisor to improve performance and efficiency of the entire system e.g. VMware software. Para virtualization modifies the OS kernel to replace non virtualizable instructions with hyper calls that communicate directly with the virtualization layer hypervisor. Here all the services are not fully available, rather the services are provided partially.

Datacenter

Datacenter is a repository of servers hosting different application. End users who requires services have to connect with the datacenter to subscribe the services.

Load Balancing in Cloud Computing

Load balancing is one of the major issue related with cloud computing. Distribution of dynamic workload evenly across the network is one of the main objectives of load balancing. So load balancing ensures that all nodes should be neutralized and served equal amount of work. In this context load may be described as memory, CPU capacity, network or delay load. Sharing loads over the distributed system ensures better utilization of resources and increasing the throughput. In brief the goal of load balancing is increasing system stability by building fault tolerance system without affecting the basic computational task. The other benefits of load balancing include:

*   **Failover:** In case of failure it may forward network traffic to other servers;
*   **Scalability:** To increase computational capacity without affecting other network/system components customers can quickly add servers under the load balancer (see Figure 4).

Types of Load Balancing Algorithm

Depending upon the initiator of the load balancing algorithm it can be divided into:

*   **Sender Initiated:** The sender is the initiator of load balancing algorithm.
*   **Receiver Initiated:** The receiver is the initiator of load balancing algorithm.
*   **Symmetric:** It is the combination of both above said strategy (Alakeel, A. M. (2010)).

Figure 4. Load balancer

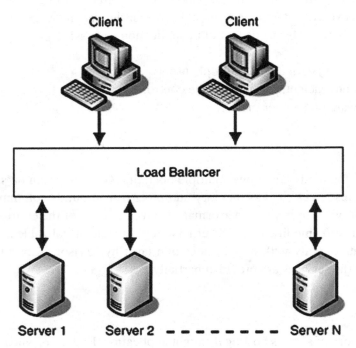

Load balancing techniques are basically two type they are (i) static and (ii) dynamic.

In static algorithm, the decisions are made at compile time where requirements are initially estimated. Prior knowledge about the system is required without depending on the systems current state. Static algorithm works properly only when effective workloads are low.

In dynamic algorithm, every resource is provisioned or deprovisioned by load balancer at run time. It uses the system's current state information to make its decisions. These load balancing algorithms are adaptive and adapt their activities by dynamically changing their parameters, policies and system state. Dynamic techniques are highly successful for load balancing among heterogeneous resources. It is further categorized into distributed approach, non distributed or centralized and hierarchical approach.

In case of distributed approach there is no centralized scheduler, scheduling of all jobs are responsibility of the recourse requesters and owners independently. This approach is scalable and distributed in nature. However individual scheduler has to co-operate with each other for scheduling decision. The decisions taken to achieve the goal state may or may not be the optimal one. This category of load balancing approach is perfect for peer-to-peer architecture in dynamic environment.

In centralized approach all jobs are submitted to single scheduler and made available to all resources at once. Easy to implement but the scheduling decisions are optimal but not scalable.

In hierarchical strategy schedulers are arranged in hierarchy, where high level resource entities are scheduled at higher level and lower level smaller entities are scheduled at lower level of the hierarchy of scheduler. This model is combination of the above two models.

Metrics for Load Balancing

1. **Throughput:** Effective load balancing strategy should increase systems throughput. Throughput is the number of tasks whose execution is completed to the total number of tasks within a time frame.
2. **Fault Tolerance:** It means recovery from failure. A good load balancing strategy must handle the fault tolerance issues.
3. **Migration Time:** The time that is required migrating a job or resources from one node to another. It should be minimized for better performance of the system.
4. **Response Time:** The time taken by the load balancing algorithm to serve the first response of the job in a system. Load balancing algorithm shouldminimize the response time for better performance.
5. **Scalability:** It is the ability of the load balancing strategy that can balance any amount of load at any point of time with finite amount of resources. The metric should be improved to increase throughput and response time.

Goals of Load Balancing

According to David Escalante and Andrew J. Korty the goals of load balancing are:

1. To improve the performance substantially at lower cost.
2. To have a backup plan in case the system fails even partially and it should be flexible enough to handle this situation.
3. To maintain the system stability by increasing the scalability.
4. Prioritization of the resources and as well as jobs are need to be done. So that high priority job gets better chance to execute.

LITERATURE SURVEY

Houle et al. (2002) proposed strategy that balance the load of the cloud using trees. Their proposed load balancing strategy is a static and they have considered the total workload as a fixed factor.

Hu et al. (1998) proposed an optimal data migration algorithm in diffusive dynamic load balancing by calculating Lagrange multiplier of the Euclidean form of transferred weight. This work proposes effective optimization and the movement of data in homogenous environments only.

Genaudet et al. (2003) proposed an enhanced the MPI Scatter primitive, to support master-slave static load balancing. They have used linear programming to optimize the computation and data distribution. However, this solution is limited to static load balancing.

Moradiet et al. (2010) proposed a scheduler that chooses the resources for the user jobs, based on better past status and least completion time. In this algorithm work class, cost, deadline and herd behavior are also considered. The work thrives to achieve load balancing and reduce the response time and task failure.

B. Yagoubi and Y. Slimani (2007) proposed strategy based on neighborhood property. This strategy privileges first local balancing then upper hierarchical balancing takes place. The uniqueness of this idea is that it decreases the amount of messages exchanged between Grid resources. The system has a hierarchical architecture totally independent of Grid architecture.

B. Yagoubi and M. Medebber (2007) proposed a tree based model to represent the grid architecture to manage the workload. This model has three different features: (i) hierarchical; (ii) heterogeneity and scalability (iii) it is totally independent from any grid physical architecture. The strategy has features such as task level load balancing, giving privilege to the local task reduced communication cost and distributed strategy with local load balancing.

Sotomayor, B et al. (2009) proposed round robin algorithm in static environment. In this policy the resources are provisioned to the user's task on first-cum-first-serve basis and scheduled in time sharing manner. The least loaded node is allocated the task.

Randles, M., Taleb-Bendiab, A., & Lamb, D. (2009) gave a comparison of some algorithms in cloud computing by checking the performance time and cost. Their work concluded that the equally spread current execution (ESCE) algorithm and throttled algorithm are better than the Round Robin algorithm.

Radojević, B et al (2011) proposed an improved algorithm over round robin called CLBDM (Central Load Balancing Decision Model). It uses the basic strategy of round robin but it also measures the duration of connection between task and resource by calculating overall execution time of task on a particular cloud resource.

Yagoubi, B., and Slimani, Y. (2007) proposed a strategy that considers three potentially viable methods for load balancing in large scale cloud systems. It uses a nature-inspired algorithm for self-organization, Secondly, the self-organization is re-engineered based on random sampling on the system domain to balance the load. Third, the system is restructured to provide ensured optimize job assignment at the server end. Recently numerous nature inspired networking and computing models are unfolding, by adapting distributed methods to address increasing scale and complexity in such systems.

M., Taleb-Bendiab, A., & Lamb, D. (2009) proposed random biased sampling methods considering individual nodes. Finally, an algorithm for connecting smile services by local rewiring is proposed that helps to improve load balancing by active system restructuring. In case of load balancing, as the web servers demand scaled up or down, the services are assigned dynamically to regulate the changing demands of the user. The actual servers are grouped under virtual servers (VS), each VS have its individual virtual service queues. Server processed a request every time from its queue and calculates a profit or reward, which is similar to the quality that the bees show in their waggle dance.

Yagoubi, B., & Slimani, Y. (2006) presented the problem of load balancing in Grid computing as a tree representation as in Alakeel, A. M. (2010). This load balancing strategy has two main objectives minimization of mean response time of tasks and reduction of the communication costs at the time of task transfer. This strategy deals with three layers of algorithms (intra-site, intra-cluster and intra-grid).

Xu, G., Pang, J., & Fu, X. (2013) proposed a novel algorithm which is totally based on the cloud partitioning concept. However, a switch mechanism is considered to set different strategies for different situations. The algorithm is an implementation of the game theory to improve the efficiency of the public cloud environment.

Liu, Z., & Wang, X. (2012) proposed a new bio–inspired strategy for task scheduling. The strategy tries to optimize the task execution time in view of both the task running time and the system resource utilization. The algorithm is based on particle swarm optimization. A simple mutation mechanism is considered with self-adapting inertia weight method for classifying the fitness values. The global search performance and convergence rate are also validated by comparative studies with other algorithm. However, the approach does not consider the restrictions from bandwidth, problems in job decomposition, energy costs of cloud datacenters etc.

K. Li et. al. (2011) describes a policy based Ant Colony Optimization (LBACO) algorithm. The approach balances the load by minimizing the make span of a given tasks set. CloudSim is used for simulation experiments results showed the proposed algorithm outperformed FCFS and the basic ACO. However limitation due to using testbed also observed here.

XChang, H., & Tang, X. (2011) introduced a resource-scheduling algorithm based on dynamic load balancing considering variable data-processing power of nodes, different data-transferring power and transfer delay between nodes in cloud. The algorithm minimizes the average response time by selecting the "best" possible node to complete the task thus increasing the efficiency of the entire system. However, limitation due to using testbed also observed here but it reduces the average response time significantly.

Šešum-Čavić, V., & Kühn, E. (2011) proposed a self-organizing approach that deals with rapidly increasing complexity due to adaption of new technologies. The work proposed uses of generic architectural pattern (SILBA) that allows the exchanging of different algorithms (intelligent and unintelligent) through plugging. The basic goal of the proposed strategy is selection of the best algorithm(s) for a certain specific problem scenario. SILBA is problem and domain independent, and can be composed towards arbitrary network topologies.

Jain, A. & Singh, R. (2014) uses Master ant colony based approach. Experiments are conducted on different data series and different conditions. The proposed algorithm shows its novelty in peer to peer environment. The Master ACO achieves better optimal solution with vanishing node concept.

Mondal, B., Dasgupta, K., & Dutta, P. (2012) proposes a soft computing based load balancing approach using Stochastic Hill Climbing. The algorithm iterates a simple loop that continuously moves in the direction of increasing value called uphill and stops when no neighbor have higher assignment or higher value. This basic operation is repeated until either a solution is found or a stopping criterion is reached. Performance of the algorithm is analyzed both qualitatively and quantitatively using Cloud Analyst. Comparison is also made with Round Robin(RR) and First Come First Serve (FCFS) algorithms. The results are quite encouraging however the disadvantages of local optimization approach needs to be corroborated.

Dasgupta, K. et.al (2013) proposed a novel load balancing strategy using Genetic Algorithm (GA) with single point crossover. By minimizing the span of a given task set the algorithm thrives to balance the load of entire system. The work outperformed approaches like First Come First Serve (FCFS), Round Robin (RR) and stochastic hill climbing. However, fault tolerance and different parameter variation of GA are not taken into consideration.

De Mello, R. F., Senger, L. J., & Yang, L. T. (2006), proposed a routing based load balancing policy in grid computing. It uses routing to define a neighborhood and search for the most adequate node or computer for load balancing. This algorithm distributes entire workload equally in parallel applications across the grid. This load balancing strategy when used in large-scale systems significantly minimizes the total execution time. However, the work does not consider critical issues like communication cost induced by load redistribution.

Mukherjee, K., & Sahoo, G. (2009, December), proposed a mathematical model of cloud computing framework using fuzzy bee colony optimization technique. The honey bee colony algorithm has been simulated with the use of fuzziness, for web services provided by web servers scattered over the entire network.

Three-phase hierarchical scheduling is proposed by Wang, S. C. et al. (2011) in their chapter. The algorithm has multiple phases of scheduling and requests monitor that acts as a head of the network and responsible for monitoring service manager. First phase uses Best Task Order scheduling, then Enhanced Opportunistic Load Balancing scheduling and finally Enhanced Min-Min scheduling.

Liu. Xi & Liu. Jun (2016) proposed a greedy approach based simulated annealing algorithm to overcome the problem of local optimum search. The greedy approach is used to generate new values. Experiments were done on physical machine by gradually increasing the number of task. It is also observed that the algorithm has direct impact on parameter convergence speed and the efficiency of the algorithm depends on the initial value. They also suggest for improving the efficiency it may be combined with deterministic algorithm.

Inferences Drawn from Literature Survey

1. In distributed applications, performance issues have become more critical due to proliferation of heterogeneous devices, large variety of communication medium and increased security concerns.
2. Researchers proposed different load balancing algorithms in order to manage the resources of service provider efficiently and effectively.
3. Workload and resource management are two essential functions provided at the service level of the distributed systems infrastructure.
4. Due to the sharing of resources and the dynamic and heterogeneous needs of the end users, the cloud computing architecture may result in wastage of resources if these resources are not properly distributed.
5. A greater challenge is minimization of response time is widely seen for each and every research chapter.

ANT COLONY OPTIMIZATION

Ant colony optimization (ACO) is a multi-agent system where every single artificial ant's behavior is inspired from real ants. It's a metaheuristic, a higher level procedure designed to find out the best possible solution to an optimization problem. In computational intelligence and operation research ACO is described as probabilistic technique. It is a variation of swarm intelligence and used for solving hard combinatorial optimization problems mediated by artificial agents (ants). ACO was initially proposed by M. Dorigo in 1992 in his PhD thesis. The inspiration of development of ACO is totally based on the behavior of the ants. Ants are social insects a simple creature and live in colonies. Their behavior is always driven to fulfill the goal to survival that in colonies rather than individually. For this reason the collectively colonies of ant performs useful task that is searching of foods for their colonies. To fulfill their goal, they start searching the shortest path for food source from their nest and shares the information to other ants by depositing pheromone, which is stigmergic communication via pheromone trails. Pheromone is a small amount of volatile chemical substance dispersed by ants when they are traveling from their nest to food or vice versa. There may be possible different length path linked to the arena of their colonies' nest to food. But after a transitory phase it is observed maximum number of ants choosing a particular path which one is most optimal. Due to high concentrated pheromone on that particular path among several possibilities, most of the ants are attracted to that particular path. By this way trails are reinforced. The pheromone trail served as distributed numerical information which are adapted by ants and probabilistically construct solutions to the problem. More precisely we can conclude this shortest path selection behavior in terms of autocatalysis (positive feedback) and differential path length. This is made possible by an indirect form of communication known as stigmergy. In the field of computational intelligence ant colony optimization (ACO), a collective intelligence of ants is transformed into useful optimization technique. It has been tried to apply on the different area of the computational problems like load balancing. To balance load in cloud environment the algorithm dispersed artificial ants when maximum nodes are overwhelmed with user jobs. These ants wander across the network to find least loaded nodes. The possibility of an isolated artificial ant to choose a particular path from an overloaded node to under loaded node among several possibilities depends on previously laid trail. By this way among several possibilities ants can separate the best possible set of optimal paths is proportion to the concentration of the path's pheromone (Dam. S et al (2014)). Divergently other paths are eliminated due to evaporation of the pheromone.

General Framework of Ant-Based Systems

The basic key idea behind any ant-based systems that are applied to a wide variety of problems, and can be characterized as follows:

Ants are regularly launched or created randomly that thrives to every part of the system for the best optimal solutions of the problem.

The paths covered randomly according to probabilities in pheromone tables for their particular destination.

Updating the probabilities of the pheromone in table always depends from the source node or location from where they launched, and increasing the pheromone probability table for a particular node always depends on the subsequent ants that traversed the node during their journey.

Figure 5. Ant colony optimization

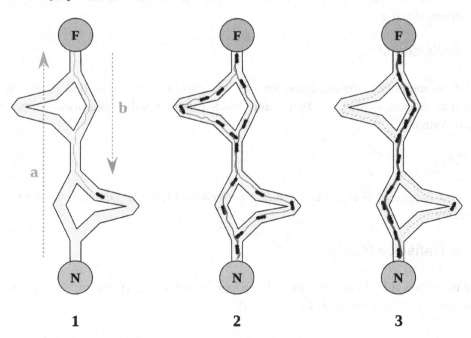

The pheromone may evaporate if the subsequent route is not followed by the other ants and decrease the probability

Increasing the probability also is a function of penalties or rewards to gathered ants on its way. It may be possible that the ants get delayed on any parts (nodes) of the system that are heavily used.

LOAD BALANCING OF VMS USING ANT COLONY OPTIMIZATION

In our proposed system we have represented our problem as a graph G= (N, E), where the nodes are basically two types represented by N they are (i) users jobs and (ii) VMs and the set of edges E is the connection between the user job and VM as shown in figure.

Problem Formulation

Ant's Creation

Initially we allocate jobs in first come first serve (FCFS) manner. The reason behind choosing FCFS initially is to reduce the overhead of the entire network due to artificial ants' creation. Ants are initiated after certain amount of time when the available VMs get exhausted by allocated user's job. We have to take care of creation of ants due to overhead issue.

Pheromone Updating

Updating of pheromone value is always required. When ants are wandering across each path of different node and after any ants visit a node updating of pheromone value of each node are initiated. This updating is necessary to declare best destination set of nodes or least loaded set of nodes on the basis of high pheromone density.

Constraint Satisfaction

Simple short term memory is implemented for Vms to satisfy the constraint that same Vms are not be visited more than once during one ACO procedure and to minimized the assignment coupling time(with user's task and Vms).

Migration Cost

A migration cost is applied if any user's job is deprovisioned from any datacenter and provisioned to another datacenter.

Probabilistic Transition Rules

Probabilistic transition rule defines the random proportional for the typical ant system. In this context it is also required to set replication cost if necessary.

Find Overhead Node

To find the overloaded node main problem is that several nodes may be found that have similar loads but not balanced at all. For this reason we are trying to set a threshold value. Initially we are try to calculate expected time of completion (ETC), where ETC[i,j]represents each task or user's job i on Vm j and also the ready time (Ready [j]) which means Vm is ready to take the next task. Next we calculate the make_span as in equation (1) which indicates maximum completion time here comp_time[i,j] means it's the time when an user's job 'i' ends on Vm 'j' and it is calculated according to equation(2)

$$makespan = MAX\left(comp_{tome[i,j]}\right)\left(1 \leq i \leq n, 1 \leq j \leq m\right) \tag{1}$$

$$comp\_time\left[i,j\right] = ready\left[j\right] + ETC\left[i,j\right] \tag{2}$$

Now for j number of Vms if we assigned I number of tasks(cloudlet) then we can say we have to set a threshold value from which we can take the decision that a node may be overloaded and we have to initiate ACO algorithm. In this context to obtain the solutions with similar makespans, we have to find the most appropriate solution with respect to load balance. If the execution time for any user job J_i is E_{time} [Ji], the average execution time (avg) for all user jobs is as shown in equation(3)

$$avg = \sum_{i=1}^{numofjobs} \left(E_{time}\left[J_i\right] \div num\_of\_VMs\right) \tag{3}$$

From equation (3) we can say that if any numbers of cloudlet n are allocated to m number of Vms then the next cloudlet *i* is provisioned to Vm$_j$ if and only if its loadbalance factor is lesser than the overall average load balance factor of the entire network. So we are taking Load balance for Vm$_j$,as CPU_LBj obtained from Equation (4)

$$CPU\_LBj = makespan + avg \tag{4}$$

To declare a certain Vm is exhausted we calculate the load balance for that Vm$_j$ and compare it with average load balance factor of the entire network (i.e. number of VMs currently available under a host). If in any case it is found that the individual load-balance factor exceeded from average load-balance factor which we set as our threshold we initiate ACO algorithm to find out the currently available Vm that is under loaded. The algorithm for finding overloaded VMs is given in Module 1.

Initializing Pheromone

Our algorithm initially assigned job which comes as request from the Cloud Service Provider (CSP) to the VMs in first-cum-first-serve manner. After a certain time due to vastness of the cloud user and their task VMs are going to cross the threshold value of their load balance. In this situation artificial ants are

Module 1.

Inputs: N number of VMs available currently present in a datacenter and m number of user's task.

Output: The certain number of overloaded VMs who are exceeding the threshold value

Step 1:   Input n number ofVms and m number cloudlets that are currently available in the entire network to calculate the average load-balanceCPU_LB$_{avg}$ for all Vm

Step 2:   for (i =1 to Vm number n)
begin

                for each and every individual Vm calculate the Load balance factor

                Step 2a: If for certain Vm CPU_LB$_I$>CPU_Lb$_{avg}$
Then declare the Vm as overloaded and select Vm_id

                        return Vm_id
                        end_if
                        Else repeat step 2 for next Vm
                end_for
        end

created and dispersed to wander across the network to search under loaded VM's. Such an artificial ant may choose a path with a certain pheromone trail intensity that is assigned same for all edges. According to Dam, S. et al (2014) we assigned the pheromone value initially given in equation (5)

$$\tau ij\big(t = 0\big) = f\big(MIPS_j, L, BW_j\big) \tag{5}$$

where, $\tau ij(t=0)$ is the pheromone value in between two node i and j at turn t=0, MIPS$_J$ (Million instructions per second) is the maximum capacity of each processor of VM$_J$ and the parameter BW$_J$ is related to the communication bandwidth ability of the VM$_J$. L is the delay cost is an estimate of penalty, which cloud service provider needs to pay to customer in the event of job finishing actual time being more than the deadline advertised.

Rule of Choosing Vm for Next Task

The basic objective of the artificial ants is to find out underloadedVms in the network. So to meet their goal they starts their trip across the network, from an overloaded node to allocate next task to new underloadedVm. In this context any ant k, where k=1,2,3,..... n (n is the number of ants) traverse from node i to node j. At each move or iteration of ACO algorithm, the kth ant starts at node I to choose node j and allocation task is based on the probabilistic transition rule as given in equation (6).

$$P_{ij}^k(t) = \begin{cases} \dfrac{\left[\tau_{ij}(t)\right]^\alpha \left[\eta_{ij}(t)\right]^\beta}{\sum_{k \in allowed_k} \left[\tau_{ik}(t)\right]^\alpha \left[\eta_{ik}(t)\right]^\beta}, if \ j \in allowed_k \end{cases} \tag{6}$$

$\tau_{ij}(t)$ defines the attractiveness, it's the pheromone concentration at time t on the path between task i and Vm_j where $allowed_k$, k={0,1,...., n-1} means allowed Vm for k^{th} ant in next step and $tabu_k$ (memory) records the updating of the pheromone value of traversed Vm by k^{th}ant, α and β are parameters to control the relative weight of the phenomenon trail and heuristic value. $\eta_{ij} = \dfrac{1}{d_{ij}}$ is the heuristic value from Tawfeek, M. et al. (April 2014), $d_{ij}$is the expected execution and transfer time of task I on Vm_j can be computed with equation (7)

$$d_{ij} = \frac{LenTask_i}{pe_{numj} * MIPS_j} + \frac{InputFileSize}{BW_j} \tag{7}$$

where, $LenTask_i$ is the total length of the task submitted to Vm_j and pe_{numj} is the number of processor present in Vm_j . $MIPS_J$ is the MIPS of each processor present in Vm_j. InputFileSize is the size of the cloudlet that is to be submitted or presented by user before execution and BW_J is the communication bandwidth of Vm_j.

Pheromone Updating

During completion of a tour, each ant lays a small amount of pheromone on the path by which its travelling. The trail is reinforced by the high concentrated pheromone on the path so we have to calculate the $\Delta\tau^k j \ (t)$ where the pheromone value of the kth ant on the edge between i and j at the time t defined by equation (8)

$$\Delta\tau_{ij}^k(t) = \begin{cases} \dfrac{Q}{Len^k(t)} & if \ (i,j) \in T^k(t) \\ 0 & otherwise \ 0 \end{cases} \tag{8}$$

where, $T^k(t)$ is the tour done by the kth ant at time of iteration number t. $Len^k(t)$ is the length of the path computed as equation (9) and Q is the adaptive parameter.

$$Len^k(t) = \arg\_\max_{J \in J}\left\{SUM_{i \in IJ}\left(d_{ij}\right)\right\} \tag{9}$$

In this context a migration cost is added with $Len^k(t)$ if and only if the kth antchooseVm belonging to different host we set a constant value as migration cost if Vm does not belong to same host.

Where, IJ is the set of tasks that are assigned to Vm_j after each iteration the value of the pheromone is going to be refreshed for all nodes connected edges the path which are choose mostly by ants the pheromone value increased and vice versa left out path's pheromone must be evaporated with the equation (10)

$$\tau_{ij}\left(t+ 1\right) = (1-\rho) * \tau_{jj}\left(t\right) + \Delta\tau_{ij} \tag{10}$$

where, $\tau ij (t+1)$ is the pheromone value of node j at time (t+1), ρ is the pheromone trail decay coefficient $0< \rho <1$. If the value of ρ is greater, then it shows less impact of past solution. $\Delta\tau_{ij}^k$ is local pheromone updating on the visited VMs when an ant completes its tour is given by equation (11).

$$\Delta\tau_{ij} = \sum_{k=1}^{n} \Delta\tau_{ij}^{\kappa}(t) \tag{11}$$

When all ants complete its tour then we select the best tour to declare most optimal path from their nest to food or to find the under loaded Vm over the overloaded one. To declare the best tour (T^+) a small amount of pheromone by a quantity $\Delta\tau ij$ are added as global update. Where $\Delta\tau ij$belongs to the best tour calculated from equation (9) by taking the minimum length distance [min (Len^k(t))]. The proposed algorithm is given below.

Proposed Algorithm

Step 1: Maintain an index table which contains VmId and its corresponding requests of job (that are allocated for execution). Initially all VMs have current request 0.

Step 2: Schedule new request to VMs according to FCFS scheduling policy.

Step 3: Make corresponding change in the index table.

Step 4: To check VM's are exhausted call **Module 1** with VMId.

Step 4a: If Module-1 return VmId then call Procedure_ACO(m no of Vm, n no of users task) Else go to Step 2.

Step 5: Stop.

CLOUD ANALYST AS A SIMULATION TOOL.

The cloud enabled infrastructure are distributed in nature and deployed on the basis of geographic location. The chosen distribution of the cloud based application, have direct impact on the performance, for the user who are far from the datacenter. So quantifying number of simultaneous user and their request, geographic location based relevant resources and requirement of network components in application. These are some of the most important multiple parameters that cannot be predicted earlier. So they cannot be controlled by the developer. Therefore, other methodologies that allow quantification of such parameters must be used. In this consequence use of testbed is very much helpful, because it helps users or researchers with practical feedback without the real world environment scenario. This section portrays the simulation of cloud environment to support application level infrastructure and services that arises from the user level and cloud computing paradigm such as virtualization of resources that may

Procedure_ACO

```
Inputs: m number of VMs returned fromModule-1, n number of user's task and a
random number of ants.
Output: The probable m number of VMs ready to take the next assignment by us-
ers.
Initiate with random number of ant with same pheromone value and place them
randomly to traverse.
Step 1: For m numbers of VMs and n numbers of user's task do
    Step 1b-1: If any ant choose a VM then check whether the ant completes
its tour or not.
    Step 1b-2: If the ant completes its tour then update the pheromone value
locally and refreshed every possible path from source node to destination.
    Step 1b-3: If the solution is optimal and go to Step 2,
    Step 1b-4: Else for non optimal solution, check all the ants have com-
pleted its tour or not. For                           non completion go to
Step 1b-2, else Step-2.
Step 2: Store the current optimal solution and update pheromone value to rein-
force the trail globally in the table.
Step 3: If all ants complete their tour then compare every local pheromone up-
dates to output best possible solution.
```

be hardware or software level but supported by cloud infrastructure. Different simulators are available today to adapt the real world scenarios like CloudSim by Calheiros, R. et al. (2011) and CloudAnalyst by Wickremasinghe, B., (2010, April).

Calheiros, R.N. et. al (2011) propose the simulation environments of CloudSim which is widely adapted today as testbeds basically very useful to allow control and repeatability of experiments. So simulation in CloudSim requires additional effort from the researches or application developers. It has to model both target infrastructure and software of specific language that can be interpreted by the simulator which may be time demanding.

Wickremasinghe, B. et .al (2010) proposed a GUI based visual modelling tool CloudAnalyst. One of the basic objectives of CloudAnalyst is to separate programming exercise from the simulation exercise. So the modeller or researchers have to focus on the simulation part without bothering about the programming and technicalities by this way it helps to save their precious time also. The CloudAnalyst also enables a modeller to execute the simulation environment and conduct series of experiment by changing the control parameters. Below the figure depicted the simulation environment in CloudAnalyst.

CONFIGURATION OF SIMULATION ENVIRONMENT

To simulate our algorithm, we use CloudAnalyst to consider the scenario of the social networking site like Facebook. Our suppositional configuration partitioned the world into six "Regions" depends upon the partition of continents as given in Table 1.

Table 1. Configuration of simulation environment

S. No.	User Base	Region	Simultaneous Online Users During Peak Hrs	Simultaneous Online Users During Off-Peak Hrs
1	UB1	0–N. America	4,70,000	80,000
2	UB2	1–S. America	6,00,000	1,10,000
3	UB3	2 – Europe	3,50,000	65,000
4	UB4	3 – Asia	8,00,000	1,25,000
5	UB5	4 – Africa	1,15,000	12,000
6	UB6	5 – Oceania	1,50,000	30,500

CloudAnalyst has the certain flexibility to set user bases(UB). In this context user base is considered as sample online users during peak or off peak hour. The proposed sample configuration has entire online users available in peak hours decreased by one tenth approximately in off peak hour.

Each simulated datacenter host has a particular amount of virtual machines (VMs) which are provided to users as resource. Each machines consists 4 GB of RAM, 100 GB storage and 1000MB of available bandwidth. Each Datacenter (DC) is assumed to be having 4 CPUs with a capacity of 10000 MIPS. Simulated hosts have x86 architecture, virtual machine monitor Xen and Linux based operating system. Each individual user's request has been considered to be requiring 100 instructions to be executed

RESULTS AND COMPARISON

The proposed algorithm is executed in several setups as tabulated in Table 2, where one DC is considered having initially 25, 50 and 75 VMs in each Cloud Configurations (CCs). Simulation scenario of Table 3 consists of two DCs with a variation of 25, 50 and 75 VMs. In Table 4, 5, 6 and 7 considers three; four, five and six DCs respectively with a mixture of 25, 50 and 75 VMs for all DCs. Average response time of the jobs are calculated for the proposed algorithm and tabulated. The performance of proposed algorithm is compared with some existing load balancing algorithm using Genetic Algorithm Gravitational Emulation Local Search(GA-GEL) (Dam, S.et al (2015)), Genetic Algorithm, Stochastic Hill

Table 2. Simulation scenario and calculated overall average response time (RT) in (ms) using one DC

Serial No.	Cloud Configuration	Data Center Specification	RT in ms for ACO	RT in ms for GA-GEL	RT in ms for SHC	RT in ms for GA	RT in ms for FCFS
1	CC1	OneDC with 25 VMs .	325.13	326	329.01	329.02	330.11
2	CC2	OneDC with 50 VMs.	323.53	324.27	328.97	329.01	329.65
3	CC3	OneDC with 75 VMs.	231.65	232.52	244	329.34	329.44

Table 3. Simulation scenario and calculated overall average response time (RT) in (ms) using two Data Center

Serial No.	Cloud Configuration	Data Center Specification	RT in ms for ACO	RT in ms for GA-GEL	RT in ms for SHC	RT in ms for GA	RT in ms for FCFS
1	CC1	Two DCs with 25 VMs each.	351.32	354.72	360.77	365.44	376.34
2	CC2	Two DCs with 50 VMs each.	346..89	349.89	355.72	360.15	372.52
3	CC3	Two DCs with 75 VMs each.	345.98	348.68	355.32	359.73	370.56
4	CC4	Two DCs with 25, 50 VMs.	343.27	346.57	350.58	356.72	368.87
5	CC5	Two DCs with 25, 75 VMs.	342.66	347.86	351.56	357.23	367.23
6	CC6	Two DCs with 75, 50 VMs.	340.37	350.47	352.01	357.04	361.01

Table 4. Simulation scenario and calculated overall average response time (RT) in (ms) result using three Data Centers

Sl. No.	Cloud Configuration	Data Center Specification	RT in ms ACO	RT in ms GA-GEL	RT in ms GA	RT in ms SHC	RT in ms FCFS
1	CC1	Each with 25 VMs.	341.85	343.25	345.68	350.32	363.34
2	CC2	Each with 50 VMs.	339.16	341.43	344.86	350.19	363.52
3	CC3	Each with 75 VMs.	336.74	338.52	340.62	346.01	361.56
4	CC4	Each with 25, 50, 75VMs.	335.43	343.25	345.68	350.32	363.34

Table 5. Simulation scenario and calculated overall average response time (RT) in (ms) using four Data Center

Serial No.	Cloud Configuration	Data Center Specification	RT in ms for ACO	RT in ms for GA-GEL	RT in ms for GA	RT in ms for SHC	RT in ms for FCFS
1	CC1	Each with 25 VMs .	335.44	337.51	348.85	354.35	359.35
2	CC2	Each with 50 VMs .	332.26	336.38	345.54	350.71	356.93
3	CC3	Each with 75 VMs	333.37	335.49	340.65	346.46	352.09
4	CC4	Each with 25, 50,75VMs.	330.23	332.61	337.88	344.31	351

Table 6. Simulation scenario and calculated overall average response time (RT) in (ms) result using five Data Center

Serial No.	Cloud Configuration	Data Center Specification	RT in ms for ACO	RT in ms for GA-GEL	RT in ms for GA	RT in ms for SHC	RT in ms for FCFS
1	CC1	Each with 25 VMs .	327.49	329.34	335.64	342.86	352.05
2	CC2	Each with 50 VMs .	315.95	317.38	326.02	332.84	345.44
3	CC3	Each with 75 VMs	314.61	316.43	322.93	329.46	342.79
4	CC4	Each with 25, 50, 75VMs.	314.37	315.53	319.98	326.64	338.01

Table 7. Simulation scenario and calculated overall average response time (RT) in (ms) result using six Data Center

Sl. No.	Cloud Configuration	Data Center Specification	RT in ms ACO	RT in ms GA-GEL	RT in ms GA	RT in ms SHC	RT in ms FCFS
1	CC1	Each with 25 VMs.	318.81	321.26	330.54	336.96	349.26
2	CC2	Each with 50 VMs.	314.01	314.23	323.01	331.56	344.04
3	CC3	Each with 75 VMs.	309.54	311.34	321.54	327.78	339.87
4	CC4	Each with 25, 50,75VMs.	301.27	302.5	315.33	323.56	338.29

Climbing Algorithm (SHC) introduced by Mondal, B., Dasgupta, K., & Dutta, P. (2012) and First Come First Serve (FCFS). Figures 2, 3, 4, 5, 6 and 7 make a comparative analysis of the proposed technique for the different scenarios and techniques. The comparative analysis confirms the novelty of the work.

Figure 6. A snapshot of the GUI of CloudAnalyst simulation toolkit is shown in (a) and its architecture is depicted in (b).

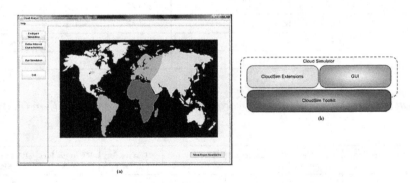

Figure 7. Performance analysis of proposed ACO with GA-GEL GA, SHC, FCFS and RR result using one Datacenter

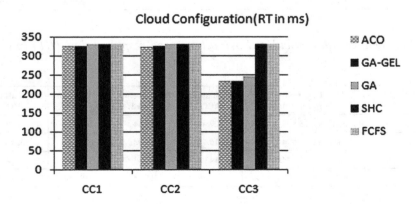

Figure 8. Performance analysis of proposed ACO with GA-GEL GA,SHC, FCFS and RR result using two Datacenter

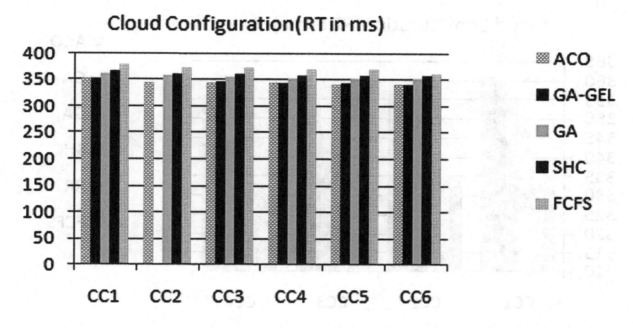

Figure 9. Performance analysis of proposed ACO with GA-GEL GA,SHC, FCFS and RR result using three Datacenter

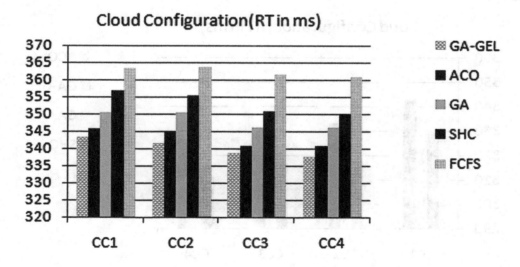

CONCLUSION AND FUTURE RESEARCH DIRECTIONS

This book chapter presents an algorithm to solve the load balancing problem in cloud computing. It's basically used ant based intelligent to distribute load among the Vm. Ant have local and also global view towards the problem space. We investigate one of the most significant strength of our algorithm is that minimum number of ants creation because of the certain threshold value calculation for all VMs,

Figure 10. Performance analysis of proposed ACO with GA-GEL GA,SHC, FCFS and RR result using four Datacenter

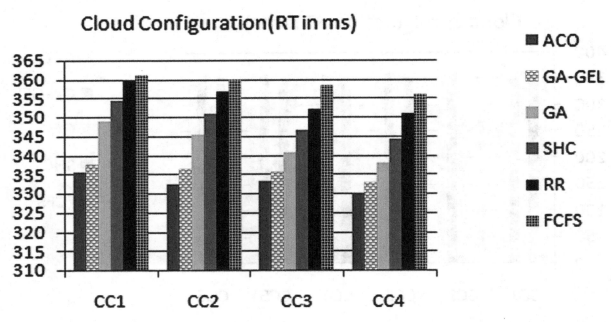

Figure 11. Performance analysis of proposed ACO with GA-GEL GA, SHC, FCFS and RR result using five Datacenter

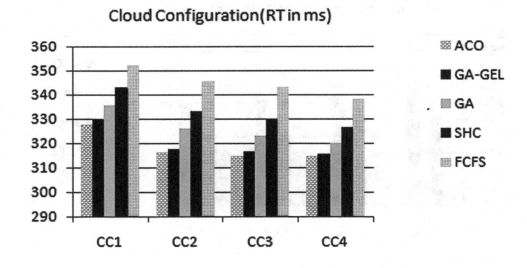

also we tries minimize the make span as well as we reduce the number of VMs who are going to miss their deadlines. Though our algorithm based on ACO have some random parameters that are not moves always according to the algorithm as well as can't predict earlier also. For this reason, it does not stop with best possible solution every time. However, fault tolerance and how to handle high priority job is not considered. We compare our proposed work with some existing technique like GA-GEL, GA,

Figure 12. Performance analysis of proposed ACO with GA-GEL GA, SHC, FCFS and RR result using six Datacenter

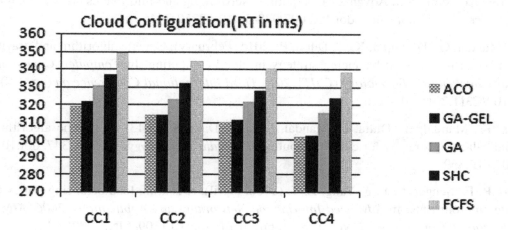

SHC and FCFS and the results out performs other algorithms and guarantees the QoS requirement of the customer job. Though a certain constant value as migration cost is taken here, this constant value is increased if the returned Vm_id belongs to different host_id and not the neighbour of the host that consists of overloaded Vm. More variation to calculate the migration cost are in anvil. So the researchers can proceed to include fault tolerance, priority of the job can be used as future research direction.

REFERENCES

Alakeel, A. M. (2010). A guide to dynamic load balancing in distributed computer systems. *International Journal of Computer Science and Network Security*, *10*(6), 153–160.

Basic concept and terminology of cloud computing. (2015, August 1). Retrieved from http://whatiscloud.com

Beckers, R., Deneubourg, J. L., & Goss, S. (1992). Trails and U-turns in the selection of a path by the ant Lasiusniger. *Journal of Theoretical Biology*, *159*(4), 397–415. doi:10.1016/S0022-5193(05)80686-1

Calheiros, R. N., Ranjan, R., Beloglazov, A., De Rose, C. A., & Buyya, R. (2011). CloudSim: A toolkit for modeling and simulation of cloud computing environments and evaluation of resource provisioning algorithms. *Software, Practice & Experience*, *41*(1), 23–50. doi:10.1002/spe.995

Chang, H., & Tang, X. (2011, January). A load-balance based resource-scheduling algorithm under cloud computing environment. In New Horizons in Web-Based Learning-ICWL 2010 Workshops (pp. 85-90). Springer Berlin Heidelberg. doi:10.1007/978-3-642-20539-2_10

Cloud Deployment Models. (2015). *A cloud deployment model represents a specific type of cloud environment, primarily distinguished by ownership, size, and access*. Retrieved from http://whatiscloud.com/cloud_deployment_models

Dam, S., Mandal, G., Dasgupta, K., & Dutta, P. (2014). An Ant Colony Based Load Balancing Strategy in Cloud Computing. In Advanced Computing, Networking and Informatics (vol. 2, pp. 403-413). Springer International Publishing. doi:10.1007/978-3-319-07350-7_45

Dam, S., Mandal, G., Dasgupta, K., & Dutta, P. (2015, February). Genetic algorithm and gravitational emulation based hybrid load balancing strategy in cloud computing. In *Computer, Communication, Control and Information Technology (C3IT), 2015 Third International Conference on* (pp. 1-7). IEEE. doi:10.1109/C3IT.2015.7060176

Dasgupta, K., Mandal, B., Dutta, P., Mandal, J. K., & Dam, S. (2013). A genetic algorithm (GA) based load balancing strategy for cloud computing. *Procedia Technology*, *10*, 340–347. doi:10.1016/j. protcy.2013.12.369

De Mello, R. F., Senger, L. J., & Yang, L. T. (2006, April). A routing load balancing policy for grid computing environments. In *Advanced Information Networking and Applications, 2006. AINA 2006. 20th International Conference on* (Vol. 1, pp. 6-pp). IEEE. doi:10.1109/AINA.2006.54

Dorigo, M. (1992). *Optimization, learning and natural algorithms* (Ph.D. Thesis). Politecnico di Milano, Italy.

Escalnte, D., & Korty, A. J. (2011). Cloud services: Policy and assessment. *EDUCAUSE Review*, *46*(4).

Gartner Highlights Five Attributes of Cloud Computing. (n.d.). Available from: http://www.gartner. com/newsroom/id/1035013

Genaud, S., Giersch, A., & Vivien, F. (2004). Load-balancing scatter operations for grid computing. *Parallel Computing*, *30*(8), 923–946. doi:10.1016/j.parco.2004.07.005

Gorelik, E. (2013). *Cloud computing models* (Doctoral dissertation). Massachusetts Institute of Technology.

Houle, M. E., Symvonis, A., & Wood, D. R. (2002, June). Dimension-Exchange Algorithms for Load Balancing on Trees. SIROCCO, 181-196.

Hu, Y. F., Blake, R. J., & Emerson, D. R. (1998). An optimal migration algorithm for dynamic load balancing. *Concurrency (Chichester, England)*, *10*(6), 467–483. doi:10.1002/(SICI)1096-9128(199805)10:6<467::AID-CPE325>3.0.CO;2-A

Jain, A., & Singh, R. (2014, February). An innovative approach of Ant Colony optimization for load balancing in peer to peer grid environment. In *Issues and Challenges in Intelligent Computing Techniques (ICICT), 2014 International Conference on* (pp. 1-5). IEEE. doi:10.1109/ICICICT.2014.6781242

Li, K., Xu, G., Zhao, G., Dong, Y., & Wang, D. (2011, August). Cloud task scheduling based on load balancing ant colony optimization. In *Chinagrid Conference (ChinaGrid), 2011 Sixth Annual* (pp. 3-9). IEEE. doi:10.1109/ChinaGrid.2011.17

Liu, X., & Liu, J. (2016). A Task Scheduling Based on Simulated Annealing Algorithm in Cloud Computing. *International Journal of Hybrid Information Technology*, *9*(6), 403–412. doi:10.14257/ ijhit.2016.9.6.36

Liu, Z., & Wang, X. (2012). A pso-based algorithm for load balancing in virtual machines of cloud computing environment. In *Advances in Swarm Intelligence* (pp. 142–147). Springer Berlin HeidelBarg. doi:10.1007/978-3-642-30976-2_17

Mell, P., & Grance, T. (2009). The NIST definition of cloud computing. *National Institute of Standards and Technology*, *53*(6), 50.

Mondal, B., Dasgupta, K., & Dutta, P. (2012). Load balancing in cloud computing using stochastic hill climbing-a soft computing approach. *Procedia Technology*, *4*, 783–789. doi:10.1016/j.protcy.2012.05.128

Moradi, M., Dezfuli, M. A., & Safavi, M. H. (2010, April). A new time optimizing probabilistic load balancing algorithm in grid computing. In *Computer Engineering and Technology (ICCET), 2010 2nd International Conference on* (Vol. 1, pp. V1-232). IEEE. doi:10.1109/ICCET.2010.5486187

Mukherjee, K., & Sahoo, G. (2009, December). Mathematical model of cloud computing framework using fuzzy bee colony optimization technique. In *Advances in Computing, Control, & Telecommunication Technologies, 2009. ACT'09. International Conference on* (pp. 664-668). IEEE. doi:10.1109/ACT.2009.168

Prerakmody. (n.d.). *Cloud Computing*. Available from: http://www.wordrandom.wordpress.com/2011/09/28/cloud-computing/

Radojević, B., & Žagar, M. (2011, May). Analysis of issues with load balancing algorithms in hosted (cloud) environments. In *MIPRO, 2011 Proceedings of the 34th International Convention* (pp. 416-420). IEEE.

Randles, M., Taleb-Bendiab, A., & Lamb, D. (2009, July). Scalable Self-Governance Using Service Communities as Ambients. In *Services-I, 2009 World Conference on* (pp. 813-820). IEEE. doi:10.1109/SERVICES-I.2009.93

Schoonderwoerd, R., Holland, O., Bruten, J., & Rothkrantz, L. (1996). *Ants for Load Balancing in Telecommunication Networks*. Hewlett Packard Lab., Bristol. UK, Tech. Rep. HPL-96-35.

Šešum-Čavić, V., & Kühn, E. (2011). Self-Organized Load Balancing through Swarm Intelligence. In *Next Generation Data Technologies for Collective Computational Intelligence* (pp. 195–224). Springer Berlin Heidelberg. doi:10.1007/978-3-642-20344-2_8

Sotomayor, B., Montero, R. S., Llorente, I. M., & Foster, I. (2009). Virtual infrastructure management in private and hybrid clouds. *IEEE Internet Computing*, *13*(5), 14–22. doi:10.1109/MIC.2009.119

Tawfeek, M., El-Sisi, A., Keshk, A. E., & Torkey, F. (2013, November). Cloud task scheduling based on ant colony optimization. In *Computer Engineering & Systems (ICCES), 2013 8th International Conference on* (pp. 64-69). IEEE. doi:10.1109/ICCES.2013.6707172

Vaquero, L. M., Rodero-Merino, L., Caceres, J., & Lindner, M. (2008). A break in the clouds: Towards a cloud definition. *Computer Communication Review*, *39*(1), 50–55. doi:10.1145/1496091.1496100

Velte, A. T., Velte, T. J., & Elsenpeter, R. (2010). *Cloud computing*. McGraw Hill.

Wang, S. C., Yan, K. Q., Wang, S. S., & Chen, C. W. (2011, April). A three-phases scheduling in a hierarchical cloud computing network. In *Communications and Mobile Computing (CMC), 2011 Third International Conference on* (pp. 114-117). IEEE. doi:10.1109/CMC.2011.28

Wickremasinghe, B., Calheiros, R. N., & Buyya, R. (2010, April). Cloudanalyst: A cloudsim-based visual modeler for analyzing cloud computing environments and applications. In *Advanced Information Networking and Applications (AINA), 2010 24th IEEE International Conference on* (pp. 446-452). IEEE. doi:10.1109/AINA.2010.32

Xu, G., Pang, J., & Fu, X. (2013). A load balancing model based on cloud partitioning for the public cloud. *Tsinghua Science and Technology, 18*(1), 34–39. doi:10.1109/TST.2013.6449405

Yagoubi, B., & Medebber, M. (2007, November). A load balancing model for grid environment. In *Computer and information sciences, 2007. ISCIS 2007. 22nd international symposium on* (pp. 1-7). IEEE. doi:10.1109/ISCIS.2007.4456873

Yagoubi, B., & Slimani, Y. (2006). Dynamic load balancing strategy for grid computing. Transactions on Engineering. *Computing and Technology, 13*, 260–265.

Yagoubi, B., & Slimani, Y. (2007). Task load balancing strategy for grid computing. *Journal of Computer Science, 3*(3), 186–194. doi:10.3844/jcssp.2007.186.194

KEY TERMS AND DEFINITIONS

Artefact: Artefact is human created thing. It is something that observed in scientifical experiments that is naturally present and occurs as a result of tangible product or procedure used in different phases of devolvement of software.

Computational Intelligence: Computational intelligence is the ability of a computer to understand the principal which helps to mimic intelligent behaviour from the nature to the artefact system to solve specific task.

Load Balancing: Distributing workload evenly in the entire system is called load balancing. In cloud computing load balancing ensures even distribution of dynamic workload.

Metaheuristic: In computer science metaheuristic is a higher level procedure which is used in optimization problem. It's proposed set of solution which may be too large to comply. Metaheuristic assumed set of solution that may be usable for optimization problem. Most literature provides empirical result about the metaheuristic experiments.

Stigmergic: Stigmergy is a term coined by French biologist Pierre-Paul Grasseits. It's a interaction through the environment where two individual interact indirectly when one of them modifies environment and other will responds to the new environment at a later time.

Chapter 10
Cloud Computing

Shailendra Singh
National Institute of Technical Teachers Training and Research Institute, India

Sunita Gond
Barkatullah University, India

ABSTRACT

As this is the age of technology and every day we are receiving the news about growing popularity of internet and its applications. Cloud computing is an emerging paradigm of today that is rapidly accepted by the industry/organizations/educational institutions etc. for various applications and purpose. As computing is related to distributed and parallel computing which are from a very long time in the market, but today is the world of cloud computing that reduces the cost of computing by focusing on personal computing to data center computing. Cloud computing architecture and standard provide a unique way for delivering computation services to cloud users. It is having a simple API (Application Platform Interface) to users for accessing storage, platform and hardware by paying-as-per-use basis. Services provided by cloud computing is as same as other utility oriented services like electricity bill, water, telephone etc. over shared network. There are many cloud services providers in the market for providing services like Google, Microsoft, Manjrasoft Aneka, etc.

FUNDAMENTAL CONCEPT

A type of computing in which demand services of a client like network, computing, and storage etc. are offered dynamically with the help of internet is known as cloud computing. A group of distributed servers is used to fulfill the demand of cloud users. Service provided by cloud computing includes shared resources, information, software, and applications etc. as per user requirements.

A conventional computer system that we are using is having a single operating system and all is system centric. Cloud computing uses standard and protocols of the network. It provides services that actually run on distributed computing server. Normally resources of cloud computing are virtual in nature. Cloud services are offered to the user on the basis of utility, users have to pay only that amount for which they have used the services. Mainly three types of services are provided by providers they are software as a service, platform as a service and infrastructure as a service.

DOI: 10.4018/978-1-5225-3129-6.ch010

Cloud delivered the application as service to the end user with the help of internet and also offer hardware and platform in the datacenters for providing that services. Every service is on metered basis and users have not to investment more capital to get this service. Interface used for accessing the services is a web browser. Single hardware resource is easily accessible and shared by more than one user using virtualization software. This virtualization technology is used for better and full resource utilization. Figure 1 shows an overview of cloud computing where various cloud users can avail the services of cloud system simultaneously which consists of services like applications and platform, hardware resources, database, storage devices etc.

With very minimum effort large or even small size business can take ubiquitous services of cloud computing. Service level agreement (SLA) define various parameters of services which are going to delivered to the cloud users which are discussed between cloud provider and user before using any type of service. Service usage conditions are also expressed in SLA. Omnipresent storage and compute power on demand basis is the main reason for popularities of cloud computing. Computing resources that are easily accessible through cloud computing are networks, servers, storage, application etc.

Cloud computing system consists of basis components as:-

- Cloud consumers
- Datacenter
- Servers.

Cloud Consumers

Cloud users can use any of the interfaces to interact with cloud for managing and fetching various information and data. Generally users can use interface using Mobile, thin and thick client.

Mobile smart phone can be used by the cloud users which make cloud accessing easy with the presence of many tools to access the information. Thin clients can be used to display the information. These

Figure 1. Overview of Cloud Computing

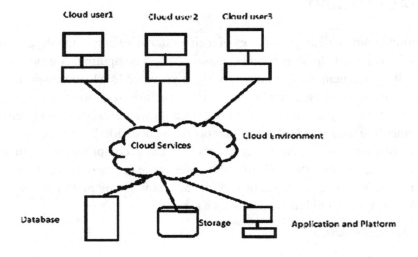

types of clients have no primary memory. Thin client is not very costly and consume very less power also. Thick clients can use various browsers for connecting with cloud.

Party those who are provided cloud services are called cloud providers and the user who consume that services are called cloud user or cloud client or cloud consumer. Cloud computing provide scaling feature to its users that means it is having the capability to increase or decrease IT resources as per the user need or demands.

An organization or an individual can be cloud consumers that have taken permission and have a formal agreement to remotely access the cloud IT resources from the cloud providers. Figure 2 shows cloud consumers of organization 1 and organization 2 who are using cloud services provided by cloud provider.

Data Center

Data Center is a storehouse consists of various IT and non IT equipment for providing services over cloud computing. IT and non IT equipment consist of servers, routers, switches, firewalls, storage and backup devices, fire control system and air conditioning for cooling.

The datacenter is actually consisted of resources and servers for hosting various applications, services etc. For using services and application cloud users have to connect with the data center which is generally kept distant from the users. As due to large or small size organization migrated to the cloud computing right now data center are consuming a large amount of energy, for providing users better service 24 hours in a day, is a challenge for cloud providers. Emission of carbon dioxide from these data center causes a disturbance in the ecological balance, which also causes human hazards.

Figure 2. Cloud consumers

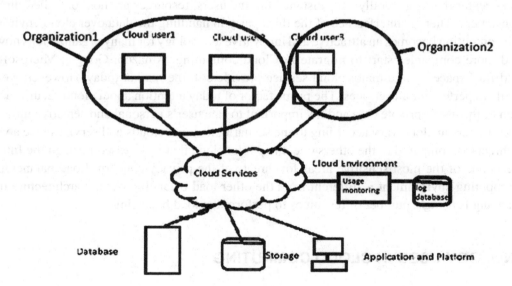

Servers

Servers are used for hosting various applications over the cloud. Users of cloud have not to worry about the complexity of servers they feel that they are accessing the local host while using cloud environment for various applications.

Apart from various services provided by cloud computing, it is having some important benefits like:

1. Data and documents can easily be accessible from anywhere, anytime and many compatible devices are available in the market to support the applications.
2. As organization always tries to concentrate on their business logic but some time they are helpless while handling the complexity of infrastructure. So, with the help of cloud computing, they can handle their business and all complexity related to computing will be handled by cloud providers experts.
3. Protocols and standards exist that allow computers to communicate with each other.
4. Cloud computing reduces the initial cost of infrastructure which is a huge investment for an organization or company who are going to setup their business. All services related to software, hardware, and platform are easily available on cloud and users can avail those services on pay per uses basis.
5. Cloud computing reduces the problem of updating of software's and hardware as cloud users have not be bothered about the software and hardware updating because updated version is made available by cloud providers. Cloud users are also not to worry about the complexity of infrastructure and hardware.

Cloud computing is having some security boundary, as IT resources are sharing by multiple cloud consumers so sometime trust boundaries between them are overlapped. Due to the geographical location of the data center that is generally very distant from the users, resources are not controlled directly by cloud consumers. There is interference of the third party in handling the data over cloud environment.

Cloud computing becomes an attractive and innovative technology for many organizations nowadays. More and more companies start to migrate in Cloud computing. Amazon, Google, Microsoft, Sales Force and Rackspace are the major cloud service providers in the market today. However, we cannot say that all are perfect for all services. The prime factor of today attention about cloud security is for the protection of the user's private data and it's important to safe user's personal and sensitive information.

Privacy threats in cloud vary according to the scenario, as some clouds and services face a very low privacy threats as compared to the others one, the public cloud that is accessed through the Internet by everyone is one of the most sensitive areas for threats of the privacy concern. Load balancing in the Cloud computing environment is different from the other load balancing. As the architecture of cloud load balancing is using a number of resources to perform the load balancing.

TECHNOLOGY USED IN CLOUD COMPUTING

Cloud services are perhaps a quickly growing and developing an approach for delivering services from anywhere any time to the customer, on various type of device. Basically, Cloud computing uses these technologies:

- Grid computing.
- Virtualization.
- Utility Computing.
- Autonomic computing.

Grid Computing

Computer resources dispersed on various locations can be used for a purpose using grid computing. Grid computing can be used for many purposes. General purpose software's can be used to make grid computing.

Virtualization

Virtualization is the strength for any computing and it initiates a layer between Hardware and operating system. Virtualization is the foundation of cloud technology. Users can use services like accessing servers or storage without worrying about server and storage and complexity details. The virtualization layer provides service to users by executing user request for computing resources and accessing proper resources. Resource utilization is also enhanced with virtualization technology.

Utility Computing

Utility computing defines billing model of computing resource like electricity bill etc. Based on the utilization users have to pay the bill to the provider. Billing for utility computing protocol is already making clear to the cloud users. Different billing models are there, some of them are:

- **Day/Hour Basis Billing:** Users have to pay for how many hours or how many days they have used the resource of computing.
- **No. of Users Basis:** This type of billing is based on how much users have used this service in an organization or company and for how time.
- **On the Basis of Data Used:** In this type of billing users have to pay for how much data or computing resource like storage space they are used.

Autonomic Computing

Computing model with self managing capabilities without any external intervention is called Autonomic computing. It is inspired and works like working of the human body nervous system.

CHARACTERISTIC OF CLOUD COMPUTING

Following are the important feature of the cloud computing that makes its distinct from others computing:

- **As per Demand Usage:** Cloud computing provide users the liberty to self provision the IT resource as per the requirements of the users.
- **Omnipresent Access of Data:** Cloud consumers can access data available on the cloud from anywhere and anytime. Resources are available at the server and multiple consumers can simultaneously use these services. Resources are well managed so the consumers have not to worry about the location or complexity of data where it is kept.
- **Pay Per Usage Basis:** Resources whether physical or virtual available in cloud environment automatically control and optimize. Detail of resource usage provides transparency for both the cloud provider and consumer of the service utilized.
- **Flexibility:** Cloud provider offers the consumer, the flexibility for availing services or facilities in any quantity at any time. They can even increase or decrease their demand as per the requirement of the company or individual.

CLOUD INFRASTRUCTURE

Cloud infrastructure mainly consist of the network, database, server and storage (devices), software for virtualization, software's for managing cloud environment and various operational(deployment) software as shown in Figure 3.

Network

For connecting cloud resources over the internet and providing seamless services and applications to the cloud users network play a vital role in cloud computing. Cloud users can even customize the services of cloud computing. The network is the key component of cloud infrastructure. It allows connecting

Figure 3. Cloud infrastructure

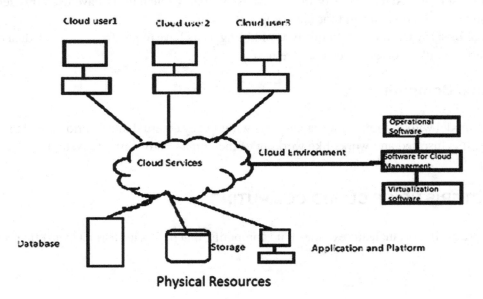

cloud services over the Internet. It is also possible to deliver network as a utility over the Internet, which means, the customer can customize various services.

Server

The server is another important component in cloud computing for providing services to the user like resource monitoring, resource granting, and also offers security services over the cloud. Virtual instances of the physical server are available for cloud users.

Virtualization Software

For offering a various instance of a physical resource to cloud users as a virtual resource, virtualization software is required. It permits various users to share a single physical resource. There is a virtual machine manager to handle the management of resources.

Software for Managing cloud

Apart from the infrastructure various software is required for managing cloud like infrastructure configuration etc.

Operational Software

The software requires for operating, handling, and integrating the services of various applications over the cloud.

Storage

For keeping data safe and secure from a malicious user, storage is replicated at different storage devices for fast accessing and recovering purpose also at the time of failure. Cloud storage devices are available for remote accessing so there is need of security and integrity. Third party involvement is there for handling a large amount of data which is a risky part of cloud storage. There is also need for amendment in legal and regulatory issues for accessing of data across a national boundary.

Commonly used cloud storage technologies for accessing logical unit are:-

- **File Access:** Data are grouped into files;
- **Block Access:** Smallest unit of data that can be accessed individually;
- **Object Access:** Metadata and data are arranged as web base;
- **Dataset Access:** Data are arranged or organized as table or record form.

In the given Figure 4 we can see that cloud user 1 accessing the same storage device as file access, while user 2 access storage for block access. User 3 uses two different storage device one for object access and other for data set access.

Figure 4. Cloud storage technologies

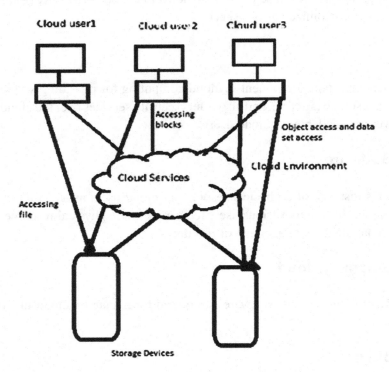

CLOUD MANAGEMENT

Management in Cloud computing means a mechanism used for coordinating resources for various cloud users demands. A virtual infrastructure manager works behind this technology for handling a virtual instance of physical resources. There are various parameters used for monitoring the cloud system like:

- **Resource Replication:** For managing and enhancing the resource required by the consumer, there is need to create and manage a various instance of the resource, and for making the resource available at the time of demand. Load on servers are always trying to evenly distribute among the virtualized resource, which guarantees the quality of services and optimized energy utilization also. As shown in Figure 5 from the virtualized resource, replication image is stored in the permanent storage device for safety purpose.
- **SLA (Service Level Agreement):** An agreement between the cloud provider and cloud user for availing various services over cloud computing. Various parameters are monitored for evaluating and ensuring services to cloud users. Cloud providers always try to fulfill QoS(Quality of services) that is already discussed and signed in contract with cloud consumer. Alternate services are also available for the cloud consumers for the fluent supply of services. Parameters of SLA may vary as per the service provider. Metrics that mainly used to define services are:-
- **Reliability of Services:** Uptime of the services provided to the users.
- **Procedure to Report Problems:** Way how to report the problems occurred during computation.

Figure 5. Cloud resource replication management

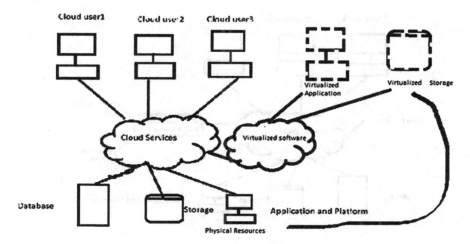

- **Exit Policy:** It defines the way to exit from a particular contract if services are not satisfactory by the cloud provider.
- Action to be taken at the time of disaster or any problem.
- Billing management system.
- Various security issues and measures adopted by the providers.
- Legal and regulatory issues.
- **Automated Scaling System:** For workload management of cloud users there is an automatic scaling management system that will actually keep tracks of various information's like status of workload, a requirement like software and hardware of the workload etc.

Various demands are requested by cloud user dynamically at the time of using applications that have to manage by cloud providers for example high capacity data storage, fast accessing processor etc. For granting and revoking all demand resources automatic scaling play an important role. Sometime a particular resource is unable to handle the required demand of the user at that time the whole workload are dynamically transferred to another machine which we called as Live migration without disturbing the user.

- **Charges Monitoring (On the Basis of Pay Per Use):** For availing various IT services from cloud computing users have to pay charges, therefore there are mechanisms used for monitoring services provided to users. For evaluating various IT resource usages parameters are always keep in the log file for future reference and for billing. Some of them are:

  ○ Amount of data to be uploaded or downloaded;
  ○ Quality of message;
  ○ Storage required;
  ○ Bandwidth required.

For handling all the above monitoring parameters there is a management system that actually calculates the charges that users have to pay. As shown in Figure 6 monitoring system and SLA management work

Figure 6. Cloud Service Level Agreement management

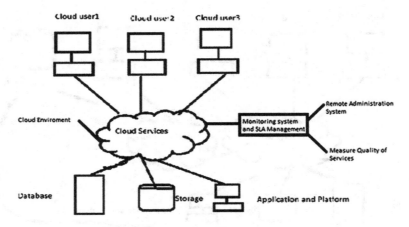

and maintain log files while providing services to the cloud user. Remote administration system and quality of services maintained as already discussed during SLA between the cloud provider and cloud user.

BENEFITS OF CLOUD COMPUTING

Cloud Computing are having abundant advantages over other computing. Some of them are:

- Utility based pay per use service is provided by cloud computing.
- Data and applications can fluently access all the time with the help of internet from the cloud computing system.
- No need to install every software and updates on client location, required software, and its updating software are easily available and kept over cloud environment.
- Various IT resource and tools are available online on demand basis.
- Cloud computing optimize the economic status of the users by charging very low for using the highly efficient resource.
- Users can even increase or decrease their demand dynamically as per the requirements
- The initial investment for accessing cloud infrastructure is very low that is offered by cloud providers as compared to the physical resource that made available at the client location.
- Hardware and software purchasing overhead costs are minimized, that are made available by cloud provider with very little operational charges.
- Cloud computing offers more than one operating platform for the cloud users on the basis of various application software.
- Users of the cloud are not to worry about the geographical location of the resource available because complexity and location of the resource are totally abstracted from the cloud users.
- Easy and simple tools are available for dynamically allocate resources to the users.
- A Higher level of data availability and reliability are there over cloud system. Proper maintenance of snapshots of various resources is kept for the time of recovery.
- High level of security features is applied to cloud data centers.

RISKS AND CHALLENGES OF CLOUD COMPUTING

As cloud computing is a growing technology of today but the biggest challenge for cloud computing is security and privacy. Various security measures are used at cloud data center for handling situations but still, there is need to improve the security features up to a certain extent. Another issue for cloud providers is of standard and platform supported by one provider need not be support applications of another cloud provider. As there are many cloud vendors in the market and each of them following different standard and protocol, so it is one of the problems for cloud user if they want to migrate from one provider to another one. Platform compatibility is also another problem sometime faced by the cloud users.

Robustness and reliability are a necessary features for the cloud system but due to third party involvement over the data storage in the data center, so it is not possible for the cloud provider to be very reliable and robust one.

There is also the risk of isolation failure in the data center as multiple users are sharing a pool of resources.

Redundant data are stored at multiple locations for high recovery and availability of data but some time the deleted data for which consumer is very sure is present at some location of the data center which breaks the trust boundary and may result in security break of highly sensitive data.

Still, businessmen are not in favors to move whole business over cloud computing system because there is always a risk of data loss. If proper security features are not used in the data center then it is very easy for the malicious users to enter in the network and break the trust boundaries. By getting sensitive and private data from the data center these suspicious users not only damage the business but used that sensitive data for some intentionally planned purpose.

CLOUD DELIVERY MODEL

Cloud Delivery is a model representing readymade combinations of IT resources and services, presented by cloud providers.

Basically, there are three types of cloud service models, Infrastructure as a service (IaaS), Platform as a service (PaaS), and Software as a service (SaaS). In the first model, the provider offers resources like servers, networking equipment, storage, backup etc. and users have only to pay for computing services they have taken. Amazon EC2 is one of the examples.

Second is Platform as a service (PaaS), in this model the cloud provider provides the platform to the users, and the users can build their own application softwares. Google Engine is an example of this type of service. The third is Software as a service (SaaS), in this model the provider offer the user's service of using software applications. Sales-Force.com is a renowned example of SaaS provider.

Applications that we are using at cloud environment are the services provided to us by distributed servers. Basically, there are three types of services:

- Software as a Service (SaaS);
- Platform as a Service (PaaS);
- Hardware as a Service (HaaS) or Infrastructure as a Service (IaaS).

Software as a Service (SaaS)

Different software for accessing various applications can be easily accessed by the user using cloud computing. The software is updated time to time by the cloud providers for giving better services to the users. Users have to pay only the rented amount without buying the whole application or software while paying very less amount. Apart from the various advantages of SaaS there are some obstacles also like:

- Sometime SaaS are not able to fulfill the need of an organization according to their demand.
- Change of Vendor by cloud users include unnecessary cost investment by the users.
- Users are attracted to move towards open source software is also challenging for the cloud providers.

Platform as a Service (PaaS)

For making applications of different types, resources are provided to the user, the software also offers to the users that need not be installed or download. Services like design, development, testing etc of software, offered at very nominal charges. Services also support teamwork services for developing various applications. Apart from the various advantages of PaaS, there are some obstacles like:

- Sometime portability is not possible among applications offered by various cloud providers.
- Some time service provider exit from the business, at that time migration, is also not possible, which result in loss of applications and data.

Hardware as a Service (HaaS)

It is commonly known by Infrastructure as a Service (IaaS). It provides hardware resource to the users on a rental basis. Users can opt:

- Any size Server space.
- Supported Network equipment.
- Memory as required.
- Large or small Storage space.

CLOUD DEPLOYMENT MODEL

A Model represents access environment of cloud, based on the parameters like size, holder etc. There are four deployment cloud models that used are Public, Private, Community and Hybrid. In Public deployment model, infrastructure and resource are available for users easily on the internet. Cloud administrator required to manage the cloud system as shown in Figure 7. Various application, database, and storage etc are available at cloud environment; users can use those services on the basis of their requirement. User1 avail applications and storage, while user2 use application and database, user3 avail facility of application and storage from the cloud computing system.

For the Private cloud, the infrastructure is made exclusively only for some private user (i.e. a company or organization) where the services can only be handled and managed locally by the cloud owner. As

Figure 7. Public Cloud

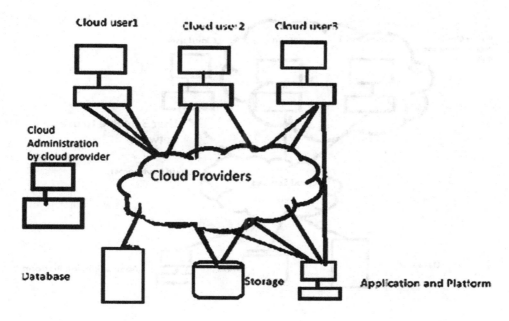

shown in Figure 8 Cloud administrator is there for managing various services over cloud computing. Services are not publicly availed by anyone.

In Community, cloud infrastructure is made available on a shared basis by several organizations that have a specific common motto. It can be managed by the organizations or a third party.

In the Hybrid cloud, the infrastructure includes two or more clouds (private, community, or public) that can communicate with one another using some standardized technologies and protocol that support data and application portability.

DATA CENTER TECHNOLOGY

Data center make IT resource a group, where all resource are kept at the location, available resources are shared among many resources for improving resource utilization and enhance accessing capability of IT resource.

Apart from the centralized IT resource like storage, network, and servers, there is some other networking equipment used in the data center for proper functioning like air conditioner, fire protection system, UPS of high voltage etc.

By using various technologies data center fulfill the demand of cloud user like:

- Remote management.
- Availability of data.
- Security issues.
- Automation system.
- Virtualization.

Figure 8. Private Cloud

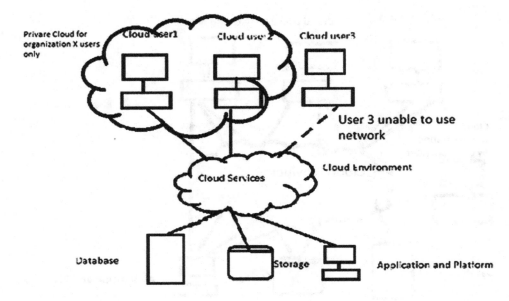

The data center is having both types of resources physical and virtual. With the help of virtualization platform, physical resources are abstracted from the cloud user and virtualized resources are available for operating and allocating the resource.

In the data center, an administrative task on IT resources is handled by remote systems. Technical persons only handled the specific tasks, and rest of the system is automatic. Specialized servers are used for handling execution that requires high processing power. Highly efficient CPU is required for handling large cloud user request. Architecture for computing mainly supports blade server technology consists of the rack, switches, power supply and cooling devices.

A storage device that consists of various hard disks uses the concept of organizing arrays. With the help of management and operational software, infrastructure in the data center is so much organized that from a single console by an operator can handle thousands of physical and virtual resource.

Storage devices commonly used the technologies like:

- Replication management.
- Hard disk.
- Virtualization(Storage).

Replication management saves the snapshot of physical and virtual memory for future reference.

Hard disk using the concept of array replicates the data in multiple destinations; the technology that mostly used with the hard disk is RAID (Redundant arrays of independent disks). The concept of virtualization and virtual device are used for accessing and storing data. For handling enormous data, backup is taken for faster recovery and future reference into removable devices like SAN (Storage area network) and NAS (Network attached storage).

- **SAN:** This type of data storage are directly connected to the dedicated network and it support block level data access.
- **NAS:** Hard disk is directly handled by this device, which supports file data access connected through a network. Both SAN and NAS are fault tolerance device.

VIRTUALIZATION TECHNOLOGY

A conventional computer system that we are using is having a single operating system. It is having a fixed architecture with tightly coupled application software with a specific hardware configuration. It is not necessary that some software that is compatible with one machine is also compatible with another machine with different operating system. The concept of the virtual machine is introduced that offers a new strategy to fully utilized resources, make application flexible, manage software easily with any running platform etc. Virtualization is a fundamental part of cloud computing technology. It provides a conceptual environment for virtual hardware and an operating system for running various applications and beyond this, it also provides environment for storage, memory, and networking. There are three major components in virtualized environment that are guest, host, and layer of virtualization. Host means the actual physical environment where guest will be managed. A layer of virtualization is responsible for creating virtualized environment for guest to operate applications, resources etc. In the process of virtualization physical IT resources is converted as a virtual resource. Resources that are mainly virtualized are servers, storage, network (e.g. routers, switches etc.)

A new virtual server is created with the help of virtualization software on the physical server, then an operating system can be installed on the new guest virtual environment, that is totally independent of the operating system is installed on the physical resource. Guest operating system and application software that is running over it are not aware of the virtualization or virtual environment. A Virtualization technique used to create a virtual instance of the physical resource is a hypervisor.

Virtualization software makes underutilized resources of physical server available to others and that's why virtualization needs virtual machine monitor to manage the environment.

The multitenant application allows multiple users to access the same application simultaneously. Users are not aware of each other and they feel that they are exclusive user of the application.

While in virtualization multiple copies of a single physical server is created. Each copy is handled by a single user that can be easily configured and managed independently having its own operating system and application.

In multitenant application, each user has to access data and configure its own application. A peculiar feature of the application that can be customized are:

- Interface provided to the user.
- Data Models used.
- Various rights and access control provided to the user.

The multitenant application maintains isolation between applications. Security issues are also seriously considered in this environment. Virtualization makes users a feel of real facilities. Two types of services are provided by the remote data center, i.e. full or partial virtualization.

Full Virtualization

One machine is completely installed on another machine in full virtualization. The virtual machine will behave and offers all the software's that are provided by the physical server. There are many reasons to adopt full virtualization like:

- Many users share a common computer system.
- Copy hardware on different machine for various purpose.

Para Virtualization

Hardware supports multiple operating systems to run on the single machine in para virtualization. Para virtualization makes efficient use of system resources. Users can work with multiple environments in this type virtualization. Complete services of a system are not available for others to use.

Benefits of Para virtualization are:

- At the time of catastrophe, this virtualization works efficiently by moving the guest to some system.
- Updating hardware or any resource is easy in this virtualization.

APPLICATIONS OF CLOUD COMPUTING

There are many cloud computing applications that are absolutely free available to use for different application point of view. Some important applications on the basis of which sites have been categorized are:

- File storage space available online.
- Applications of twitter.
- Create image album online and editing.
- Application of Anti-virus.
- Documentation software, spreadsheets, and power points.
- Direction through map.
- Application of e-commerce.
- Other varied applications.

For file storage purpose many tools are available that are used to host files and share any type of file like image, document file etc. Some free spaces are also available for storage and having uploaded and download facility.

Some online file sharing applications are Rapidshare, depositfiles, Yourfilehost, zshare, NowDownloadAll, easy-share, etc. Many tools are available for free downloading movies, vedios TV shows which are compatible with the browsers.

For creating and organizing images and albums on the website, tools are available online; some of them are flickr, Fotolog, photobucket, webshots etc. Some free available online software for photo editing are a picnic, pixlr etc. which has many vital features like cropping, resizing and rotation of images with special effects. Softwares are easily available and easy to use.

For security purpose, various updated antivirus applications are also available that can be used to protect the system from virus and malwares. Writeboard, slideshare etc. are some applications tools used for editing various documents, spreadsheets, and powerpoints.

Googlemaps is the one of the popular web application used to get direction map of any location. Various other miscellaneous free Software as Service applications are also available for checking the status of letters and packages. Free Softwares are available to check package and track it.

VENDORS OF CLOUD COMPUTING

Amazon AWS leading cloud providers, it has having the highest computing power. In the infrastructure viewpoint, Amazon is a public cloud so it can be easily accessible from anywhere through the internet. Amazon is different Cloud Computing provider that is having distinguished innovative cloud features. Amazon has a set of cloud services which is offered by Amazon AWS, that is including computation, storage, and other features. Amazon AWS facilitate company and individuals to organize applications and services on requirement and demand basis. Amazon offer services like Mechanical Turk, Simple Storage Service (S3), Elastic Compute Cloud (EC2), SimpleDB, and Relational Data Service (RDS).

Google App Engine GAE is Google's application development and hosting platform. GAE offer services to build web applications devoid of managing infrastructure. All application that is built on GAE, uses the technology that supports Google's websites for speed and reliability. GAE also support virtualizations of applications across various servers and data centers. GAE is free up to a certain level of use resources. The amount is charged for additional usage like storage, bandwidth etc. as required by the application.

Windows Azure is actually Cloud Operating System and it helps to run windows applications and storing the data on servers in data centers. Windows Azure supports many languages such as.NET Framework, C#, Visual Basic, C++, SOAP, REST, XML, Java, PHP, and Ruby etc that can be used as applications development tool.

Rackspace offer services to all kind of businesses. It offers Cloud hosting, Email, and application. Language supported by Cloud Sites is PHP 5, Perl, Python, MySQL, NET 2.0+, ASP and Microsoft SQL Server 2008. Other popular applications are WordPress, Drupal, Joomla, and DotNet-Nuke.

CONCLUSION

With the speedy advances of Cloud technologies, there's a brand new demand for tools to review and analyze the advantages of the technology and therefore the best practices to use the technology to large-scaled applications by configuring it as per the requirement of the organization. Cloud Service Broker, can increase or decreases the number of resources on the market. Develop and evaluate new mechanisms and algorithms for resource management, is important as per the performance of rising Cloud applications. Load balancing is one amongst the most challenges in cloud computing. It's needed to distribute the dynamic work equally across all the nodes to attain a high user satisfaction and resource utilization. The quality result can be achieved by ensuring that each computing resource is distributed fairly.

Cloud Computing is having a necessity to develop related adjustive algorithmic that is appropriate for heterogeneous atmosphere and may cut back the price. There are varied techniques that are projected by the varied researchers to beat the challenge of load balancing.

Still, there is need to minimize the whole energy consumption of servers by scheduling uncertain client requests and switch server modes. Backlogging can also help us to scale back the whole consumed energy by permitting servers to consolidate requests to later periods. The power allocated to every server is adjusted in terms of current demand level, to reduce energy consumption and meet QoS needs. In Cloud, Computing infrastructures develop heuristic-based algorithms for deriving good-quality possible solutions.

Finally, we can also think about self-service environments in Clouds, and modify the environment to handle dynamic job arrives with unknown distributions. CloudAnalyst could be a new tool developed to deal with this demand.

LITERATURE REVIEW

Weijia Song et al. propose, present an approach that uses virtualization technology for allocating resources dynamically in the data center on the basis of application demands and it also optimizing the number of servers actively used for achieving green computing. An alternative of on-line bin packing problem and develop a realistic, competent algorithm that works well in a real environment. Broad simulation results reveal that system achieves good performance as compared to the existing work.

Lin Wang et al. propose a new frame by combining some unique features of data centers through traffic engineering. On the basis of which they illustrate the energy efficiency problem with time aware model and prove that it is NP hard problem with a solution having two steps. Initially, the problem of virtual machines assignment to the server is solved by reducing traffic and to make positive conditions for traffic engineering. Three important principles are proposed for problem solution. Subsequent, the active switches are diminished and balance traffic flows which depend upon power consumption and routing. Fifty percent energy savings can be achieved by this framework.

Yi-Ju Chang et al. propose three power-saving policies which are applied in a cloud environment to reduce the idle power of servers. An efficient green control (EGC) algorithm is proposed for solving constrained optimization problems. N-policy is applied to optimize operational cost within a performance guarantee. The operational costs of power consumption, system congestion, and mode-switching are all considered while developing cost function.

Wassim Itani et al. present an autonomic service routing protocol for constructing energy-efficient service provider paths in mutual cloud computing architectures, G-Route (Green Route). The principal part of this work is separately selecting the optimal set of merged service components behind the most efficient energy consumption. Energy saving is the major goal of G-Route for enhancing the energy savings in cloud computing infrastructure. The protocol design and tested in a real cloud computing environment with the Amazon EC2 cloud platform.

LI Hongyou et al. propose two algorithms (ESWCT) Energy aware scheduling algorithm using workload aware consolidation techniques and (ELMWCT) Energy aware live migration algorithm using workload aware consolidation techniques. Physical machine considered here are consist of multiple compositions of CPU, memory and network cards. Both algorithms focused on the problem of consolidating diverse workloads and executing all virtual machines while using the minimum physical machine, then unused physical machines are switched off.

Mahdi Ghamkhari et al. propose a systematic approach to maximize green data center's profit. Practical service-level agreements (SLAs) between service providers and their customers are considered. Various factors such as availability of local renewable power generation at data centers are studied. A novel optimization-based profit maximization strategy for data centers with basically two cases, without and with behind-the-meter renewable generators is also proposed.

Rasoul Beik proposes, an energy aware layer in software architecture. This layer is responsible for evaluating micro and macro metrics of energy consumption. Micro metrics evaluate energy consumption on CPU; macro metrics evaluate overall energy consumption in a data center. A task that should be done for achieving mentioned layer are defining micro and macro metrics, weighting above metrics, locate the best hosts which consume energy efficiently.

Awada Uchechukwu et al. present Green Cloud Environments (GCE) to minimize its energy consumption by considering static and dynamic portions of cloud components. Energy consumption is basically divided into two parts:

- Fixed energy consumption.
- Dynamic energy consumption.

They investigate energy consumption patterns. They also described an energy consumption tools and empirical analysis approach. They also provide models for server idle and server active states.

Mayank Mishra et al. illustrate the role of live virtual machine migration in dynamic resource management in cloud data centers. They also discussed when to migrate, which VM to migrate and where to migrate during migration. Different approaches can be applied in migration techniques like server consolidation, Load balancing, and hotspot migration.

Yuvapriya Ponnusamy et al. propose framework and principles to provide green enhancements in a Cloud computing architecture. A new energy efficient scheduling is presented. With power-aware scheduling techniques, variable resource management, live migration, and a minimal virtual machine design, overall system efficiency will be enormously improved. Power aware and thermal aware scheduling system is future opportunities for the researcher to minimize energy consumption.

Nidhi Jain Kansal et al. discussed the advantage of energy efficient load balancing techniques in details. Various parameters like performance, scalability and associated overheads are explained in detail. Existing load balancing techniques are discussed which mainly focused on reducing overhead, service response time and improving performance etc. but none of them are discussed while considering and reducing carbon emission.

N. Xiong et al. presented survey report on green Cloud computing. Provisioning cloud service while considering energy consumption under a set of energy consumption criteria and it is called GCC. Recent work is done in GCC based on networks, including microprocessors, task scheduling algorithms, virtualization technology, cooling systems, networks and disk storage etc. also discussed. The works on GCC from their research group was presented at Georgia State University.

Jue Wang et al proposed, the models dynamically monitor and predict customer requests for each period, and proactively switch servers on/off according to estimated customer requests. QoS levels are maintained by either enforcing zero unsatisfied requests, or imposing a joint chance constraint to bound possible failures in a backlogging model. The models also handle dynamic job arrives with unknown distributions.

Qingwen Chen et al. presented a linear power model to analyze the behavior of a single work node and understand the contribution of components like CPU, memory, and HDD. Five important metrics that are considered are performance, power consumption, execution time, power efficiency and energy consumption. Test type like floating point operation, Integer operation and hyper threading are used. Investigation on effects on energy consumption and performance of running multiple VMs with different workloads are also done.

Qiang Huang et al. presented, a power consumption evaluation on the effects lives migration on VMs. Paper mainly focused on VM live migration in which a VM is transferred from a physical server to another while running continuously.

Jayant Baliga et al. present an analysis of energy consumption in cloud computing. It considers both public and private clouds and also analyzes energy consumption in switching and transmission as well as data processing and data storage. Energy consumption in transport and switching have a major percentage of total energy consumption in cloud computing. Cloud computing consume more energy-efficient when the computing tasks are of low intensity or infrequent. Sometimes cloud computing can consume more energy than conventional computing when every user performs all computing on their own personal computer (PC).

Woongki Back et al. propose the Green system that supports a programming which is energy conscious using controlled approximation for expensive loops and functions. Green is evaluated by building a prototype with phoenix compiler framework. The same is applied in real work search application.

Keijiang Ye et al. presented a study of energy efficiency from the performance perspective. Initially, they present a virtual machine based energy-efficient data center architecture for cloud computing. They investigate then the potential performance overheads caused by server consolidation and live migration of virtual machine technology. Technologies can effectively implement energy-saving goals with little performance overheads.

Young Choon Lee et al. presented two energy conscious task consolidation heuristics approach to maximize resource utilization and minimize energy consumption. Cost functions are incorporated into heuristics, capture energy saving possibilities.

Bo Li, Jianxin Huai et al. proposed, a novel approach named EnaCloud, which enables application live placement dynamically with consideration of energy efficiency in a cloud platform. Virtual Machine is used to encapsulate the application, that supports applications scheduling and lives migration to minimize the number of running machines, for energy saving. The application placement is treated as a bin packing problem, and an energy-aware heuristic algorithm is proposed to get an appropriate solution. An over-provision approach is presented to deal with the changeable applications demands for various resources.

Uwe Schmidtmann et al. discussed the ongoing research project LK3S an agent platform is under construction which enables optimization and flexibility. Since the agent platform needs full access to all field level information a new concept of this part is needed. The paper discusses how this concept can be used to optimize the whole system with respect to the constraints of energy consumption and throughput.

Andrew J. Younge et al. propose new cloud computing architecture with efficient green enhancements. To show the potential of the framework they presented a new energy efficient scheduling, VM system image, and image management components that expose new power consumption ways.

FUTURE RESEARCH DIRECTIONS

Following are some vital research area of cloud computing that needs further enhancement for providing better services to the cloud users.

Quality Management in Cloud Computing

Cloud service suppliers aren't totally different to ancient IT service suppliers in relevancy there have to be compelled to provide quality, efficient, secure and on the market IT services. A key worth plan of cloud based mostly service suppliers is that the provision of IT infrastructure and services beneath a utility or pay-per-use model. Cloud service suppliers ought to be targeted on planning quality services customers and shoppers require. Cloud service provider tries to supply worth to customers by facilitating outcomes customers need to realize. For example, Platform as a Service (PaaS) might cut back the general possession and prices (capital and operational) to the client, concerning their back-end infrastructure. It's obligatory the client analyze the whole prices and examine the potential for price savings. The cloud service supplier is predictable to supply high levels of quality and repair assurance so as to:

- Increase the client share.
- Deliver the services.
- Ensure the integrity, security, convenience and continuity of the services.

However, quality and maintenance might not be open for discussion or negotiation with the client. Therefore, it's sensible for the client to know if the client will outline the amount of service quality and assurance they need in a much negotiated service level agreement. Customers of cloud computing and cloud based mostly services ought to expect, and demand, a minimum of similar levels of service as that's provided by ancient IT service suppliers and internal IT organizations.

In several cases, it's common for customers to expect even higher levels of service from cloud service suppliers. There are varieties of reasons for this, Company information currently resides outside of the organization and should be managed confidently issues like:

- Security issues.
- Availability needs.
- Guarantee service stability.

Cloud computing is unfamiliar with the organization Fear, uncertainty and doubt.

Capacity Management Cloud Computing

Cloud computing provides the illusion of a seamless, infinite resource pool with versatile on-demand accessibility. However, behind this illusion thousands of servers and peta-bytes of storage are used, running tens of thousands of applications accessed by several users. The management of such systems is non-trivial as a result of they face elastic demand, have heterogeneous resources, should fulfill numerous management objectives, and are a unit immense in scale. Autonomic computing techniques are familiar to tackle the drawback of resource management in cloud computing centers by introducing self-managing components known as automatic managers.

Every automatic manager ought to be capable of managing itself whereas at the same time to the fulfillment of high level system wide objectives. A large varies of approaches and mechanisms with familiar outline and design are used, moreover to organize data centers and coordinate the actions so as to achieve specific goals.

The resource management is developed with reference to one or a lot of management objectives like value, profit, or data center utilization, moreover as performance considerations like latency, quality of service, and rejection rates. Mains problems are of efficient elastic resource provisioning unified management of cloud resources, and measurability in cloud resource management.

Cloud Migration Issues in Cloud Computing

A hypervisor is a virtual machine manager or monitoring system (VMM), or virtualization manager, may be a program that permits multiple operational systems to share one hardware host. Each guest package seems to possess the host's processor, memory, and alternative resources all to it. However, the hypervisor is really dominant the host processor and resources, allocating what's required to every package successively and ensuring that the guest operational systems (called virtual machines) cannot disrupt one another.

- Sharing of resources helps price reduction.
- Virtual machines maintenance isolation.
- Virtual machines encapsulate a whole computing setting.
- Virtual machines run severally underlying hardware.
- Virtual machines will be migrated between totally different hosts.

Cloud Resource Virtualization

The foundation for the bulk of high-performing clouds could be a virtualized infrastructure. Virtualization has been in data centers for many years as an eminent IT strategy for consolidating servers. Today, the first focus for virtualization continues to on servers. However, virtualizing storage and networks is rising as a general strategy. Resource virtualizations tools are available for achieving desktop virtualization, compute virtualizations, network and storage virtualizations.

Workload Management in Cloud Computing

Cloud computing is a technology through that package, platforms and infrastructure are often provided as services. Managing resources that alter this technology may be a vital task to maximize performance and edges all connected parties. Demand for resources starts with application requests initiated by the users. These trigger the creation of virtual machines that successively trigger the allocation of physical resources.

License Management in Cloud Computing

The 3 basic types of license used in cloud computing are measure per-user, per-device, and enterprise. Paying per user is a technique whereby a user is granted a license to use the appliance or server. This can be divided into concurrent users and total users. A concurrent-user license merely implies that they authorized up to a certain range of users at the same time. Per-device licenses vary wide. Licenses management supported the overall range of processors in a host system.

Big Data in Cloud Computing

The cloud computing and cloud data centers are a pioneer and result emergence of huge knowledge. Cloud computing is that the commoditization of computing time and knowledge storage by suggests that of standardized technologies.

It has vital benefits over ancient physical deployments. However, cloud platforms are available in many forms and generally have to be compelled to be integrated with ancient architectures.

Vertical scaling achieves physical property by adding further instances for serving the demand of users. A package like Hadoop specifically designed as distributed systems to take advantage of vertical scaling. Distributed systems support SQL databases, like Cassandra or HBase, and file systems like Hadoop's HDFS. Instantiating thousands of those machines to attain a lot of requests per day is simple with the help of the available tools. Of course, mining operations from the large database ought to be conscious of the resources of the online sites or through the application interface. A poorly planned data processing operation some have an attack like denial of service.

Data Handling with Map-Reduce

MapReduce a programming model with an associated implementation for process and generating giant data sets. Users specify a map operate that processes a key or value combine to come up with a group of intermediate value pairs and a cut back operate that merges all intermediate values related to the identical intermediate key.

The run-time system takes care of the details of partitioning the computer file, programming the program's execution across a group of machines, handling machine failures, and managing the desired inter-machine communication. This permits programmers with none experience with parallel and distributed systems to simply utilize the resources of an oversized distributed system

In the massive information community, MapReduce has been seen joined of the key authoritative approaches for meeting continuously increasing demands on computing resources imposed by huge information sets. The basis for this is often the high scalability of the MapReduce paradigm that permits for massively parallel and distributed execution over an oversized a number of computing nodes. Moreover, current efforts aimed toward rising and extending MapReduce to handle known challenges. Consequently, distinguishing problems and challenges MapReduce faces handling massive information, this study encourages future massive information analysis.

Virtual Machine Consolidation in Cloud Computing

Improving the energy effectiveness of cloud computing systems has become a crucial issue as a result of the electrical energy bill for 24/7 operation of those systems is quite massive. Virtual machine (VM) consolidation in an exceedingly cloud automatic data processing system as the way of lowering energy consumption of the system.

Risk Assessment in Cloud Computing

With the advancement in cloud technologies and increasing variety of cloud users, businesses jointly ought to sustain with the prevailing technology to supply real business solutions. Additionally, predictions for growth indicate huge developments and implementations of cloud computing services, together with that the cloud computing services market is probably going to increase. From the business perspective, cloud computing becomes one in key technologies that give real promise to business with real benefits in term of price and machine power. In spite of the advancement in cloud technologies and increasing variety of cloud users, Cloud computing is a completely unique technology introduces new security risks that require being assessing and satisfying. Consequently, assessment of security risks is important, the normal technical methodology of risk assessment that centers on the assets ought to fall down to the business centered on the particular nature of cloud computing and on the changes in technology that have resulted replacement ways that for cloud suppliers to deliver their services to cloud customers

Recovery Management and Disaster Recovery in Cloud Computing

Cloud computing transforms the approach info technology (IT) is consumed and managed, promising improved price efficiencies, accelerated innovation, quicker time-to-market, and also the ability to scale applications on demand. Because cloud computing is rising and developing very fast. Each conceptually and truly, the legal/contractual, economic, service quality, ability, security and privacy problems still create vital challenges. Especially, we have a tendency to discuss 3 vital challenges: restrictive, security and privacy problems in cloud computing. Some solutions to mitigate these challenges also are planned beside a short presentation on the longer term trends in cloud computing.

Economic, Business and ROI Models for Cloud Computing

Cloud Computing has been defining as a technological amendment and union of a variety of latest and existing technologies. The promise of Cloud Computing is primarily the subsequent key technical characteristics like the flexibility to make the illusion of infinite capacity. The performance is that the same if scaled for one to many or one thousand users with consistent service-level characteristics.

Abstraction of the infrastructure, therefore, applications aren't latched into devices or locations. You merely get hold of what you utilize and with no or borderline up-front investment prices. The service is on-demand and access to applications and data from any end.

Green Cloud Computing

Cloud computing is having the extremely efficient infrastructure for running HPC, enterprise, and applications. However, the growing demand for Cloud infrastructure has drastically increased the energy consumption of information centers that has become a vital issue. High energy consumption does not solely interpret to high operational price, however conjointly results in high carbon emissions that aren't environmentally friendly. Hence, energy-efficient solutions needed to reduce the impact of Cloud computing.

Energy-Aware Scheduling of Map Reduce

The majority of large-scale knowledge intensive applications dead by knowledge centers measure supported Map Reduce or its ASCII text file implementation, Hadoop. Heuristic algorithms referred to as energy-aware MapReduce programming algorithms (EMRSA-I and EMRSA-II), that notice the assignments of map and scale back tasks to the machine slots so as to reduce the energy consumed once capital punishment the applying.

REFERENCES

Back & Chilimbi (2010). *Green: A Framework for Supporting Energy – Conscious Programming using Controlled Approximation.* ACM.

Baliga, J., Ayre, R. W. A., Hinton, K., & Tucker, R. S. (2010). Green Cloud Computing: Balancing Energy in Processing, Storage and Transport. *Proceeding of the IEEE.*

Beik. (2012). *Green Cloud Computing: An Energy-Aware Layer in Software Architecture.* IEEE.

Buyya, R., Vecchhiola, C., & Thamarai Selvi, S. (2008). *Mastering Cloud Computing.* Tata McGraw Hill Education Private Limited.

Chang, Ouyang, & Hsu. (2014). An Efficient Green Control Algorithm in Cloud Computing for Cost Optimization. *IEEE Transactions on Cloud Computing.*

Chee & Franklin, Jr. (2010). *Cloud Computing Technologies and Strategies.* CRC Press.

Chen, Q., Grosso, P., van der Veldt, K., de Laat, C., Hofman, R., & Bal, H. (2011). Profiling energy consumption of VMs for green computing. *IEEE Ninth International Conference.*

Ghamkhari & Rad. (2013). Energy and Performance Management of Green Data Centers: A Profit Maximization Approach. *IEEE Transactions on Smart Grid, 4*(2).

Harmon & Auseklis. (2009). Sustainable IT Services: Assessing the Impact of Green Computing Practices. *IEEE Xplore.*

Huang, Q., Gao, F., Wang, R., & Qi, Z. (n.d.). Power Consumption of Virtual Machine Live Migration in Clouds. *IEEE 3rd International conference on Communication and Mobile Computing.*

Hurwitz, Bloor, Kaufman, & Halper. (2009). *Cloud computing for dummies.* Wiley Publication.

Itani, W., Ghali, C., Chehab, A., & Kayssi, A. (2013). Accountable Energy Monitoring for Green Service Routing in the Cloud. *3rd International conference on communications and information technology.*

Jue, S. S. (2012). Risk and Energy Consumption Tradeoffs in Cloud Computing Service via Stochastic Optimization Models. *IEEE/ACM Fifth International Conference on Utility and Cloud Computing.*

Kansal, N. J., & Chana, I. (2012). Cloud Load Balancing Techniques: A Step towards Green Computing. IJCSI, 9(1).

Katarina, S. S. T. W. S. R. (2009). *Grid and Cloud Computing.* Springer.

Krutz, R. L., & Vines, R. D. (2010). *Cloud Security: A Comprehensive Guide to Secure Cloud Computing.* Wiley Publication.

Lee & Zomaya. (2010). *Energy efficient utilization of resources in cloud computing systems.* Springer.

Li, B., Huai, J., Wo, T., & Qin, L. L. Z. (2009). IEEE International Conference on Cloud Computing. *EnaCloud: An Energy Saving Application Live Placement Approach for Cloud Computing Environments.*

Li, Wang, Peng, Wang, & Liu. (2013, December). Energy Aware scheduling scheme using workload-Aware consolidation technique in cloud data centers. *China Communication.*

Mishra, M., Das, A., Kulkarni, P., & Sahoo, A. (2012, September). Dynamic Resource Management Using Virtual Machine Migrations. *IEEE Communication Magazine.*

Ponnusamy & Sasikumar. (2012). Application of Green Cloud Computing for Efficient Resource Energy Management in Data Centers. *IJCSIT, 3*(5).

Rajeswara Rao, V., & Shubba Ramaiah, V. (2014). Cloud computing and Virtualization. BS Publications.

Sarna. (2010). *Implementing and Developing cloud applications.* Auerbach Publications.

Schmidtmann, Kreutz, Barkhoff, Virkus, Stockmann, & Jovic. (2009). *Material Flow Optimization under Aspects of Energy Efficiency.* IEEE.

Song, W., Xiao, Z., Chen, Q., & Luo, H. (2014). Adaptive Resource Provisioning for the Cloud Using Online Bin Packing. IEEE Transactions on Computers, 63.

Uchechukwu, Li, & Shen. (2012). *Improving Cloud Computing Energy Efficiency.* IEEE.

Velte, A. T., Velte, T. J., & Elsenpeter, R. (2009). *Cloud Computing: A Practical Approach.* McGraw-Hill Publication.

Wang, L., Zhang, F., Aroca, J. A., Vasilakos, A. V., Zheng, K., Hou, C., . . . Liu, Z. (2014). GreenDCN: A General Framework for Achieving Energy Efficiency in Data Center Networks. IEEE Journal, 32.

Xiong, , Han, , & Vandenberg, . (2012). Green Cloud computing schemes based on networks survey. The Institution of Engineering and Technology.

Ye, K., Huang, D., Jiang, X., & Chen, H. (2010). Virtual Machine Based Energy-Efficient Data Center Architecture for Cloud Computing: A Performance perspective. *IEEE/ACM International conference on Green Computing and Communication.*

Younge, von Laszewski, Wang, Lopez-Alarcon, & Carithers. (n.d.). *Efficient Resource Management Cloud Computing Environments.* Academic Press.

KEY TERMS AND DEFINITIONS

Autonomic Computing: A computing model with self managing capabilities without any external intervention. It is inspired and works like working of human body nervous system.

Data Center: Data Center is a storehouse consists of various IT and non IT equipment for providing services over cloud computing.

Delivery Model: A model representing readymade combinations of IT resources and services, presented by cloud providers.

Deployment Model: A Model represents access environment of cloud, based on the parameters like size, holder, etc.

Hypervisor: A Virtualization technique used to create a virtual instance of the physical resource.

Live Migration: A mechanism that supports runtime transfer of virtual server from one to another is called Live Migration of virtual machine.

SLA (Service Level Agreement): An agreement between the cloud provider and cloud user for availing various services over cloud computing.

Utility Computing: Utility computing defines billing model of the computing resource.

Chapter 11
Survey of Unknown Malware Attack Finding

Murugan Sethuraman Sethuraman
Wolkite University, Ethiopia

ABSTRACT

Intrusion detection system(IDS) has played a vital role as a device to guard our networks from unknown malware attacks. However, since it still suffers from detecting an unknown attack, i.e., 0-day attack, the ultimate challenge in intrusion detection field is how we can precisely identify such an attack. This chapter will analyze the various unknown malware activities while networking, internet or remote connection. For identifying known malware various tools are available but that does not detect Unknown malware exactly. It will vary according to connectivity and using tools and finding strategies what they used. Anyhow like known Malware few of unknown malware listed according to their abnormal activities and changes in the system. In this chapter, we will see the various Unknown methods and avoiding preventions as birds eye view manner.

INTRODUCTION

This chapter surveys proposed solutions for the problem of Unknown Malware attack appearing in the computer security research literature. After describing the challenges of this problem and highlighting current approaches and techniques pursued by the research community for insider attack detection, suggest directions for future research.

Recent news articles have reported that Every year to year time to time an enormous increase of known and unknown malware variants . This has made it even more difficult for the anti-malware vendors to maintain protection against the vast amount of Unknown threats. Various obfuscation techniques, such as reverse engineering, honeypot, and intelligence intrusion detection prevention, contribute to this trend. The ongoing battle between malware creators and anti-virus vendors causes an increasing signature, which leads to vulnerable end-systems for home users as well as in corporate environments.

DOI: 10.4018/978-1-5225-3129-6.ch011

Data Mining Basics

Recent progress in scientific and engineering applications has accumulated huge volumes of data. The fast growing, tremendous amount of data, collected and stored in large databases has far exceeded our human ability to comprehend it without proper tools. Coverage and volume of digital geographic data sets and multidimensional data have grown rapidly in recent years. These data sets include digital data of all sorts created and disseminated by government and private agencies on land use, climate data and vast amounts of data acquired through remote sensing systems and other monitoring devices. It is estimated that multimedia data is growing at about 70% per year. Therefore, there is a critical need for data analysis systems that can automatically analyze the data, to summarize it and predict future trends. Data Mining is a necessary technology for collecting information from distributed databases and then performing data analysis.

The process of knowledge discovery in databases is explained and it consists of the following steps:

- Data cleaning to remove noise and inconsistencies.
- Data integration to get data from multiple sources.
- Data selection step where data relevant for the task is retrieved.
- Data transformation step where data is transformed into an appropriate form for data analysis.
- Data Analysis where complex queries are executed for in depth analysis.

The following are different kinds of techniques and algorithms that data mining can provide:

Association Analysis involves discovery of association rules showing attribute value conditions that occur frequently together in a given set of data. This is used frequently for transaction data analysis.

A popular algorithm for discovering association rules is the Apriori method. This algorithm uses an iterative approach known as level-wise search where k-itemsets are used to explore (k+1) itemsets. Association rules are widely used for prediction.

Classification and Prediction are two forms of data analysis that can be used to extract models describing important data classes or to predict future data trends. The basic techniques for data classification are decision tree induction, Bayesian classification, and neural networks. These techniques find a set of models that describe the different classes of objects. These models can be used to predict the class of an object for which the class is unknown. The derived model can be represented as rules (IF-THEN), decision trees or other formulae.

Clustering involves grouping objects so that objects within a cluster have high similarity but are very dissimilar to objects in other clusters. Clustering is based on the principle of maximizing the intraclass similarity and minimizing the interclass similarity. Due to a large amount of data collected, cluster analysis has recently become a highly active topic in Data Mining research. As a branch of statistics, cluster analysis has been extensively studied for many years, focusing primarily on distance based cluster analysis. These techniques have been built into statistical analysis packages such as S-PLUS and SAS. In machine learning, clustering is an example of unsupervised learning. For this reason, clustering is an example of learning by observation.

A database may contain data objects that do not comply with the general model or behavior of data. These data objects are called outliers. Most Data Mining methods discard outliers as noise or exceptions.

These outliers are useful for applications such as fraud detection and network intrusion detection. The analysis of outlier data is referred to as outlier mining. Outliers may be detected using statistical tests that assume a distribution or probability model for the data, or using distance measures where objects that are a substantial distance from other clusters are considered outliers.

Data Mining Intrusion Detection Models

Since the cost of information processing and Internet accessibility is dropping, more and more organizations are becoming vulnerable to a wide variety of cyber threats. According to a recent survey by CERT, the rate of cyber attacks has been doubling every year in recent times.

Therefore, it has become increasingly important to make our information systems, especially those used for critical functions such as military and commercial purpose, resistant to and tolerant of such attacks. IDS are an integral part of any security package of a modern networked information system. An IDS detects intrusions by monitoring a network or system and analyzing an audit stream collected from the network or system to look for clues of malicious behavior.

Intrusion detection systems can be classified into the following two categories:

Misuse Detection method finds intrusions by monitoring network traffic in search of direct matches to known patterns of attack. A disadvantage of this approach is that it can only detect intrusions that match a pre-defined rule. One advantage of these systems is that they have low false alarm rates.

Anomaly Detection approach defines the expected behavior of the network in advance. The profile of normal behavior is built using techniques that include statistical methods, association rules, and neural networks. Any significant deviations from this expected behavior are reported as possible attacks. In principle, the primary advantage of anomaly based detection is the ability to detect novel attacks for which signatures have not been defined yet. However, in practice, this is difficult to achieve because it is hard to obtain accurate and comprehensive profiles of normal behavior. This makes an anomaly detection system generate too many false alarms and it can be very time to consume and labor intensive to sift through this data.

IDS can also be categorized according to the kind of information they analyze. This leads to the distinction between host-based and network based IDS. A host based IDS analyzes host bound audit sources such as operating system audit trails, system logs or application logs. Since host based systems directly monitor the host data files and operating system processes, they can determine exactly which host resources are targets of a particular attack. Due to the rapid development of computer networks, traditional single host intrusion detection systems have been modified to monitor a number of hosts on a network. They transfer the monitored information from multiple monitored hosts to a central site for processing. These are termed as distributed intrusion detection systems.

Network based IDS analyzes network packets that are captured on a network. This involves placing a set of traffic sensors within the network. The sensors typically perform local analysis and detection and report suspicious events to a central location. Recently, there is a great interest in application of Data Mining techniques to intrusion detection systems. The problem of intrusion detection can be reduced to a Data Mining task of classifying data. Briefly, one is given a set of data points belonging to different classes (normal activity, different attacks) and aims to separate them as accurately as possible by means of a model.

Knowledge Discovery in Database (KDD)

KDD is an automatic, exploratory analysis and modeling of large data repositories. It is an organized process of identifying valid, novel, useful, and understandable patterns from large and complex data sets.

Data Mining (DM) is the core of the KDD process, involving the inferring of algorithms that explore the data, develop the model and discover previously unknown patterns. The model is used for understanding phenomena from the data, analysis, and prediction.

The accessibility and abundance of data today makes Knowledge Discovery and Data Mining a matter of considerable importance and necessity. Given the recent growth of the field, it is not surprising that a wide variety of methods is now available to the researchers and practitioners.

The special recent aspects of data availability that are promoting the rapid development of KDD and DM are the electronically readiness of data (though of different types and reliability). The internet and intranet fast development in particular data accessibility (as formatted or unformatted, voice or video, etc.). Methods that were developed before the Internet revolution considered smaller amounts of data with less variability in data types and reliability. Since the information age, the accumulation of data has become easier and less costly. It has been estimated that the amount of stored information doubles every twenty months. Unfortunately, as the amount of electronically stored information increases, the ability to understand and make use of it does not keep pace with its growth. Data Mining is a term coined to describe the process of sifting through large databases for interesting patterns and relationships. The studies today aim at evidence-based modeling and analysis, as is the leading practice in medicine, finance, security and many other fields. The data availability is increasing exponentially, while the human processing level is almost constant. Thus the potential gap increases exponentially. This gap is the opportunity for the KDD or DM field, which therefore becomes increasingly important and necessary.

KDD Process

The knowledge discovery process is iterative and interactive, consisting of nine steps. Note that the process is iterative at each step, meaning that moving back to adjust previous steps may be required. The process has many artistic aspects in the sense that one cannot present one formula or make a complete taxonomy for the right choices for each step and application type. Thus it is required to deeply understand the process and the different needs and possibilities in each step. Taxonomy for the Data Mining methods is helping in this process.

The process starts with determining the KDD goals and ends with the implementation of the discovered knowledge. As a result, changes would have to be made in the application domain. This closes the loop, and the effects are then measured on the new data repositories, and the KDD process is launched again.

Knowledge-Based ID

Knowledge based detection Technique can be used for both signature based IDS as well as anomaly based IDS. It accumulates the knowledge about specific attacks and system vulnerabilities. It uses this knowledge to exploit the attacks and vulnerabilities to generate the alarm. Any other event that is not recognized as an attack is accepted. Therefore the accuracy of knowledge based intrusion detection systems is considered good. However, their completeness requires that their knowledge of attacks be updated regularly.

Knowledge-based intrusion-detection techniques apply the knowledge accumulated about specific attacks and system vulnerabilities. The intrusion-detection system contains information about these vulnerabilities and looks for attempts to exploit them. When such an attempt is detected, an alarm is raised. In other words, any action that is not explicitly recognized as an attack is considered acceptable. Therefore, the accuracy of knowledge-based intrusion-detection systems is considered good. However, their completeness depends on the regular update of knowledge about attacks.

Knowledge based detection Techniques can be classified into a) State Transition Analysis b) Signature Analysis c) Petrinet and d) Expert Systems.

State Transition Analysis

State transition analysis, a technique proposed by Porras and Kemmerer was implemented first in UNIX and later in other environments. The technique is conceptually identical to model based reasoning, it describes the attacks with a set of goals and transitions, and represents them as state transition diagrams. State transition diagram is a graphical representation of the actions performed by an intruder to archive a system compromise. In state transition analysis, an intrusion is viewed as a sequence of actions performed by an intruder that leads from some initial state to a computer system to a target compromised state. State transition analysis diagrams identify the requirements and the compromise of the penetration. They also list the key actions that have to occur for the successful completion of an intrusion.

Signature Analysis

The signature analysis follows exactly the same knowledge-acquisition approach as expert systems, but the knowledge acquired is exploited in a different way. The semantic description of the attacks is transformed into information that can be found in the audit trail in a straightforward way. For example, attack scenarios might be translated into the sequences of audit events they generate, or into patterns of data that can be sought in the audit trail generated by the system. This method decreases the semantic level of the attacks description. This technique allows a very efficient implementation and is therefore applied in various commercial intrusion-detection products e.g. Haystack.

Petri Nets

To represent signatures of intrusions, IDIOT, a knowledge-based intrusion-detection system developed at Purdue University, uses Colored Petri Nets (CPN). The advantages of CPNs are their generality, their conceptual simplicity, and their graphical representation. System administrators are assisted in writing their own signatures of attacks and integrating them in IDIOT. Owing to the generality of CPNs, quite complex signatures can be written easily. However, matching a complex signature against the audit trail may become computationally very expensive.

Expert Systems

Expert systems can be used for both signature based IDS as well as anomaly based IDS. Expert Systems are used primarily by knowledge-based intrusion-detection techniques. The expert system contains a set of rules that describe attacks. Audit events are then translated into facts carrying their semantic signification in the expert system, and the inference engine draws conclusions using these rules and facts. This method increases the abstraction level of the audit data by attaching semantic to it. It also encodes knowledge about past intrusions, known system vulnerabilities, and the security policy. As information is gathered, the expert system determines whether any rules have been satisfied.

Rule based languages are a natural tool for modeling the knowledge that experts have collected about attacks. This approach allows a systematic browsing of the audit trail in search of evidence of attempts to exploit known vulnerabilities. They are also used to verify the proper application of the security policy of an organization.

Model based reasoning which also uses expert systems. Knowledge about the behavior of an attacker is described by the attacker's goals, the actions he takes to reach these goals, and his usage of the system which sometimes reveals a certain level of fear. The tool then scans the audits for evidence of these actions and transitions.

Machine Learning for Detecting and Classifying Malwares

Various machine learning approaches like Association Rule, Support Vector Machine, Decision Tree, Random Forest, Naive Bayes, and Clustering have been proposed for detecting and classifying unknown samples into either known malware families or underline those samples that exhibit unseen behavior, for detailed analysis. A few of these used in the literature are discussed in this section. Schultz *et al.* were the first to introduce the concept of data mining for detecting malwares. They used three different static features for malware classification: Portable Executable (PE), strings and byte sequences.

In the PE approach, the features are extracted from DLL information inside PE files. Strings are extracted from the executables based on the text strings that are encoded in program files. The byte sequence approach uses sequences of n bytes extracted from an executable file. They used a data set consisted of 4266 files including 3265 malicious and 1001 benign programs. A rule induction algorithm called Ripper was applied to find patterns in the DLL data. A learning algorithm Naive Bayes was used to finding patterns in the string data and n-grams of byte sequences were used as input data for the Multinomial Naive Bayes algorithm. The Naive Bayes algorithm, taking strings as input data, gives the highest classification accuracy of 97.11%. The authors claimed that the rate of detection of malwares using data mining method is twice as compared to signature based method.

Later on, their results were improved by Kolter *et al.* They used n-gram and data mining method to detect malicious executables. They used different classifiers including Naive-Bayes, Support Vector Machine, Decision Tree, and their boosted versions. They concluded that boosted decision tree gives the best classification results.

Nataraj *et al.* proposed a method for visualizing and classifying malwares using image processing techniques, which visualize malware binaries as gray-scale images. A K-nearest neighbor technique with Euclidean distance method is used for malware classification. Though it is a very fast method as compared to other malware analysis methods, the limitation is that an attacker can adopt countermeasures to beat the system because this method uses global image based features. They found that classification using this method is faster, scalable and is comparable to dynamic analysis in terms of accuracy. They also found that this approach can robustly classify a large number of malwares with both packed and unpacked samples. The limitation is that this method is vulnerable to knowledgeable adversaries who can obfuscate their malicious code to defeat texture analysis.

Kong *et al.* presented a framework for automated malware classification based on structural information (function call graph) of malwares. After extracting the fine grained features based on function call graph for each malware sample, the similarity is evaluated for two malware programs by applying discriminate distance metric learning which clusters the malware samples belonging to the same family while keeping the different clusters separate by a marginal distance. The authors then used an ensemble of classifiers that learn from pair wise malware distances to classify malwares into their respective families.

Tian *et al.* used function length frequency to classify Trojans. Function length is measured by the number of bytes in the code. Their results indicate that the function length along with its frequency is significant in identifying malware family and can be combined with other features for fast and scalable malware classification.

Further, they noted that usually an obfuscated file does not have any string consisting of words or sentences and thus used printable string information contained within the executables. They used machine learning algorithms available in WEKA library for classifying malwares.

Santos *et al.* pointed out that supervised learning requires a significant amount of labeled executables for both classes (malicious as well as benign datasets) and proposed a semi-supervised learning approach for detecting unknown malwares. It is designed to build a machine learning classifier using a lot of labeled and unlabelled instances. A semi-supervised algorithm LLGC (Learning with Local and Global Consistency) is used, which is able to learn from labeled and unlabelled data and provides a solution with respect to the intrinsic structure displayed by both labeled and unlabelled instances. Executables are represented by using n-gram distribution technique. They also determine and evaluate the optimal number of labeled instances and effect of this parameter on the accuracy of the model. The main contribution of this research is to reduce the number of required labeled instances while maintaining high precision. The limitation is that the previously supervised learning approaches presented in and obtain better results (above 90% of accuracy) than the presented semi supervised approach. Further in, the authors proposed a collective learning approach to detect unknown malwares. It is a type of semi-supervised learning that presents the method for optimizing the classification of partially-labeled data. Collective classification algorithms are used to build different machine learning classifiers using a set of labeled and unlabelled instances. It is validated that the labeling efforts are lower than when supervised learning is used while maintaining the high accuracy rate.

Siddiqui *et al.* used variable length instruction sequence along with machine learning for detecting worms in the wild. Before disassembling the files, they detect compilers, packers. Sequence reduction was done and decision tree and random forest machine learning models were used for classification. They tested their method on a data set of 2774 including 1444 worms and 1330 benign files. Many researchers now prefer to work on dynamic techniques so as to improve the accuracy and effectiveness of malware classification.

Zolkipli *et al.* presented an approach for malware behavior analysis. They used Honey Clients and Amun as security tools to collect malwares. Behaviors of these malwares are identified by executing every sample on both CWSandbox and Anubis on virtual machine platform. The results generated by both of these analyzers are customized using human based behavior analysis. Then the malwares are grouped into malware families Worms and Trojans. The limitation of this work is that customization using human analysis is not possible for today's real time traffic which is voluminous and having a variety of threats.

Rieck *et al.* proposed a framework for the automatic analysis of malware behavior using machine learning. This framework collected a large number of malware samples and monitored their behavior using a sandbox environment. By embedding the observed behavior in a vector space, they apply the learning algorithms. Clustering is used to identify the novel classes of malware with similar behavior. Assigning unknown malware to these discovered classes is done by classification. Based on both, clustering and classification, an incremental approach is used for behavior-based analysis, capable of processing the behavior of thousands of malware binaries on daily basis.

Anderson *et al.* presented a malware detection algorithm based on the analysis of graphs constructed from dynamically collected instruction traces. A modified version of Ether malware analysis framework is used to collect data. The method uses 2-grams to condition the transition probabilities of a markov chain (treated as a graph). The machinery of graph kernels is used to construct a similarity matrix between instances in the training set. Kernel matrix is constructed by using two distinct measures of similarity: a Gaussian kernel, which measures the local similarity between the graph edges and a spectral kernel which measures the global similarity between the graphs. From the kernel matrix, a support vector machine is trained to classify the test data. The performance of multiple kernel learning method used in this work is demonstrated by discriminating different instances of malware and benign software. Limitation of this approach is that the computation complexity is very high, thus limiting its use in real world setting.

Bayer *et al.* proposed a system that clusters large sets of malicious binaries based on their behavior effectively and automatically. The proposed technique relies on Anubis to generate execution traces of all the samples. Anubis was extended in this work with taint-propagation capabilities, to make use of additional information sources. After creating the extraction traces along with taint information, a behavioral profile is extracted for each trace, which serves as input to the clustering algorithm. The clustering algorithm used is based on Locality Sensitive Hashing (LSH), which is a sub linear (efficient) approach to the approximate nearest neighbor problem. LSH can be used to perform an approximate clustering while computing only a small fraction of the n2/2 distances between pairs of points. The authors demonstrate the scalability of their approach by clustering a set of 75,000 malware samples in three hours.

Tian *et al.* used an automated tool for extracting API call sequences from executables while these are running in a virtual environment. They used the classifiers available in WEKA library to discriminate malware files from clean files as well as for classifying malwares into their families. They used a data set of 1368 malwares to demonstrate their work and achieved an accuracy of over 97%.

Biley *et al.* pointed out that the antivirus (AV) products characterize the malwares in ways that are not consistent across various AV products, not complete across malwares and are not concise in their semantics. They developed a classification technique that describes malwares behavior in terms of system state changes.

Park *et al.* proposed a malware classification method which is based on maximal component subgraph detection. After executing the malware samples in sandboxed environment, system calls along with parameter values of these calls are captured and a directed graph is generated from these system call traces. The maximal common subgraph is computed to compare two programs. The drawback of this method is that there are some known malware samples that manage to gain kernel-mode privileges without making use of system call interface and can evade the analysis method.

Firdausi *et al.* presented a proof of concept of a malware detection method. Firstly the behavior of malware samples is analyzed in sandbox environment using Anubis. The reports generated are preprocessed into sparse vector models for classification using machine learning. The performance comparison of 5 different classifiers *i.e.* *k*-Nearest Neighbors (*k*NN), Naive Bayes, J48 Decision Tree, Support Vector Machine (SVM), and Multilayer Perceptron Neural Network (MLP) is done on a small data set of 220 malicious samples and 250 benign samples with and without feature selection. The obtained results depicted that overall best performance is achieved by J48 decision tree with a recall of 95.9%, a false positive rate of 2.4%, a precision of 97.3%, and an accuracy of 96.8%. The researcher presented a framework for automated malware classification into their respective families based on network behavior. Network traces are taken as input to the framework in the form of pcap files, from which the network flows are extracted. Then a behavior graph is created to represent the network activities of malwares and dependencies between network flows. From these behavior graphs, the features like graph size, root out-degree, average out-degree, maximum out-degree, the number of specific nodes are extracted. These features are then used to classify malwares using classification algorithms available in WEKA library and it is concluded that J48 decision tree performs better than other classifiers.

Lee *et al.* proposed a method that clusters the malicious programs by using machine learning method. All the samples of data set are executed in a virtual environment and system calls along with their arguments are monitored. A behavioral profile is created on the basis of information recorded regarding sample's interaction with system resources like registry keys, writing files, and network activities. The similarity between two profiles is calculated and then by applying k-method, different samples are grouped into different clusters. After completing the training process, the new and unknown samples are assigned to the cluster having method closer to the sample *i.e.* nearest neighbor.

It is clear that a single view either static or dynamic is not sufficient for efficiently and accurately classifying malicious programs because of the obfuscation and execution-stalling techniques. So, researches have adapted a hybrid technique which incorporates both static and dynamic features simultaneously for better malware detection and classification.

Santos *et al.* proposed a hybrid unknown malware detector called OPEM, which utilizes a set of features obtained from both static and dynamic analysis of malicious code. The static features are obtained by modeling an executable as a sequence of operational codes and dynamic features are obtained by monitoring system calls, operations and raised exceptions. The approach is then validated over two different data sets by considering different learning algorithms for classifiers Decision Tree, K-nearest neighbor, a Bayesian network, and Support Vector Machine and it has been found that this hybrid approach enhances the performance of both approaches when running separately.

The machine-learning technologies that are being used in detecting and classifying malwares are not adequate to handle challenges arising from the huge amount of dynamic and severely imbalanced network data. These should be transformed so that their potential can be leveraged to address the challenges posed in cyber security.

ZASMIN

ZASMIN (Zero-day Attack Signature Management Infrastructure), for novel network attack protection. This system provides early detection function and validation of attack at the moment the attacks start to spread on the network. In order to detect unknown network attack, the ZASMIN system has adopted various of new technologies, which are composed of suspicious traffic monitoring, attack validation, polymorphic worm recognition, signature generation. Some of these functionalities are implemented with the hardware-based accelerator to be able to deal with giga-bit speed traffic, therefore, it can be applicable to Internet backbone or the bottle-neck point of high-speed enterprise network without any loss of traffic. In order to check the feasibility of ZASMIN, installed it on the real honey net environment, then analyzed the result of detection of an unknown attack.

Zeroday-Attack Signature Management Infrastructure (ZASMIN) system for novel network attack detection system provides early detection function and validation of attack at the moment the attacks start to spread on the network. After installing the ZASMIN on the real honey-net environment in the internet exchange point (IX), has analyzed the results of the ZASMIN about detection of unknown attack for two days with CERT expert group. Even if the two-day analysis is not enough long to detect various unknown attacks, find some attacks without any well-known signature through the case study. Even if these vulnerabilities which the attacks used were released a long time ago, these kinds of attacks still exist in the public domain with polymorphic form. Through this case study has convinced that new attack or polymorphic Authorized known attack can be detected by the ZASMIN system. It's hard to evaluate the exact system-level false positive rate in the real environment, but the ZASMIN system has a relatively low false rate with this case study. And also need to focus on reducing its false rate as the further study.

The false rate of the detection methods which are based on abnormal traffic behavior is a little high and the accuracy of the signature generation is relatively low. Moreover, it is not suitable to detect exploits and generate its signature. ZASMIN provides an early warning at the moment the attacks start to spread on the network and to block the spread of the cyber attacks by automatically generating a signature that could be used by the network security appliance such as IPS. This system has adopted various technologies suspicious traffic monitoring, attack validation, polymorphic worm recognition, signature generation for unknown network attack detection. And also, researcher introduce two concepts to validate the preprocessing of the suspicious traffic. The one is attack-based validation and the other is signature-based validation. These validation functions can reduce the false rate of the unknown attack detection. In order to check the feasibility of the validation functions in ZASMIN, researcher has installed it on the real honey net environment, then researcher has analyzed the result of detection of an unknown attack. Even though short–period analysis is not enough long to detect various unknown attacks, researcher confirmed that ZASMIN can detect some attacks without any well-known signature.

Even if the two-day analysis is not enough long to detect various unknown attacks, a researcher could find some attacks without any well-known signature through the case study. Even if these vulnerabilities which the attacks used were released a long time ago, these kinds of attacks still exist in the public domain with polymorphic form. Through this case study, researcher has convinced that new attack or polymorphic known attack can be detected by the ZASMIN system.

Malware Forensics: Detecting the Unknown

The increasing speed of new malware strains being written and released means that security professionals are more likely than ever before to see new malware. This means new malware which is not detected by the anti-malware solutions they have deployed in their infrastructure, be it a workstation, server, PDA or at the gateway. Imagine this scenario: An end-user calls the helpdesk and reports that their system is running very sluggishly when it wasn't a week ago and that they can't access the Windows 'Task Manager' or open a command prompt any more. The virus scanner is right up to date and active, and it says the system is clean; the personal firewall is active too. It will focus on a step by step approach of what tools to use, what to look for and what to do with any suspicious files. It will also discuss the use of forensic tools in such a scenario, as the last port of call.

As with other security threat, especially malware related ones, deploy a multi-layered approach to minimize the chance of malware getting onto your computers. This means not only need good technological solutions and overlapping technologies at that, but these need to be backed up with good security policies, procedures, education and constant vigilance.

Active Learning

Detecting unknown worms is a challenging task, an innovative technique for detecting the presence of an unknown worm based on the computer measurements extracted from the operating system. An experiment to test the new technique employing several computer configurations and background applications activity. During the experiments, 323 computer features were monitored. Four feature selection measures were used to reduce the number of features. Applied support vector machines on the resulting feature subsets. In addition, used active learning as a selective sampling method to increase the performance of the classifier and improve its robustness in noisy data. The results indicate that using the proposed approach resulted in a mean accuracy in excess of 90%, and for specific unknown worms accuracy reached above 94%, using just 20 features while maintaining a low false positive rate.

The concept of detecting *unknown* computer worms based on a host behavior, using the SVM classification algorithm based on several kernels. Based on the results shown in this study, the use of support vector machines in the task of detecting unknown computer worms is possible. A feature-selection method which enabled to identify the most important computer features in order to detect unknown worm activity, currently performed by human experts. Based on the initial experiment (*e1*), the *GainRatio* feature selection measure was most suitable to this task. On average the *Top20* features produced the highest results and the *RBF kernel* commonly outperformed other kernels. In the detection of unknown worms (*e2*), the results show that it is possible to achieve a high level of accuracy (exceeding 80% on average); as more worms were included in the training set the accuracy improved. To reduce the noise in the training set and improve the learning researcher argued that the use of the active learning approach as a selective method would improve the performance, which actually happened, increasing the accuracy after selecting 50 examples to above 90% accuracy and 94% when the training set contained four worms. When selected 100 and 150 examples no improvement was observed in the performance after selecting 50 examples.

These results are highly encouraging and show that unknown worms, which commonly spread intensively, can be stopped from propagating in real time. The advantage of the suggested approach is the automatic acquisition and maintenance of knowledge, based on inductive learning. This avoids the need for a human expert who is not always available and familiar with the general rules. This is possible these days, based on the existing amount of known worms, as well as on the generalization capabilities of classification algorithms. Currently in the process of extending a number of worms in the dataset, as well as extending the suggested approach to other types of malicious code using temporal data mining.

Collective Classification

Malware is any type of computer software harmful to computers and networks. The amount of malware is increasing every year and poses a serious global security threat. Signature-based detection is the most broadly used commercial antivirus method, however, it fails to detect new and previously unseen malware. Supervised machine-learning models have been proposed in order to solve this issue, but the usefulness of supervised learning is far to be perfect because it requires a significant amount of malicious code and benign software to be identified and labelled in beforehand. Santos et.al proposed a new method that adopts a collective learning approach to detect unknown malware. Collective classification is a type of semi-supervised learning that presents an interesting method for optimizing the classification of partially-labeled data. In this way, for the first time, collective classification algorithms are proposed to build different machine-learning classifiers using a set of labeled (as malware and legitimate software) and unlabelled instances. An empirical validation demonstrating that the labeling efforts are lower than when supervised learning is used while maintaining high accuracy rates.

The obtained results validate our initial hypothesis that building an unknown malware detector based on collective classification is feasible. The classifiers achieved high performance in classifying unknown malware, improving our previous results using LLGC (Santos et al., 2011), which achieved a 86% of accuracy in its best configuration. Therefore, researcher believes that our results will have a strong impact in the area of unknown malware detection, which usually relies on supervised machine learning (Schultz et al., 2001; Kolter and Maloof, 2004). Training the model through supervised machine-learning algorithms can be a problem itself because supervised learning requires each instance in the dataset to be properly labeled.

This demands a large amount of time and resources. In this way, the researcher tried to find among our results the number of labeled malware that is needed to assure a certain performance in unknown malware detection.

Classification Technique on OpCode Patterns

In previous studies, classification algorithms were employed successfully for the detection of unknown malicious code. Most of these studies extracted features based on byte n-gram patterns in order to represent the inspected files. In this study, researcher represents the inspected files using OpCode n-gram patterns which are extracted from the files after disassembly. The OpCode n-gram patterns are used as features for the classification process. The classification process main goal is to detect unknown malware within a set of suspected files which will later be included in antivirus software as signatures. A rigorous evaluation was performed using a test collection comprising of more than 30,000 files, in which various settings of OpCode n-gram patterns of various size representations and eight types of classifiers were evaluated.

A typical problem of this domain is the imbalance problem in which the distribution of the classes in real life varies. The researcher investigated the imbalance problem, referring to several real-life scenarios in which malicious files are expected to be about 10% of the total inspected files. Lastly, researcher presents a chronological evaluation in which the frequent need for updating the training set was evaluated. Evaluation results indicate that the evaluated methodology achieves a level of accuracy higher than 96% (with TPR above 0.95 and FPR approximately 0.1), which slightly improves the results in previous studies that use byte n-gram representation. The chronological evaluation showed a clear trend in which the performance improves as the training set is more updated.

In this study researcher used OpCode n-gram patterns generated by disassembling the inspected executable files to extract features from the inspected files. OpCode n-grams are used as features during the classification process with the aim of identifying unknown malicious code. Researcher performed an extensive evaluation using a test collection comprising more than 30,000 files.

SUMMARY

In this chapter, the basic concepts of data mining, knowledge database discovery, Data mining based Intrusion Detection Models and Malware databases are discussed. These are existing technologies helps a lot to design a new model to detect and prevent unknown malware in network security.

This chapter describes in depth many of the popular Computational Intelligence techniques found in malware detection research. Several existing intelligence techniques show promise in the malware detection problem. Many of the machine learning techniques have application to both continuous and discrete datasets. As signature- based solutions become overwhelmed by an exponential growth in malware, pattern recognition based solutions are gaining popularity.

REFERENCES

Anderson, Lunt, Javitz, Tamaru, & Valdes. (1993). *Safeguard Final Report: Detecting Unusual Program Behavior Using the NIDES Statistical Component*. Computer Science Laboratory, SRI International.

Anderson, Storlie, & Lane. (2012). Improving Malware Classification: Bridging the Static/Dynamic Gap. *Proceedings of 5th ACM Workshop on Security and Artificial Intelligence (AISec)*, 3-14.

Axelsson. (1998). *Research in Intrusion-Detection Systems: A survey*. Chalmers University of Technology.

Axelsson. (2000). *Intrusion Detection Systems: A Survey and Taxonomy*. Chalmers University.

Balakrishnan, G., & Reps, T. (2004). Analyzing memory accesses in x86 executable. *International Conference on Compiler Construction*.

Barbara, D., Wu, N., & Jajodia, S. (2001). Detecting novel network intrusions using bayes estimators. *Proc. First SIAM Conference on Data Mining*. doi:10.1137/1.9781611972719.28

Barbara, Couto, Jajodia, & Wu. (2001). Detecting Intrusions by Data Mining. *Proc. 2nd Annual IEEE Information Assurance Workshop*.

Barbara, Domeniconi, & Rogers. (2006). Detecting outliers using transduction and statistical testing. *Proceedings of the 12th Annual SIGKDD International Conference on Knowledge Discovery and Data Mining*, 54–60.

Bayer, U., Moser, A., Kruegel, C., & Kirda, E. (2006). Dynamic Analysis of Malicious Code. *Journal in Computer Virology*, 2(1), 67–77. doi:10.1007/s11416-006-0012-2

Biley, Oberheid, Andersen, Morley Mao, Jahanian, & Nazario. (2007). Automated Classification and Analysis of Internet Malware. *Proceedings of the 10th International Conference on Recent Advances in Intrusion Detection, 4637*, 178-197.

Braverman, Williams, & Mador. (2006). *Microsoft security intelligence report*. Microsoft.

Christodorescu & Jha. (2004). Testing malware detectors. *Proceedings of the 2004 ACM SIGSOFT International Symposium on Software Testing and Analysis*, 34–44.

Christodorescu, Jha, Seshia, Song, & Bryant. (2005). Semantics-aware malware detection. *Proceedings of the 26th IEEE Symposium on Security and Privacy.*

Cohen, F. (1987). Computer viruses: Theory and experiments. *Computers & Security, 6*(1), 22–35. doi:10.1016/0167-4048(87)90122-2

Cohen. (1995). Protection, and Security on the Information Superhighway. New York, NY: John Wiley & Sons.

Cuppens & Miege. (2002). Alert Correlation in a Cooperative Intrusion Detection Framework. *Proc. IEEE Symposium on Security and Privacy.*

Dorothy, E. (1987). Denning, An Intrusion-Detection Model. *IEEE Transactions on Software Engineering, SE-13*(2), 222–232. doi:10.1109/TSE.1987.232894

Eckmann, S. T., Vigna, G., & Kemmerer, R. A. (2000). An attack language for state-based intrusion detection. *Proceedings of the 2000 ACM Workshop on Intrusion Detection.*

Egele, Kruegel, Kirda, Yin, & Song. (2007). Dynamic spyware analysis. *Proceedings of the 2007 USENIX Annual Technical Conference.*

Ertoz, Eilertson, Lazarevic, Tan, Dokes, Kumar, & Srivastava. (2003). Detection of Novel Attacks using Data Mining. *Proc. IEEE Workshop on Data Mining and Computer Security.*

Firdausi, Lim, & Erwin. (2010). Analysis of Machine Learning Techniques Used in Behavior Based Malware Detection. *Proceedings of 2nd International Conference on Advances in Computing, Control and Telecommunication Technologies (ACT)*, 201-203.

Garfinkel & Rosenblum. (2003). A virtual machine introspection based architecture for intrusion detection. *Proceedings of the 10th Network and Distributed System Security Symposium (NDSS).*

Goudey, H. (2004). Watch the money-go-round, watch the malware-go round. *Proceedings of the 2004 Virus Bulletin Conference.*

Hile, Gray, & Wakelin. (1994). *In transit detection of a computer virus with safeguard.* Academic Press.

Ilgun, K., Kemmerer, R. A., & Porras, P. A. (1995). State Transition Analysis: A Rule-Based Intrusion Detection Approach. *IEEE Transactions on Software Engineering, 21*(3), 181–199. doi:10.1109/32.372146

Wang, J. (2007). Internet Worm Early Detection and Response Mechanism. *Journal of China Universities of Posts and Telecommunications, 14*(3).

Jiang, X., Wang, X., & Xu, D. (2007). Stealthy malware detection through vmm-based out-of-the-box-semantic view reconstruction. *Proceedings of the 14th ACM Conference on Computer and Communications Security.* doi:10.1145/1315245.1315262

Kang, Poosankam, & Yin. (2007). Renovo: A hidden code extractor for packed executables. *Proceedings of the 2007 ACM workshop on Recurring Malcode*, 46–53.

Kirda, Kruegel, Banks, Vigna, & Kemmerer. (2006). Behavior-based spyware detection. *Proceedings of the 15th USENIX Security Symposium.*

Kolter & Maloof. (2004). Learning to Detect Malicious Executable in the Wild. *Proceedings of the 10th ACM SIGKDD International Conference on Knowledge Discovery and Data Mining*, 470-478.

Kong & Yan. (2013). Discriminant Malware Distance Learning on Structural Information for Automated Malware Classification. *Proceedings of the ACM SIGMETRICS/International Conference on Measurement and Modeling of Computer Systems*, 347-348.

Kruegel & Toth. (2001). Sparta, A mobile agent based intrusion detection system. *Proceedings of the IFIP Conference on Network Security*.

Kruegel. (2004). *Intrusion Detection and Correlation: Challenges and Solutions*. Springer.

Krugel & Toth. (2000). *A Survey on Intrusion Detection Systems*. TUV-1841-00-11 Technical University of Vienna, Information Systems Institute, Distributed Systems Group.

Kumar, V., Lazarevic, A., Ertoz, L., Ozgur, A., & Srivastava, J. (2003). A Comparative Study of Anomaly Detection Schemes in Network Intrusion Detection. *Proc. Third SIAM International Conference on Data Mining*.

Lakhotia, A., & Kumar, E. U. (2004). Abstract stack graph to detect obfuscated calls in binaries. *4th IEEE International Workshop on Source Code Analysis and manipulation.* doi:10.1109/SCAM.2004.2

Lakhotia, A., & Mohammed, M. (2004). Imposing order on program statements to assist anti-virus scanners. *11th Working Conference.* doi:10.1109/WCRE.2004.24

Lee, W., & Stolfo, S. J. (1998). Data Mining approaches for intrusion detection. *Proc. Seventh USENIX Security Symposium*.

Lee, W., Stolfo, S. J., & Kwok, K. W. (1998). Mining audit data to build intrusion detection models. *Proc. Fourth International Conference on Knowledge Discovery and Data Mining*.

Li, Srinivasan, & Zhou. (2004). C-miner: Mining block correlations in storage systems. *Proceedings of the 3rd USENIX Conference on File and Storage Technologies (FAST)*.

Li, S., Salour, M., & Su, X. (2008). A Survey of Internet Worm Detection and Containment. *IEEE Communications Surveys and Tutorials*, *10*(1), 20–35. doi:10.1109/COMST.2008.4483668

Liu & Motoda. (2001). *Instance selection and construction for data mining*. Kluwer Academic Pub.

Liu, H., & Motoda, H. (2008). Computational methods of feature selection. Chapman & Hall/CRC.

Mahoney, M., & Chan, P. (2002). Learning non stationary models of normal network traffic for detecting novel attacks. *Proceedings of SIGKDD*, 376–385.

Mahoney & Chan. (n.d.a). *Learning models of network traffic for detecting the novel attack*. Technical report, Florida Tech., CS-2002-8.

Mahoney & Chan. (n.d.b). *PHAD: Packet header anomaly detection for identifying hostile network traffic*. Technical report, Florida Tech., CS-2001-4.

Martignoni, , Christodorescu, & Jha. (2007). (Omniunpack): Fast, generic, and safe unpacking of malware. *Proceedings of the 23rd Annual Computer Security Applications Conference (ACSAC)*, 431–441.

Moser, A., Kruegel, C., & Kirda, E. (2007a). Exploring multiple execution paths for malware analysis. *Proceedings of the 2007 IEEE Symposium on Security and Privacy*. doi:10.1109/SP.2007.17

Moser, A., Kruegel, C., & Kirda, E. (2007b). Limits of static analysis for malware detection. *Proceedings of the 23rd Annual Computer Security Applications Conference (ACSAC)*. doi:10.1109/ACSAC.2007.21

Nataraj, Karthikeyan, Jacob, & Manjunath. (2011). Malware Images: Visualization and Automatic Classification. *Proceedings of the 8th International Symposium on Visualization for Cyber Security*.

Nataraj, Yegneswaran, Porras, & Zhang. (2011). A Comparative Assessment of Malware Classification Using Binary Texture Analysis and Dynamic Analysis. *Proceedings of the 4th ACM Workshop on Security and Artificial Intelligence*, 21-30.

Ning, Cui, & Reeves. (2002). Constructing Attack Scenarios through Correlation of Intrusion Alerts. *Proc. ACM Computer and Communications Security Conf*.

Park, Reeves, Mulukutla, & Sundaravel. (2010). Fast Malware Classification by Automated Behavioral Graph Matching. *Proceedings of the 6th Annual Workshop on Cyber Security and Information Intelligence Research*.

Petroni, Monlina, & Arbaugh. (2004). Copilot - a coprocessor-based kernel runtime integrity monitor. *Proceedings of the 13th USENIX Security Symposium*.

Petroni & Hicks. (2007). Automated detection of the persistent kernel and control-flow attacks. *Proceedings of the 14th ACM Conference on Computer and Communications Security*.

Portnoy, & Stolfo. (2001). Intrusion Detection with unlabeled data using clustering. *Proceedings of ACM Workshop on Data Mining Applied to Security*.

Pyle, D. (1999). *Data preparation for data mining*. Morgan Kaufmann.

Rieck, K., Trinius, P., Willems, C., & Holz, T. (2011). Automatic Analysis of Malware Behavior Using Machine Learning. *Journal of Computer Security*, 19(4), 639–668. doi:10.3233/JCS-2010-0410

Royal, P., Halpin, M., Dagon, D., Edmonds, R., & Lee, W. (2006). Polyunpack: Automating the hidden-code extraction of unpack-executing malware. *Proceedings of the 22nd Annual Computer Security Applications Conference (ACSAC)*, 289–300. doi:10.1109/ACSAC.2006.38

Santos, I., Devesa, J., Brezo, F., Nieves, J., & Bringas, P. G. (2013). OPEM: A Static-Dynamic Approach for Machine Learning Based Malware Detection. *Proceedings of International Conference CISIS'12-ICEUTE'12, Special Sessions Advances in Intelligent Systems and Computing, 189*, 271-280. doi:10.1007/978-3-642-33018-6_28

Santos, Nieves, & Bringas. (2011). Collective Classification for Unknown Malware Detection. *Proceedings of the International Conference on Security and Cryptography*, 251-256.

Schultz, Eskin, Zadok, & Stolfo. (2001). Data Mining Methods for Detection of New Malicious Executables. *Proceedings of the IEEE Symposium on Security and Privacy*, 178-184.

Sharif, M., Yegneswaran, V., & Saidi, H. (2008). Eureka: A Framework for Enabling Static Malware Analysis. *Proceedings of the European Symposium on Research in Computer Security (ESORICS)*, 481–500.

Siddiqui, Wang, & Lee. (2009). Detecting Internet Worms Using Data Mining Techniques. *Journal of Systemics, Cybernetics, and Informatics*, 6, 48–53.

Silberstein. (2004). *Designing a cam-based coprocessor for boosting the performance of antivirus software*. Academic Press.

Axelsson. (1999). Research in Intrusion –Detection System: Survey. Department of Computer Engineering, Chalmers University of Technology.

Symantec. (1997). *Understanding heuristics: Symantec's bloodhound technology*. Author.

Szor. (2005). *Metamorphic computer virus detection*. Academic Press.

Szor, P., & Ferrie, P. (2005). *Hunting for metamorphic, The Art of Computer Virus Research and Defense*. Addison-Wesley.

Tarari. (2006). *Anti-virus content processor*. Retrieved from http://www.tarari.com/antivirus/index.html

Taylor & Alves-Foss. (2001). Network analysis of anomalous traffic events, a low-cost approach. *NSPW '01: Proceedings of the 2001 workshop on New security paradigms*, 89–96.

Tian, R., Batten, L., & Versteeg, S. (2008). Function Length as a Tool for Malware Classification. *Proceedings of the 3rd International Conference on Malicious and Unwanted Software*, 57-64. doi:10.1109/MALWARE.2008.4690860

Tsang, E. C. C., Yeung, D. S., & Wang, X. Z. (2003). OFFSS: Optimal fuzzy-valued feature subset selection. *IEEE Transactions on Fuzzy Systems*, *11*(2), 202–213. doi:10.1109/TFUZZ.2003.809895

Turner. (2006). *Spamming malware: Parite.b and irc backdoor disable anti-spyware programs*. Academic Press.

Wagner, D., & Soto, P. (2002). Mimicry attacks on host-based intrusion detection systems. *Proceedings of the 9th ACM Conference on Computer and communications Security*. doi:10.1145/586110.586145

Wang. (2005). *The intelligent proactive information assurance, and security technology*. Academic Press.

Wang, F.-Y. (2005). Agent-based control for networked traffic management systems. *IEEE Intelligent Systems*, *19*(5), 92–96. doi:10.1109/MIS.2005.80

Zhang, X., van Doorn, L., Jaeger, T., Perez, R., & Sailer, R. (2002). Secure coprocessor-based intrusion detection. *10th Workshop on ACM Special Interest Group on Operating Systems (SIGOPS)*. doi:10.1145/1133373.1133423

Zolkipli & Jantan. (2011). An Approach for Malware Behavior Identification and Classification. *Proceeding of 3rd International Conference on Computer Research and Development*, 191-194.

Chapter 12
Machine Learning Data Analysis for On-Line Education Environments:
A Roadmap to System Design

Marian Cristian Mihaescu
University of Craiova, Romania

ABSTRACT

The increase of e-Learning resources such as interactive learning environments, learning management systems or intelligent tutoring systems has created huge repositories of educational data that can be explored. This increase generated the need of integrating machine learning methodologies into the currently existing e-Learning environments. The integration of such procedures focuses on working with a wide range of data analysis algorithms and their various implementations in form of tools or technologies. This paper aims to present a self-contained roadmap for practitioners who want to have basic knowledge about a core set of algorithms and who want to apply them on educational data. The background of this research domain is represented by state-of-the-art data analysis algorithms found in the areas of Machine Learning, Information Retrieval or Data Mining that are adapted to work on educational data. The main goal of the research efforts in the domain of Intelligent Data Analysis on Educational Data is to provide tools that enhance the quality of the on-line educational systems.

INTRODUCTION

Data Analysis for on-line educational environments as well as Educational Data Mining (EDM) may be applied to extract knowledge from educational assets. In this context educational assets may be represented by educational content such as documents, images, quizzes, etc. or activity data such number of sessions, time spent on line, number/dimension of sent or received messages, etc. The intelligent data analysis of this huge amount of data in an attempt of finding information, knowledge or even wisdom may become very useful for the e-Learning environment that manages and produces the analyzed data.

DOI: 10.4018/978-1-5225-3129-6.ch012

The main goal is to carry out information retrieval activities as an integrated functional part of the beneficiary e-Learning system.

It is a well-known fact that data understanding and pre-processing constitutes the main work of the data analysis and mining process. Although learning algorithms are not especially designed for data mining or information retrieval these three data analysis techniques share a lot of common fundamental approaches. Even if many e-Learning software systems do store huge amounts of usage and educational data and they are designed to support learning and teaching, they usually do not analyze the data they store. However, the field of educational data mining is emerging precisely because valuable information may be obtained from analyzing and mining the data stored by the educational software. As a consequence, the process of IR on educational data becomes sometimes long and tedious but the outcomes may be surprisingly useful.

Since its inception as a domain, educational data mining requires domain experts who use machine learning rather than machine learning experts who study education. The most commonly used methods are thus highly dependent on domain expertise. Examples include domain experts constructing data features, generating priors, and developing initial seed models. An expertise-based approach is highly effective for educational data, but a reliance on domain experts has risks: if the domain expert's prior beliefs are wrong then the results will tend to be biased. The process can also be time-consuming and difficult for other researchers to replicate.

The chapter is self-contained and consists of six sections. The next section of the chapter presents the IR on educational data and EDM related works and state of the art achievements in the domain. The third section provides an introduction of the main classes of algorithms with an emphasis on the guidelines of how they may be integrated into IR systems. The fourth section presents the main tools and technologies that may be used for designing successful IR system that work with educational data. The final section provides the conclusions and the main promising roads in the domain of IR on educational data.

RELATED WORK AND CURRENT STATE OF THE ART RESEARCH

Applying advanced algorithms on educational data started back in 1995 as in Barnes (2005) or Choquet et al. (2009). At that moment, models that were used in psychometrics literature made a shift towards educational data mining. Right from the beginning EDM domain defined itself as in interdisciplinary field. Theoretical as well as practical aspects from machine learning, statistics, information retrieval and visualization, and computational modeling are usually found in EDM research area.

An important step forward was made by Romero and Ventura (2007) in the attempt to categorize the main directions of the work that needs to be performed in EDM. At that moment there were defined the main types of procedures that may be applied for solving different problems from EDM. The two categories of procedures were defined: web mining (i.e., clustering, classification, association rule mining, and text mining) and visualization. From this perspective it is obvious that a main source of data that was envisioned to be analyzed was represented by the logs (i.e., the activity) of student-computer interaction. On the other hand, IR on educational data tackles with other types of data: databases (i.e., classical IR), documents, images as in works of Stanescu et al. (2010).

Later, Baker (2010) presented a more refined taxonomy of research work in EDM. The main tracks were prediction, clustering, relationship mining, distillation of data for human judgment and discovery with models. Among the subcategories there were set classification, regression, association rule mining. This more refined taxonomy was due to the advances in the fundamental areas of advanced data analysis algorithms.

The rise of the EDM domain was supported by a wide range of libraries that implement data analysis algorithms. 1994 is the year of the first internal release of Weka by Hall et al. (2009) and 1996 is the year of the first public release. In 1999 Weka 3 is released as a version to complement the Data Mining book by Witten et. al. (2016). The second edition of the book appeared in 2005 and the third edition in 2011. Of course, there is a large number of other free open-source data mining software and applications. Among them, the most well-known are R by Ihaka and Gentleman (1996) or RapidMiner by Mierswa et al. (2006). As an interesting detail, RapidMiner uses learning schemes and attribute evaluators from the Weka machine learning environment and statistical modeling schemes from R-Project. Still, the latest and maybe the one of the most powerful machine learning library is Apache Mahout (2010). The Apache Mahaout becomes a top level project in April of 2010 and its original goal was to implement all ten algorithms described in Chu et al. (2006). Still, the commercial data-mining software and applications have are there well defined place. Oracle Data Mining presented by Hamm and Burleson (2006) or Clementine by Wang and Ren (2011) are just two data mining toolkits from a very large number of similar products.

The progress in the area should not have been possible without the great development of on-line educational environments. Among the most well-known Learning Management Systems there are Moodle by Dougiamas and Taylor (2003), ATututor (2017), Claroline (2017), and many more. On the other hand, among the most well known proprietary systems there are Blackboard in Bradford et al. (2007), Desire2Learn (2017) and many more.

Surprisingly, from historical point of view the great development of open source as well as proprietary solutions for LMSs coincides with the rapid development of advanced data analysis technologies. Thus, on the realm of open-source solutions Moodle was released in 2002 as well as ATutor. Blackboard founded in 1997 and become a public company in 2004. Desire2Learn company was founded in 1999 and currently is among the fastest growing technology companies in Canada.

The simultaneous development of data mining tools and e-Learning environments lead to the arise of the new EDM domain. From the business perspective this meant the development of modules that run along the e-Learning environments and use various data analysis algorithms for enhancing the educational environment. Two such modules are Blackboard Analytics for Learn module or Moodle analytics with MocLog - Monitoring Online Courses with Log files. The overall goal is to improve the quality of teaching and learning by answering to questions like "Which are the students that need support and what kind of support should be offered?" or "What should be changed in course design to offer a better experience to students?" From the previously presented perspective the advances in educational on-line environments may need also important support from HCI (Human-Computer Interaction) research domain. EDM and HCI may be the domains that can make a big step forward for the currently existing on-line educational environments.

The advances in EDM domain created the possibility of creating large repositories of data. Among the most well-known is the Pittsburgh Science of Learning Center DataShop, the world's largest public repository for data on the interaction between students and educational software in Koedinger et al. (2010). Another example is National Center for Educational Statistics under the authority of Institute of Education Sciences - National Center for Educational Statistics (2017), Department of Education Washington D.C..

The latest progress in domain regards the classical goals of student modeling, mining student behavior patterns or building a recommender system. All this progress is mainly based on the important improvements of data analysis methodologies that were integrated into currently used software libraries of toolkits. In Koedinger et al. (2012) there is presented a technique for automated improvement of student models that leverages the DataShop repository, crowd sourcing, and a version of the Learning Factors Analysis algorithm.

Collaborative Filtering (CF) as well as Item Response Theory (IRT) has been recently used in Bergner et al. (23) to model the student response data. This is a clear proof that latest progress in Recommender Systems theory and psychometrics may be successfully integrated to work on educational data.

KEY TERM (KT)

Following are the key terms, which will help the readers for understanding this chapter and related issues.

- **Machine Learning:** The term machine learning is a fundamental concept. Broadly, it may be used as the mathematical foundation on which learning from data may be accomplished. The main tasks are prediction and representation.
  - **Classification:** This term regards a particular approach in machine learning. A data analysis process may be seen as a classification problem if instances are labeled.
  - **Clustering:** This term regards another particular type of approach in machine learning, particularly when instances are not labeled.
  - **Association Rules:** This term regards third type of learning, when items are described as transactions composed of item sets.
- **Information Retrieval:** This term relates to tasks as indexing and retrieving of various data types such as web pages, images, etc. The machine learning algorithms are fundamentals of this domain, but their context of usage is related with databases.

FUNDAMENTAL AIDA ALGORITHMS

This section presents a roadmap of how Data Analysis Procedures may be successfully integrated to work with educational data. There are two issues that need to be addressed for a successful integration. One regards an understanding of the general classes of Data Analysis algorithms. The second issue regards understanding how each class of algorithms may be used in an educational context. The main error is trying to use a certain algorithm in a wrong context. This may be very bad since it consumes large amounts of time and the results may not have any meaning due to bad data analysis system design.

A successful approach is to use unsupervised algorithms that incorporate student-level educational measures directly into the learning process, biasing the model search towards models that predict learning gain. Domain experts are only involved with the post-hoc interpretation of results. Further, in addition to predicting learning gain, the algorithm's models of student behavior suggest that the students who learn best tend to make persistent attempts rather than using software help. As a general concept Educational data mining processes often involve retrieving and analyzing multiple data attributes that spread across several tables or databases.

Figure 1 presents the general overview of Intelligent Data.

The employed algorithm of any Intelligent Data Computing system represents the core of the system. In general, there are known two types of algorithms: supervised and unsupervised. Supervised algorithms (e.g., classification algorithms like decision trees, Bayesian classifiers, SVM, Neural Networks) assume that one feature from the feature vector represents the so called target class. From this perspective, all other features represent input features while the target feature is regarded as output. The most common use of supervised learning is to predict the target feature. If the predicted feature has real values then we have a regression problem. On the other hand, if the predicted feature (also called target class) takes values from a discrete set of values then we have a classification problem.

If there is no feature defined as target class it means all the features have equal importance and therefore we are in the situation of unsupervised learning. In this situation we say that algorithms just try to find patterns in data without having access to any previous labeling of data. The algorithms that follow this approach are called clustering algorithms. There are known several types of clustering algorithms such as: flat clustering, fuzzy clustering, hierarchical clustering, etc.

- **Indexing of Source Data:** This activity assumes that available data is stored within the Information Retrieval system. From machine learning perspective, the source data represents the "training data".
- **Retrieval of Data (e.g., Textual Documents):** This is the output of the Information Retrieval system. The data that is offered as output is data that actually resides on the Information Retrieval system and has been previously indexed. This activity is concerned mainly with retrieving relevant documents to a query that has been provided as input. From machine learning perspective, the query represents the input data given to the hypothesis.

The main specific issues of Information Retrieval systems regard content analysis and information modeling (or structuring). Content analysis is mainly concerned with describing the contents of data sources (e.g., documents) in a form suitable for computer processing. In machine learning and data mining this step is known as pre-processing, which means parsing the raw data (e.g., files, databases, etc.)

Figure 1. Intelligent data computing

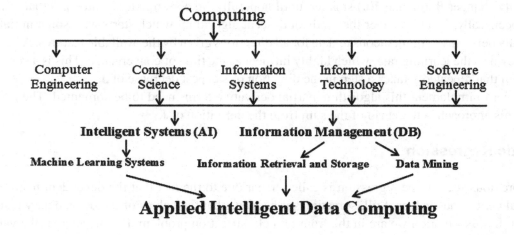

Figure 2. General architecture of an Information Retrieval system

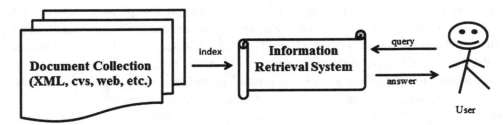

and producing the training data that is ready to be provided as input for machine learning algorithm. Information modeling or structuring regards finding and exploiting relationships between documents in order to improve the efficiency and effectiveness of retrieval strategies.

The quality of the machine learning or information retrieval system is assessed through evaluation. This implies the measurement of the effectiveness of retrieval for an information retrieval system or the value of the cost function for an obtained hypothesis. This step is often regarded as the most important one because it gives confidence to the end-user that the build system is effective and reliable. The effectiveness and reliability of the obtained hypothesis for machine learning systems or obtained results for information retrieval systems are usually measured by objective cost functions and metrics.

Linear Regression with Gradient Descent

Linear regression is probably the most widely used, and useful, statistical technique for finding a straight line that generalizes in best possible way a set of items defined by two numerical values. Linear regression models have the power to determine very complicated relationships between two or more numerical features. Among features, one is called dependent feature and is noted with y and all others are considered observed features and are noted $x_1, x_2, ..., x_n$.

The direct linear regression computes the parameters θ directly from the input dataset. The gradient descent has a different approach in the way that it iteratively estimates parameters θ such that the cost function $J(\theta)$ has minimum value. So, the learning problem is to fit θ parameters so as to minimize the cost function $J(\theta)$. To do so, a search algorithm is used. It starts with some "initial guess" for θ, and that repeatedly changes θ to make $J(\theta)$ smaller, until hopefully we converge to a value of θ that minimizes $J(\theta)$. Specifically, let us consider the gradient descent algorithm, which starts with some initial θ, and repeatedly performs a simultaneous update for all directions given by the available features. A key aspect is α, known as the learning rate, which highly influences the time of convergence. This is a very natural algorithm that repeatedly takes a step in the direction of steepest decrease of J.

In order to implement this algorithm, partial derivative terms need to be computed. The reason for having this approach is to get rid of the sum from the definition of J.

Logistic Regression

In the previous section the regression is called linear due to the fact that the dependent feature **y** may have real continuous values. Still, sometimes it happens that the values of the dependent **y** feature are nominal. In this situation we are in the front of a classification problem. For instance, if the values for the dependent feature may be only 0 or 1 we are in the front of a binary classification problem. This is in fact a special type of regression problem in which the predicted values are nominal, not continuous. The generalization of a binary classifier is a multi-class classifier and this situation occurs when the dependent feature may take a small number of discrete values.

For instance, if we are trying to build a spam classifier for email, then observed features **x(i)** may be some features of a piece of email, and predicted **y** may be 1 if it is a piece of spam mail, and 0 otherwise. 0 is also called the negative class, and 1 the positive class, and they are sometimes also denoted by the symbols "-"and "+." From this perspective we are dealing with positive items and negative items. Given **x(i)**, the corresponding **y(i)** is also called the label for the item. Having this in mind there is a wide range of problems that may be described as classification problems: image classification (e.g., optical character recognition), text classification (e.g., categorization, genre detection), etc.

One option would be to use the linear regression approach, ignoring the fact that **y** is discrete-valued. In the situation when linear regression is used to predict **y** values given **x** we may be in the situation to predict values larger than 1 or or smaller than 0 when we know that $y \in \{0, 1\}$. These situations do not make sense and conduct to models that perform very poorly.

Classification Algorithms

Classification is one of the major intelligent data analysis tasks. Although this task is accomplished by generating a predictive model of data, interpreting the model frequently provides information for discriminating labeled classes in data. Decision trees provide a predictive model that is easy to interpret to provide a description of data.

Classification algorithms belong to the large class of supervised learning algorithms. This means that items from the input dataset are labeled and the labels are also known as classes. The goal of the learning procedure is to obtain a hypothesis (which in this case is the classifier) that may be further used to predict the label (or the class) of a new item for which all other feature values are known. As in the case of any other learning methodology the concepts of input dataset, item (representing the vector of feature values and the associated label), and feature value, hypothesis, cost function have the same meaning. In this chapter there are presented the most common classification algorithms that may be used for training a classifier.

Decision Trees

Decision tree induction is one of the most well-known and used classification algorithms. Some of the application areas where it may be successfully uses are medical diagnosis, credit risk analysis, modeling calendar scheduling preferences or student classification in on-line educational environments.

A decision tree may be integrated into very useful tools in helping a financial institution decide whether a person should be offered a loan or not. In this context a person which applies for getting a loan may be defined by the following features: income range, criminal record, years in present job, etc. The target class has two values: *loan* and *no loan*.

One of the critical issues regards choosing the tree size. Using the obtained maximum trees is not practical due to very high complexity of the structure and the large (possible hundreds) of levels. Under these circumstances an optimization is required before actual usage of the tree. Therefore, they have to be optimized before being used for classification of new data. Tree optimization implies choosing the right size of tree (i.e., cutting off insignificant nodes and even subtrees). In practice there are mostly used two pruning algorithms: optimization by number of points in each node and cross-validation.

Once the classification tree is constructed, it can be used for classification of new data. In fact, this is the main goal of the whole procedure. The output of this stage is an assigned class or response value to each of the new items. By applying the set of splitting rules in the tree, each of the new items will get to one of the leaf nodes of the tree. A new item is assigned to the dominating class/response value of leaf node, where this observation belongs to. As you may observe the approach is similar with the one used for decision trees.

Bayesian Classifiers

The Bayesian classifiers belong to supervised learning procedures that are based on statistical methods. From mathematical point of view it is assumed the underlying probabilistic model that allows us to capture uncertainty about the model by determining probabilities of the outcomes. As any other classification methodology it is mainly used for solving predictive problems.

Bayesian classification provides a practical learning framework which makes intensive use of prior knowledge and the currently observed data. The output of Bayesian classifiers is in the form of explicit probabilities for derived hypothesis.

Some of the most common usages of Bayesian classifiers are for text classification, spam filtering, recommender systems or even sentiment detection. In on-line educational environments they are currently used for classifying users, e-Learning assets, etc.

Naive Bayes classifiers are among the most successful known algorithms for learning to classify text documents. The classifier determines the probability that a term t_k occurs in a document of class C. In this setup once a training dataset is provided new documents may be classified with a certain probability as belonging to a class (e.g., Computer Science, history, etc.).

Spam filtering is another well-known use of Naive Bayesian text classification. It makes use of a naive Bayes classifier to identify spam e-mail. Bayesian spam filtering has become a popular mechanism to distinguish illegitimate spam email from legitimate email.

Vector Space Classification

The data representation in previously presented classification scheme (i.e., Naive Bayes) is a sequence of terms or a vector $(x_1, x_2, ..., x_n)$ where all x_i have binary or nominal values (i.e., belonging to a small finite set of discrete values). In this section there is presented a different approach that works for vector representation of data in which the x_i terms are real-valued. For this type of data representation there need to be used different classification methods specially designed for operating on real-valued continuous variables making up vectors of data.

The basic hypothesis in using the vector space model for classification, under the previously presented data representation setup, is the contiguity hypothesis.

1. **Contiguity Hypothesis:** Items in the same class form a contiguous region and regions of different classes do not overlap.

The above hypothesis is quite strong and may not be usually found in input datasets. Still, for better understanding of the concept it is assumed that this hypothesis holds for the input dataset.

There are many classification tasks, in particular the type of student classification within on-line educational environments, where classes can be distinguished by activity patterns. For example, students in the class LOW tend to have low values on attributes like average grade on testing activities or messaging activity while students in the class HIGH tend to have high values for same attributes. Students of the two classes therefore form distinct contiguous regions as shown in below figure and we can set boundaries that separate them and classify new students. Building a classifier starting from an input dataset that has the characteristics presented above is the topic of this chapter.

Whether or not a set of items (e.g., students) is mapped into a contiguous region depends on the particular choices we make for the data representation.

If the data representation chosen is unfavorable, the contiguity hypothesis will not hold and successful vector space classification is not possible or may not generalize well. Generalization is the main goal for the classifier we are building and it characterizes how well it classifies new instances that were not used for building up the classifier.

The most representative algorithms that perform vector space classification are kNN and Rocchio. Intuitively, Rocchio classification divides the vector space into regions centered on centroids, one for each class, computed as the center of mass of all items (e.g., students) in the class. Rocchio classification is simple and efficient, but inaccurate if classes are not approximately spheres with similar radii values.

On the other hand, kNN or k nearest neighbor classification assigns the majority class of the **k** nearest neighbors to a test document. Intuitively, for the discussed item (the item for which we want to determine its class) there are considered the closest **n** items and the majority class of these **n** items decides the class of the discussed item. kNN requires no explicit training and can use the unprocessed training set directly in classification. Of course, it is much less efficient than other classification methods especially when the input dataset is large and when large value of **n** is considered in order of obtain greater accuracy. The advantage of kNN is that it can handle non-spherical and other complex classes better than Rocchio.

Clustering Algorithms

Clustering is an unsupervised machine learning technique used for data modeling. As compared with the supervised learning methodology in unsupervised learning there is no indication regarding the class to which an item belongs to. This means that for a data representation there is no such thing as target class or variable. From this point of view all features that describe an instance have equal importance. The first

Figure 3. Vector space classification into three classes

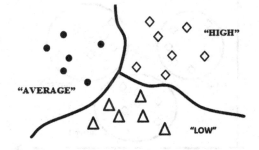

consequence of this approach is that the unsupervised modeling does not have as goal prediction (e.g., classification for nominal or discrete values or regression for continuous real-valued features) of values for the target feature given the values of all other features. The main task of unsupervised algorithms is to determine patterns in data. The main goal is to determine some structure within input dataset.

The different flavors of clustering algorithms need to take into consideration the data types of the features representing the items, the need for crisp or overlapping clusters, the hierarchical and flat representations or the access method to data. For crisp clustering each item may belong to only one cluster. This is a hard constrained as compared to soft computing paradigms where an item may belong simultaneously to many clusters. In hierarchical clustering the output presents a "parent-child relation" between clusters as in classical tree data structures as compared to flat clustering where there is no relation between obtained clusters. The access method to data may be full or incremental. In full access mode all the data is available and is processed as compared to incremental learning (or on-line learning) when the algorithm builds the clusters with each instance that is available.

The classical examples of clustering algorithms are k-Means which is a flat crisp clustering, EM which is also flat crisp but for which the number of clusters is not known in advance, fuzzy c-means which is a flat soft clustering and hierarchical clustering which is crisp but non-flat.

K-Means Clustering

K-Means is perhaps the most well-known clustering algorithm and is among the top ten data mining algorithms. The key inputs to a k-Means clustering algorithm (besides the data itself) are the number of clusters and the distance/similarity measure. The basic approach of k-Means assumes that the data analyst knows from advance the number of clusters that he wants to obtain from an input dataset. Of course, there are also standard methodologies for determining the optimal number of clusters that produces the highest quality of cluster distributions but this is an issue that needs a proper data analysis procedure. The second input represents the distance measure and is closely related to the defined distance between analyzed items. The most used function is normalized Euclidian distance but other distances such as squared Euclidian, Minkowski, Manhattan or previously presented cosine similarity. These distances are well suited for items defined by a set of real valued feature vectors. In the situation when the items have other type (e.g., images, sounds, etc.) custom similarity functions need to be used in the clustering process.

In Figure 4, the distance measure is Euclidian distance in the two-dimensional (2D) plane. This measure suggests three different clusters in for the available data. In this case each rhombus represents an item which is defined by two real valued features. If a vector representation is used in a document clustering

Figure 4. Sample output of a clustering process

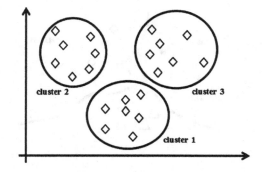

application the distance measures is often normalized Euclidean distance or cosine similarity. Still, different distance measures give rise to different cluster distributions and are the task of the data analyst and the domain knowledge person to actually specify the one which is obtains the most significant results.

In data analysis, k-Means clustering is a method of cluster analysis which aims to partition n items into k clusters in which each item belongs to the cluster with the nearest mean. The k-Means algorithm takes the input parameter **k**, and partitions a set of n items into **k** clusters so that the resulting intracluster similarity is high but the intercluster similarity is low. Cluster intra and inter similarity may be seen as a cost function which guides the algorithm towards the solution. The similarity is always measured in regard to the mean value of the items (also known as centroid) in a cluster and can be intuitively be seen as the center of gravity.

EM Clustering

The EM clustering algorithm is similar to previously presented the k-Means algorithm.

The EM (expectation maximization) algorithm extends and generalizes the basic approach of k-Means in two important ways:

1. Instead of assigning items to clusters in order to maximize the differences in means for continuous variables, the EM clustering algorithm computes probabilities of cluster memberships based on one or more probability distributions. The goal of the clustering algorithm is therefore to maximize the overall probability or likelihood of the data items, given the (final) clusters.
2. Unlike the classic implementation of k-Means clustering, the general EM algorithm can be applied to both continuous and categorical variables.
    a. **Mixtures of Distributions:** Figure 5 shows two normal distributions with different means and different standard deviations, and the sum of the two distributions. The dot line and the thin continuous line are the distributions and the thick continuous line represents their sum. We are in the situation in which only the mixture (i.e. the sum) of the two normal distributions (with different means and standard deviations) is given as input dataset. The goal of EM clustering is to estimate the means and standard deviations for each cluster so as to maximize the likelihood of the observed data (distribution). In other words, the EM algorithm attempts to estimate the contributing normal distributions (i.e. the dot and thin lines) having as input only their sum.
    b. **Nominal Variables:** The EM algorithm can also accommodate categorical variables. Clustering algorithms (especially k-Means) are more suited to work on continuous real valued variables. To accommodate also nominal variables EM method will at first randomly assign different probabilities (i.e., weights) to each class or category, for each cluster. In successive iterations, these probabilities are recomputed (adjusted) to maximize the likelihood of the data given the specified number of clusters.
    c. **Clustering Probabilities:** The results of EM clustering are different from those computed by k-Means clustering. The k-Means assigns items to clusters in order to maximize the distances between clusters and maximize the similarity between items from the same cluster. The EM algorithm does not compute actual assignments of items to clusters, but clustering probabilities. In other words, each item belongs to each cluster with a certain probability. Of course, as a final result you can usually review an actual assignment of items to clusters, based on the (largest) clustering probability.

Figure 5. Two normal distributions and their sum

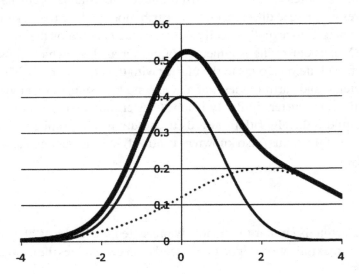

The algorithm's input are the data set (**X**), the total number of clusters (**M**), the accepted error to converge (**e**) and the maximum number of iterations. For each iteration, first is executed the E-Step (Expectation), that estimates the probability of each point belongs to each cluster, followed by the M-step (Maximization), that re-estimate the parameter vector of the probability distribution of each class after the iteration relocation. The algorithm finishes when the distribution parameters converge or reach the maximum number of iterations.

Association Rules and Link Analysis Algorithms

Association rules and link analysis are unsupervised algorithms that have certain characteristics apart from already presented ones. The main characteristic of these algorithms is that they take into consideration a temporal ordering in of the items that belong to the input dataset. So far, an item is viewed as a set of variables (or features) for which values are set. Still, a new perspective opens if we think of an item as a sequence of events that are ordered in time. Having this new perspective in mind a natural predictive problem arises: having a repository of experiences, each of them represented as an ordered sequence of actions and a list of actions that are already performed what action is most likely to be performed next?

Apriori Algorithm

In intelligent data analysis, association rule learning/mining is among the top ten algorithms used for discovering interesting relations between variables defining items that make up large input datasets. Piatetsky-Shapiro describes analyzing and presenting strong rules discovered in databases using different measures of interestingness. Based on the concept of strong rules, Agrawal introduced association rules for discovering regularities between products in large scale transaction data recorded by point-of-sale (POS) systems in supermarkets. Following the original definition by Agrawal the problem of association rule mining is defined as:

Let $I = \{i_1, i_2, ..., i_n\}$ be a set of **n** binary attributes called *items*. Let $D = \{t_1, t_2, ...t_m\}$ be a set of transactions called the database. Each transaction in **D** has a unique transaction **ID** and contains a subset of the items from **I**. A rule is defined as an implication of the form $X \rightarrow$. where X, $Y \subseteq I$ and $X \cap$. $Y \oslash$. The sets of items (for short item sets) **X** and **Y** are called *antecedent* (left-hand-side or LHS) and *consequent* (right-hand-side or RHS) of the rule respectively.

To illustrate the concepts, we use a small example from the educational domain. The set of items is $I = \{BST, OPT, AVL, SPLAY, RB\}$ and a small database containing the items where 1 codes presence and 0 absence of an item in a pool of studied concepts as in the table below. An example rule for the educational domain could be *{BST, OPT}=>{AVL}* meaning that if BST and OPT are already studied, students may also want to study AVL. The abbreviations are from tree data structures: BST – Binary Search Tree, OPT – Optimal Binary Search Tree, AVL – height balanced tree, SPLAY – Splay tree and RB – Red-Black tree.

In practical applications, a rule needs a support of several hundred transactions before it can be considered statistically significant and datasets often contain thousands or millions of transactions.

In Table 1 each transaction contains the information regarding the studied concepts for one student. For example, the first row contains the data regarding the successfully studied concepts of one student: BST and OPT are well studied concepts and AVL, SPLAY and RB are not well studied. The output of Apriori algorithm is in the form of rules that have high quality and therefore may be given as advice to students. For example, if the previously presented rule *{BST, OPT}=>{AVL}* is selected by Apriori algorithm as having a high quality that for students that already have studied well the BST and OPT concepts it may be given an advice that it's time to study AVL.

To select interesting rules from the set of all possible rules, constraints on various measures of significance and interest can be used. The best-known constraints are minimum thresholds on support and confidence.

BUILDING INTELLIGENT DATA ANALYSIS SYSTEMS

Building intelligent data analysis systems may be a difficult task due to the large number of ingredients that are necessary. First of all, we need data and of course a system that produces that data. This assertion leads us to the idea that the data analysis system will be somehow need to be designed having in mind a specific application domain. Throughout this book the data came from on-line educational environments and thus we may say more precisely that we are trying to build educational data mining

Table 1. Sample input dataset for Apriori Algorithm

ID	BST	OPT	AVL	SPLAY	RB
1	1	1	0	0	0
2	0	1	1	0	1
3	0	0	0	1	1
4	1	1	1	0	1
5	0	1	0	0	0
...					

systems. Secondly we need a goal for the data analysis system. Of course, the goal needs to in very close relation to the application domain and thus a domain knowledge person is needed. For educational environments this may be a reachable task but for genetics or agricultural domains the domain knowledge person becomes a critical asset.

In between the two presented *ingredients* (i.e., data and goal) there is the data processing and results visualization. The data processing regards feature definition and selection, algorithm selection, problem statement from the algorithmic point of view, data pipeline setup, results visualization, evaluation and interpretation.

This chapter tries to present a roadmap along with several examples of building such systems. This may help the reader to design and develop similar systems for educational domain or for any other application domain where such procedures may bring the *intelligent* character for the system.

Evaluation in Machine Learning

Evaluation may be considered the pitfall of any Data Analysis System. It is the moment when the data analyst assesses the quality of his work. The evaluation may sometimes reveal that we have not discovered anything important of we cannot rely on the findings. Generally speaking, validation gives the data analyst an objective measure regarding the confidence with which he may use the findings on future data. If the confidence is high it means that the data analysis procedure generalizes well. The generalization is the key aspect for what has been learned. For example, in educational environments we may employ a classification algorithm to decide whether or not an educational resource (e.g., document, quiz, etc.) is interesting or not for students. Once the data is modeled the system is supposed to obtain interesting resources for new students. If students will also find the resources useful and their knowledge will increase with a higher rate it means that the data modeling generalizes well and we are in the front of successful system. This is the reason why evaluation of what has been learned is a critical step in an intelligent data analysis system. In the following sections there will be presented the most important evaluation metrics currently used when designing such systems.

Let us suppose that we want to build a student binary classifier. The task is to classify students in two classes: *low* and *high*. These classes correspond to low level of acquired knowledge and high level of acquired knowledge. Once the classifier is built it will work in the following way: given a new item (i.e., a student) the classifier will determine his class: *low* or *high*. From validation point of view the question is how much to trust the prediction of the classifier. Intuitively, we need an objective measure that gives us an intuition regarding how well the classifier will perform on new data.

One of mostly used evaluation methods is training/testing procedure. This procedure splits the input dataset into two disjunctive dataset: *training dataset* and *testing dataset*. The main idea is to build the classifier using only the items from the training dataset and thereafter to compute the test set error. This is similar to checking how obtained classifier generalizes or how it performs on new data. The most important idea is that the items from the testing dataset were not involved in any way in building the model. This is the reason why we may consider this procedure as a *pseudo-generalization* procedure. It is a pseudo-generalization because the test dataset does not really contain new data and is just a percentage of the input dataset. When splitting the input dataset the general approach is to have 70% of the instances in the training dataset and 30% of the instances in the test dataset.

The above approach is useful but is quite simplistic and is very close to cheating. The main goal is to optimize our model's training procedures to result in the best generalization. A first improvement that we can do is to assume that the training data set and testing data set are drawn randomly from the same data set. In this way, any sub-set of the training data that we do not use to train the classifier can be used to estimate what the performance on the testing data set will be. This approach leads us closer to the true notion of generalization. The portion of the data we have available for training that is withheld from the classifier training is called the validation data set, and the remainder of the data is called the training data set. This approach is called the *hold out method*.

The idea is that available data is firstly split into more training and validation pairs of sets. Thereafter, classifiers are trained using each training set and are tested on the validation set. Finally, the best classifier is validated with data from testing dataset set.

For short, the intuition regarding this approach is that the best model is selected as the one with lowest validation error and for this model the generalization error is computed on the test data set.

In *k-fold cross-validation* the training data set is divided at random into k distinct subsets. The classifier is trained using k–1 subsets and the testing is performed on the remaining subset. The process of training and testing is then repeated for each of the **k** possible choices of the subset omitted from the training. The average performance on the k omitted subsets is the estimate of the generalization performance.

This procedure has the advantage that is allows us to use a high proportion of the available training data for training, while making use of all the data items in estimating the generalization error. The disadvantage is that we need to train the classifier k times. A typical and reasonable value fork is 10.

If k is made equal to the full dataset size the method is called *leave-one-out cross validation*.

Plotting Curves

When designing, developing and implementing intelligent data analysis systems it appears a continuous need for debugging. The general recommended approach is to start with a simple algorithm and setup ant to test it on the cross validation data. Once this initial step has been performed the improvement of

Figure 6. Training/testing data distribution

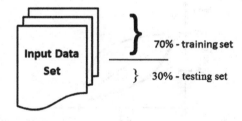

Figure 7. Training/validation/testing data distribution

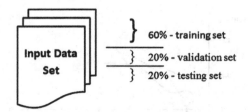

the data analysis system implies plotting error curves, performing error analysis and debugging. Thus, the big issue that arises after prototyping a data analysis system is to decide what you should try next. This is a hard issue which may have several answers: get more items in the input data set, try a smaller/ larger set of features describing the items, try a more complex (e.g., polynomial) shape of the hypothesis, tweak the parameters of the algorithm.

The main idea is that a data analyst is not advised to try all these possible solutions because it may end up working for some time with very little progress. It is not also advisable to take any decisions based on the *feeling* (or intuition) of the data analyst. The best option is to diagnose the system such that to obtain objective guidance of how to do in order to improve the performance. The diagnosis of the system may take to implement but taking this approach is a very good use of time. It is most likely that the conclusions will guide you to the proper actions that need to be performed in order to improve the performance of the system.

The precision/recall curve and possibly F-measure is a very effective way of getting an intuition on which model is best suited for our problem.

The plotting of the precision/recall curve is a very good way of effectively trading off their values. In this way the data analyst may choose the parameters for which a classifier (e.g., high recall and acceptable precision) best fits the requirements of the machine learning problem.

Plotting the training size/accuracy curve is an effective way for deciding whether or not more data may increase the accuracy. It is often the case when data analysts quickly decide that poor accuracy results are due to small size of the training dataset. Still, before spending a lot of effort for obtaining more data it is advisable to get information on how the system is likely to perform once more data is available. This can be quickly done by plotting a training size/accuracy curve for employed algorithm and possibly for other algorithms.

In Figure 9 there are plotted the training set size/precision curves for three algorithms. A quick inspection of these curves leads to the conclusion that accuracy of the algorithm with big dashes and

Figure 8. Plot of the precision/recall curve

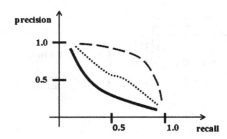

Figure 9. Plot of the training set size/precision curve

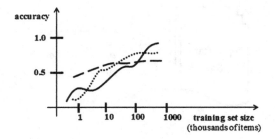

even of the one with small dots is very unlikely to improve accuracy by increasing the size of the training dataset. Still, the accuracy of the model plotted with continuous line may increase if more data are available. This plot leads to the conclusion that more data may be needed but the model that should be used is the one with continuous line.

The shape of the hypothesis has a great importance on the accuracy of the model. A simple hypothesis may have the shape of a linear model but more complicated polynomial shapes may also be obtained. Intuitively for low degree of polynomial the error may be high. Once the degree of the polynomial increases the accuracy increases because the model fits the data in a better way. Once the degree is too high the model over-fits the data and the accuracy decreases.

Figure 10 presents the concepts of under-fit and over-fit. The model (e.g., the classifier) under-fits the data if both its training error and cross validation error are high. This means that the hypothesis just poorly models the data and thus it is not useful. This situation corresponds to a high bias of the hypothesis.

The model over-fits the data if the training error is low but the cross validation error is high. The low training error looks like very appealing situation but the fact that the cross validation error is high means the model is unlikely to generalize well. In other words, it means that the model performs very well on the data that was used for building the model but it performs poorly on other data. The model just fits very well the training data (i.e., over-fitting) but fails to generalize. This situation corresponds to a high variance hypothesis.

This plotting helps a lot in trading off bias versus variance and thus choosing the proper value of **d** (i.e., the degree of polynomial) for which acceptable error rates for training and cross validation are acceptable.

Plotting learning curves is often very useful for visualizing the cross validation error rates and training error rates for the same training set size. Intuitively, for a certain hypothesis an increase in the training set size will increase the error on the training dataset but will decrease the cross validation error. The general situation is presented in Figure 11.

The presented learning curves may also reveal the high bias (i.e., under-fit) or high variance (i.e., over-fit) of the obtained model. Figures 12 and 13 present such situations.

Figure 12 presents a situation when both training set error and cross-validation error values quickly converge towards a high error value. This is a clear indication that the classifier just performs poorly, under-fits the data and thus has a high bias.

Figure 10. Plot of the hypothesis shape/error curve

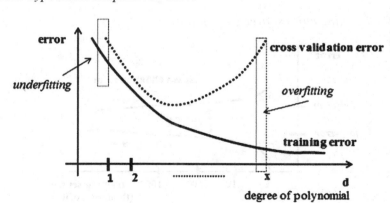

Figure 11. Plot of the learning curves

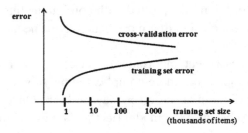

Figure 12. Plot of the learning curves: under-fit situation

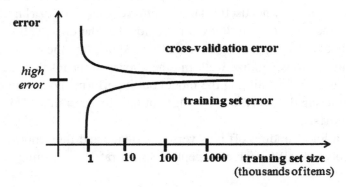

Figure 13 presents the situation in which the training set error converges towards a low value but, unfortunately, the cross validation error converges towards a high value. This situation is characterized by a large gap between the two curves. The large gap is an indication of a over-fit model which performs fine on the training set but fails for generalize even for the cross validation set. This is a clear indication that the classifier will fail to generalize on the test dataset, over-fits the training set data and thus has a high variance.

Once the learning curves are plotted the data analyst may have a more clear indication regarding what he should try next for improving the performance of the hypothesis. Here are few simple rules of thumb.

Figure 13. Plot of the learning curves: over-fit situation

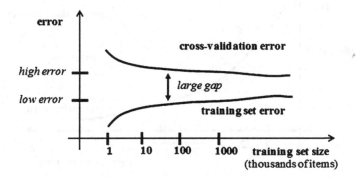

High variance (over-fitting) may be fixed by getting more training samples or by simplifying the hypothesis (e.g., a lower degree polynomial or a smaller set of features).

High bias (under-fit) may be fixed by having a more complex hypothesis. This may be done by using additional features or adding polynomial features (e.g., x_1^2, x_2^2, $x_1 x_2$ etc...)

Although plotting curves and computing accuracy rates (e.g., precision, recall, etc.) is very important the data analyst needs to answer some simple questions. One of the questions may be: "Do we have enough features for modeling the data?" For example, in an on-line educational environment we may want to predict the final grade for a student and we have available only one feature, the time spent on-line. Given this problem, the data analyst may also raise another question: "Can a human expert confidently predict the final grade given the available input?". For this particular situation the answer is definitely "NO". This approach proves that a human domain expert is a very valuable asset for building a high quality data analysis system.

General Roadmap for Building Intelligent Data Analysis Systems

The main steps that need to be performed when prototyping Data Analysis Systems are:

Task description. This is the first step in which the requirements of the system are specified. The requirements elicitation phase needs to be managed by an on-line educational domain knowledge person along with a data analyst. The first one should be very familiar with the capabilities of the on-line educational environment for which the system is being designed as well as with the requirements represented in unstructured form.

A sample task description may be: "*Build a system that advice learner regarding the resources and activities that need to be performed*". This may be only the top representation of the task.

General setup. This is the second step in which the all the needed data is specified. The first thing to be done is specifying the data that may be available from the on-line educational environment. More than this, the relations between different features need to be specified. The general setup represents the storyboard of the data pipeline. At this step, there is no need for any algorithm specification, but all data that will participate needs to be well defined as well as the output of the system.

The general setup may an xml representation. Below it is presented a sample of the xml file representing Computer Science program, Algorithms and Data Structures discipline, Binary Search Trees and Height Balanced Trees chapters.

```
<module><id>1</id> <name>Computer Science</name>
<discipline> <id>1</id><name>Algorithms and Data Structures</name>
  <chapter>        <id>1</id>            <name>Binary Search Trees</
name>        <concepts>
              <concept>        <id>1</id>        <name>BST</name>
              </concept>
<concept><id>2</id>        <name>Node</name>
              </concept>
                    ....
              </concepts>
              <quiz>        <id>1</id>  <text>text quiz 1</text>
                <visibleAns>abcd</visibleAns>
```

```
                    <cotectAns>a</ cotectAns >
                    <conceptId>1</ conceptId >
                </quiz>
                ......
    </chapter>
    ......
</discipline>
</module>
```

It may be observed that each chapter has associated a set of concepts and each quiz has associated a certain concept.

Figure 14 presents the concept map associated with the Binary Search Tree chapter. The data representing the activities performed by learners needs to be obtained. Firstly, the parameters that represent a learner and their possible values must be defined. For this study, the parameters are *nLogings* – the number of entries on the e-Learning platform; *nTests* – the number of tests taken by the learner; *noOfSentMessages* – the number of sent messages to professors; *chapterCoverage* – the weighted chapter coverage from the testing activities.

Their computed values a scaled to one of the following possibilities: VF – very few, F – few, A – average, M – many, VM – very many. The number of attributes and their meaning has a great importance for the whole process since irrelevant attributes may degrade classification performance in sense of relevance. On the other hand, the more attributes we have the more time the algorithm will take to produce a result. Domain knowledge and of course common sense are crucial assets for obtaining relevant results.

Figure 14. Binary search tree concept map

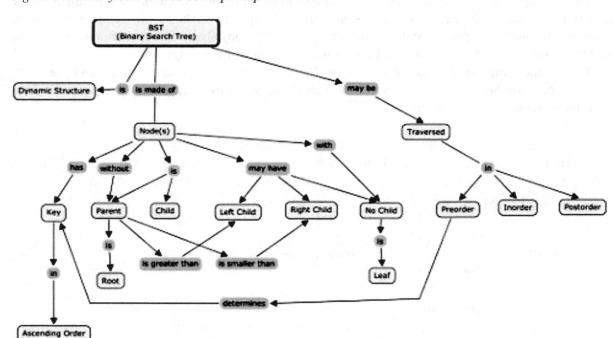

- **Data Analysis Process:** This step represents the design of the data analysis system. A sample design of a pipeline data analysis process may consist of following four layers.

  ○ **Experience Repository:** This layer is represented by the raw input data that is managed by the system. It consists of two realms: context representation and activity data. The context representation is closely related to the e-Learning environment and consists of chapter information, documents, test and exam questions, etc. The activity data consists of a homogenous representation of actions performed by learners.

  ○ **Constraints Representation:** This layer is represented by the constraints set up by users (e.g. e-Learning environment administrator, professor or learner). Each stakeholder may have and may set up parameters such that specific objectives are met.

  ○ **Learner's Request:** This is a wrapper for the request sent by the learner. It consists of learner's identity, the task to be performed and the associated parameters.

  ○ **Knowledge Repository:** This layer represents the transformed experience repository data into knowledge.

  ○ **Knowledge Miner:** This layer consists of the business logic that builds a response for the learner according to with the input data provided by the Knowledge Repository, Constraints Representation, and Learner's Request.

The software architecture is mapped on the data workflow in Figure 15. Each layer becomes a module that performs a set of associated tasks. The Experience Repository module implements functionalities of transforming data received from the e-Learning environment into a custom format that may be used by the Knowledge Repository module.

The Knowledge Repository module consists of a wrapper for a set of data mining algorithms that may be used for building in-memory models of data provided by Experience Repository.

Figure 15. Data workflow

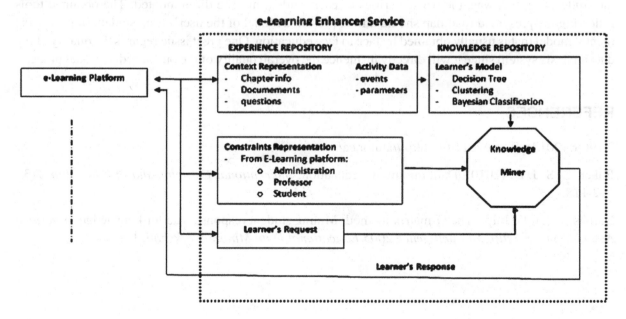

The Constraints Representation module offers the functionality for managing the constraints set up by stakeholders. The Knowledge Miner module offers functionalities for creating a knowledge work-flow with the shape of a pipeline with input from all other modules and with an output in the form of a learner's response.

The analysis process runs along the served e-Learning platform. The e-Learning platform is supposed to be able to provide in a standard format data regarding the context, the performed activity by learners and the aims/constraints provided by learners, professors or system administrator itself.

CONCLUSION AND PROMISING ROADS

The chapter presents a roadmap for designing intelligent data analysis systems that use educational data. The main ingredient of this endeavor is represented by the available educational data. Around this critical asset, there are several other important prerequisites. One regards the existence of an on-line educational system that produces data in the required format. Another prerequisite regards an educational domain knowledge person who may specify the requirements from the educational point of view. Finally, but not less important is the data analyst who may formally represent the requirements in an analytical form such that a data analysis pipeline may be designed.

A big plus in this approach is that the main three stakeholders (i.e., on-line educational system developer or administrator, educational domain knowledge person and data analysis) have at least an intuition regarding one each other's knowledge.

The data analyst should be aware of core available data analysis algorithms and classes of an algorithm such that he may formulate the requirement as a data analysis problem. For the development of applications that implement the data analysis system, there is needed knowledge about libraries that implement necessary algorithms. In extreme cases, development or adaptation of existing algorithms should be taken into consideration.

One of the key issues regards integrating a wider range of parameters that describe the activity of the students. In this way, the particularities of each student may be differentiated. The obtained tools following the presented roadmap should aim to present a model of the user's (i.e., student or professor) mental model that is usually obtained by face to face education. One great issue regards the quality of the data analysis system since it will directly influence the overall quality of the on-line educational process.

REFERENCES

ATutor. (2017). Retrieved from http://atutor.ca/

Baker, R. S. J. D. (2010). Data mining for education. *International Encyclopedia of Education*, 7(3), 112-118.

Barnes, T. (2005, July). The Q-matrix method: Mining student response data for knowledge. *American Association for Artificial Intelligence 2005 Educational Data Mining Workshop*, 1-8.

Bergner, Y., Droschler, S., Kortemeyer, G., Rayyan, S., Seaton, D., & Pritchard, D. E. (2012). *Model-Based Collaborative Filtering Analysis of Student Response Data: Machine-Learning Item Response Theory*. International Educational Data Mining Society.

Bradford, P., Porciello, M., Balkon, N., & Backus, D. (2007). The Blackboard learning system: The be all and end all in educational instruction?. *Journal of Educational Technology Systems*, *35*(3), 301–314. doi:10.2190/X137-X73L-5261-5656

Choquet, C., Luengo, V., & Yacef, K. (2009). Usage analysis in learning systems. *Usage Analysis in Learning Systems*, 7.

Chu, C. T., Kim, S. K., Lin, Y. A., Yu, Y., Bradski, G., Ng, A. Y., & Olukotun, K. (2006, December). *Map-reduce for machine learning on multicore*. NIPS.

Claroline. (2017). Retrieved from http://www.claroline.net/

Desire2Learn. (2017). Retrieved from http://www.desire2learn.com/

Dougiamas, M., & Taylor, P. (2003). *Moodle: Using learning communities to create an open source course management system*. doi:10.4028/www.scientific.net/AMR.211-212.1082

Hall, M., Frank, E., Holmes, G., Pfahringer, B., Reutemann, P., & Witten, I. H. (2009). The WEKA data mining software: An update. *ACM SIGKDD Explorations Newsletter*, *11*(1), 10-18.

Hamm, C., & Burleson, D. K. (2006). *Oracle Data Mining: Mining Gold from Your Warehouse*. Rampant TechPress.

Ihaka, R., & Gentleman, R. (1996). R: a language for data analysis and graphics. *Journal of Computational and Graphical Statistics*, *5*(3), 299–314.

Koedinger, K. R., Baker, R. S., Cunningham, K., Skogsholm, A., Leber, B., & Stamper, J. (2010). A data repository for the EDM community: The PSLC DataShop. In *Handbook of educational data mining*. National Center for Educational Statistics. Retrieved from http://nces.ed.gov/

Koedinger, K. R., McLaughlin, E. A., & Stamper, J. C. (2012). *Automated Student Model Improvement*. International Educational Data Mining Society.

Mahout, A. (2012). *Scalable machine learning and data mining. 2013-4-24*. Retrieved from http://mahout.apache.org

Mierswa, I., Wurst, M., Klinkenberg, R., Scholz, M., & Euler, T. (2006, August). Yale: Rapid prototyping for complex data mining tasks. In *Proceedings of the 12th ACM SIGKDD international conference on Knowledge discovery and data mining* (pp. 935-940). ACM. doi:10.1145/1150402.1150531

Romero, C., & Ventura, S. (2007). Educational data mining: A survey from 1995 to 2005. *Expert Systems with Applications*, *33*(1), 135–146. doi:10.1016/j.eswa.2006.04.005

Stanescu, L., Mihai, G., Burdescu, D., Brezovan, M., & Spahiu, C. S. (2010). A software system for viewing and querying automatically generated Topic Maps in the e-learning domain. *Informatica: An International Journal of Computing and Informatics, 34*(4), 441–450.

Wang, D. Y., & Ren, Z. J. (2011). The Solution of Datamining Based on Clementine. In *Advanced* []. Trans Tech Publications.]. *Materials Research, 211*, 1082–1086.

Witten, I. H., Frank, E., Hall, M. A., & Pal, C. J. (2016). *Data Mining: Practical machine learning tools and techniques*. Morgan Kaufmann.

Compilation of References

Abdul Hasib, A., & Hew Wooi, P. (2002). Fuzzy Logic Control of a three phasInduction Motor using Field Oriented Control Method. *Society of Instrument and Control Engineers, SICE Annual Conference*, 264-267.

Abramson, M. A., Asaki, T. J., Dennis, J. E., Magallanez, R., & Sottile, M. (2012). An efficient class of direct search surrogate methods for solving expensive optimization problems with CPU-time-related functions. *Structural Optimization*, *45*(1), 53–64. doi:10.1007/s00158-011-0658-3

Acar, E. (2010). Various approaches for constructing an ensemble of metamodels using local measures. *Structural and Multidisciplinary Optimization*, *42*(6), 879–896. doi:10.1007/s00158-010-0520-z

Achard, S., Salvador, R., Whitcher, B., Suckling, J., & Bullmore, E. D. (2006). A resilient, low-frequency, small-world human brain functional network with highly connected association cortical hubs. *The Journal of Neuroscience*, *26*(1), 63–72. doi:10.1523/JNEUROSCI.3874-05.2006 PMID:16399673

Ackermann, T., Andersson, G., & Söder, L. (2001). Distributed generation: A definition. *Electric Power Systems Research*, *57*(3), 195–204. doi:10.1016/S0378-7796(01)00101-8

Afonso, J. L., F. J. (1998). Genetic Algorithm Techniques Applied to the Control of a Three-Phase Induction Motor. *UK Mechatronics Forum International Conference*, 142-146.

Agustriyanto, R., & Zhang, J. (2009). Control structure selection for the ALSTOM gasifier benchmark process using GRDG analysis. *International Journal of Modelling Identification and Control*, *6*(2), 126–135. doi:10.1504/IJMIC.2009.024329

Ahmed, A. H., & Nahla, E. Z. G. Y. (2009). Fuzzy Logic Controlled Shunt Active Power Filter for Three-phase Four-wire Systems with Balanced and Unbalanced Loads. World Academy of Science, Engineering, and Technology, 58, 621-626.

Ahuja, M. K., & Singh, A. (2015). A Survey of Hand Gesture Recognition. *International Journal (Toronto, Ont.)*, *3*(5).

Al Seyab, R. K., Cao, Y., & Yang, S. H. (2006). Predictive control for the ALSTOM gasifier problem. *IEEE Proceedings - Control Theory and Application, 153*(3), 293-301. doi:10.1049/ip-cta:20050049

Al Seyab, R. K., & Cao, Y. (2006). Nonlinear model predictive control for the ALSTOM Gasifier. *Journal of Process Control*, *16*(8), 795–808. doi:10.1016/j.jprocont.2006.03.003

Alakeel, A. M. (2010). A guide to dynamic load balancing in distributed computer systems. *International Journal of Computer Science and Network Security*, *10*(6), 153–160.

Alon, J., Athitsos, V., Yuan, Q., & Sclaroff, S. (2009). A Unified Framework for Gesture Recognition and Spatiotemporal Gesture Segmentation. *IEEE Transactions on Pattern Analysis and Machine Intelligence*, *31*(9), 1685–1699. doi:10.1109/TPAMI.2008.203 PMID:19574627

Amrane, A., Louri, M., Larabi, A., & Hamzaoui, A. (2013). A fuzzy model reference adaptive system control for induction motor drives. *Systems and Control (ICSC), 2013 3rd International Conference on*, 177-182. doi:10.1109/ICoSC.2013.6750855

Anderson, Lunt, Javitz, Tamaru, & Valdes. (1993). *Safeguard Final Report: Detecting Unusual Program Behavior Using the NIDES Statistical Component*. Computer Science Laboratory, SRI International.

Anderson, Storlie, & Lane. (2012). Improving Malware Classification: Bridging the Static/Dynamic Gap. *Proceedings of 5th ACM Workshop on Security and Artificial Intelligence (AISec)*, 3-14.

Asmer, B. N., Jones, W. E., & Wilson, J. A. (2000). A process engineering approach to the ALSTOM gasifier problem. *Proceedings of the Institution of Mechanical Engineers. Part I, Journal of Systems and Control Engineering*, *214*(6), 441–452. doi:10.1177/095965180021400601

Astrom, K. J. (1983). Theory and applications of adaptive control: A survey. *Automatica*, *19*(5), 471–486. doi:10.1016/0005-1098(83)90002-X

Astrom, K. J., & Eykhoff, P. (1971). Systems identification-a survey. *Automatica*, *7*(2), 123–162. doi:10.1016/0005-1098(71)90059-8

ATutor. (2017). Retrieved from http://atutor.ca/

Axelsson. (1998). *Research in Intrusion-Detection Systems: A survey*. Chalmers University of Technology.

Axelsson. (1999). Research in Intrusion –Detection System: Survey. Department of Computer Engineering, Chalmers University of Technology.

Axelsson. (2000). *Intrusion Detection Systems: A Survey and Taxonomy*. Chalmers University.

Ayaz, H., Shewokis, P. A., Bunce, S., Schultheis, M., & Onaral, B. (2009). Assessment of cognitive neural correlates for a functional near infrared-based brain computer interface system. In Foundations of Augmented Cognition. Neuroergonomics and Operational Neuroscience (pp. 699-708). Springer Berlin Heidelberg. doi:10.1007/978-3-642-02812-0_79

Baccalá, L. A., & Sameshima, K. (2001). Overcoming the limitations of correlation analysis for many simultaneously processed neural structures. *Progress in Brain Research*, *130*, 33–47. doi:10.1016/S0079-6123(01)30004-3 PMID:11480285

Back & Chilimbi (2010). *Green: A Framework for Supporting Energy – Conscious Programming using Controlled Approximation*. ACM.

Bahrami, S., & Imari, A. (2014). Optimal placement of distributed generation units for constructing virtual power plant using binary particle swarm optimization algorithm. *Journal of Electrical & Electronics*, *3*(2), 1.

Bailey, L. M. (1984). The use of songs in music therapy with cancer patients and their families. *Music Therapy*, *4*(1), 5–17. doi:10.1093/mt/4.1.5

Baker, R. S. J. D. (2010). Data mining for education. *International Encyclopedia of Education*, *7*(3), 112-118.

Balakrishnan, G., & Reps, T. (2004). Analyzing memory accesses in x86 executable. *International Conference on Compiler Construction*.

Baliga, J., Ayre, R. W. A., Hinton, K., & Tucker, R. S. (2010). Green Cloud Computing: Balancing Energy in Processing, Storage and Transport. *Proceeding of the IEEE*.

Bansal, N. K., & Hake, J. (2000). Energy needs and supply option for developing countries. Proceedings of World Engineer's Convocation, 65-96.

Barbara, Couto, Jajodia, & Wu. (2001). Detecting Intrusions by Data Mining. *Proc. 2nd Annual IEEE Information Assurance Workshop.*

Barbara, Domeniconi, & Rogers. (2006). Detecting outliers using transduction and statistical testing. *Proceedings of the 12th Annual SIGKDD International Conference on Knowledge Discovery and Data Mining*, 54–60.

Barbara, D., Wu, N., & Jajodia, S. (2001). Detecting novel network intrusions using bayes estimators. *Proc. First SIAM Conference on Data Mining.* doi:10.1137/1.9781611972719.28

Barnes, T. (2005, July). The Q-matrix method: Mining student response data for knowledge. *American Association for Artificial Intelligence 2005 Educational Data Mining Workshop*, 1-8.

Basar, E., Basar-Eroglu, C., Karakas, S., & Schürmann, M. (1999). Oscillatory brain theory: A new trend in neuroscience. *Engineering in Medicine and Biology Magazine, IEEE, 18*(3), 56–66. doi:10.1109/51.765190 PMID:10337564

Basic concept and terminology of cloud computing. (2015, August 1). Retrieved from http://whatiscloud.com

Bauer, M., Oostenveld, R., Peeters, M., & Fries, P. (2006). Tactile spatial attention enhances gamma-band activity in somatosensory cortex and reduces low-frequency activity in parieto-occipital areas. *The Journal of Neuroscience, 26*(2), 490–501. doi:10.1523/JNEUROSCI.5228-04.2006 PMID:16407546

Bayer, U., Moser, A., Kruegel, C., & Kirda, E. (2006). Dynamic Analysis of Malicious Code. *Journal in Computer Virology, 2*(1), 67–77. doi:10.1007/s11416-006-0012-2

Beckers, R., Deneubourg, J. L., & Goss, S. (1992). Trails and U-turns in the selection of a path by the ant Lasiusniger. *Journal of Theoretical Biology, 159*(4), 397–415. doi:10.1016/S0022-5193(05)80686-1

Beik. (2012). *Green Cloud Computing: An Energy-Aware Layer in Software Architecture.* IEEE.

Bellman, R. (1957). *Dynamic Programming.* Princeton University Press.

Bergner, Y., Droschler, S., Kortemeyer, G., Rayyan, S., Seaton, D., & Pritchard, D. E. (2012). *Model-Based Collaborative Filtering Analysis of Student Response Data: Machine-Learning Item Response Theory.* International Educational Data Mining Society.

Berndt, D. J., & Clifford, J. (1994). Using Dynamic Time Warping to Find Patterns in Time Series. *KDD Workshop*, 359–70.

Bickel, P. J., & Li, B. (1977). Mathematical Statistics. Test. Citeseer.

Biley, Oberheid, Andersen, Morley Mao, Jahanian, & Nazario. (2007). Automated Classification and Analysis of Internet Malware. *Proceedings of the 10th International Conference on Recent Advances in Intrusion Detection, 4637*, 178-197.

Black, M. J., & Jepson, A. D. (1998). A Probabilistic Framework for Matching Temporal Trajectories: Condensation-Based Recognition of Gestures and Expressions. *European Conference on Computer Vision*, 909–24. doi:10.1007/BFb0055712

Blasco, F. X. (1999). *Model based predictive control using heuristic optimization techniques: Application to non- linear multivariable processes* (Ph.D. thesis). Universidad Politecnica de Valencia, Valencia, Spain.

Bobick, A. F., & Wilson, A. D. (1997). A State-Based Approach to the Representation and Recognition of Gesture. *IEEE Transactions on Pattern Analysis and Machine Intelligence, 19*(12), 1325–1337. doi:10.1109/34.643892

Bobick, A., & Davis, J. (2001). The Representation and Recognition of Action Using Temporal Activities. *IEEE Transactions on Pattern Analysis and Machine Intelligence, 23*(3), 257–267. doi:10.1109/34.910878

Bolt, R. A. (1980). *14 "Put-That-There": Voice and Gesture at the Graphics Interface.* ACM.

Booker, A. J., Dennis, J. E. Jr, Frank, P. D., Serafini, D. B., Torczon, V., & Trosset, M. W. (1999). A rigorous framework for optimization of expensive functions by surrogates. *Structural Optimization, 17*(1), 1–13. doi:10.1007/BF01197708

Borges, C. L., & Falcao, D. M. (2006). Optimal distributed generation allocation for reliability, losses, and voltage improvement. *International Journal of Electrical Power & Energy Systems, 28*(6), 413–420. doi:10.1016/j.ijepes.2006.02.003

Bradford, P., Porciello, M., Balkon, N., & Backus, D. (2007). The Blackboard learning system: The be all and end all in educational instruction?. *Journal of Educational Technology Systems, 35*(3), 301–314. doi:10.2190/X137-X73L-5261-5656

Bradley, M. M., & Lang, P. J. (1994). Measuring emotion: The self-assessment manikin and the semantic differential. *Journal of Behavior Therapy and Experimental Psychiatry, 25*(1), 49–59. doi:10.1016/0005-7916(94)90063-9 PMID:7962581

Braverman, Williams, & Mador. (2006). *Microsoft security intelligence report*. Microsoft.

Bretzner, L., Laptev, I., & Lindeberg, T. (2002). Hand Gesture Recognition Using Multi-Scale Colour Features, Hierarchical Models, and Particle Filtering. *Automatic Face and Gesture Recognition, 2002. Proceedings. Fifth IEEE International Conference on*, 423–28. doi:10.1109/AFGR.2002.1004190

Buchanan, B. G. (1998). Applications of artificial intelligence for chemical inference. XXII. Automatic rule formation in mass spectrometry by means of the meta-DENDRAL program. J. ACS, 61-68.

Büche, D., Schraudolph, N. N., & Koumoutsakos, P. (2005). Accelerating evolutionary algorithms with Gaussian process fitness function models. *IEEE Transactions on Systems, Man, and Cybernetics–Part C, 35*(2), 183–194. doi:10.1109/TSMCC.2004.841917

Bullmore, E., & Sporns, O. (2012). The economy of brain network organization. *Nature Reviews. Neuroscience, 13*(5), 336–349. PMID:22498897

Buyya, R., Vecchhiola, C., & Thamarai Selvi, S. (2008). *Mastering Cloud Computing*. Tata McGraw Hill Education Private Limited.

Calheiros, R. N., Ranjan, R., Beloglazov, A., De Rose, C. A., & Buyya, R. (2011). CloudSim: A toolkit for modeling and simulation of cloud computing environments and evaluation of resource provisioning algorithms. *Software, Practice & Experience, 41*(1), 23–50. doi:10.1002/spe.995

Calinon, S., & Billard, A. (2007). Incremental Learning of Gestures by Imitation in a Humanoid Robot. *Proceedings of the ACM/IEEE International Conference on Human-Robot Interaction*, 255–62. doi:10.1145/1228716.1228751

Can, M. T. (2011). *What is music therapy?*. Academic Press.

Capirci, O., Contaldo, A., Caselli, M. C., & Volterra, V. (2005). From Action to Language through Gesture: A Longitudinal Perspective. *Gesture, 5*(1–2), 155–177. doi:10.1075/gest.5.1-2.12cap

Caponio, A., Cascella, G. L., Neri, F., Salvatore, N., & Sumner, M. (2007). A fast adaptive memetic algorithm for online and offline control design of PMSM drives. *IEEE Transactions on Systems, Man, and Cybernetics. Part B, Cybernetics, 37*(1), 28–41. doi:10.1109/TSMCB.2006.883271 PMID:17278556

Carreras-Sospedra, M., Vutukuru, S., Brouwer, J., & Dabdub, D. (2010). Central power generation versus distributed generation–An air quality assessment in the South Coast Air Basin of California. *Atmospheric Environment, 44*(26), 3215–3223. doi:10.1016/j.atmosenv.2010.05.017

Chakravorty, M., & Das, D. (2001). Voltage stability analysis of radial distribution networks. *International Journal of Electrical Power & Energy Systems, 23*(2), 129–135. doi:10.1016/S0142-0615(00)00040-5

Chang, H., & Tang, X. (2011, January). A load-balance based resource-scheduling algorithm under cloud computing environment. In New Horizons in Web-Based Learning-ICWL 2010 Workshops (pp. 85-90). Springer Berlin Heidelberg. doi:10.1007/978-3-642-20539-2_10

Chang, Ouyang, & Hsu. (2014). An Efficient Green Control Algorithm in Cloud Computing for Cost Optimization. *IEEE Transactions on Cloud Computing.*

Chapman, C. E. (1994). Active versus passive touch: Factors influencing the transmission of somatosensory signals to primary somatosensory cortex. *Canadian Journal of Physiology and Pharmacology, 72*(5), 558–570. doi:10.1139/y94-080 PMID:7954086

Chee & Franklin, Jr. (2010). *Cloud Computing Technologies and Strategies.* CRC Press.

Chen Donghua, T. G. (2005). Shunt Active Power Filters Applied in the Aircraft Power Utility. *36th Power Electronics Specialists Conference,* 59-63.

Chen, L., Wang, F., Deng, H., & Ji, K. (2013). A Survey on Hand Gesture Recognition. *Computer Sciences and Applications (CSA), 2013 International Conference on,* 313–16. doi:10.1109/CSA.2013.79

Chen, Q., Grosso, P., van der Veldt, K., de Laat, C., Hofman, R., & Bal, H. (2011). Profiling energy consumption of VMs for green computing. *IEEE Ninth International Conference.*

Chen-Ching, Y. (2007). *Auto tuning of PID controllers: A relay feedback approach* (2nd ed.). Springer Publication.

Chen, F.-S., Fu, C.-M., & Huang, C.-L. (2003). Hand Gesture Recognition Using a Real-Time Tracking Method and Hidden Markov Models. *Image and Vision Computing, 21*(8), 745–758. doi:10.1016/S0262-8856(03)00070-2

Chen, Q. (2008). Hand Gesture Recognition Using Haar-like Features and a Stochastic Context-Free Grammar. *IEEE Transactions on Instrumentation and Measurement, 57*(8), 1562–1571. doi:10.1109/TIM.2008.922070

Chen, S., Cowan, C. F., & Grant, P. M. (1991). Orthogonal least squares learning algorithm for radial basis function networks. *IEEE Transactions on Neural Networks, 2*(2), 302–309. doi:10.1109/72.80341 PMID:18276384

Chen, V. P., Barton, R. R., Meckesheimer, M., & Tsui, K.-L. (2006). A review on design, modeling, and applications of computer experiments. *IIE Transactions, 38*(4), 273–291. doi:10.1080/07408170500232495

Cheyne, D., Gaetz, W., Garnero, L., Lachaux, J. P., Ducorps, A., Schwartz, D., & Varela, F. J. (2003). Neuromagnetic imaging of cortical oscillations accompanying tactile stimulation. *Brain Research. Cognitive Brain Research, 17*(3), 599–611. doi:10.1016/S0926-6410(03)00173-3 PMID:14561448

Chiewchitboon, T., Soonthomphisaj, & Piyarat. (2003). Speed Control of Three-phase Induction Motor Online Tuning by Genetic Algorithm. *Fifth International Conference on Power Electronics and Drive Systems, PEDS 2003,* 184-188. doi:10.1109/PEDS.2003.1282751

Chin, C. S., & Munro, N. (2003). Control of the ALSTOM Gasifier benchmark problem using H2 methodology. *Journal of Process Control, 13*(8), 759–768. doi:10.1016/S0959-1524(03)00008-8

Chiou, J.-S., Tsai, S.-H., & Liu, M.-T. (2012). A pso-based adaptive fuzzy pid-controllers. *Simulation Modelling Practice and Theory, 26,* 49–59. doi:10.1016/j.simpat.2012.04.001

Chipperfield, A., Fleming, P., Pohlheim, H., & Fonseca, C. (1994). *Genetic algorithm toolbox for use with matlab, version 1.2 User's Guide.* Sheffield, UK: Academic Press.

Choquet, C., Luengo, V., & Yacef, K. (2009). Usage analysis in learning systems. *Usage Analysis in Learning Systems, 7.*

Christodorescu & Jha. (2004). Testing malware detectors. *Proceedings of the 2004 ACM SIGSOFT International Symposium on Software Testing and Analysis*, 34–44.

Christodorescu, Jha, Seshia, Song, & Bryant. (2005). Semantics-aware malware detection. *Proceedings of the 26ᵗʰ IEEE Symposium on Security and Privacy.*

Chu, C. T., Kim, S. K., Lin, Y. A., Yu, Y., Bradski, G., Ng, A. Y., & Olukotun, K. (2006, December). *Map-reduce for machine learning on multicore.* NIPS.

Clark, R. C., & Mayer, R. E. (2011). *E-Learning and the Science of Instruction: Proven Guidelines for Consumers and Designers of Multimedia Learning.* Wiley.com.

Claroline. (2017). Retrieved from http://www.claroline.net/

Cloud Deployment Models. (2015). *A cloud deployment model represents a specific type of cloud environment, primarily distinguished by ownership, size, and access.* Retrieved from http://whatiscloud.com/cloud_deployment_models

Cohen. (1995). Protection, and Security on the Information Superhighway. New York, NY: John Wiley & Sons.

Cohen, F. (1987). Computer viruses: Theory and experiments. *Computers & Security, 6*(1), 22–35. doi:10.1016/0167-4048(87)90122-2

Correia, V. M. F., Madeira, J. F. A., Aeaujo, A. L., & Soares, C. M. M. (n.d.). Multiobjective design optimization of laminated composite plates with piezoelectric layers. *Composite Structures.*

Cortes, C., & Vapnik, V. (1995). Support Vector Machine. *Machine Learning, 20*(3), 273–297. doi:10.1007/BF00994018

Costantini, G., Todisco, M., Casali, D., Carota, M., Saggio, G., Bianchi, L., & Quitadamo, L. et al. (2009, July).SVM Classification of EEG Signals for Brain Computer Interface. *2009 conference on Neural Nets WIRN09: Proceedings of the 19th Italian Workshop on Neural Nets*, 229-233.

Cristianini, N., & Shawe-Taylor, J. (2000). *An introduction to support vector machines and other kernel-based learning methods.* Cambridge University Press. doi:10.1017/CBO9780511801389

Crone, N. E., Miglioretti, D. L., Gordon, B., Sieracki, J. M., Wilson, M. T., Uematsu, S., & Lesser, R. P. (1998). Functional mapping of human sensorimotor cortex with electrocorticographic spectral analysis. *Brain, 121*(Pt 12), 2271–2299. doi:10.1093/brain/121.12.2271 PMID:9874480

Cuppens & Miege. (2002). Alert Correlation in a Cooperative Intrusion Detection Framework. *Proc. IEEE Symposium on Security and Privacy.*

Dam, S., Mandal, G., Dasgupta, K., & Dutta, P. (2014). An Ant Colony Based Load Balancing Strategy in Cloud Computing. In Advanced Computing, Networking and Informatics (vol. 2, pp. 403-413). Springer International Publishing. doi:10.1007/978-3-319-07350-7_45

Dam, S., Mandal, G., Dasgupta, K., & Dutta, P. (2015, February). Genetic algorithm and gravitational emulation based hybrid load balancing strategy in cloud computing. In *Computer, Communication, Control and Information Technology (C3IT), 2015 Third International Conference on* (pp. 1-7). IEEE. doi:10.1109/C3IT.2015.7060176

Dasgupta, K., Mandal, B., Dutta, P., Mandal, J. K., & Dam, S. (2013). A genetic algorithm (GA) based load balancing strategy for cloud computing. *Procedia Technology, 10*, 340–347. doi:10.1016/j.protcy.2013.12.369

Das, S., Abraham, A., Chakraborty, U. K., & Konar, A. (2009). Differential evolution using a neighborhood-based mutation operator. *IEEE Transactions on Evolutionary Computation, 13*(3), 526–553. doi:10.1109/TEVC.2008.2009457

de Jong, K. A. (2006). *Evolutionary computation: A unified approach*. Cambridge, MA: MIT Press.

De Mello, R. F., Senger, L. J., & Yang, L. T. (2006, April). A routing load balancing policy for grid computing environments. In *Advanced Information Networking and Applications, 2006. AINA 2006. 20th International Conference on* (Vol. 1, pp. 6-pp). IEEE. doi:10.1109/AINA.2006.54

De Schotten, M. T., DellAcqua, F., Forkel, S. J., Simmons, A., Vergani, F., Murphy, D. G., & Catani, M. (2011). A lateralized brain network for visuospatial attention. *Nature Neuroscience*, *14*(10), 1245–1246. doi:10.1038/nn.2905 PMID:21926985

De Silva, L. C., & Ng, P. C. (2000). Bimodal emotion recognition. In *Automatic Face and Gesture Recognition, 2000. Proceedings. Fourth IEEE International Conference on* (pp. 332-335). IEEE. doi:10.1109/AFGR.2000.840655

Dennis, T. A., & Solomon, B. (2010). Frontal EEG and emotion regulation: Electrocortical activity in response to emotional film clips is associated with reduced mood induction and attention interference effects. *Biological Psychology*, *85*(3), 456–464. doi:10.1016/j.biopsycho.2010.09.008 PMID:20863872

Desborough & Honeywell. (2001). PID control. *Proceedings of the Sixth International Conference on Chemical Process Control*.

Desire2Learn. (2017). Retrieved from http://www.desire2learn.com/

Devi, S., & Geethanjali, M. (2014). Optimal location and sizing determination of Distributed Generation and DSTAT-COM using Particle Swarm Optimization algorithm. *International Journal of Electrical Power & Energy Systems*, *62*, 562–570. doi:10.1016/j.ijepes.2014.05.015

Dharageshwari, K., & Nayanatara, C. (2015). *Multiobjective optimal placement of multiple distributed generations in IEEE 33 bus radial system using simulated annealing*. Paper presented at the Circuit, Power and Computing Technologies (ICCPCT), 2015 International Conference on.

Dickerson, B. C., Salat, D. H., Bates, J. F., Atiya, M., Killiany, R. J., Greve, D. N., & Sperling, R. A. (2004). Medial temporal lobe function and structure in mild cognitive impairment. *Annals of Neurology*, *56*(1), 27–35. doi:10.1002/ana.20163 PMID:15236399

Dietterich, T. G. (1998). Approximate Statistical Tests for Comparing Supervised Classification Learning Algorithms. *Neural Computation*, *10*(7), 1895–1923. doi:10.1162/089976698300017197 PMID:9744903

Dixon, R., & Pike, A. W. (2006). ALSTOM Benchmark Challenge II on Gasifier Control. *IEEE Proceedings. Control Theory and Applications*, *153*(3), 254–261. doi:10.1049/ip-cta:20050062

Doagou-Mojarrad, H., Gharehpetian, G., Rastegar, H., & Olamaei, J. (2013). Optimal placement and sizing of DG (distributed generation) units in distribution networks by novel hybrid evolutionary algorithm. *Energy*, *54*, 129–138. doi:10.1016/j.energy.2013.01.043

Doane, D. P., & Seward, L. E. (2011). Measuring skewness: A forgotten statistic. *Journal of Statistics Education*, *19*(2), 1–18.

Do, H. T., Park, H. G., & Ahn, K. K. (2014). Application of an adaptive fuzzy sliding mode controller in velocity control of a secondary controlled hydrostatic transmission system. *Mechatronics*, *24*(8), 1157–1165. doi:10.1016/j.mechatronics.2014.09.003

Dorigo, M. (1992). *Optimization, learning and natural algorithms* (Ph.D. Thesis). Politecnico di Milano, Italy.

Dorothy, E. (1987). Denning, An Intrusion-Detection Model. *IEEE Transactions on Software Engineering, SE-13*(2), 222–232. doi:10.1109/TSE.1987.232894

Dougiamas, M., & Taylor, P. (2003). *Moodle: Using learning communities to create an open source course management system.* doi:10.4028/www.scientific.net/AMR.211-212.1082

Draper, C., & Li, Y. (1951). *Principles of optimizalizing control systems and an application to the internal combustion engine.* ASME Publication.

Drela, M., & Youngren, H. (2001). Xfoil 6.9 user primer [Computer software manual]. Cambridge, MA: Academic Press.

Dugan, R. C. M. F. (1996). Electrical Power Systems Quality. New York: McGraw-Hill.

Eberhart, R. C., & Shi, Y. (2000). Comparing inertia weights and constriction factors in particle swarm optimization. *Proceedings of the 2000 Congress on Evolutionary Computation.* doi:10.1109/CEC.2000.870279

Eckmann, S. T., Vigna, G., & Kemmerer, R. A. (2000). An attack language for state-based intrusion detection. *Proceedings of the 2000 ACM Workshop on Intrusion Detection.*

Edward, A. (2003). Some Challenges and Grand Challenges for Computational Intelligence. *Journal of the ACM, 50*(1), 32–40. doi:10.1145/602382.602400

Egele, Kruegel, Kirda, Yin, & Song. (2007). Dynamic spyware analysis. *Proceedings of the 2007 USENIX Annual Technical Conference.*

Eid, A., El-Kishky, H., Abdel-Salam, M., & El-Mohandes, T. (2010). VSCF Aircraft Electric Power System Performance with Active Power Filters. *42nd South Eastern Symposium on the System Theory,* 182-187. doi:10.1109/SSST.2010.5442838

El-Fergany, A. (2015a). Multi-objective Allocation of Multi-type Distributed Generators along Distribution Networks Using Backtracking Search Algorithm and Fuzzy Expert Rules. *Electric Power Components and Systems,* 1-16.

El-Fergany, A. (2015b). Optimal allocation of multi-type distributed generators using backtracking search optimization algorithm. *International Journal of Electrical Power & Energy Systems, 64,* 1197–1205. doi:10.1016/j.ijepes.2014.09.020

Ertoz, Eilertson, Lazarevic, Tan, Dokes, Kumar, & Srivastava. (2003). Detection of Novel Attacks using Data Mining. *Proc. IEEE Workshop on Data Mining and Computer Security.*

Escalnte, D., & Korty, A. J. (2011). Cloud services: Policy and assessment. *EDUCAUSE Review, 46*(4).

Essick, G. K., McGlone, F., Dancer, C., Fabricant, D., Ragin, Y., Phillips, N., & Guest, S. et al. (2010). Quantitative assessment of pleasant touch. *Neuroscience and Biobehavioral Reviews, 34*(2), 192–203. doi:10.1016/j.neubiorev.2009.02.003 PMID:19896001

Exadaktylos, V., Taylor, C. J., Wang, L., & Young, P. C. (2009). Forward path model predictive control using a non-minimal state-space form. *Proceedings of the Institution of Mechanical Engineers. Part I, Journal of Systems and Control Engineering, 223*(3), 353–369. doi:10.1243/09596518JSCE674

Feldbaum, A. A. (1960-1961). Dual control theory I-IV. *Aut & Remote Control.*

Fels, S., & Hinton, G. E. (1993). Glove-Talk: A Neural Network Interface between a Data-Glove and a Speech Synthesizer. *IEEE Transactions on Neural Networks, 4*(1), 2–8. doi:10.1109/72.182690 PMID:18267698

Feurra, M., Paulus, W., Walsh, V., & Kanai, R. (2011). Frequency specific modulation of human somatosensory cortex. *Frontiers in Psychology, 2.* PMID:21713181

Figueroa, C. J., Estevez, R. A., & Hernandez, R. E. (2005). Nonlinear mappings based on particle swarm optimization. *Proceedings of the 2005 International Joint Conference on Neural Networks.*

Firdausi, Lim, & Erwin. (2010). Analysis of Machine Learning Techniques Used in Behavior Based Malware Detection. *Proceedings of 2nd International Conference on Advances in Computing, Control and Telecommunication Technologies (ACT)*, 201-203.

Fogassi, L., Ferrari, P. F., Gesierich, B., Rozzi, S., Chersi, F., & Rizzolatti, G. (2005). Parietal lobe: From action organization to intention understanding. *Science, 308*(5722), 662–667. doi:10.1126/science.1106138 PMID:15860620

Fogassi, L., & Luppino, G. (2005). Motor functions of the parietal lobe. *Current Opinion in Neurobiology, 15*(6), 626–631. doi:10.1016/j.conb.2005.10.015 PMID:16271458

Forrester, A. I. J., & Keane, A. J. (2008). Recent advances in surrogate-based optimization. *Progress in Aerospace Sciences, 45*(1–3), 50–79.

Freeman, W. T., & Roth, M. (1995). Orientation Histograms for Hand Gesture Recognition. *International Workshop on Automatic Face and Gesture Recognition*, 296–301.

Friston, K. J., Harrison, L., & Penny, W. (2003). Dynamic causal modeling. *NeuroImage, 19*(4), 1273–1302. doi:10.1016/S1053-8119(03)00202-7 PMID:12948688

Fuhrhop, C., Mercorelli, P., & Georgiadis, A. (2013). Combining model predictive and adaptive control for an atomic force microscope piezo-scanner-cantilever system. *Sensorless Control for Electrical Drives and Predictive Control of Electrical Drives and Power Electronics (SLED/PRECEDE), 2013 IEEE International Symposium on*, 1–6. doi:10.1109/SLED-PRECEDE.2013.6684499

Fuster, J. M. (1988). *Prefrontal cortex. In Comparative neuroscience and neurobiology* (pp. 107–109). Birkhäuser Boston. doi:10.1007/978-1-4899-6776-3_43

Gallace, A., & Spence, C. (2010). The science of interpersonal touch: An overview. *Neuroscience and Biobehavioral Reviews, 34*(2), 246–259. doi:10.1016/j.neubiorev.2008.10.004 PMID:18992276

Gao, Y., Wang, H., & Liu, Y.-J. (2015). Adaptive fuzzy control with minimal leaning parameters for electric induction motors. *Neurocomputing, 156*, 143–150. doi:10.1016/j.neucom.2014.12.071

García, S., Molina, D., Lozano, M., & Herrera, F. (2009). A Study on the Use of Non-Parametric Tests for Analyzing the Evolutionary Algorithms' Behaviour: A Case Study on the CEC'2005 Special Session on Real Parameter Optimization. *Journal of Heuristics, 15*(6), 617–644.

Garfinkel & Rosenblum. (2003). A virtual machine introspection based architecture for intrusion detection. *Proceedings of the 10ʰ Network and Distributed System Security Symposium (NDSS).*

Gartner Highlights Five Attributes of Cloud Computing. (n.d.). Available from: http://www.gartner.com/newsroom/id/1035013

Gavrila, D. M. (1999). The Visual Analysis of Human Movement: A Survey. *Computer Vision and Image Understanding, 73*(1), 82–98. doi:10.1006/cviu.1998.0716

Genaud, S., Giersch, A., & Vivien, F. (2004). Load-balancing scatter operations for grid computing. *Parallel Computing, 30*(8), 923–946. doi:10.1016/j.parco.2004.07.005

Gentili, R., Cahouet, V., & Papaxanthis, C. (2007). Motor planning of arm movements is direction-dependent in the gravity field. *Neuroscience, 145*(1), 20–32. doi:10.1016/j.neuroscience.2006.11.035 PMID:17224242

Gentiner, D. (2003). Why we're so smart. In *Language in Mind: Advances in the Study of Language and Thought.* Cambridge, MA: MIT Press.

Ghamkhari & Rad. (2013). Energy and Performance Management of Green Data Centers: A Profit Maximization Approach. *IEEE Transactions on Smart Grid, 4*(2).

Ghosh, A., & Ledwich, G. (2002). *Power Quality Enhancement Using Custom Power Devices.* Boston, MA: Kluwer. doi:10.1007/978-1-4615-1153-3

Ghosh, S., Ghoshal, S. P., & Ghosh, S. (2010). Optimal sizing and placement of distributed generation in a network system. *International Journal of Electrical Power & Energy Systems, 32*(8), 849–856. doi:10.1016/j.ijepes.2010.01.029

Goel, T., Haftka, R. T., Shyy, W., & Queipo, N. V. (2007). Ensembles of surrogates. *Structural and Multidisciplinary Optimization, 33*(3), 199–216. doi:10.1007/s00158-006-0051-9

Goldberg, D. E. (2000). *Genetic Algorithms in search, optimization and machine learning.* New Delhi: Pearson Education Asia Ltd.

Golińska, A. K. (2011). Coherence function in biomedical signal processing: A short review of applications in Neurology, Cardiology, and Gynecology. *Studies in Logic, Grammar, and Rhetoric, 25*(38), 73–82.

Gorelik, E. (2013). *Cloud computing models* (Doctoral dissertation). Massachusetts Institute of Technology.

Gorissen, D., Coukuyt, I., Demeester, P., & Dhaene, T. (2010). A surrogate modeling and adaptive sampling toolbox for computer based design. *Machine Learning, 11*, 2051–2055.

Gorissen, D., Dhaene, T., & De Turck, F. (2009). Evolutionary model type selection for global surrogate modeling. *Journal of Machine Learning Research, 10*, 2039–2078.

Goudey, H. (2004). Watch the money-go-round, watch the malware-go round. *Proceedings of the 2004 Virus Bulletin Conference.*

Gözel, T., & Hocaoglu, M. H. (2009). An analytical method for the sizing and siting of distributed generators in radial systems. *Electric Power Systems Research, 79*(6), 912–918. doi:10.1016/j.epsr.2008.12.007

Graetzel, Fong, Grange, & Baur. (2004). A Non-Contact Mouse for Surgeon-Computer Interaction. *Technology and Health Care, 12.*

Gray, J. (1950). What Next? A Dozen Information-Technology Research Goals. *Journal of the ACM*, 41–57.

Griffin, I. A., Schroder, P., Chipperfield, A. J., & Fleming, P. J. (2000). Multi-objective optimization approach to the ALSTOM gasifier problem. *Proceedings of the Institution of Mechanical Engineers. Part I, Journal of Systems and Control Engineering, 214*(6), 453–469. doi:10.1243/0959651001540807

Guillermin, P. (1996). Fuzzy logic Applied to Motor Control. *IEEE Transactions on Industrial Application, 32*(1), 51–56. doi:10.1109/28.485812

Guo, M., Yu, Y., Yang, J., & Wu, J. (2012). The Crossmodal between the Visual and Tactile for Motion Perception. *Biomedical Engineering and Cognitive Neuroscience for Healthcare: Interdisciplinary Applications: Interdisciplinary Applications*, 99.

Hajebi, P., & AlModarresi, S. (2013). Online adaptive fuzzy logic controller using a genetic algorithm and neural network for networked control systems. *Advanced Communication Technology (ICACT), 2013 15th International Conference on*, 88–98.

Hajebi, P., & AlModarresi, S. M. T. (2013). Online adaptive fuzzy logic controller using a genetic algorithm and neural network for Networked Control Systems. *Advanced Communication Technology (ICACT), 2013 15th International Conference on*, 88-98.

Hall, M., Frank, E., Holmes, G., Pfahringer, B., Reutemann, P., & Witten, I. H. (2009). The WEKA data mining software: An update. *ACM SIGKDD Explorations Newsletter, 11*(1), 10-18.

Hameed, I. A. (2011). Using Gaussian Membership Functions for Improving the Reliability and Robustness of Students Evaluation Systems. *Expert Systems with Applications, 38*(6), 7135–7142. doi:10.1016/j.eswa.2010.12.048

Hamm, C., & Burleson, D. K. (2006). *Oracle Data Mining: Mining Gold from Your Warehouse*. Rampant TechPress.

Han, J., Shao, L., Xu, D., & Shotton, J. (2013). Enhanced Computer Vision With Microsoft Kinect Sensor: A Review. *Cybernetics, IEEE Transactions on, 43*(5), 1318–1334. doi:10.1109/TCYB.2013.2265378 PMID:23807480

Hariharan, D., Acharya, T., & Mitra, S. (2011). Recognizing Hand Gestures of a Dancer. In *Pattern Recognition and Machine Intelligence* (pp. 186–192). Springer. doi:10.1007/978-3-642-21786-9_32

Harmon & Auseklis. (2009). Sustainable IT Services: Assessing the Impact of Green Computing Practices. *IEEE Xplore*.

Haryanto, P., Siregar, D., Kurniadi, & Hong, K-S. (2008). Development of Integrated Alstom Gasification Simulator for Implementation Using DCS CS3000. *Proceedings of the 17th World Congress, the International Federation of Automatic Control*, 6-11.

Hasan & , Mishra. (2012). Hand Gesture Modeling and Recognition Using Geometric Features: A Review. *Canadian Journal of Image Processing and Computer Vision, 3*(1), 12–26.

Hasan, H. S., & Abdul Kareem, S. (2012). Human Computer Interaction for Vision Based Hand Gesture Recognition: A Survey. *Advanced Computer Science Applications and Technologies (ACSAT), 2012 International Conference on*, 55–60. doi:10.1109/ACSAT.2012.37

Hayakawa, Y., Miki, H., Takada, K., & Tanaka, K. (2000). Effects of music on mood during bench stepping exercise. *Perceptual and Motor Skills, 90*(1), 307–311. doi:10.2466/pms.2000.90.1.307 PMID:10769915

Haykin, S., & Lippmann, R. (1994). Neural networks, a comprehensive foundation. *International Journal of Neural Systems, 5*(4), 363–364. doi:10.1142/S0129065794000372

Henry, P., Krainin, M., Herbst, E., Ren, X., & Fox, D. (2012). RGB-D Mapping: Using Kinect-Style Depth Cameras for Dense 3D Modeling of Indoor Environments. *The International Journal of Robotics Research, 31*(5), 647–663. doi:10.1177/0278364911434148

Hernandez-Lopez, J.-J., Quintanilla-Olvera, A.-L., López-Ramírez, J.-L., Rangel-Butanda, F.-J., Ibarra-Manzano, M.-A., & Almanza-Ojeda, D.-L. (2012). Detecting Objects Using Color and Depth Segmentation with Kinect Sensor. *Procedia Technology, 3*, 196–204. doi:10.1016/j.protcy.2012.03.021

Hertenstein, M. J., Holmes, R., McCullough, M., & Keltner, D. (2009). The communication of emotion via touch. *Emotion (Washington, D.C.), 9*(4), 566–573. doi:10.1037/a0016108 PMID:19653781

Hicks, R. M., & Henne, P. A. (1978). Wing design by numerical optimization. *Journal of Aircraft, 15*(7), 407–412. doi:10.2514/3.58379

Hile, Gray, & Wakelin. (1994). *In transit detection of a computer virus with safeguard*. Academic Press.

Horlings, R., Datcu, D., & Rothkrantz, L. J. (2008, June). Emotion recognition using brain activity. In Proceedings of the 9th international conference on computer systems and technologies and workshop for Ph.D. students in computing (p. 6). ACM. doi:10.1007/978-3-642-24571-8_58

Hornak, J., Rolls, E. T., & Wade, D. (1996). Face and voice expression identification in patients with emotional and behavioural changes following ventral frontal lobe damage. *Neuropsychologia*, *34*(4), 247–261. doi:10.1016/0028-3932(95)00106-9 PMID:8657356

Hosovsky, A., Michal, P., Tothova, M., & Biros, O. (2014). Fuzzy adaptive control for pneumatic muscle actuator with simulated annealing tuning. *Applied Machine Intelligence and Informatics (SAMI), 2014 IEEE 12th International Symposium on*, 205–209. doi:10.1109/SAMI.2014.6822408

Houle, M. E., Symvonis, A., & Wood, D. R. (2002, June). Dimension-Exchange Algorithms for Load Balancing on Trees. SIROCCO, 181-196.

http://www.nihonkohden.com/products/products_en/type/eeg/eeg1200.html

Huang, Donghai, Li, & Xue. (2013). Active disturbance rejection control for the ALSTOM gasifier benchmark problem. *Control Engineering Practice, 21*(4), 556–564.

Huang, Q., Gao, F., Wang, R., & Qi, Z. (n.d.). Power Consumption of Virtual Machine Live Migration in Clouds. *IEEE 3rd International conference on Communication and Mobile Computing*.

Huang, W., Yang, J., & Yan, L. (2014, January). Multiobjective design optimization of the transverse gaseous jet in supersonic flows. *Acta Astronautica*, *93*, 13–22. doi:10.1016/j.actaastro.2013.06.027

Hurwitz, Bloor, Kaufman, & Halper. (2009). *Cloud computing for dummies*. Wiley Publication.

Hu, Y. F., Blake, R. J., & Emerson, D. R. (1998). An optimal migration algorithm for dynamic load balancing. *Concurrency (Chichester, England)*, *10*(6), 467–483. doi:10.1002/(SICI)1096-9128(199805)10:6<467::AID-CPE325>3.0.CO;2-A

IEEE Standard 519-1992 *1992 IEEE Recommended Practices and Requirements for Harmonic Control in Electrical Power Systems*. IEEE.

Ihaka, R., & Gentleman, R. (1996). R: a language for data analysis and graphics. *Journal of Computational and Graphical Statistics*, *5*(3), 299–314.

Ilgun, K., Kemmerer, R. A., & Porras, P. A. (1995). State Transition Analysis: A Rule-Based Intrusion Detection Approach. *IEEE Transactions on Software Engineering*, *21*(3), 181–199. doi:10.1109/32.372146

Ismail, B., Abdeldjebar, H., Abdelkrim, B., Mazari, B., & Rahli, M. (2008). Optimal Fuzzy Self-Tuning of PI Controller Using Genetic Algorithm for Induction Motor Speed Control. *International Journal of Automotive Technology*, *2*(2), 85–95. doi:10.20965/ijat.2008.p0085

Itani, W., Ghali, C., Chehab, A., & Kayssi, A. (2013). Accountable Energy Monitoring for Green Service Routing in the Cloud. *3rd International conference on communications and information technology*.

Jacquot, R. (1995). *Modern Digital Control Systems*. Marcel Dekker.

Jaimes, A., & Sebe, N. (2007). Multimodal Human–computer Interaction: A Survey. *Computer Vision and Image Understanding*, *108*(1), 116–134. doi:10.1016/j.cviu.2006.10.019

Jain, A., & Singh, R. (2014, February). An innovative approach of Ant Colony optimization for load balancing in peer to peer grid environment. In *Issues and Challenges in Intelligent Computing Techniques (ICICT), 2014 International Conference on* (pp. 1-5). IEEE. doi:10.1109/ICICICT.2014.6781242

Jain, S., Agrawal, P., & Gupta, H. (2002). Fuzzy logic controlled shunt active power filter for power quality improvement. *IEE Proceedings. Electric Power Applications, 149*(5), 317–328. doi:10.1049/ip-epa:20020511

Jech, T. (2013). *Set Theory*. Springer Science & Business Media.

Jiang, X., Wang, X., & Xu, D. (2007). Stealthy malware detection through vmm-based out-of-the-box-semantic view reconstruction. *Proceedings of the 14th ACM Conference on Computer and Communications Security.* doi:10.1145/1315245.1315262

Jin, R., Chen, W., & Sudjianto, A. (2005). An efficient algorithm for constructing optimal design of computer experiments. *Journal of Statistical Planning and Inference, 134*(1), 268–287. doi:10.1016/j.jspi.2004.02.014

Jin, Y. (2005). A comprehensive survey of fitness approximation in evolutionary computation. *Journal of Soft Computing, 9*(1), 3–12. doi:10.1007/s00500-003-0328-5

Jones, D. R., Schonlau, M., & Welch, W. J. (1998). Efficient global optimization of expensive black-box functions. *Journal of Global Optimization, 13*(4), 455–492. doi:10.1023/A:1008306431147

Jones, M. J., & Rehg, J. M. (2002). Statistical Color Models with Application to Skin Detection. *International Journal of Computer Vision, 46*(1), 81–96. doi:10.1023/A:1013200319198

Juang, C.-F., Chiu, S.-H., & Shiu, S.-J. (2007). Fuzzy System Learned through Fuzzy Clustering and Support Vector Machine for Human Skin Color Segmentation. *Systems, Man and Cybernetics, Part A: Systems and Humans, IEEE Transactions on, 37*(6), 1077–1087. doi:10.1109/TSMCA.2007.904579

Jue, S. S. (2012). Risk and Energy Consumption Tradeoffs in Cloud Computing Service via Stochastic Optimization Models. *IEEE/ACM Fifth International Conference on Utility and Cloud Computing.*

Kang, Poosankam, & Yin. (2007). Renovo: A hidden code extractor for packed executables. *Proceedings of the 2007 ACM workshop on Recurring Malcode,* 46–53.

Kansal, N. J., & Chana, I. (2012). Cloud Load Balancing Techniques: A Step towards Green Computing. IJCSI, 9(1).

Kansal, S., Kumar, V., & Tyagi, B. (2013). Optimal placement of different type of DG sources in distribution networks. *International Journal of Electrical Power & Energy Systems, 53,* 752–760. doi:10.1016/j.ijepes.2013.05.040

Kar, R., Konar, A., Chakraborty, A., & Nagar, A. K. (2014). Detection of signaling pathways in the human brain during arousal of a specific emotion. In *Neural Networks (IJCNN), 2014 International Joint Conference on* (pp. 3950-3957). IEEE. doi:10.1109/IJCNN.2014.6889939

Kar, R., Konar, A., Chakraborty, A., Sen Bhattacharya, B., & Nagar, A. (2015). EEG Source Localization by Memory Network Analysis of Subjects Engaged in Perceiving Emotions from Facial Expressions, International Joint Conference on Neural Networks. In *Neural Networks (IJCNN),* 2015 *International Joint Conference on.* IEEE.

Karni, A., Meyer, G., Rey-Hipolito, C., Jezzard, P., Adams, M. M., Turner, R., & Ungerleider, L. G. (1998). The acquisition of skilled motor performance: Fast and slow experience-driven changes in primary motor cortex. *Proceedings of the National Academy of Sciences of the United States of America, 95*(3), 861–868. doi:10.1073/pnas.95.3.861 PMID:9448252

Kar, R., Chakraborty, A., Konar, A., & Janarthanan, R. (2013). Emotion recognition system by gesture analysis using fuzzy sets. In *International Conference on Swarm, Evolutionary, and Memetic Computing* (pp. 354-363). Springer International Publishing. doi:10.1007/978-3-319-03756-1_32

Katarina, S. S. T. W. S. R. (2009). *Grid and Cloud Computing*. Springer.

Keil, A., Müller, M. M., Gruber, T., Wienbruch, C., Stolarova, M., & Elbert, T. (2001). Effects of emotional arousal in the cerebral hemispheres: A study of oscillatory brain activity and event-related potentials. [Chicago.]. *Clinical Neurophysiology*, *112*(11), 2057–2068. doi:10.1016/S1388-2457(01)00654-X PMID:11682344

Kennedy, J. E. R. (1995). *Particle swarm optimization*. Paper presented at the Particle Swarm Optim. doi:10.1109/ICNN.1995.488968

Khalid, S. N. (2009). Application of Power Electronics to Power System. New Delhi: University Science Press.

Khalid, S., & Dwivedi, B. (2007). A Review of State of Art Techniques in Active Power Filters and Reactive Power Compensation. *National Journal of Technology*, *3*(1), 10–18.

Khalid, S., & Dwivedi, B. (2013). Power quality improvement of constant frequency aircraft electric power system using Fuzzy Logic, Genetic Algorithm and Neural network control based control scheme. *International Electrical Engineering Journal*, *4*(3), 1098–1104.

Kim, S. G., Ashe, J., Hendrich, K., Ellermann, J. M., Merkle, H., Ugurbil, K., & Georgopoulos, A. P. (1993). Functional magnetic resonance imaging of motor cortex: Hemispheric asymmetry and handedness. *Science*, *261*(5121), 615–617. doi:10.1126/science.8342027 PMID:8342027

Kim, Y. E., Schmidt, E. M., Migneco, R., Morton, B. G., Richardson, P., Scott, J., & Turnbull, D. et al. (2010, August). Music emotion recognition: A state of the art review. *Proc. ISMIR*, 255-266.

Kirda, Kruegel, Banks, Vigna, & Kemmerer. (2006). Behavior-based spyware detection. *Proceedings of the 15th USENIX Security Symposium*.

Koedinger, K. R., Baker, R. S., Cunningham, K., Skogsholm, A., Leber, B., & Stamper, J. (2010). A data repository for the EDM community: The PSLC DataShop. In *Handbook of educational data mining*. National Center for Educational Statistics. Retrieved from http://nces.ed.gov/

Koedinger, K. R., McLaughlin, E. A., & Stamper, J. C. (2012). *Automated Student Model Improvement*. International Educational Data Mining Society.

Koelsch, S. (2010). Towards a neural basis of music-evoked emotions. *Trends in Cognitive Sciences*, *14*(3), 131–137. doi:10.1016/j.tics.2010.01.002 PMID:20153242

Kolter & Maloof. (2004). Learning to Detect Malicious Executable in the Wild. *Proceedings of the 10th ACM SIGKDD International Conference on Knowledge Discovery and Data Mining*, 470-478.

Konar, A. (1999). *Artificial Intelligence and Soft Computing: Behavioral and Cognitive Modeling of the Human Brain*. CRC Press. doi:10.1201/9781420049138

Konar, A. (2005). *Computational Intelligence: Principles, Techniques, and Applications*. Springer. doi:10.1007/b138935

Konar, A., Chakraborty, A., Halder, A., Mandal, R., & Janarthanan, R. (2012). Interval type-2 fuzzy model for emotion recognition from facial expression. In *Perception and Machine Intelligence* (pp. 114–121). Springer Berlin Heidelberg. doi:10.1007/978-3-642-27387-2_15

Kong & Yan. (2013). Discriminant Malware Distance Learning on Structural Information for Automated Malware Classification. *Proceedings of the ACM SIGMETRICS/International Conference on Measurement and Modeling of Computer Systems*, 347-348.

Kong, X., Thakor, N., & Goel, V. (1995, September). Characterization of EEG signal changes via Itakura distance. In *Engineering in Medicine and Biology Society, 1995., IEEE 17th Annual Conference* (Vol. 2, pp. 873-874). IEEE. doi:10.1109/IEMBS.1995.579247

Körner, E., & Matsumoto, G. (2002). Cortical architecture and self-referential control for brain-like computation. *Engineering in Medicine and Biology Magazine, IEEE, 21*(5), 121–133. doi:10.1109/MEMB.2002.1044182 PMID:12405066

Koshel, R. J. (2005). Simplex optimization method for illumination design. *Optics Letters, 30*(6), 649–651. doi:10.1364/OL.30.000649 PMID:15792005

Kothari, S. (1979). *Bharata Natyam: Indian Classical Dance Art*. Marg Publications.

Kothari, S. (1989). *Kathak, Indian Classical Dance Art*. Abhinav Publications.

Kotteeswaran & Sivakumar. (2016). Coal Gasifier Control - A Heuristic Algorithm Based Optimization Approach. *Australian Journal of Basic and Applied Sciences, 10*(5), 161-167.

Kotteeswaran, R., & Sivakumar, L. (2013). Normalized Normal Constraint algorithm based Multi- Objective optimal tuning of Decentralised PI controller of Nonlinear Multivariable Process – Coal gasifier, SEMCCO 2013. *Lecture Notes in Computer Science, 8297*, 333–344. doi:10.1007/978-3-319-03753-0_30

Kotteeswaran, R., & Sivakumar, L. (2013). Optimal Partial-retuning of decentralized PI controller of coal gasifier using Bat Algorithm, SEMCCO 2013. *Lecture Notes in Computer Science, 8297*, 750–761. doi:10.1007/978-3-319-03753-0_66

Kotteeswaran, R., & Sivakumar, L. (2013). Partial-retuning of decentralized PI Controller of nonlinear multivariable process using Firefly algorithm. *IEEE International Conference on Human Computer Interactions (ICHCI'13)*.

Kotze, J. J., & Van Schalkwyk, J. J. D. (1992). Image Coding through Skeletonization. *Communications and Signal Processing, 1992. COMSIG'92., Proceedings of the 1992 South African Symposium on*, 87–90. doi:10.1109/COMSIG.1992.274306

Kreinovich, V., Quintana, Ch., & Reznik, L. (1992). Gaussian Membership Functions Are Most Adequate in Representing Uncertainty in Measurements. *Proceedings of NAFIPS*, 15–17.

Kresch, R., & Malah, D. (1998). Skeleton-Based Morphological Coding of Binary Images. *Image Processing, IEEE Transactions on, 7*(10), 1387–1399. doi:10.1109/83.718480 PMID:18276206

Krishnakumar, K. (1989). Micro-genetic algorithms for stationary and nonstationary function optimization. In G. E. Rodriguez (Ed.), *Intelligent control and adaptive systems*. Bellingham, WA: SPIE.

Kroupi, E., Yazdani, A., & Ebrahimi, T. (2011). EEG correlates of different emotional states elicited during watching music videos. In *Affective Computing and Intelligent Interaction* (pp. 457–466). Springer Berlin Heidelberg.

Kruegel & Toth. (2001). Sparta, A mobile agent based intrusion detection system. *Proceedings of the IFIP Conference on Network Security*.

Kruegel. (2004). *Intrusion Detection and Correlation: Challenges and Solutions*. Springer.

Krugel & Toth. (2000). *A Survey on Intrusion Detection Systems*. TUV-1841-00-11 Technical University of Vienna, Information Systems Institute, Distributed Systems Group.

Krutz, R. L., & Vines, R. D. (2010). *Cloud Security: A Comprehensive Guide to Secure Cloud Computing*. Wiley Publication.

Kuipers, S. D., & Bramham, C. R. (2006). Brain-derived neurotrophic factor mechanisms and function in adult synaptic plasticity: New insights and implications for therapy. *Current Opinion in Drug Discovery & Development, 9*(5), 580–586. PMID:17002218

Kumar, P., & Mahajan, A. (2009). Soft Computing Techniques for the Control of an Active Power Filter. *IEEE Transactions on Power Delivery, 24*(1), 452–461. doi:10.1109/TPWRD.2008.2005881

Kumar, V., Lazarevic, A., Ertoz, L., Ozgur, A., & Srivastava, J. (2003). A Comparative Study of Anomaly Detection Schemes in Network Intrusion Detection. *Proc. Third SIAM International Conference on Data Mining.*

Labate, D., Palamara, I., Mammone, N., Morabito, G., La Foresta, F., & Morabito, F. C. (2013, August). SVM classification of epileptic EEG recordings through multiscalepermutation entropy. *Proceedings of the 2013 International Joint Conference on Neural Networks (IJCNN)*, (pp. 1-5). IEEE. doi:10.1109/IJCNN.2013.6706869

Lakhotia, A., & Kumar, E. U. (2004). Abstract stack graph to detect obfuscated calls in binaries. *4th IEEE International Workshop on Source Code Analysis and manipulation.* doi:10.1109/SCAM.2004.2

Lakhotia, A., & Mohammed, M. (2004). Imposing order on program statements to assist anti-virus scanners. *11th Working Conference.* doi:10.1109/WCRE.2004.24

Lang, Y., Malacina, A., Blegler, L. R., Munteanu, S., Madsen, J. L., & Zitney, S. E. (2009, March 19). lReduced Order Model Based on Principal Component Analyis for Process Simulation and Optimization. *Energy & Fuels, 23*(3), 1695–1706. doi:10.1021/ef800984v

Laurenceau, J., & Sagaut, P. (2008). Building efficient response surfaces of aerodynamic functions with Kriging and Cokriging. *AIAA Journal, 46*(2), 498–507. doi:10.2514/1.32308

Lavopa, E., Zanchetta, P., Sumner, M., & Cupertino, F. (2009). Real-time estimation of Fundamental Frequency and harmonics for active shunt power filters in aircraft Electrical Systems. *IEEE Transactions on Industrial Electronics, 56*(8), 412–416. doi:10.1109/TIE.2009.2015292

Laws, K. I. (1980). *Textured Image Segmentation.* DTIC Document.

Lee & Zomaya. (2010). *Energy efficient utilization of resources in cloud computing systems.* Springer.

Lee Rodgers, J., & Nicewander, W. A. (1988). Thirteen ways to look at the correlation coefficient. *The American Statistician, 42*(1), 59–66. doi:10.1080/00031305.1988.10475524

Lee, W., Stolfo, S. J., & Kwok, K. W. (1998). Mining audit data to build intrusion detection models. *Proc. Fourth International Conference on Knowledge Discovery and Data Mining.*

Lee, Y., & Jung, K. (2009). Non-Temporal Mutliple Silhouettes in Hidden Markov Model for View Independent Posture Recognition. *Computer Engineering and Technology, 2009. ICCET'09. International Conference on*, 466–70. doi:10.1109/ICCET.2009.113

Lee, H.-K., & Kim, J.-H. (1999). An HMM-Based Threshold Model Approach for Gesture Recognition. *IEEE Transactions on Pattern Analysis and Machine Intelligence, 21*(10), 961–973. doi:10.1109/34.799904

Lee, W., & Stolfo, S. J. (1998). Data Mining approaches for intrusion detection. *Proc. Seventh USENIX Security Symposium.*

Li, B., Huai, J., Wo, T., & Qin, L. L. Z. (2009). IEEE International Conference on Cloud Computing. *EnaCloud: An Energy Saving Application Live Placement Approach for Cloud Computing Environments.*

Li, K., Xu, G., Zhao, G., Dong, Y., & Wang, D. (2011, August). Cloud task scheduling based on load balancing ant colony optimization. In *Chinagrid Conference (ChinaGrid), 2011 Sixth Annual* (pp. 3-9). IEEE. doi:10.1109/ChinaGrid.2011.17

Li, Srinivasan, & Zhou. (2004). C-miner: Mining block correlations in storage systems. *Proceedings of the 3rd USENIX Conference on File and Storage Technologies (FAST)*.

Li, Wang, Peng, Wang, & Liu. (2013, December). Energy Aware scheduling scheme using workload- Aware consolidation technique in cloud data centers. *China Communication*.

Liang, K.-H., Yao, X., & Newton, C. (2000). Evolutionary search of approximated N-dimensional landscapes. *International Journal of Knowledge-Based Intelligent Engineering Systems*, *4*(3), 172–183.

Lian, R. J. (2014, March). Adaptive Self-Organizing Fuzzy Sliding-Mode Radial Basis-Function Neural-Network Controller for Robotic Systems. *Industrial Electronics. IEEE Transactions on*, *61*(3), 1493–1503.

Liddell, S. K., & Johnson, R. E. (1989). American Sign Language: The Phonological Base. *Sign Language Studies*, *64*(1), 195–277. doi:10.1353/sls.1989.0027

Lien, C.-C., & Huang, C.-L. (1998). Model-Based Articulated Hand Motion Tracking for Gesture Recognition. *Image and Vision Computing*, *16*(2), 121–134. doi:10.1016/S0262-8856(97)00041-3

Lin, J., & Ding, Y. (2013). A Temporal Hand Gesture Recognition System Based on Hog and Motion Trajectory. *Optik-International Journal for Light and Electron Optics*, *124*(24), 6795–6798. doi:10.1016/j.ijleo.2013.05.097

Lin, Y. P., Wang, C. H., Jung, T. P., Wu, T. L., Jeng, S. K., Duann, J. R., & Chen, J. H. (2010). EEG-based emotion recognition in music listening. *Biomedical Engineering. IEEE Transactions on*, *57*(7), 1798–1806.

Lin, Y. P., Wang, C. H., Wu, T. L., Jeng, S. K., & Chen, J. H. (2008, October). Support vector machine for EEG signal classification during listening to emotional music. *10th Workshop on Multimedia Signal Processing*, (pp. 127-130). IEEE. doi:10.1109/MMSP.2008.4665061

Li, S., Salour, M., & Su, X. (2008). A Survey of Internet Worm Detection and Containment. *IEEE Communications Surveys and Tutorials*, *10*(1), 20–35. doi:10.1109/COMST.2008.4483668

Li, S., Zhou, W., Cai, D., Liu, K., & Zhao, J. (2011). EEG signal classification based on EMD and SVM. *Journal of Biomedical Engineering*, *28*(5), 891–894. PMID:22097250

Litovitz, T. A., Krause, D., & Mullins, J. M. (1991). Effect of coherence time of the applied magnetic field on ornithine decarboxylase activity. *Biochemical and Biophysical Research Communications*, *178*(3), 862–865. doi:10.1016/0006-291X(91)90970-I PMID:1872866

Liu & Motoda. (2001). *Instance selection and construction for data mining*. Kluwer Academic Pub.

Liu, H., & Motoda, H. (2008). Computational methods of feature selection. Chapman & Hall/CRC.

Liu, G. P., Dixon, R., & Daley, S. (2000). Multi-objective optimal-tuning proportional-integral controller design for the ALSTOM gasifier problem. *Proceedings of the Institution of Mechanical Engineers. Part I, Journal of Systems and Control Engineering*, *214*(6), 395–404. doi:10.1243/0959651001540753

Liu, X., & Liu, J. (2016). A Task Scheduling Based on Simulated Annealing Algorithm in Cloud Computing. *International Journal of Hybrid Information Technology*, *9*(6), 403–412. doi:10.14257/ijhit.2016.9.6.36

Liu, Z., & Wang, X. (2012). A pso-based algorithm for load balancing in virtual machines of cloud computing environment. In *Advances in Swarm Intelligence* (pp. 142–147). Springer Berlin HeidelBarg. doi:10.1007/978-3-642-30976-2_17

Li, Y., Tong, S., Liu, Y., & Li, T. (2014). Adaptive Fuzzy Robust Output Feedback Control of Nonlinear Systems With Unknown Dead Zones Based on a Small-Gain Approach. *Fuzzy Systems. IEEE Transactions on*, *22*(1), 164–176.

Mahesh, K., Nallagownden, P. A., & Elamvazuthi, I. A. (2015). *Optimal placement and sizing of DG in distribution system using accelerated PSO for power loss minimization.* Paper presented at the 2015 IEEE Conference on Energy Conversion (CENCON). doi:10.1109/CENCON.2015.7409538

Mahesh, K., Nallagownden, P., & Elamvazuthi, I. (2016). Advanced Pareto Front Non-Dominated Sorting Multi-Objective Particle Swarm Optimization for Optimal Placement and Sizing of Distributed Generation. *Energies, 9*(12), 982. doi:10.3390/en9120982

Mahoney & Chan. (n.d.a). *Learning models of network traffic for detecting the novel attack.* Technical report, Florida Tech., CS-2002-8.

Mahoney & Chan. (n.d.b). *PHAD: Packet header anomaly detection for identifying hostile network traffic.* Technical report, Florida Tech., CS-2001-4.

Mahoney, M., & Chan, P. (2002). Learning non stationary models of normal network traffic for detecting novel attacks. *Proceedings of SIGKDD,* 376–385.

Mahout, A. (2012). *Scalable machine learning and data mining. 2013-4-24.* Retrieved from http://mahout.apache.org

Maini, R., & Aggarwal, H. (2009). Study and Comparison of Various Image Edge Detection Techniques. *International Journal of Image Processing, 3*(1), 1–11.

Maragos, P., & Schafer, R. (1986). Morphological Skeleton Representation and Coding of Binary Images. *Acoustics, Speech and Signal Processing, IEEE Transactions on, 34*(5), 1228–1244. doi:10.1109/TASSP.1986.1164959

Martignoni, , Christodorescu, & Jha. (2007). (Omniunpack): Fast, generic, and safe unpacking of malware. *Proceedings of the 23rd Annual Computer Security Applications Conference (ACSAC),* 431–441.

Martinez, H. P., Bengio, Y., & Yannakakis, G. N. (2013). Learning deep physiological models of affect. *IEEE Computational Intelligence Magazine, 8*(2), 20–33. doi:10.1109/MCI.2013.2247823

Masumpoor, S., Yaghobi, H., & Khanesar, M. A. (2015). Adaptive sliding mode type-2 neuro-fuzzy control of an induction motor. *Expert Systems with Applications, 42*(19), 6635–6647. doi:10.1016/j.eswa.2015.04.046

Mauricio Aredes, J. H. (1997, March). Three-Phase Four-Wire Shunt Active Filter Control Strategies. *IEEE Transactions on Power Electronics, 12*(2), 311–318. doi:10.1109/63.558748

McKay, M. D., Beckman, R. J., & Conover, W. J. (1979). A comparison of three methods for selecting values of input variables in the analysis of output from a computer code. *Technometrics, 21*(2), 239–245.

McKetta, J. J., Jr. (1976). Encyclopedia of Chemical Processing and Design: Volume 1-Abrasives to Acrylonitrile. CRC Press.

McNeill, D. (2000). *Language and Gesture.* Cambridge University Press. doi:10.1017/CBO9780511620850

Meckesheimer, M., Booker, A. J., Barton, R. R., & Simpson, T. W. (2002). Computationally inexpensive metamodel assessment strategies. *AIAA Journal, 40*(10), 2053–2060. doi:10.2514/2.1538

Melinger, A., & Levelt, W. J. M. (2004). Gesture and the Communicative Intention of the Speaker. *Gesture, 4*(2), 119–141. doi:10.1075/gest.4.2.02mel

Mell, P., & Grance, T. (2009). The NIST definition of cloud computing. *National Institute of Standards and Technology, 53*(6), 50.

Mendes, N., & Neto, P. (2015). Indirect adaptive fuzzy control for industrial robots: A solution for contact applications. *Expert Systems with Applications, 42*(22), 8929–8935. doi:10.1016/j.eswa.2015.07.047

Mierswa, I., Wurst, M., Klinkenberg, R., Scholz, M., & Euler, T. (2006, August). Yale: Rapid prototyping for complex data mining tasks. In *Proceedings of the 12th ACM SIGKDD international conference on Knowledge discovery and data mining* (pp. 935-940). ACM. doi:10.1145/1150402.1150531

Miller, E. K., & Cohen, J. D. (2001). An integrative theory of prefrontal cortex function. *Annual Review of Neuroscience, 24*(1), 167–202. doi:10.1146/annurev.neuro.24.1.167 PMID:11283309

Min, Y. K., Chung, S. C., & Min, B. C. (2005). Physiological evaluation of emotional change induced by imagination. *Applied Psychophysiology and Biofeedback, 30*(2), 137–150. doi:10.1007/s10484-005-4310-0 PMID:16013786

Mishra, M., Das, A., Kulkarni, P., & Sahoo, A. (2012, September). Dynamic Resource Management Using Virtual Machine Migrations. *IEEE Communication Magazine.*

Mitchell, T. M. (1999). Machine Learning and Data Mining. *Communications of the ACM, 42*(11), 30–36. doi:10.1145/319382.319388

Mitra, S., & Acharya, T. (2007). Gesture Recognition: A Survey. *Systems, Man, and Cybernetics, Part C: Applications and Reviews, IEEE Transactions on, 37*(3), 311–324. doi:10.1109/TSMCC.2007.893280

Moeslund, T. B., & Granum, E. (2001). A Survey of Computer Vision-Based Human Motion Capture. *Computer Vision and Image Understanding, 81*(3), 231–268. doi:10.1006/cviu.2000.0897

Mohandas, N., Balamurugan, R., & Lakshminarasimman, L. (2015). Optimal location and sizing of real power DG units to improve the voltage stability in the distribution system using ABC algorithm united with chaos. *International Journal of Electrical Power & Energy Systems, 66*, 41–52. doi:10.1016/j.ijepes.2014.10.033

Mondal, B., Dasgupta, K., & Dutta, P. (2012). Load balancing in cloud computing using stochastic hill climbing-a soft computing approach. *Procedia Technology, 4*, 783–789. doi:10.1016/j.protcy.2012.05.128

Moradi, M., Dezfuli, M. A., & Safavi, M. H. (2010, April). A new time optimizing probabilistic load balancing algorithm in grid computing. In *Computer Engineering and Technology (ICCET), 2010 2nd International Conference on* (Vol. 1, pp. V1-232). IEEE. doi:10.1109/ICCET.2010.5486187

Moradi, M. H., & Abedini, M. (2012). A combination of genetic algorithm and particle swarm optimization for optimal DG location and sizing in distribution systems. *International Journal of Electrical Power & Energy Systems, 34*(1), 66–74. doi:10.1016/j.ijepes.2011.08.023

Moser, A., Kruegel, C., & Kirda, E. (2007a). Exploring multiple execution paths for malware analysis. *Proceedings of the 2007 IEEE Symposium on Security and Privacy.* doi:10.1109/SP.2007.17

Moser, A., Kruegel, C., & Kirda, E. (2007b). Limits of static analysis for malware detection. *Proceedings of the 23rd Annual Computer Security Applications Conference (ACSAC).* doi:10.1109/ACSAC.2007.21

Moses, P. M., Mbuthia, J., & Odero, N. A. (2012). *Reducing real and reactive power losses in the distribution system by DFIG placement and sizing using ordinary PSO and HGPSO: A comparison.* University of Nairobi.

Mugunthan, P., & Shoemaker, C. A. (2006). Assessing the impacts of parameter uncertainty for computationally expensive groundwater models. *Water Resources Research, 42*(10). doi:10.1029/2005WR004640

Mukherjee, K., & Sahoo, G. (2009, December). Mathematical model of cloud computing framework using fuzzy bee colony optimization technique. In *Advances in Computing, Control, & Telecommunication Technologies, 2009. ACT'09. International Conference on* (pp. 664-668). IEEE. doi:10.1109/ACT.2009.168

Muller, J., & Piché, R. (2011). Mixture surrogate models based on Dempster-Shafer theory for global optimization problems. *Journal of Global Optimization, 51*(1), 79–104. doi:10.1007/s10898-010-9620-y

Müller, M. M., Keil, A., Gruber, T., & Elbert, T. (1999). Processing of affective pictures modulates right-hemispheric gamma band EEG activity. *Clinical Neurophysiology, 110*(11), 1913–1920. doi:10.1016/S1388-2457(99)00151-0 PMID:10576487

Munro, N., Edmunds, J. M., Kontogiannis, E., & Impram, I. M. (2000). A sequential loop closing approach to the ALSTOM gasifier problem. *Proceedings of the Institution of Mechanical Engineers. Part I, Journal of Systems and Control Engineering, 214*(6), 427–439. doi:10.1243/0959651001540780

Murthy, G. R. S., & Jadon, R. S. (2009). A Review of Vision Based Hand Gestures Recognition. *International Journal of Information Technology and Knowledge Management, 2*(2), 405–410.

Myers, R. H., & Montgomery, D. C. (1995). *Response surface methodology: Process and product optimization using designed experiments*. New York: John Wiley and Sons.

Nair, R.R. & Behera, L. & Kumar, V. & Jamshidi, M. (2015). Multisatellite Formation Control for Remote Sensing Applications Using Artificial Potential Field and Adaptive Fuzzy Sliding Mode Control. *Systems Journal, IEEE, 9*(2), 508-518.

Nakamura, T., Tomita, Y., Ito, S. I., &Mitsukura, Y. (2010, September). A method of obtaining sense of touch by using EEG. In *RO-MAN*, (pp. 276-281). IEEE.

Nataraj, Karthikeyan, Jacob, & Manjunath. (2011). Malware Images: Visualization and Automatic Classification. *Proceedings of the 8th International Symposium on Visualization for Cyber Security*.

Nataraj, Yegneswaran, Porras, & Zhang. (2011). A Comparative Assessment of Malware Classification Using Binary Texture Analysis and Dynamic Analysis. *Proceedings of the 4th ACM Workshop on Security and Artificial Intelligence*, 21-30.

Nelder, J. A., & Mead, R. (1965). A simplex method for function minimisation. *The Computer Journal, 7*(4), 308–313. doi:10.1093/comjnl/7.4.308

Ng, C. W., & Ranganath, S. (2002). Real-Time Gesture Recognition System and Application. *Image and Vision Computing, 20*(13), 993–1007. doi:10.1016/S0262-8856(02)00113-0

Nickel, K., & Stiefelhagen, R. (2007). Visual Recognition of Pointing Gestures for Human–robot Interaction. *Image and Vision Computing, 25*(12), 1875–1884. doi:10.1016/j.imavis.2005.12.020

Nie, D., Wang, X. W., Shi, L. C., & Lu, B. L. (2011, April). EEG-based emotion recognition during watching movies. In *Neural Engineering (NER), 2011 5th International IEEE/EMBS Conference on* (pp. 667-670). IEEE. doi:10.1109/NER.2011.5910636

Ning, Cui, & Reeves. (2002). Constructing Attack Scenarios through Correlation of Intrusion Alerts. *Proc. ACM Computer and Communications Security Conf.*

Nise, N. S. (2006). *Control System Engineering* (3rd ed.). CECSA.

Niu, Y., Li, X., Lin, Z., & Li, M. (2014). Adaptive decentralized-coordinated neural control of hybrid wind-thermal power system. Innovative Smart Grid Technologies Conference Europe (ISGT-Europe), 2014 IEEE PES, 1–6. doi:10.1109/ISGTEurope.2014.7028981

Nobakhti, A., & Wang, H. (2008). A simple self-adaptive Differential Evolution algorithm with application on the AL-STOM gasifier. *Applied Soft Computing, 8*(1), 350–370. doi:10.1016/j.asoc.2006.12.005

Norman, M., Samsul, B., Mohd, N., & Jasronita, J., & B., O. S. (2004). A Fuzzy logic Controller for an Indirect vector Controlled Three Phase Induction. *Proceedings of Analog And Digital Techniques In Electrical Engineering*, 1–4.

Nothdurft, H. C. (1991). Texture Segmentation and Pop-out from Orientation Contrast. *Vision Research, 31*(6), 1073–1078. doi:10.1016/0042-6989(91)90211-M PMID:1858322

O'Dwyer, A. (2009). Handbook of PI and PID Controller Tuning Rules (3rd ed.). Imperial College Press.

Ogata, K. (2003). *Modern Control Engineering* (4th ed.). Person Prentice Hall.

OHara, K., Dastur, N., Carrell, T., Gonzalez, G., Sellen, A., Penney, G., & Rouncefield, M. et al. (2014). Touchless Interaction in Surgery. *Communications of the ACM, 57*(1), 70–77. doi:10.1145/2541883.2541899

Oszust, M., & Wysocki, M. (2013). Recognition of Signed Expressions Observed by Kinect Sensor. *Advanced Video and Signal Based Surveillance (AVSS), 2013 10th IEEE International Conference on*, 220–25. doi:10.1109/AVSS.2013.6636643

P, P. J., K, B. B., & Eduardo, B. d. (2001). A Stator-Flux-Oriented Vector-Controlled Induction Motor Drive with Space-Vector PWM and Flux-Vector Synthesis by Neural Networks. *IEEE Transaction on Industry Applications, 37*(5), 1308-1318.

Panda, R., Khobragade, P. S., Jambhule, P. D., Jengthe, S. N., Pal, P. R., & Gandhi, T. K. (2010, December). Classification of EEG signal using wavelet transform and support vector machine for epileptic seizure diction. *Proceedings of International Conference on Systems in Medicine and Biology (ICSMB)*, (pp. 405-408). IEEE. doi:10.1109/ICSMB.2010.5735413

Park, Reeves, Mulukutla, & Sundaravel. (2010). Fast Malware Classification by Automated Behavioral Graph Matching. *Proceedings of the 6th Annual Workshop on Cyber Security and Information Intelligence Research*.

Parr, J. M., Holden, C. M. E., Forrester, A. I. J., & Keane, A. J. (2010). Review of efficient surrogate infill sampling criteria with constraint handling. In H. Rodrigues et al. (Eds.), *Second international conference on engineering optimization*. Academic Press.

Patra, B. G., Maitra, P., Das, D., & Bandyopadhyay, S. (2015). MediaEval 2015: Feed-Forward Neural Network based Music Emotion Recognition. *MediaEval 2015 Workshop*.

Patra, B. G., Das, D., & Bandyopadhyay, S. (2013). Automatic Music Mood Classification of Hindi Songs. *Sixth International Joint Conference on Natural Language Processing*, 24.

Pavlovic, Sharma, & Huang. (1997). Visual Interpretation of Hand Gestures for Human-Computer Interaction: A Review. *Pattern Analysis and Machine Intelligence, IEEE Transactions on, 19*(7), 677–95.

Peli, T., & Malah, D. (1982). A Study of Edge Detection Algorithms. *Computer Graphics and Image Processing, 20*(1), 1–21. doi:10.1016/0146-664X(82)90070-3

Peltoranta, M., & Pfurtscheller, G. (1994). Neural network based classification of non-averaged event-related EEG responses. *Medical & Biological Engineering & Computing, 32*(2), 189–196. doi:10.1007/BF02518917 PMID:8022216

Pepermans, G., Driesen, J., Haeseldonckx, D., Belmans, R., & Dhaeseleer, W. (2005). Distributed generation: Definition, benefits and issues. *Energy Policy, 33*(6), 787–798. doi:10.1016/j.enpol.2003.10.004

Petrantonakis, P. C., & Hadjileontiadis, L. J. (2010). Emotion recognition from brain signals using hybrid adaptive filtering and higher order crossings analysis. *Affective Computing. IEEE Transactions on, 1*(2), 81–97.

Petrantonakis, P. C., & Hadjileontiadis, L. J. (2010). Emotion recognition from EEG using higher order crossings. *IEEE Transactions on Information Technology in Biomedicine, 14*(2), 186–197. doi:10.1109/TITB.2009.2034649 PMID:19858033

Petrantonakis, P. C., & Hadjileontiadis, L. J. (2012). Adaptive emotional information retrieval from EEG signals in the time-frequency domain. *IEEE Transactions on Signal Processing, 60*(5), 2604–2616. doi:10.1109/TSP.2012.2187647

Petroni & Hicks. (2007). Automated detection of the persistent kernel and control-flow attacks. *Proceedings of the 14th ACM Conference on Computer and Communications Security.*

Petroni, Monlina, & Arbaugh. (2004). Copilot - a coprocessor-based kernel runtime integrity monitor. *Proceedings of the 13th USENIX Security Symposium.*

Phillips, J. (2006). Different types of gasifiers and their integration with gas turbines. In The Gas Turbine Handbook. U.S. Department of Energy, Office of Fossil energy, National Energy Technology Laboratory, DOE/NETL-2006-1230.

Phung, Bouzerdoum, & Chai. (2005). Skin Segmentation Using Color Pixel Classification: Analysis and Comparison. *Pattern Analysis and Machine Intelligence, IEEE Transactions on, 27*(1), 148–54.

Pike, A. W., Donne, M. S., & Dixon, R. (1998). Dynamic modelling and simulation of the air blown gasification cycle prototype publication. *Proceedings of the International Conference on Simulation*, 354-361.

Ploner, M., Gross, J., Timmermann, L., & Schnitzler, A. (2002). Cortical representation of first and second pain sensation in humans. *Proceedings of the National Academy of Sciences of the United States of America, 99*(19), 12444–12448. doi:10.1073/pnas.182272899 PMID:12209003

Ponnusamy & Sasikumar. (2012). Application of Green Cloud Computing for Efficient Resource Energy Management in Data Centers. *IJCSIT, 3*(5).

Ponnusamy, P., Sivakumar, L., & Sankaran, S. V. (1983). Low-order dynamic model of a complete thermal power plant loop. *Proceedings of the Power Plant Dynamics, Control and Testing Symposium*, 1.

Poongodi, P., & Victor, S. (2009). *Genetic algorithm based PID controller design for LTI system via reduced order model.* International Conference on Instrumentation, Control & Automation ICA2009, Bandung, Indonesia.

Portnoy, & Stolfo. (2001). Intrusion Detection with unlabeled data using clustering. *Proceedings of ACM Workshop on Data Mining Applied to Security.*

Powell, M. J. D. (1998). Direct search algorithms for optimization calculations. *Acta Numerica, A*, 287–336.

Prempain, P., Postlethwaite, I., & Sun, X. D. (2000). Robust control of the gasifier using a mixed-sensitivity H∞ approach. *Proceedings of the Institution of Mechanical Engineers Part I: Journal of Systems and Control Engineering, 214*(6), 415-427.

Prerakmody. (n.d.). *Cloud Computing.* Available from: http://www.wordrandom.wordpress.com/2011/09/28/cloud-computing/

Procyk, T., & Mamdani, E. (1979). A linguistic self-organizing process controller. *Automatica, 15*(1), 15–30. doi:10.1016/0005-1098(79)90084-0

Pullen, K., & Bregler, C. (2002). Motion Capture Assisted Animation: Texturing and Synthesis. In *ACM Transactions on Graphics (TOG)* (pp. 501–508). ACM. doi:10.1145/566570.566608

Purves, D., Augustine, G. J., Fitzpatrick, D., Katz, L. C., LaMantia, A. S., McNamara, J. O., & Williams, S. M. (2001). *The Primary Motor Cortex: Upper Motor Neurons That Initiate Complex Voluntary Movements*. Academic Press.

Pyle, D. (1999). *Data preparation for data mining*. Morgan Kaufmann.

Queipo, N. V., Haftka, R. T., Shyy, W., Goel, T., Vaidyanathan, R., & Tucker, K. P. (2005). Surrogate-based analysis and optimization. *Progress in Aerospace Sciences, 41*(1), 1–28. doi:10.1016/j.paerosci.2005.02.001

Quttineh, N.-H., & Holmström, K. (2009). The influence of experimental designs on the performance of surrogate model based costly global optimization solvers. *Studies in Informatics and Control, 18*(1), 87–95.

Radojević, B., & Žagar, M. (2011, May). Analysis of issues with load balancing algorithms in hosted (cloud) environments. In *MIPRO, 2011 Proceedings of the 34th International Convention* (pp. 416-420). IEEE.

Rajasekaran, S. P. (2005). *Neural Networks, Fuzzy Logic, and Genetic Algorithm: Synthesis and Applications*. New Delhi: Prentice Hall of India.

Rajeswara Rao, V., & Shubba Ramaiah, V. (2014). Cloud computing and Virtualization. BS Publications.

Ramamoorthy, A., Vaswani, N., Chaudhury, S., & Banerjee, S. (2003). Recognition of Dynamic Hand Gestures. *Pattern Recognition, 36*(9), 2069–2081. doi:10.1016/S0031-3203(03)00042-6

Ramezan & Stiegel. (2006). Integrated coal gasification combined cycle. In *The gas turbine handbook*. Retrieved from http://www.netl.doe.gov/technologies/ coalpower/turbines/refshelf/handbok/1.2.pdf

Randles, M., Taleb-Bendiab, A., & Lamb, D. (2009, July). Scalable Self-Governance Using Service Communities as Ambients. In *Services-I, 2009 World Conference on* (pp. 813-820). IEEE. doi:10.1109/SERVICES-I.2009.93

Ratle, A. (1999). Optimal sampling strategies for learning a fitness model. In *The 1999 IEEE congress on evolutionary computation–CEC 1999* (pp. 2078–2085). Piscataway, NJ: IEEE. doi:10.1109/CEC.1999.785531

Reed-Geaghan, E. G., & Maricich, S. M. (2011). Peripheral somatosensation: A touch of genetics. *Current Opinion in Genetics & Development, 21*(3), 240–248. doi:10.1016/j.gde.2010.12.009 PMID:21277195

Reed, T. R., & Hans Dubuf, J. M. (1993). A Review of Recent Texture Segmentation and Feature Extraction Techniques. *CVGIP. Image Understanding, 57*(3), 359–372. doi:10.1006/ciun.1993.1024

Regis, R. G., & Shoemaker, C. A. (2013). A quasi-multistart framework for global optimization of expensive functions using response surface models. *Journal of Global Optimization, 56*(4), 1719–1753. doi:10.1007/s10898-012-9940-1

Ren, Z., Meng, J., Yuan, J., & Zhang, Z. (2011). Robust Hand Gesture Recognition with Kinect Sensor. *Proceedings of the 19th ACM International Conference on Multimedia*, 759–60. doi:10.1145/2072298.2072443

Ren, Z., Yuan, J., Meng, J., & Zhang, Z. (2013). Robust Part-Based Hand Gesture Recognition Using Kinect Sensor. *Multimedia, IEEE Transactions on, 15*(5), 1110–1120. doi:10.1109/TMM.2013.2246148

Rice, M., Rosster, J., & Schurmans, J. (2000). An advanced predictive control approach to the Alstom gasifier problem. *Proceedings of the Institution of Mechanical Engineers Part I: Journal of Systems and Control Engineering, 214*(6), 405-413.

Rieck, K., Trinius, P., Willems, C., & Holz, T. (2011). Automatic Analysis of Malware Behavior Using Machine Learning. *Journal of Computer Security, 19*(4), 639–668. doi:10.3233/JCS-2010-0410

Rizzolatti, G., Fadiga, L., Gallese, V., & Fogassi, L. (1996). Premotor cortex and the recognition of motor actions. *Brain Research. Cognitive Brain Research, 3*(2), 131–141. doi:10.1016/0926-6410(95)00038-0 PMID:8713554

Rojas, R. (1996). *Neural Network- A Systematic Introduction*. Berlin: Spriger-Verlag.

Roland, P. E., Larsen, B., Lassen, N. A., & Skinhoj, E. (1980). Supplementary motor area and other cortical areas in organization of voluntary movements in man. *Journal of Neurophysiology*, *43*(1), 118–136. PMID:7351547

Romero, C., & Ventura, S. (2007). Educational data mining: A survey from 1995 to 2005. *Expert Systems with Applications*, *33*(1), 135–146. doi:10.1016/j.eswa.2006.04.005

Rosenberg, M. J. (2001). *E-Learning: Strategies for Delivering Knowledge in the Digital Age*. McGraw-Hill New York.

Royal, P., Halpin, M., Dagon, D., Edmonds, R., & Lee, W. (2006). Polyunpack: Automating the hidden-code extraction of unpack-executing malware. *Proceedings of the 22nd Annual Computer Security Applications Conference (ACSAC)*, 289–300. doi:10.1109/ACSAC.2006.38

Sabeti, L., & Jonathan Wu, Q. M. (2007). High-Speed Skin Color Segmentation for Real-Time Human Tracking. *Systems, Man, and Cybernetics, 2007. ISIC. IEEE International Conference on*, 2378–82. doi:10.1109/ICSMC.2007.4413744

Sacks, J., Welch, W. J., Mitchell, T. J., & Wynn, H. P. (1989). Design and analysis of computer experiments. *Statistical Science*, *4*(4), 409–435. doi:10.1214/ss/1177012413

Saha, A., Konar, A., Rakshit, P., Ralescu, A. L., & Nagar, A. K. (2013, August). Olfaction recognition by EEG analysis using differential evolution induced Hopfield neural net. In *Neural Networks (IJCNN), The 2013 International Joint Conference on* (pp. 1-8). IEEE.

Saha, Ghosh, Konar, & Nagar. (2013). Gesture Recognition from Indian Classical Dance Using Kinect Sensor. *Computational Intelligence, Communication Systems and Networks (CICSyN), 2013 Fifth International Conference on*, 3–8.

Saha, S., & Banerjee, A. (2013). Fuzzy Image Matching for Posture Recognition in Ballet Dance. *Fuzzy Systems (FUZZ), 2013 IEEE International Conference on*, 1–8. doi:10.1109/FUZZ-IEEE.2013.6622401

Saha, S., & Konar, A. (2014). Bharatanatyam Hand Gesture Recognition Using Polygon Representation. *Control, Instrumentation, Energy, and Communication (CIEC), 2014 International Conference on*, 563–67. doi:10.1109/CIEC.2014.6959152

Saha, S., Datta, S., Konar, A., & Janarthanan, R. (2014). A Study on Emotion Recognition from Body Gestures Using Kinect Sensor. *Communications and Signal Processing (ICCSP), 2014 International Conference on*, 56–60. doi:10.1109/ICCSP.2014.6949798

Saha, S., Ghosh, L., Konar, A., & Janarthanan, R. (2013). Fuzzy L Membership Function Based Hand Gesture Recognition for Bharatanatyam Dance. *Computational Intelligence and Communication Networks (CICN), 2013 5th International Conference on*, 331–35. doi:10.1109/CICN.2013.75

Saha, A., Konar, A., Chatterjee, A., Ralescu, A., & Nagar, A. K. (2014). EEG analysis for olfactory perceptual-ability measurement using a recurrent neural classifier. *IEEE Transactions on Human-Machine Systems*, *44*(6), 717–730. doi:10.1109/THMS.2014.2344003

Saha, A., Konar, A., Das, P., Sen Bhattacharya, B., & Nagar, A. (2015b). Data-point and Feature Selection of Motor Imagery EEG Signals for Neural Classification of Cognitive Tasks in Car-Driving. *Proceedings of International Joint Conference on Neural Networks (IJCNN)*, (pp. 1-8). IEEE.

Saha, A., Konar, A., Sen Bhattacharya, B., & Nagar, A. (2015a). EEG Classification to Determine the Degree of Pleasure Levels in TouchPerception of Human Subjects. *Proceedings of International Joint Conference on Neural Networks (IJCNN)*, (pp. 1-8). IEEE.

Saha, S., Konar, A., & Janarthanan, R. (2015). Two Person Interaction Detection Using Kinect Sensor. In *Facets of Uncertainties and Applications* (pp. 167–176). Springer. doi:10.1007/978-81-322-2301-6_13

Saifullah Khalid, B. D. (2013). Application of AI techniques in implementing Shunt APF in Aircraft Supply System. *SOCROPROS Conference on Dec 26-28* (pp. 333-341). Roorkee: Springer Lecture Notes.

Saifullah Khalid, B. D. (2013). Comparative critical analysis of SAF using soft computing and conventional control techniques for high frequency (400 Hz) aircraft system. *IEEE 1st International Conference on Condition Assessment Techniques in Electrical Systems (CATCON)* (pp. 100-110). Kolkata: IEEE.

Saifullah Khalid, B. D. (2010). Power Quality: An Important Aspect. *International Journal of Engineering Science and Technology, 2*(11), 6485–6490.

Saifullah Khalid, B. D. (2011). Power Quality Issues, Problems, Standards & their Effects in Industry with Corrective Means. *International Journal of Advances in Engineering & Technology, 1*(2), 1–11.

Saifullah Khalid, B. D. (2013). Comparison of Control Strategies for Shunt Active Power Filter under balanced, unbalanced and distorted supply conditions. *IEEE Sponsored National Conference on Advances in Electrical Power and Energy Systems (AEPES-2013)*, 37-41.

Saifullah, K., & Bharti, D. (2014). Comparative Evaluation of Various Control Strategies for Shunt Active Power Filters in Aircraft Power Utility of 400 Hz. *Majlesi Journal of Mechatronic Systems, 3*(2), 1–5.

Sajjadi, S. M., Haghifam, M.-R., & Salehi, J. (2013). Simultaneous placement of distributed generation and capacitors in distribution networks considering voltage stability index. *International Journal of Electrical Power & Energy Systems, 46*, 366–375. doi:10.1016/j.ijepes.2012.10.027

Sakkalis, V. (2011). Review of advanced techniques for the estimation of brain connectivity measured with EEG/MEG. *Computers in Biology and Medicine, 41*(12), 1110–1117. doi:10.1016/j.compbiomed.2011.06.020 PMID:21794851

Sánchez-Nielsen, Antón-Canalís, & Hernández-Tejera. (2004). *Hand Gesture Recognition for Human-Machine Interaction*. Academic Press.

Santos, I., Devesa, J., Brezo, F., Nieves, J., & Bringas, P. G. (2013). OPEM: A Static-Dynamic Approach for Machine Learning Based Malware Detection. *Proceedings of International Conference CISIS'12-ICEUTE'12, Special Sessions Advances in Intelligent Systems and Computing, 189*, 271-280. doi:10.1007/978-3-642-33018-6_28

Santos, Nieves, & Bringas. (2011). Collective Classification for Unknown Malware Detection. *Proceedings of the International Conference on Security and Cryptography*, 251-256.

Sarna. (2010). *Implementing and Developing cloud applications*. Auerbach Publications.

Schlögl, A., Lugger, K., & Pfurtscheller, G. (1997, November). Using adaptive autoregressive parameters for a brain-computer-interface experiment. *Proceedings of 19th International Conference IEEE Engineering in Medicine and Biology Society (IEEE/EMBS)*, (pp. 1533-1535). IEEE. doi:10.1109/IEMBS.1997.757002

Schmidtmann, Kreutz, Barkhoff, Virkus, Stockmann, & Jovic. (2009). *Material Flow Optimization under Aspects of Energy Efficiency*. IEEE.

Schölkopf, B., & Smola, A. J. (2002). *Learning with kernels: Support vector machines, regularization, optimization, and beyond*. MIT Press.

Schoonderwoerd, R., Holland, O., Bruten, J., & Rothkrantz, L. (1996). *Ants for Load Balancing in Telecommunication Networks*. Hewlett Packard Lab., Bristol. UK, Tech. Rep. HPL-96-35.

Schore, A. N. (2005). A neuropsychoanalytic viewpoint: Commentary on paper by Steven H. Knoblauch. *Psychoanalytic Dialogues*, *15*(6), 829–854. doi:10.2513/s10481885pd1506_3

Schuller, B., Valster, M., Eyben, F., Cowie, R., & Pantic, M. (2012, October). Avec 2012: the continuous audio/visual emotion challenge. In *Proceedings of the 14th ACM international conference on Multimodal interaction* (pp. 449-456). ACM. doi:10.1145/2388676.2388776

Schultz, Eskin, Zadok, & Stolfo. (2001). Data Mining Methods for Detection of New Malicious Executables. *Proceedings of the IEEE Symposium on Security and Privacy*, 178-184.

Segen, J., & Kumar, S. (1998). Human-Computer Interaction Using Gesture Recognition and 3D Hand Tracking. *Image Processing, 1998. ICIP 98. Proceedings. 1998 International Conference on*, 188–92. doi:10.1109/ICIP.1998.727164

Senecal, P. K. (2000). *Numerical optimization using the GEN4 micro-genetic algorithm code (Tech. Rep.)*. Engine Research Center, University Of Wisconsin-Madison.

Senthilkumaran, N., & Rajesh, R. (2009). Edge Detection Techniques for Image Segmentation–a Survey of Soft Computing Approaches. *International Journal of Recent Trends in Engineering*, *1*(2), 250–254.

Seong-Hwan, K., & Tae-Sik, P. (2001). Speed-Sensorless Vector Control of an Induction Motor Using Neural Network Speed Estimation. *IEEE Transactions on Industrial Electronics*, *48*(3), 609–614. doi:10.1109/41.925588

Serra, G. L. O. (Ed.). (2012). *Highlighted Aspects From Black Box Fuzzy Modeling For Advanced Control Systems Design, Frontiers in Advanced Control Systems*. InTech; doi:10.5772/45717

Šešum-Čavić, V., & Kühn, E. (2011). Self-Organized Load Balancing through Swarm Intelligence. In *Next Generation Data Technologies for Collective Computational Intelligence* (pp. 195–224). Springer Berlin Heidelberg. doi:10.1007/978-3-642-20344-2_8

Sevakula & Verma. (2012). Support Vector Machine for Large Databases as Classifier. In *Swarm, Evolutionary, and Memetic Computing*. Springer.

Sharif, M., Yegneswaran, V., & Saidi, H. (2008). Eureka: A Framework for Enabling Static Malware Analysis. *Proceedings of the European Symposium on Research in Computer Security (ESORICS)*, 481–500.

Sheskin, D. J. (2007). *Handbook of parametric and nonparametric statistical procedures* (4th ed.). Boca Raton, FL: Chapman and Hall.

Shi & Ritter. (1995). A New Parallel Binary Image Shrinking Algorithm. *Image Processing, IEEE Transactions on*, *4*(2), 224–26.

Shi, L. C., & Lu, B. L. (2010, August). Off-line and on-line vigilance estimation based on linear dynamical system and manifold learning. In *Engineering in Medicine and Biology Society (EMBC), 2010 Annual International Conference of the IEEE* (pp. 6587-6590). IEEE.

Shi, Y., & Eberhart, R. (1998). A modified particle swarm optimizer. *Proceedings, 1998. IEEE World Congress on Computational Intelligence., The 1998 IEEE International Conference on*. doi:10.1109/ICEC.1998.699146

Siddiqui, Wang, & Lee. (2009). Detecting Internet Worms Using Data Mining Techniques. *Journal of Systemics, Cybernetics, and Informatics*, *6*, 48–53.

Silapasuphakornwong, Phimoltares, Lursinsap, & Hansuebsai. (2010). Posture Recognition Invariant to Background, Cloth Textures, Body Size, and Camera Distance Using Morphological Geometry. *Machine Learning and Cybernetics (ICMLC), 2010 International Conference on*, 1130–35.

Silberstein. (2004). *Designing a cam-based coprocessor for boosting the performance of antivirus software*. Academic Press.

Simm, A., & Liu, G. P. (2006). Improving the performance of the ALSTOM baseline controller using multiobjective optimisation. *IEEE Proceedings. Control Theory and Applications, 153*(3), 286–292. doi:10.1049/ip-cta:20050131

Simpson, T. W., Lin, D. K. J., & Chen, W. (2001). Sampling strategies for computer experiments: Design and analysis. *International Journal of Reliability and Applications, 2*(3), 209–240.

Singh, H., Bauer, M., Chowanski, W., Sui, Y., Atkinson, D., Baurley, S., & Bianchi-Berthouze, N. et al. (2014). The brain's response to pleasant touch: An EEG investigation of tactile caressing. *Frontiers in Human Neuroscience, 8.* PMID:25426047

Singh, R., & Goswami, S. (2010). Optimum allocation of distributed generations based on nodal pricing for profit, loss reduction, and voltage improvement including voltage rise issue. *International Journal of Electrical Power & Energy Systems, 32*(6), 637–644. doi:10.1016/j.ijepes.2009.11.021

Sivakumar, L., & Kotteeswaran, R. (2014). Soft computing based partial-retuning of decentralized PI Controller of non-linear multivariable process. *ICT and Critical Infrastructure: Proceedings of the 48th Annual Convention of Computer Society of India*, 117-124.

Sivanandam, S.N., & Deepa, S.N. (2009). A Comparative Study Using Genetic Algorithm and Particle Swarm Optimization for Lower Order System Modelling. *International Journal of the Computer, the Internet and Management, 17*(3), 1-10.

Smith, L. I. (2002). A tutorial on principal components analysis. *Cornell University, USA, 51*, 52.

Sobel, I. (1978). Neighborhood Coding of Binary Images for Fast Contour Following and General Binary Array Processing. *Computer Graphics and Image Processing, 8*(1), 127–135. doi:10.1016/S0146-664X(78)80020-3

Sóbester, A., Leary, S. J., & Keane, A. J. (2005). On the design of optimization strategies based on global response surface approximation models. *Journal of Global Optimization, 33*(1), 31–59. doi:10.1007/s10898-004-6733-1

Soleymani, M., Lichtenauer, J., Pun, T., & Pantic, M. (2012). A multimodal database for affect recognition and implicit tagging. *IEEE Transactions on Affective Computing, 3*(1), 42–55. doi:10.1109/T-AFFC.2011.25

Song, W., Xiao, Z., Chen, Q., & Luo, H. (2014). Adaptive Resource Provisioning for the Cloud Using Online Bin Packing. IEEE Transactions on Computers, 63.

Sotomayor, B., Montero, R. S., Llorente, I. M., & Foster, I. (2009). Virtual infrastructure management in private and hybrid clouds. *IEEE Internet Computing, 13*(5), 14–22. doi:10.1109/MIC.2009.119

Squire, L. R., & Zola-Morgan, S. (1991). The medial temporal lobe memory system. *Science, 253*(5026), 1380–1386. doi:10.1126/science.1896849 PMID:1896849

Srinivasan, V., Eswaran, C., & Sriraam, N. (2007). Approximate entropy-based epileptic EEG detection using artificial neural networks. *IEEE Transactions on Information Technology in Biomedicine, 11*(3), 288–295. doi:10.1109/TITB.2006.884369 PMID:17521078

Stanescu, L., Mihai, G., Burdescu, D., Brezovan, M., & Spahiu, C. S. (2010). A software system for viewing and querying automatically generated Topic Maps in the e-learning domain. *Informatica: An International Journal of Computing and Informatics, 34*(4), 441–450.

Starner, T., & Pentland, A. (1997). Real-Time American Sign Language Recognition from Video Using Hidden Markov Models. In *Motion-Based Recognition* (pp. 227–243). Springer. doi:10.1007/978-94-015-8935-2_10

Starner, T., Weaver, J., & Pentland, A. (1998). Real-Time American Sign Language Recognition Using Desk and Wearable Computer Based Video. *Pattern Analysis and Machine Intelligence, IEEE Transactions on*, *20*(12), 1371–1375. doi:10.1109/34.735811

Stergiopoulou, E., & Papamarkos, N. (2009). Hand Gesture Recognition Using a Neural Network Shape Fitting Technique. *Engineering Applications of Artificial Intelligence*, *22*(8), 1141–1158. doi:10.1016/j.engappai.2009.03.008

Stoica, P., & Moses, R. L. (1997). *Introduction to spectral analysis*. Upper Saddle River, NJ: Prentice Hall.

Stokoe, W. C. (1978). *Sign Language Structure*. Academic Press.

Storn, R., & Price, K. (1997). Differential evolution–a simple and efficient heuristic for global optimization over continuous spaces. *Journal of Global Optimization*, *11*(4), 341–359. doi:10.1023/A:1008202821328

Suarez & Murphy. (2012). Hand Gesture Recognition with Depth Images: A Review. *RO-MAN, 2012 IEEE*, 411–17.

Suk, H.-I., Sin, B.-K., & Lee, S.-W. (2010). Hand Gesture Recognition Based on Dynamic Bayesian Network Framework. *Pattern Recognition*, *43*(9), 3059–3072. doi:10.1016/j.patcog.2010.03.016

Symantec. (1997). *Understanding heuristics: Symantec's bloodhound technology*. Author.

Szor. (2005). *Metamorphic computer virus detection*. Academic Press.

Szor, P., & Ferrie, P. (2005). *Hunting for metamorphic, The Art of Computer Virus Research and Defense*. Addison-Wesley.

Tamminga, C. A., & Buchsbaum, M. S. (2004). Frontal cortex function. *The American Journal of Psychiatry*, *161*(12), 2178. doi:10.1176/appi.ajp.161.12.2178 PMID:15569885

Tan, W., Lou, G., & Liang, L. (2011). Partially decentralized control for ALSTOM gasifier. *ISA Transactions*, *50*(3), 397–408. doi:10.1016/j.isatra.2011.01.008 PMID:21356534

Tarari. (2006). *Anti-virus content processor*. Retrieved from http://www.tarari.com/antivirus/index.html

Tari, Z., Shah, J., & Pien, H. (1997). Extraction of Shape Skeletons from Grayscale Images. *Computer Vision and Image Understanding*, *66*(2), 133–146. doi:10.1006/cviu.1997.0612

Tawfeek, M., El-Sisi, A., Keshk, A. E., & Torkey, F. (2013, November). Cloud task scheduling based on ant colony optimization. In *Computer Engineering & Systems (ICCES), 2013 8th International Conference on* (pp. 64-69). IEEE. doi:10.1109/ICCES.2013.6707172

Taylor & Alves-Foss. (2001). Network analysis of anomalous traffic events, a low-cost approach. *NSPW '01: Proceedings of the 2001 workshop on New security paradigms*, 89–96.

Taylor, C. J., McCabe, A. P., Young, P. C., & Chotai, A. (2000). Proportional integral-plus (PIP) control of the ALSTOM gasifier problem. *Proceedings of the Institution of Mechanical Engineers. Part I, Journal of Systems and Control Engineering*, *214*(6), 469–481. doi:10.1243/0959651001540816

Taylor, C. J., & Shaban, E. M. (2006). Multivariable proportional-integralplus (PIP) control of the ALSTOM nonlinear gasifier simulation. *IEEE Proceedings. Control Theory and Applications*, *153*(3), 277–285. doi:10.1049/ip-cta:20050058

Tenenbaum, J. B., De Silva, V., & Langford, J. C. (2000). A global geometric framework for nonlinear dimensionality reduction. *Science*, *290*(5500), 2319–2323. doi:10.1126/science.290.5500.2319 PMID:11125149

Tenne, Y., & Armfield, S. W. (2009). A framework for memetic optimization using variable global and local surrogate models. *Journal of Soft Computing*, *13*(8), 781–793. doi:10.1007/s00500-008-0348-2

Tenne, Y., & Goh, C. K. (Eds.). (2010a). *Computational intelligence in expensive optimization problems* (Vol. 2). Berlin: Springer. doi:10.1007/978-3-642-10701-6

Tenne, Y., & Goh, C. K. (Eds.). (2010b). *Computational intelligence in optimization* (Vol. 7). Springer. doi:10.1007/978-3-642-12775-5

Thangaraj, R., Thanga, R. C., Pant, M., Ajit, A., & Grosan, C. (2010). Optimal gain tuning of PI speed controller in induction motor drives using particle swarm optimization. *Logic Journal of IGPL Advance Access*, 1-4.

Tian, R., Batten, L., & Versteeg, S. (2008). Function Length as a Tool for Malware Classification. *Proceedings of the 3rd International Conference on Malicious and Unwanted Software*, 57-64. doi:10.1109/MALWARE.2008.4690860

Toal, D. J. J., Bressloff, N. W., & Keane, A. J. (2008). Kriging hyperparameter tuning strategies. *AIAA Journal*, *46*(5), 1240–1252. doi:10.2514/1.34822

Trigueiros, Ribeiro, & Reis. (2014). Generic System for Human-Computer Gesture Interaction. *Autonomous Robot Systems and Competitions (ICARSC), 2014 IEEE International Conference on*, 175–80.

Tsang, E. C. C., Yeung, D. S., & Wang, X. Z. (2003). OFFSS: Optimal fuzzy-valued feature subset selection. *IEEE Transactions on Fuzzy Systems*, *11*(2), 202–213. doi:10.1109/TFUZZ.2003.809895

Tsypkin, Ya. Z. (1971). *Adaptation and Learning in Automatic Systems*. New York: Academic Press.

Turing, A. M. (1950). Computing machinery and intelligence. *Mind*, 59.

Turner. (2006). *Spamming malware: Parite.b and irc backdoor disable anti-spyware programs*. Academic Press.

Uchechukwu, Li, & Shen. (2012). *Improving Cloud Computing Energy Efficiency*. IEEE.

Van Den Heuvel, M. P., & Pol, H. E. H. (2010). Exploring the brain network: A review on resting-state fMRI functional connectivity. [PubMed]. *European Neuropsychopharmacology*, *20*(8), 519–534.

Van Ede, F., de Lange, F., Jensen, O., & Maris, E. (2011). Orienting attention to an upcoming tactile event involves a spatially and temporally specific modulation of sensorimotor alpha-and beta-band oscillations. *The Journal of Neuroscience*, *31*(6), 2016–2024. doi:10.1523/JNEUROSCI.5630-10.2011 PMID:21307240

Vaquero, L. M., Rodero-Merino, L., Caceres, J., & Lindner, M. (2008). A break in the clouds: Towards a cloud definition. *Computer Communication Review*, *39*(1), 50–55. doi:10.1145/1496091.1496100

Velte, A. T., Velte, T. J., & Elsenpeter, R. (2009). *Cloud Computing: A Practical Approach*. McGraw-Hill Publication.

Velte, A. T., Velte, T. J., & Elsenpeter, R. (2010). *Cloud computing*. McGraw Hill.

Vijay, P. K., Suhas, N. N., Chandrashekhar, C. S., & Dhananjay, D. K. (2012). Recent Developments in Sign Language Recognition: A Review. *Int J Adv Comput Eng Commun Technol*, *1*, 21–26.

Viral, R., & Khatod, D. (2015). An analytical approach for sizing and siting of DGs in balanced radial distribution networks for loss minimization. *International Journal of Electrical Power & Energy Systems*, *67*, 191–201. doi:10.1016/j.ijepes.2014.11.017

Vogler, C., & Metaxas, D. (2001). A Framework for Recognizing the Simultaneous Aspects of American Sign Language. *Computer Vision and Image Understanding*, *81*(3), 358–384. doi:10.1006/cviu.2000.0895

Vourkas, M., Micheloyannis, S., & Papadourakis, G. (2000). Use of ann and hjorth parameters in mental-task discrimination. *First International Conference on Advances in Medical Signal and Information Processing*, (pp. 327-332). IET. doi:10.1049/cp:20000356

Wagner, A. D., Shannon, B. J., Kahn, I., & Buckner, R. L. (2005). Parietal lobe contributions to episodic memory retrieval. [Chicago.]. *Trends in Cognitive Sciences*, *9*(9), 445–453. doi:10.1016/j.tics.2005.07.001 PMID:16054861

Wagner, D., & Soto, P. (2002). Mimicry attacks on host-based intrusion detection systems. *Proceedings of the 9th ACM Conference on Computer and communications Security*. doi:10.1145/586110.586145

Wang, G., Zhang, M., Xu, X., & Jiang, C. (2006). Optimization of Controller Parameters based on the Improved Genetic Algorithms. *IEEE Proceedings of the 6th World Congress on Intelligent Control and Automation*, 3695-3698.

Wang, H., Tanaka, K., & Griffin, M. (1995). Parallel distributed compensation of nonlinear systems by takagi-sugeno fuzzy model. *Fuzzy Systems. International Joint Conference of the Fourth IEEE International Conference on Fuzzy Systems and The Second International Fuzzy Engineering Symposium., Proceedings of 1995 IEEE Int*, *2*, 531–538. doi:10.1109/FUZZY.1995.409737

Wang, J. (2007). Internet Worm Early Detection and Response Mechanism. *Journal of China Universities of Posts and Telecommunications*, *14*(3).

Wang, L., Zhang, F., Aroca, J. A., Vasilakos, A. V., Zheng, K., Hou, C., . . . Liu, Z. (2014). GreenDCN: A General Framework for Achieving Energy Efficiency in Data Center Networks. IEEE Journal, 32.

Wang, S. C., Yan, K. Q., Wang, S. S., & Chen, C. W. (2011, April). A three-phases scheduling in a hierarchical cloud computing network. In *Communications and Mobile Computing (CMC), 2011 Third International Conference on* (pp. 114-117). IEEE. doi:10.1109/CMC.2011.28

Wang. (2005). *The intelligent proactive information assurance, and security technology*. Academic Press.

Wang, C., Liu, Z., & Chan, S.-C. (2015). Superpixel-Based Hand Gesture Recognition With Kinect Depth Camera. *Multimedia, IEEE Transactions on*, *17*(1), 29–39. doi:10.1109/TMM.2014.2374357

Wang, D. Y., & Ren, Z. J. (2011). The Solution of Datamining Based on Clementine. In *Advanced []. Trans Tech Publications.]. Materials Research*, *211*, 1082–1086.

Wang, F.-Y. (2005). Agent-based control for networked traffic management systems. *IEEE Intelligent Systems*, *19*(5), 92–96. doi:10.1109/MIS.2005.80

Wang, G. G., & Shan, S. (2007). Review of metamodeling techniques in support of engineering design optimization. *Journal of Mechanical Design*, *129*(4), 370–380. doi:10.1115/1.2429697

Whitaker, H., Yamron, J., & Kezer, A. (1958). *Design of model reference adaptive control systems for aircraft. Reporter No. R-164. Instrumentation Lab*. MIT.

Whitemore, H. (1987). *Breaking the Code*. Amber Lane Press.

Wickremasinghe, B., Calheiros, R. N., & Buyya, R. (2010, April). Cloudanalyst: A cloudsim-based visual modeler for analyzing cloud computing environments and applications. In *Advanced Information Networking and Applications (AINA), 2010 24th IEEE International Conference on* (pp. 446-452). IEEE. doi:10.1109/AINA.2010.32

Wilson, J. A., Chew, M., & Jones, W. E. (2006). A state estimation based approach to gasifier control. *IEE Proceedings. Control Theory and Applications*, *153*(3), 268–276. doi:10.1049/ip-cta:20050071

Witten, I. H., Frank, E., Hall, M. A., & Pal, C. J. (2016). *Data Mining: Practical machine learning tools and techniques*. Morgan Kaufmann.

Wolpaw, J. R., McFarland, D. J., Neat, G. W., & Forneris, C. A. (1991). An EEG-based brain-computer interface for cursor control. *Electroencephalography and Clinical Neurophysiology, 78*(3), 252–259. doi:10.1016/0013-4694(91)90040-B PMID:1707798

Woods, E. J. (1990). Aircraft Electrical System computer Simulation. *Proceedings of the 25th Intersociety Energy Conversion Engineering Conference, IECEC-90*, 84-89. doi:10.1109/IECEC.1990.716551

Wu, Q., Li, C., Takahashi, S., & Wu, J. (2012). Visual-Tactile Bottom-Up and Top-Down Attention. *Biomedical Engineering and Cognitive Neuroscience for Healthcare: Interdisciplinary Applications: Interdisciplinary Applications*, 183.

Xiang, Pan, & Tong. (2011). Depth Camera in Computer Vision and Computer Graphics: An Overview. *Jisuanji Kexue yu Tansuo, 5*(6), 481–92.

Xiong, , Han, , & Vandenberg, . (2012). Green Cloud computing schemes based on networks survey. The Institution of Engineering and Technology.

Xue, Y., Donghai, L., & Gao, F. (2010). Multi-objective optimization and selection for the PI control of ALSTOM gasifier problem. *Control Engineering Practice, 18*(1), 67-76.

Xu, G., Pang, J., & Fu, X. (2013). A load balancing model based on cloud partitioning for the public cloud. *Tsinghua Science and Technology, 18*(1), 34–39. doi:10.1109/TST.2013.6449405

Xu, J. W., Bakardjian, H., Cichocki, A., & Principe, J. C. (2008). A new nonlinear similarity measure for multichannel signals. *Neural Networks, 21*(2), 222–231. doi:10.1016/j.neunet.2007.12.039 PMID:18272331

Yagoubi, B., & Medebber, M. (2007, November). A load balancing model for grid environment. In *Computer and information sciences, 2007. ISCIS 2007. 22nd international symposium on* (pp. 1-7). IEEE. doi:10.1109/ISCIS.2007.4456873

Yagoubi, B., & Slimani, Y. (2006). Dynamic load balancing strategy for grid computing. Transactions on Engineering. *Computing and Technology, 13*, 260–265.

Yagoubi, B., & Slimani, Y. (2007). Task load balancing strategy for grid computing. *Journal of Computer Science, 3*(3), 186–194. doi:10.3844/jcssp.2007.186.194

Yang, U., Kim, B., & Sohn, K. (2009). Illumination Invariant Skin Color Segmentation. *Industrial Electronics and Applications, 2009. ICIEA 2009. 4th IEEE Conference on*, 636–41.

Yang, M.-H., Ahuja, N., & Tabb, M. (2002). Extraction of 2d Motion Trajectories and Its Application to Hand Gesture Recognition. *Pattern Analysis and Machine Intelligence, IEEE Transactions on, 24*(8), 1061–1074. doi:10.1109/TPAMI.2002.1023803

Ye, K., Huang, D., Jiang, X., & Chen, H. (2010). Virtual Machine Based Energy-Efficient Data Center Architecture for Cloud Computing: A Performance perspective. *IEEE/ACM International conference on Green Computing and Communication*.

Yingpeng Luo, Z. C. (2011). *A cascaded shunt active power filter with high performance for aircraft electric power system. In Energy Conversion Congress and Exposition (ECCE)* (pp. 1143–1149). IEEE.

Yoon, H.-S., Soh, J., Bae, Y. J., & Seung Yang, H. (2001). Hand Gesture Recognition Using Combined Features of Location, Angle, and Velocity. *Pattern Recognition, 34*(7), 1491–1501. doi:10.1016/S0031-3203(00)00096-0

You, H., Yang, M., Wang, D., & Jia, X. (2009). Kriging model combined with Latin hypercube sampling for surrogate modeling of analog integrated circuit performance. In *Proceedings of the tenth international symposium on quality electronic design–ISQED 2009* (pp. 554–558). Piscataway, NJ: IEEE. doi:10.1109/ISQED.2009.4810354

Younge, von Laszewski, Wang, Lopez-Alarcon, & Carithers. (n.d.). *Efficient Resource Management Cloud Computing Environments*. Academic Press.

Yu, Z., & Lusan, D. (2004). Optimal placement of FACTs devices in deregulated systems considering line losses. *International Journal of Electrical Power & Energy Systems, 26*(10), 813–819. doi:10.1016/j.ijepes.2004.07.003

Zahara, E., & Kao, Y.-T. (2009). Hybrid Nelder-Mead simplex search and particle swarm optimization for constrained engineering design problems. *Expert Systems with Applications, 36*(2), 3880–3886. doi:10.1016/j.eswa.2008.02.039

Zald, D. H., & Pardo, J. V. (1997). Emotion, olfaction, and the human amygdala: Amygdala activation during aversive olfactory stimulation. *Proceedings of the National Academy of Sciences of the United States of America, 94*(8), 4119–4124. doi:10.1073/pnas.94.8.4119 PMID:9108115

Zar, J. H. (1999). *Biostatistical Analysis*. Pearson Education India.

Zatorre, R. J. (1988). Pitch perception of complex tones and human temporal-lobe function. *The Journal of the Acoustical Society of America, 84*(2), 566–572. doi:10.1121/1.396834 PMID:3170948

Zerikat, M., & Chekroun, S. (2008). Adaptation Learning Speed Control for a High-Performance Induction Motor using Neural Networks. Proceedings of World Academy of Science, Engineering and Technology, 294-299.

Zhang, X., van Doorn, L., Jaeger, T., Perez, R., & Sailer, R. (2002). Secure coprocessor-based intrusion detection. *10th Workshop on ACM Special Interest Group on Operating Systems (SIGOPS)*. doi:10.1145/1133373.1133423

Zhang, Z. (2012). Microsoft Kinect Sensor and Its Effect. *Multimedia, IEEE, 19*(2), 4–10. doi:10.1109/MMUL.2012.24

Zhong Chen, Y. L., Yingpeng Luo, , & Miao Chen, . (2012). Control and Performance of a Cascaded Shunt Active Power Filter for Aircraft Electric Power System. *IEEE Transactions on Industrial Electronics, 59*(9), 3614–3623. doi:10.1109/TIE.2011.2166231

Zhong, M., Lotte, F., Girolami, M., & Lécuyer, A. (2008). Classifying EEG for brain computer interfaces using Gaussian processes. *Pattern Recognition Letters, 29*(3), 354–359. doi:10.1016/j.patrec.2007.10.009

Zhou, Lin, & Huang. (2004). Static Hand Gesture Recognition Based on Local Orientation Histogram Feature Distribution Model. *Computer Vision and Pattern Recognition Workshop, 2004. CVPRW'04. Conference on*, 161.

Ziou & Tabbone. (1998). Edge Detection Techniques-an Overview. *Pattern Recognition and Image Analysis, 8*, 537–59.

Zolkipli & Jantan. (2011). An Approach for Malware Behavior Identification and Classification. *Proceeding of 3rd International Conference on Computer Research and Development*, 191-194.

About the Contributors

Saifullah Khalid obtained two PhD degrees: one in Electronics and Communication Engineering and another in Electrical Engineering from Institute of Engineering and Technology, Lucknow. He worked at IIT BHU, Varanasi and different Universities before joining the dynamic job of Air Traffic Control officer at Airports Authority of India in 2008. Currently, he is working as Manager (Air Traffic control) at Lucknow Airport. He is Senior Member of International Association of Computer Science and Information Technology (IACSIT), Singapore, International Association of Engineers (IAENG), and IEEE. His research interests are in the area of Optimization Algorithms applications for power quality improvement. He has developed three novel optimization algorithms Adaptive Spider Net search Algorithm, Adaptive Mosquito Blood Search Algorithm and Adaptive blanket body cover search algorithm. Dr. Khalid has published around 100 research papers in various International Journals and Conferences including IEEE, Elsevier, and Springer etc. in India and abroad. He has contributed Chapters in many edited books. He is on the editorial board of many International Journals and also in the reviewer's panel of many International Journals (Including IEEE Transactions, Elsevier, Springer, Wiley, etc.). Dr Khalid has authored four books published by University Science Press, USA.

* * *

Aruna Chakraborty received the M.A. degree in cognitive science and the PhD degree in emotional intelligence and human–computer interactions from Jadavpur University, Kolkata, India, in 2000 and 2005, respectively. She is currently an Associate Professor in the Department of Computer Science and Engineering, St. Thomas' College of Engineering and Technology, Kolkata. She is also a Visiting Faculty at Jadavpur University, where she offers graduate-level courses on intelligent automation and robotics and cognitive science. She, with Prof. A. Konar, has written a book entitled Emotional Intelligence: A Cybernetic Approach (Heidelberg, Germany: Springer, 2009). Sheis also co-editing a book with Prof. A. Konar entitled Advances in Emotion Recognition (Wiley-Interscience; to be published). Her current research interest includes artificial intelligence, emotion modeling, and their applications in next-generation human–machine interactive systems.Dr. Chakraborty serves as an Editor of the International Journal of Artificial Intelligence and Soft Computing, Inderscience, U.K.

Edson B. M. Costa was born in São Luis, Maranhão, Brazil, in 1989. He received the B.Sc. degree in electrical engineering from Federal Institute of Maranhão and M.Sc. degree in electrical engineering from Federal University of Maranhão, Maranhão, Brazil, in 2014 and 2016, respectively. Currently, Mr

Costa is a PhD candidate in electrical engineering at the Federal University of Maranhão and is a professor in the Department of ElectroElectronics at Federal Institute of Maranhão, Imperatriz, Brazil. His research interests include fuzzy systems, evolving fuzzy control, adaptive control and swarm intelligence.

Santanu Dam received his M. Tech degree in Computer Technology from the Jadavpur University, of Jadavpur, Kolkata-32, West Bengal, India, in 2010. Presently he is working as Assistant Professor in Computer Science and Engineering department of the Future Institute of Engineering & Management, located in Sonarpur, Kolkata, West Bengal, India, Pin-700150.His area of interest for research work includes cloud computing and natural language processing. He has publications in the area of cloud computing.

Kousik Dasgupta did his Bachelors of Engineering from Nagpur University and Masters from the West Bengal University of Technology. He is presently on submission of his Doctor of Philosophy in Engineering from the University of Kalyani, Kalyani. He has served Industry like ABB, L&T, Llyods Steel, Wardha for three years in various capacity. Mr Dasgupta is now Assistant Professor in the Department of Computer Sciences of the Kalyani Government Engineering College. Apart from this, he has remained associated with University of Kalyani, Kalyani, Barrackpore Rastraguru Surendranath College, Barrackpore, as guest faculty from time to time. Mr Dasgupta has been involved as the principal investigator for the externally funded projects by the All India Council for Technical Education and Department of Science and Technology, Govt. of West Bengal. He has coauthored three books. He has published about twenty-five papers in various journals and conference proceedings, both international and national. Mr Dasgupta is a Life Fellow of the Optical Society of India (OSI), Indian Society for Technical Education (ISTE), Member of Associated Computing Machinery (ACM), Associate Member of the Institute of Engineers (India), Charted Engineer [India] of The Institute of Engineers (India).

Paramartha Dutta did his Bachelors and Masters in Statistics from the Indian Statistical Institute, Calcutta in the years 1988 and 1990 respectively. He afterwards completed his Master of Technology in Computer science from the same Institute in the year 1993 and Doctor of Philosophy in Engineering from the Bengal Engineering and Science University, Shibpur in 2005 respectively. He has served in the capacity of research personnel in various projects funded by Govt. of India, which include Defence Research and Development Organization, Council of Scientific and Industrial Research, Indian Statistical Institute, Calcutta etc. Dr Dutta is now a Professor in the Department of Computer and system Sciences of the Visva Bharati University, West Bengal, India. He has coauthored four books and has also one edited book to his credit. He has published about hundred papers in various journals and conference proceedings, both international and national. Dr. Dutta is a Life Fellow of the Optical Society of India (OSI), Life Member of Institution of Electronics and Telecommunication Engineers (OSI), Computer Society of India (CSI), Indian Science Congress Association (ISCA), Indian Society for Technical Education (ISTE), Indian Unit of Pattern Recognition and Artificial Intelligence (IUPRAI) - the Indian affiliate of the International Association for Pattern Recognition (IAPR), Member of Associated Computing Machinery (ACM), IEEE, Computer Society, USA.

Irraivan Elamvazuthi obtained his PhD degree from Department of Automatic Control and System Engineering, University of Sheffield, UK in 2002. He is currently an Associate Professor at the Department of Electrical and Electronics Engineering, Universiti Teknologi PETRONAS (UTP), Malaysia. His research interests include Control, Robotics, Mechatronics, Power System and Bio -medical Applications.

Sunita Gond received the MCA degree from Bhoj University, Bhopal and MCM & M. Tech. degree in Information Technology from Barkatullah University Institute of Technology Bhopal, India. She is currently pursuing her PhD degree in Computer Science & Engineering from Barkatullah University Bhopal. She has authored 2 books and contributed one book Chapter. She has published more than 25 papers in International and National Journals and has presented in prestigious International and National Conferences.

Reshma Kar completed her B.Tech. in Information Technology from North Eastern Hill University, Shillong in 2010. She received her M.Tech. degree from National Institute of Technology, Agartala in 2012. She is currently pursuing her PhD degree at Jadavpur University under the joint guidance of Dr Amit Konar and Dr Aruna Chakraborty. Her current research interests include EEG Analysis, Emotion Recognition, Artificial Intelligence and Human-Computer Interactions. She has also authored publications in reputed national and international conferences.

Amit Konar is currently a Professor in the dept. of Electronics and Tele-Communication Engineering (ETCE), Jadavpur University. He is the founding coordinator of the M.Tech. program on Intelligent Automation and Robotics, offered by ETCE department, Jadavpur University. He received his B. E degree from Bengal Engineering and Science University (B. E. College), Shibpur in 1983 and his M. E. Tel E, M. Phil. and PhD (Engineering) degrees from Jadavpur University in 1985, 1988, and 1994 respectively. Dr Konar's research areas include the study of computational intelligence algorithms and their applications to various domains of electrical engineering and computer science. Specifically he worked on fuzzy sets and logic, neuro-computing, evolutionary algorithms, Dempster-Shafer theory and Kalman filtering, and applied the principles of computational intelligence in image understanding, gesture recognition, VLSI design, mobile robotics and pattern recognition Specifically he worked on fuzzy sets and logic, neuro-computing, evolutionary algorithms, Dempster-Shafer theory and Kalman filtering, and applied the principles of computational intelligence in image understanding, VLSI design, mobile robotics and pattern recognition. Dr Konar has supervised 15 PhD theses. He has over 300 publications in international journal and conferences. He is an author of 8 books, including two popular texts: Artificial Intelligence and Soft Computing, from CRC Press in 2000 and Computational Intelligence: Principles, Techniques and Applications from Springer in 2005. Dr Konar served as the founding Editor-in-Chief of the International Journal of Artificial Intelligence and Soft Computing, Inderscience, U.K. He also served as a member of the editorial board of 5 other international journals. Currently, he is serving as an associate editor of two journals: IEEE Trans. on Fuzzy Systems and Neurocomputing. He was a recipient of AICTE-accredited 1997-2000 Career Award for Young Teachers for his significant contribution in teaching and research. He was a Visiting Professor for the Summer Courses in University of Missouri, St. Louis, USA in 2006. Dr Konar served as Principal Investigator or Co-Principal Investigator of Government funded projects. His current research projects include brain-computer interfacing for rehabilitative applications, gesture recognition for elderly healthcare systems, economic time-series prediction and forecasting, shape perception by tactile analysis and cognitive models for visual and tactile perception.

Mahesh Kumar is Lecturer in Department of Electrical Engineering, Mehran University of Engineering and Technology Jamshoro, Pakistan. Mr. Kumar currently registered as PhD student in Department of Electrical and Electronics Engineering, Universiti Teknologi Petronas, Malaysia. His research interest is distributed generation in the distribution system, distribution automation, and its efficiency.

Gopa Mandal did her Bachelor Degree from Govt. College of Engineering & Textile Technology in computer science & engineering and M.E in Computer Science & Engineering from the West Bengal University of Technology presently she is working as assistant professor in Kalyani Government Engineering College. She is serving Computer science & Engineering Department since 2006. Apart from this, she has remained associated with University of Kalyani, Kalyani. She has published papers in various conference proceedings.

Marian Cristian Mihăescu is an Associate Professor at Computers and Information Technology Department, University of Craiova, Romania. He received his PhD in 2009 for thesis 'Data Traffic Monitoring in Information Systems' and his research interests are educational data mining and machine learning. He develops Tesys e-Learning system and a data driven research infrastructure based on activities performed by users. He is involved in developing official open-source packages that implement new algorithms for clustering and classification within Weka workbench. He has served as Chair for IDAIR Workshop at IEEE IISA Conference since 2013.

S. Murugan is a Research Scholar in Alagappa University, Karaikudi, Tamilnadu, India. He received BSc in Physics from Madurai Kamaraj University, Madurai, in 1989 and MCA degree in Computer Applications from Alagappa University, Karaikudi, Tamilnadu, India and MPhil(CS) from Manonmaniam Sundaranar University, Tirunelveli, Tamilnadu, India. He has 22 years of teaching and admin experience at UG &PG level in the field of Computer Science. He has published 10 papers in the National Level and 17 in International Level. His research interests include Intelligence Network Security Algorithms, Malware prevention and Detection mechanism and algorithm. He has published various books and courseware in the field of Computer Science.

Perumal Nallagownden currently Associate Professor in the department of Electrical and Electronics Engineering at Universiti Teknologi Petronas, Malaysia. He has a significant published work in the journal articles/conferences. His special area of interest is an electrical power system, deregulated operation of power system, power quality and renewable energy. He is a member of the Institution of Engineers Malaysia and is a Professional Engineer registered with the Board of Engineers Malaysia.

Luqman Hakeem Rehman currently graduated from Universiti Teknologi PETRONAS in Malaysia. His research interest is DG in the distribution system.

Anuradha Saha received the B. Tech. degree in Electronics and Communication Engineering (ECE) from West Bengal University of Technology, India and M. Tech. degree in Mechatronics from National Institute of Technical Teachers' Training and Research, Kolkata, India in 2006 and 2009 respectively. She has submitted her Ph.D. on Brain-Signal Decoding in Human Perception and Cognition from Artificial Intelligence Lab, Jadavpur University, supervised by Prof. Amit Konar and funded by UGC. Her principal research interests include Artificial Intelligence, Pattern Recognition, Cognitive Science and Human-Computer-Interaction.

Sriparna Saha received her B.Tech degree (2011) in Electronics & Communication Engineering (ECE) Department from RCC Institute of Information Technology under West Bengal University of Technology and M.E. degree (2013) in Electronics and Tele-Communication Engineering (ETCE) Department from Jadavpur University. She has submitted her Ph.D. (2017) on Machine Intelligence from Artificial Intelligence Laboratory, ETCE department, Jadavpur University, India. All though her masters, she is a recipient of GATE fellowship and awarded UGC fellowship to pursue her Ph.D. She has offered currently post-graduate level courses in Intelligent Automation and Robotics, Jadavpur University, Calcutta. Currently, She is the assistant professor of Maulana Abul Kalam Azad University (formerly known as West Bengal University of Technology), Salt Lake, India.

Ginalber Serra was born in São Luis, Brazil, in 1976. He received the B.Sc. and M. Sc. degrees in electrical engineering from Federal University of Maranhão, Maranhão, Brazil, in 1999 and 2001, respectively. He received the PhD degree in electrical engineering from State University of Campinas (UNICAMP), Campinas, Brazil, on September 2005. He finished his Postdoctoral research on multivariable neuro-fuzzy adaptive control of nonlinear systems, Department of Machines, Components and Intelligent Systems, State University of Campinas, Campinas, Brazil, on September 2006. From 2006 to 2007, he was a researcher at Department of Electrical Engineering, University of Santiago, Santiago, Chile. He is Associate Professor and head of the research group in Computational Intelligence Applied to Technology, at Federal Institute of Education, Sciences and Technology (IFMA), Maranhão, Brazil. He is also the advisor of several students who is working in Master and PhD thesis from Master/PhD Program in Electricity Engineering at the Federal University of Maranhão, Maranhão, Brasil. Dr Serra is Editor of the Book "Frontiers in Advanced Control Systems" published by INTECH, in 2012. Dr Serra is a reviewer for many prestigious international journals and conferences. His research interest includes topics on Fuzzy Inference Systems, Neural Networks, Evolutionary Computation, Signal Processing, Adaptive Control, Robust Control, Optimal Control, Systems Modeling, Evolving Systems, Industrial Automation, Real Time Applications and Instrumentation for High-Performance Modeling/Control.

Shailendra Singh is currently Professor & Head in Department of Computer Engineering and Applications at National Institute of Technical Teachers' Training and Research, Bhopal. He has more than 20 years of experience in Teaching, Industry and research as well as education and training for human resource and development. Dr. Singh has supervised two PhD thesis. He is a member of many professional bodies including a senior member of IEEE, USA. His current research interests are Machine learning and Cloud Computing. He has also delivered expert talks and chaired the session in International Conferences in India and abroad. He is a member of editorial board and reviewer of various prestigious journals and conference proceedings. He has organized a number of international and national conferences. He has authored 2 books and contributed one book Chapter. He has served as Technical Chair IEEE international conferences held in India and abroad. Dr. Singh has published more than 47 papers in International and National Journals and has presented in prestigious International and National Conferences. His research publications have been referred by many research articles during the last 6 years. He has been keenly involved in various consultancy projects.

Yoel Tenne obtained his PhD at Sydney University and has been an Endeavour post-doctoral fellow at KAIST (S. Korea) and a JSPS Post-doctoral Fellow at Kyoto University (Japan). He is currently a Senior Lecturer at Ariel University. His research fields include systems engineering, applied optimization, and applied computational intelligence. In these respective fields, he has authored multiple publications which include edited volumes, book chapters, and journal and conference papers.

Pandian Vasant is a senior lecturer at Department of Fundamental and Applied Sciences, Faculty of Science and Information Technology, Universiti Teknologi PETRONAS in Malaysia. He holds PhD (UNEM, Costa Rica) in Computational Intelligence, MSc (UMS, Malaysia, Engineering Mathematics) and BSc (Hons, Mathematics, University of Malaya, Malaysia) in Mathematics. His research interests include Soft Computing, Hybrid Optimization, Holistic Optimization, Innovative Computing and Applications. He has co-authored research papers and articles in national journals, international journals, conference proceedings, conference paper presentation, and special issues lead guest editor, lead guest editor for book chapters' project, conference abstracts, edited books, keynote lecture and book chapters (176 publications indexed in SCOPUS). In the year 2009, Dr. Pandian Vasant was awarded top reviewer for the journal Applied Soft Computing (Elsevier) and awarded outstanding reviewer in the year 2015 for ASOC (Elsevier) journal. He has 25 years of working experience at the various universities from 1989-2016. Currently he is Editor-in-Chief of IJCO, IJSIEC, IEM, IJEOE, Associate Editor of IJFSA and Editor of GJTO and Cogent Engineering.

Anitha Mary X completed her B.E Electronics and Instrumentation Engineeing from Karunya University, Coimbatore in the year 2001 and M.E in VLSI Design from ANNA University, Coimbatore in the year 2009. She has completed PhD in control system from Karunya University. She has published several papers in reputed journals.

Index

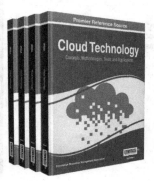

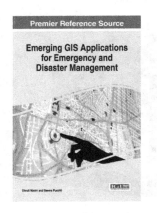 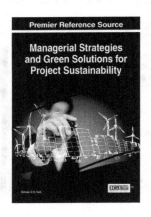  

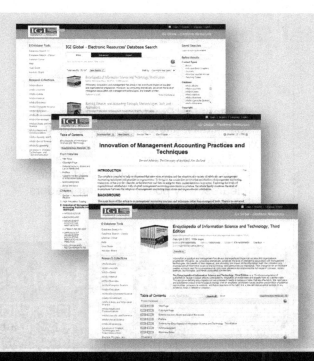

Information Resources Management Association

Become an IRMA Member

Members of the **Information Resources Management Association (IRMA)** understand the importance of community within their field of study. The Information Resources Management Association is an ideal venue through which professionals, students, and academicians can convene and share the latest industry innovations and scholarly research that is changing the field of information science and technology. Become a member today and enjoy the benefits of membership as well as the opportunity to collaborate and network with fellow experts in the field.

IRMA Membership Benefits:

- **One FREE Journal Subscription**
- **30% Off Additional Journal Subscriptions**
- **20% Off Book Purchases**
- Updates on the latest events and research on Information Resources Management through the IRMA-L listserv.
- Updates on new open access and downloadable content added to Research IRM.
- A copy of the Information Technology Management Newsletter twice a year.
- A certificate of membership.

IRMA Membership $195

Scan code or visit **irma-international.org** and begin by selecting your free journal subscription.

Membership is good for one full year.

Printed in the United States
By Bookmasters